PARAS VERSUS
THE REICH

D0556083

PARAS VERSUS THE REICH

Canada's Paratroopers at War, 1942–45

Lieutenant-Colonel Bernd Horn and Michel Wyczynski

THE DUNDURN GROUP
TORONTO · OXFORD

Copy-Editor: Andrea Pruss
Design: Jennifer Scott
Printer: University of Toronto Press

National Library of Canada Cataloguing in Publication Data

Horn, Bernd, 1959-
Paras versus the Reich : Canada's paratroopers at war, 1942-45 / Bernd Horn and Michel Wyczynski.

Includes bibliographical references and index.
ISBN 1-55002-470-1

1. Canada. Canadian Army. Canadian Parachute Battalion, 1st — History. 2. World War, 1939-1945 — Regimental histories — Canada. I. Wyczynski, Michel, 1953- II. Title.

D792.C2H66 2003   940.54'1271   C2003-903529-8

1   2   3   4   5   07   06   05   04   03

THE CANADA COUNCIL | LE CONSEIL DES ARTS
FOR THE ARTS | DU CANADA
SINCE 1957 | DEPUIS 1957

Canadä

ONTARIO ARTS COUNCIL
CONSEIL DES ARTS DE L'ONTARIO

We acknowledge the support of the **Canada Council for the Arts** and the **Ontario Arts Council** for our publishing program. We also acknowledge the financial support of the **Government of Canada** through the **Book Publishing Industry Development Program** and **The Association for the Export of Canadian Books**, and the **Government of Ontario** through the **Ontario Book Publishers Tax Credit** program.

Care has been taken to trace the ownership of copyright material used in this book. The author and the publisher welcome any information enabling them to rectify any references or credit in subsequent editions.

J. Kirk Howard, President

Printed and bound in Canada.⊕
Printed on recycled paper.
www.dundurn.com

Dundurn Press
8 Market Street
Suite 200
Toronto, Ontario, Canada
M5E 1M6

Dundurn Press
73 Lime Walk
Headington, Oxford,
England
OX3 7AD

Dundurn Press
2250 Military Road
Tonawanda NY
U.S.A. 14150

This book is dedicated to all those who have answered their country's call to arms.

ACKNOWLEDGEMENTS

Initially, we must thank the Department of National Defence Academic Research Program (ARP) for their generous support of this project. Without their assistance, the final product would never have been as complete or as timely. In addition, as with any project of this scope, there is an enormous debt owed to an innumerable number of individuals who contributed their expertise, memories, resources, and time. Our sincere thanks are extended to all those who assisted, either directly or indirectly, with this book.

Although it would be impossible to individually acknowledge everyone, the significant contributions of some oblige us to make special mention of their efforts. In this regard, we wish to convey our sincere gratitude to: Jan and Joanne de Vries, Reina Lahtinen (Image Services CWM), John David Reinhard, Ed Storey, Michael Wheatley (Collection Manager CAFM/CFB Petawawa Museum), and Ted Zuber (Zuber Galleries).

We must also make special mention of the selfless efforts and enormous support of the staff of the DND Directorate of History and Heritage, the National Archives of Canada, the National Library of Canada, the Canadian Airborne Forces Museum, the Canadian War Museum, the 1st Canadian Parachute Battalion Association, and the Royal Military College of Canada.

Finally, as always, the completion of this project was also dependant on two special individuals, without whose constant support and understanding we would not have been able to finish. As such, we wish to acknowledge our deepest gratitude to our wives, Kim and Suzanne, who consistently, patiently, and tolerantly accept our toil and continue to provide the necessary encouragement. It is to them that we owe our largest debt for all that we achieve.

TABLE OF CONTENTS

FOREWORD

I *consider it a great* privilege to once again be given the opportunity to acknowledge the contribution of the 1st Canadian Parachute Battalion, a group that Sir Winston Churchill described as "those formidable Canadians." I still recall the pride and joy I felt when I welcomed the Battalion into my brigade at Bulford in the summer of 1943. I could not help feeling in those far-off days that I had been entrusted with, and had a great responsibility for, a magnificent body of fighting men who were Canada's answer to Winston Churchill's stirring call in August 1940 for a great parachute force.

They were a great band of brothers, all volunteers, drawn together by the challenge of a new adventure and the desire to fight for freedom and destroy the tyranny of Hitler. They were drawn from across Canada and represented the wealth and breadth of that splendid Dominion. Their youth was unquestionable, the average age being twenty-two. But their strength was equally apparent. Our divisional commander, General Richard Gale, inspected them on July 29, 1943, and recorded in his diary, "Any man with two eyes in his head could not fail to see that here is a fine Battalion — with all the makings of something good — something magnificent."

Magnificent they were, especially their "joie de vivre." The Battalion as a whole had a remarkable vitality to it. Here lay what I believed to be the difference between the Old World and the New. They were always ready to "have a go." Although this unbridled enthusiasm sometimes created mischief, overall it provided the Battalion with an unconquerable spirit.

This spirit was responsible for the genesis of a great confidence in themselves, as well as in their brothers in arms in the Brigade and Division, and in their superiors.

They soon lived up to everyone's expectations. Their baptism of fire came at night in the early hours of D-Day when they were given the task of capturing the brigade dropping zone, destroying the enemy command post on its edge, and then assisting in the destruction of two bridges. Upon completion of these tasks, they were responsible for seizing the vital Le Mesnil crossroads on the ridge that overlooked the valley of the River Dives to the north and the left flank of 21st Army Group to the south. It is a matter of record that the Battalion's performance was superb. But this came with a cost — the Battalion lost nearly half its strength in the bloody battle.

The experienced and battle-hardened soldiers of the 1st Canadian Parachute Battalion continued to build on their achievements and distinguished record. They were the only Canadian unit to participate in the battle of the Ardennes during the Christmas of 1944. They were also an integral part of the greatest and most successful Airborne operation in history as part of the Allied Airborne Corps (6th British and 17th American Airborne Divisions) that breached the German defences across the Rhine at Wesel. And they played their full part in the final battle — the pursuit of the German Army and the collapse of the Reich.

This battle marked the beginning of the end. It also highlighted the strength and tenacity of the airborne soldier. The final victory was achieved only through a fighting trek across 275 miles of German territory when we more than kept pace with the armoured division on our flank. It ended with our lead battalion, the Canadian paratroopers, entering the town of Wismar on the Baltic Sea a scant three hours ahead of the Russians, as Sir Winston Churchill had personally demanded.

And so ended the war for the 1st Canadian Parachute Battalion, one of the truly great fighting battalions of the Second World War. They proved to be splendid ambassadors for Canada as their enthusiasm, indomitable spirit, and unquestioned valour were repeatedly demonstrated both in the United Kingdom and on the field of battle. I feel both honoured and privileged to have had the opportunity to have been their commander.

The record of this magnificent battalion is ably captured in the pages that follow. The authors, who have written and researched extensively on airborne forces, have meticulously recorded the entire scope of the Battalion's history from its inception, its training, and its combat experience. Importantly, they have also related the political debate and hesitancy that existed during the tumultuous times in regard to the adoption of paratroops. But most significantly, they have captured the spirit of the Canadian paratroopers and their battalion: intrepid soldiers who dared to take up the challenge of a bold new form of warfare. This book is a great tribute to all those who served. These are the individuals who forged the legacy that Canada's paratroopers have proudly emulated. Their story in its entirety is vividly recounted here.

S. James L. Hill
Brigadier (Retired)
Commander, 3rd Parachute Brigade 1943–1945

INTRODUCTION

On July 1, 2002, the veterans of the 1st Canadian Parachute Battalion (1 Cdn Para Bn) celebrated the sixtieth anniversary of the establishment of their wartime unit. Predictably, they were not great in number and all were of advanced age. Nevertheless, the surviving members still possessed the fiery spirit and pride that had become their hallmark. These were the intrepid individuals who created the proud Canadian airborne legacy that is carried on by the nation's parachute soldiers today.

Their story is one of courage, perseverance, and tenacity. The idea of raising a parachute capability within Canada was not one that was readily supported in those dark early days of the Second World War. B.H. Liddell Hart, the renowned British military theorist, once observed, "There are over two thousand years of experience to tell us that the only thing harder than getting a new idea into the military mind is to get an old one out." Canadian military commanders were no exception. Echoing the sentiments of their allies, Canada's military and political leadership believed paratroops to be nothing more than a stunt, albeit a spectacular one.

But this would eventually change. The German Blitzkrieg that overwhelmed Poland in September 1939 and stormed through Europe in the spring of 1940 shocked the Western allies. Particularly, it was the use of small numbers of *Fallschirmjäger* (paratroopers) to achieve strategic results that finally forced the Americans and the British to reconsider their indifference for airborne forces. Nonetheless, for armies that only now fully discovered how woefully unprepared they were for modern warfare, paratroops were a luxury far down the list of requirements. As a result, a cautious and slow program was undertaken, and even this limited foray was carried out only because of the aggressive prompting of individuals such as British Prime Minister Winston Churchill and American Army Chief of Staff General George C. Marshall.

For Canada, the idea of creating an airborne force was dismissed outright. The Canadian Army was anything but a modern one, numbering approximately four thousand regular forces and fifty thousand militia personnel and devoid of even the most rudimentary equipment. Canada's military commanders were more concerned with developing a mechanized force capable of combatting the German panzers than a corps of avant-garde paratroopers. Moreover, neither the politicians nor the generals believed, despite the chaos in Europe and the peril hanging over England, that there existed any threat to Canada. Military appreciations consistently discounted the need for or utility of airborne forces for home defence. And to raise a specialized paratroop unit only to attach them to a foreign army was not palatable to politicians and military commanders who worked so hard at maintaining their national autonomy. Moreover, an assessment of the sluggish advancement of the programs of their allies led them to believe that the use of paratroopers was a flash in the pan.

The fall of the Mediterranean island of Crete in May 1941 to German Fallschirmjäger, however, dramatically changed perceptions. This latest German coup convinced Prime Minister Churchill of the strategic value of airborne forces. Angry with the slow development of the British program, he now forced his will onto his intractable military commanders. By November 1941, the first airborne division was formed in England. The Americans, too, accelerated their program, and in the summer of 1942 they converted the 82nd Motorized Division into the 82nd Airborne Division. Ironically, the Allies now defined a modern army as one that included paratroopers. Furthermore, their doctrine now predicted success of operations based on the ability to unleash thousands of airborne soldiers who could descend onto the enemy's flanks and rear.

Not to be left out of the club, Canadian military commanders reversed their previous arguments and convinced their political masters that Canada, too, needed parachute soldiers. As a result, on July 1, 1942, the War Cabinet authorized the establishment of 1 Cdn Para Bn. The Canadian Army was back in the game. Although hesitant to develop an airborne capability at first, the Army, having made its decision, now worked hard at creating a distinct military elite. Selection standards were quite demanding. Only volunteers were accepted, and on average 50 percent of those were rejected. And that was just the beginning. A further 35 percent of successful applicants were lost due to the normal parachute training injuries and course failures.

Once a nucleus of volunteers was assembled, they started training in England and the United States until such time as a core of instructors was qualified and the necessary infrastructure could be built in Canada. But as the unit started to take shape, the original question once again arose — what exactly did Canada need airborne forces for?

The answer was a difficult one. As argued from the beginning, there was no real home defence role. Overseas duty for the aggressive, action-seeking paratroops seemed to be the only real solution. Therefore, the neophyte paratroopers were attached to the 3rd Parachute Brigade (3 Para Bde) in the British 6th Airborne Division (6 AB Div) and were very quickly forgotten by their own government and army. Not surprisingly they called themselves the "Forgotten Battalion." Lieutenant-Colonel Fraser Eadie lamented, "They really had nothing to do with us, ever." He added, "Canada had forsaken us for everything but pay and clothing."[1] Quite simply, the paratroopers were never fully integrated with the Canadian Army overseas. For all intents and purposes, they were orphans.[2]

Despite the perceived abandonment, or possibly because of it, the Canadian paratroopers were imbued with an adventurous spirit and a desire to continually prove themselves. And prove themselves they did. "All eyes were naturally upon them," reminisced Brigadier S. James L. Hill, their beloved brigade commander, "and what splendid ambassadors for Canada they proved to be, both in the United Kingdom and on the field of battle where their spirit and valour was the admiration of us all."[3]

The members of 1 Cdn Para Bn quickly settled into Bulford Camp and became an integral component of their British airborne division. They made history as the first Canadian unit to land in Occupied Europe in the inky darkness of June 6, 1944, as the "tip of the spear" that cracked the outer crust of the Reich. Their courage and valour earned them a reputation as premier fighting troops. But this came at a cost. Casualties for the 89-day Normandy campaign numbered 270 all ranks, with an additional 87 captured. But it was the Battalion's tenacity in accomplishing its D-Day tasks and holding the vital Le Mesnil crossroads that helped ensure the Allied success.

Repatriated to England in September, it was not very long before the unit was once again thrown into battle. In the bitter cold of December 1944, Hitler attempted one last gamble — a massive offensive strike through the quiet Ardennes front in a bid for Antwerp. The German panzer force rapidly sliced through the unprepared American troops holding the front; however, the initial Allied surprise very quickly transformed itself into the mobilization of forces for a counterstroke. The 6th Airborne Division was expeditiously thrown in to help plug the gap. As such, the members of 1 Cdn Para Bn became the only Canadian unit to participate in the infamous Battle of the Bulge. For almost two months the paratroopers chased an elusive German enemy that continually melted away as the paratroopers advanced through Belgium and Holland.

Their return to England in late February 1945, however, was short-lived. Within a month they left Britain's shores one more time to participate in the largest airborne operation of the war — Operation Varsity, the crossing of the Rhine. "It was during the parachute drop over the Rhine River in March 1945, that the Battalion became a truly professional fighting unit, skilled in its execution of its specific battle plans," proclaimed Lieutenant-Colonel Eadie, "and readily adaptable to the ever-changing challenges placed before it."[4]

The battle was a true test of its worth. Dropping onto the objective, the Canadians were met with murderous fire the moment their aircraft arrived over the drop zone (DZ). Well-entrenched enemy machine guns, flak cannons, and artillery unleashed a torrent of fire. The paratroopers had no choice but to assault the moment they hit the ground. The battle quickly turned into a vicious struggle for survival, one that the paratroopers quickly won. It was the initiative, aggressiveness, and tenacity of the airborne soldier that made the difference. As individuals or small groups, the paratroopers continually carried out their missions regardless of whether their non-commissioned officers (NCOs) or officers were present. They took the fight to the enemy without hesitation, living the credo "no mission too daunting, no task too great." As such, within ninety minutes the Battalion had achieved its objectives.

Having pierced the very Reich itself, the Battalion now participated in an epic fighting trek across almost 450 kilometres of northwest Germany to complete the collapse of Hitler's Third Reich. In a whirlwind advance, riding on tanks and in trucks and marching, the unit, as part of the 6th Airborne Division, smashed through roadblocks and swept through villages as they fought their way to Wismar on the Baltic Sea. In the end, the Canadians were given the honour of leading the assault into the final objective — Wismar. They arrived mere hours before the Russians, as personally demanded by Prime Minister Churchill himself.

But the price for success in war is always blood. And the Battalion paid its fair share. The toll amounted to 122 killed, 286 carried off the field of battle wounded, and 86 who suffered in German prisoner of war camps — "[almost] 500 men from the 650 who had marched into Bulford Camp with great elan two years before."[5]

On September 30, 1945, the 1st Canadian Parachute Battalion was officially disbanded. The nation's first airborne soldiers had earned a proud and remarkable reputation. Their legacy would become the standard that would challenge Canada's future paratroopers and imbue them with a special pride. The Battalion never failed to complete an assigned mission, nor did it ever lose or surrender an objective once taken. The Canadian paratroopers were among the first Allied soldiers to have landed in Occupied Europe, the only Canadians to have participated in the Battle of the Bulge in the Ardennes, and by the end of the war had advanced deeper into Germany than any other Canadian unit. "The Battalion," wrote Field Marshal Sir Allan Brooke, Chief of the Imperial General Staff, "played a vital part in the heavy fighting which followed their descent onto French soil on June 6, 1944, during the subsequent critical days and in the pursuit to the Seine. Finally, it played a great part in the lightning pursuit of the German Army right up the shores of the Baltic. It can indeed be proud of its record."[6] Unquestionably, the paratroopers of 1st Canadian Parachute Battalion, as well as their supporting airborne organizations, the 1st Canadian Parachute Training Company/Battalion and the A-35 Canadian Parachute Training Centre, established, at great cost and personal sacrifice, the foundation of the Canadian Airborne experience.

PART I

Creation of a
Canadian Airborne Capability

CHAPTER ONE

Deep Battle — The Maturation of the Concept of Airborne Warfare

Where is the Prince who can afford so to cover his country with troops for its defence, as that ten thousand men descending from the clouds might not, in many places, do an infinite deal of mischief before a force could be brought together to repel them?

Benjamin Franklin, 1784[7]

B enjamin Franklin wrote these prescient words to a friend after witnessing the second ascension in history of a balloon in 1784, in Paris. The vehicle in question was a Charles hydrogen balloon that used a mix of both hydrogen and hot air. It was made of silk and consequently was extremely expensive. Nonetheless, the implications of this innovative technology were not lost on Franklin. "Five thousand balloons," he argued, "capable of raising two men each could not cost more than five ships of the line." More importantly, the freedom of movement and mobility would give a marked advantage to those who dared to wage war from the heavens. This "magnificent experiment," believed Franklin, "appears to be a discovery of great importance, and what may possibly give a new turn to human events."[8]

Franklin's concept was not entirely profound. Waging war from the heavens was already contemplated in antiquity. The Greek warrior Bellerophon, astride his winged steed Pegasus, was but the earliest manifestation of this idea. The advantage bestowed to a combatant who could utilize the "third dimension" was plainly apparent. Remarkably, this potential was grasped by Friar Joseph Galien even prior to the invention of the balloon. The concept of such a device led Galien to propose that it could be used "to transport a whole army and all their munitions of war from place to place as desired."[9]

This musing was not lost on the victorious French under the reign of Napoleon. Although incapable of matching Britain's naval power, the new technology provided an alternate means of striking at their English foe. The experimentation with balloons led to the establishment, on March 23, 1794, of a special formation designated the Compagnie d'Aérostiers. The unit consisted of four balloons: *l' Entreprenant, Céleste, Hercule,* and *Intrépide.* Each had a permanently assigned crew. French military planners placed such great faith in the potential of this idea that they later contemplated an invasion of England with the assistance of an aerial armada of these contraptions. They pondered the idea that 2,500 of these four-man balloons, launched prior to a sea invasion, would create chaos, if not the complete surrender of England.[10] This new threat was such that even the British considered it a possibility. A popular contemporary English song, "Invasion! A Song for 1803," included the verse, "Or should they try their Grand Balloon, And Soar as high as larks can, Our musquets shall convince them soon John Bull's a knowing marksman."[11] In the end, however, the futuristic scheme, similar to Napoleon's invasion plans, failed to be realized.

Although the concept of unleashing assault troops from the skies subsequently underwent a lengthy hiatus, experimentation with balloons and parachutes, and the fascination they engendered, continued. Throughout the 1800s daredevils, acrobats, and circus performers in Europe and North America were lifted up by balloons at outdoor events such as fairs, and then jumped and floated to the ground by way of crude static line parachutes.[12] The military application never disappeared. In the spring of 1889, American balloonist Charles Leroux demonstrated his new parachute harness and technique to a group of senior German officers in Berlin. Jumping from one thousand metres, Leroux successfully landed safely in front of the impressed officers. "If one could only steer these things," General Graf von Schlieffen of the Great General Staff reportedly commented, "parachutes could provide a new means of exploiting surprise in war, as it would be feasible for a few men to wipe out an enemy headquarters."[13]

Schlieffen's speculation, like that before him, was still premature. However, the military application of parachuting quickly became apparent with the invention of the airplane. In 1912, Captain Albert Berry of the United States Army made the first successful jump from an aircraft in St. Louis, Missouri. Two years later, William Lewis became the first British parachutist to drop from an airplane. Indeed, during the First World War the parachute, often referred to by its commercial name "Guardian Angel," was used universally by aerial observers to jump to safety when their observation balloons were shot down by fighters. Logically, the parachute was later adopted as emergency equipment for aircraft as well.[14]

It was the use of parachutes by German pilots to escape their stricken aircraft that supposedly sparked the next great event in airborne history. In the fall of 1918, Colonel William "Billy" Mitchell, the commander of the United States Army Air Corps in France, listened carefully to accounts of the German aviators' use of parachutes. This not only spurred his efforts at getting parachutes for his own pilots, but also provided the genesis of an idea that would revolutionize the concept of warfare on the costly and stagnant European battlefields of the First World War.[15]

On October 17, 1918, during a meeting with General John "Black Jack" Pershing, the commander of the American Expeditionary Force in Europe, Colonel Mitchell proposed that Pershing "assign one of the infantry divisions permanently to the Air Service, preferably the 1st U.S. Infantry Division [Big Red One]; that we should arm the men with a great number of machine guns and train them to go over the front in our large airplanes, which would carry ten or fifteen of these soldiers." The crux of his plan hinged on an aerial assault. "We could equip each man with a parachute," he insisted, "so that when we desired to make a rear attack on the enemy, we could carry these men over the lines and drop them off in parachutes behind the German position." He further asserted that "they could assemble at a prearranged strong point, fortify it, and we could supply them by aircraft with food and ammunition." Mitchell's visionary plan further elucidated, "Our low flying attack aviation would then cover every road in their vicinity, both day and night, so as to prevent the Germans falling on them before they could thoroughly organize the position." Then, he added, "we could attack the Germans from the rear, aided by an attack from our army on the front, and support the whole maneuver with our great air force."[16]

Amazingly, the innovative plan was accepted. However, the armistice announced less than a month later put Mitchell's daring scheme to rest. Notwithstanding the brilliance of the idea, in reality, the plan was actually premature for its time. Colonel Mitchell assigned the task of planning the mission to an officer on his staff, Major Lewis Brereton.[17] The enormity of the project quickly engulfed the young staff officer, who realized it was beyond their present capability. First, the sheer logistics were overwhelming. Brereton would need twelve thousand parachutes and the entire holdings and factory output of the British Handley-Page four-engine bomber to lift the assault force. Furthermore, the organization for controlling the assembly, transit, and dropping procedures on a single target for such a large body of aircraft was non-existent.[18] The simple problem of marshalling the bombers on airfields across England and France and coordinating rendezvous points (RV) from which all aircraft could proceed as one single formation was beyond the available doctrine of the time. And there were even more hurdles. Each man in the Division would require a rudimentary instruction on exiting the aircraft and parachuting. Moreover, once on the ground, communications and the resupply of ammunition and rations posed further difficulties. Luckily for Brereton, the Armistice put an end to the mission, and thus, to his incubus.

Although Mitchell's idea of an airborne army assaulting the enemy's rear area never made it beyond the initial planning stage, the concept itself did not die. The Italians, strongly influenced by their own General Guilio Douhet, the well-known and respected author of *The Command of the Air*, published in 1921, quickly seized every opportunity that air power offered. Such advantage was displayed in 1927, when the Italians demonstrated the practical application of Colonel Mitchell's earlier plan, albeit on a much smaller scale, simultaneously dropping nine men with their equipment. The next year, they dropped supplies to the stranded crew of the dirigible *Italia* in the North Pole. Shortly thereafter, the Italians established several battalions of parachutists and reportedly conducted several mass drops in North Africa in 1929 and 1930.[19]

The Italian experimentation, however, was quickly dwarfed by a more aggressive and wide-sweeping program. It was the Russians who pioneered the modern theory of airborne warfare. Their experimentation and vision advanced the idea to unprecedented heights.

Undeniably, the Russian experience in the First World War, as well as their subsequent Civil War, left an indelible mark on the psyche of its army commanders. Soviet military planners and strategists quickly grasped the importance of manoeuvre, speed, and surprise. Consequently, a belief in aggressive and bold action emerged. All these ideas together necessitated the development of doctrine that inherently embraced and nurtured the offensive. Clearly, mechanization became an obvious and pivotal ingredient to the new Soviet way of thinking. *Desanty*, the use of air mechanization to air-land forces and/or deploy parachute troops, was another.[20]

The individual who became key to the development of the avant-garde Soviet military doctrine was Marshal of the Soviet Union Mikhail Tukhachevsky. After fighting with the Bolsheviks during the Russian Civil War, Tukhachevsky emerged from the conflict with the idea that successful military operations depended on the principle of simultaneity — or simply put, the simultaneous neutralization of the enemy's entire tactical depth.[21] In his 1926 article entitled "War," Tukhachevsky articulated, "Modern operations involve the concentration of the forces necessary for an assault and the infliction of continual and uninterrupted strikes by these forces against the opponent throughout an extremely deep area."[22] Airborne forces were viewed as an integral element of this philosophy, named "Deep Battle."

The Soviet concept of Deep Battle envisioned that aviation, airborne, mechanized, and motorized formations would be organized to cooperate together but, importantly, still operate independently of the main force, allowing severe penetration of the enemy's operational depth.[23] The Soviet construct went well beyond the theoretical. It was actually put into practice. In 1929, fifteen heavily armed soldiers were air-landed into Tadzhikistan in an operation against Afghan Basmachi Moslem rebels.[24] That same year, Russian soldiers were selected for parachute training, and subsequently a parachute battalion was established. In 1930 and 1931, a number of these airborne troops were dropped during large exercises with some success.[25] By the summer of 1933, the official Soviet military publication, *Temporary Instructions on the Combat Use of Aviation Landing Units*, emphasized the requirement for airborne forces to engage in bold manoeuvres, to capitalize on the element of surprise, and to effect the speedy employment and rapid concentration of force. Significantly, all Soviet field exercises from 1933 onwards included airborne operations.

It was approximately two years later that an entire battalion conducted a mass drop in the Ukraine. Improvements increased exponentially. In 1935, the Soviets inserted two battalions under the command of General Jonah Yakir during an exercise in Kiev to seize an airstrip, allowing 2,300 reinforcements, including 16 artillery pieces, to be air-landed. The next year, they stunned the world when a regiment, totaling in excess of one thousand men, was dropped in front of an array of foreign military attachés. Major-General Archibald Wavell, the British military attaché to the Soviet Union, witnessed the Soviet demonstration in Kiev and was fully impressed. "If I had not witnessed the descents," he reported to his superiors, "I could not have believed such an operation possible."[26] Its significance, however, completely escaped him. "This Parachute descent," he wrote, "though its tactical value may be doubtful, was a most spectacular performance."[27]

The potential of this new capability, however, was not lost on Marshal Mikhail Tukhachevsky. The commander of the Leningrad Military District actively promoted further Soviet experimentation. As stated earlier, Tukhachevsky envisioned joint, as well as combined-arms, offensive operations. He stressed the coordinated utilization of motorized rifle units, self-propelled artillery, and aviation to crack the enemy's outer defences. To support the main effort, Tukhachevsky proposed the use of bombers to attack enemy reserves. But more importantly, he believed that paratroopers could be used to seize vital targets and block an enemy's withdrawal. Their utilization, he insisted, would allow "a crushing blow to be delivered by the second echelon of forces."[28]

By 1936, Tukhachevsky and his cohorts had conceptually refined their idea of Deep Battle. Moreover, they had validated their theory by implementation during field exercises. Their ideas were now entrenched in their operational doctrine. "Major units of parachute forces," stated the *1936 Red Army Field Regulations*, "provide an effective means of disrupting the enemy's command, control and logistics. In conjunction with frontal attack, parachute units may play a decisive part in achieving complete destruction of the enemy on a given thrust line."[29] Clearly, for the Soviets, airborne forces were a critical element in creating "operational shock" in the opponent's rear areas. As the 1936 regulations articulated:

> Modern offensive forces, above all the large-scale employment of tanks, aviation, and *desanty* by mechanized forces open up the possibility of attacking the enemy simultaneously over the entire depth of the field force layout, with a view to isolating him, and completely surrounding him ... with all arms and forms of support acting in concert, an offensive operation should be based on simultaneous neutralization of the entire depth of the enemy defence.[30]

The People's Commissar of Defence, Marshal of the Soviet Union Kliment Voroshilov, could rightly boast to the first All-Union Congress of Stakhanovites in 1936 that "Parachute jumping is the field of aviation in which the monopoly belongs to the Soviet Union." Furthermore, "there is no country in the world," he correctly asserted, "which can say that in this field it can even nearly be equal to the Soviet Union or that it puts before it the task to catch up in the near future."[31] Incredibly, the Soviet developments were quickly lost in the turmoil of the Stalinist purges of 1937. The architect of the Soviet operational doctrine, Marshal Tukhachevsky, was the first "key" victim. With his death, his ideas and dramatic developments fell into disrepute. As a result, the concept of Deep Battle quickly dissipated.

The momentum gained, however, was not entirely lost. During the 1936 manoeuvres in Minsk, a German Air Force major, Kurt Student, witnessed the same airborne spectacle as Major-General Wavell. Curiously, Student went away with an entirely different outlook. If not already philosophically committed, Student now became a strong proponent of the large-scale use of airborne troops. But the Soviet demonstration was not the catalyst for German parachute development. Experimentation was already underway.

In February 1933, Hermann Göring, as the Prussian minister of the interior, ordered the formation of a special police parachute unit with a strength of fourteen officers and four hundred men for internal security operations. *Polizeimajor* Hans Wecke, of the Prussian *Landespolizeigruppe* "General Göring," utilized a small task force that parachuted into suspected Communist hideouts. The shock and surprise effect of this small formation was exceedingly successful.[32] In September of the same year, Göring announced, "It is my objective to transform the Prussian Police Force into a sharp-edged weapon, equal to the Reichswehr, which I can deliver to the Führer when the day comes to fight our external enemies."[33] Not surprisingly, in April 1935, Wecke's organization was renamed the "General Göring" Regiment, designated a military unit, and in October of the same year absorbed into the Luftwaffe. That autumn, the Luftwaffe Chief of Staff, General Walther Wever, successfully persuaded now Air Marshal Hermann Göring that the newly formed regiment should be trained as parachutists. This led to the establishment of the first German parachute battalion and provided the catalyst for the creation of a parachute school in Stendal a year later.

The first operational parachute company made its debut in the autumn of 1937, during the Wehrmacht manoeuvres in Mecklenburg. Its role was limited to that of a commando-type force. Fourteen demolition teams were dropped on the first night of the exercise. Their task was to destroy railway installations and communications in the enemy rear area. The mission was judged a success by both the exercise umpires and the senior observers present.[34] Despite this apparent success, however, the German effort was still experiencing growing pains. First, there was no clear articulation of the war role for the parachutists. Second, there was not a clear delineation of who was in charge of the ongoing endeavour. Both the Wehrmacht and the Luftwaffe had elements undergoing parachute training. In addition, Heinrich Himmler's *Schutzstaffeln* (SS) and Ernst Röhm's Nazi "Brownshirts," or the *Sturmabteilung* (SA), also sent troops to Stendal for training. The effort was clearly confused. There were four different organizations competing for a limited number of vacancies at the single training facility.

In June 1938, in an effort to clarify the situation, Air Marshal Göring appointed Major-General Student as the overall commander of German airborne forces. Before long, he would become the preeminent and undisputed champion of the German airborne movement. Kurt Student began his military career in 1911 in an elite Jäger (light infantry) unit but transferred to the new Army Air Force just prior to the First World War. Göring described him as an "energetic, intelligent officer with a reputation for achieving results." He was, as Göring confided to Hitler, "a man who thinks up the cleverest things." Student's "efficiency and taste for the unorthodox appealed to Hitler," but more importantly, he "could be relied upon to translate the Fuhrer's dreams into military reality."[35]

Student's new command was designated the 7th Air Division and included all existing airborne (air-landing) and parachute units, as well as the requisite air transport force.[36] The motive behind this long-needed direction was the impending operations to annex the Sudetenland from Czechoslovakia. A political solution negated the use of the airborne formation, and the Wehrmacht quickly reclaimed its troops. Student maintained nominal command of the hollowed-out 7th Air Division and was appointed inspector of the Airborne forces. His efforts, as well as those of the megalomaniac Göring, finally resulted in achieving a unified German effort. After all, the first mass drop of German paratroops on October 7, 1938, prompted Field Marshal Göring to declare that "this weapon has a great future."[37] Not surprisingly then, in January 1939 the Army parachute battalion changed services and 7th Air Division was designated a parachute division. Furthermore, the 22nd Infantry Division was placed under Student's operational control in the air-landing role as part of the 7th Air Division.

Germany's airborne effort was now moving in the right direction. But Student disagreed from the beginning with the apparent role others in the German military envisioned for parachute troops. "I could not accept," he acknowledged, "the saboteur force concept."[38] Student explained:

It was a daredevil idea but I did not see minor operations
of this kind as worthwhile — they wasted individual soldiers and were not tasks for a properly constituted force.
The chances of getting back after such missions appeared
to be strictly limited; those taking part who survived
would probably be captured and the prospect of then
being treated as terrorists or spies would undermine the
morale of even the best troops. Casualties are inevitable
in war. But soldiers must be able to assume a real chance
of survival, and an eventual return home. The employment of airborne troops on such limited missions did not
seem to take account of their immense potential.[39]

This debate represented a fundamental point of divergence between
army and air force comprehension of how to utilize airborne forces. The
army believed the role was much like Mitchell had envisioned in 1918,
the landing of a large body of troops behind enemy lines to conduct, in
essence, conventional attacks. The air force, however, focused on the use
of highly trained commando teams that could attack and destroy high-
value strategic targets.[40]

Student, however, had always clearly understood the value of his
Fallschirmjäger. "Airborne troops," he insisted, "could become a battle winning factor of prime importance." He believed that "airborne forces made
third dimensional warfare possible in land operations. An adversary could
never be sure of a stable front because paratroops could simply jump in
and attack it from the rear where and when they decided." He emphasized
the effect of the psychological shock that a sudden attack from the sky, a
so-called "vertical envelopment," would produce on an adversary.
Airborne soldiers, he explained, could "pounce down and take over before
the foe knows what is going on." Student insisted, "The element of surprise
and shock action of paratroopers dropping in what was considered a safe
area instilled panic in the defender prior to the first shot being fired."[41]

Despite widespread knowledge of the ongoing airborne experimentation, parallel developments in the other major powers were virtually
nonexistent. The French had limited their foray into airborne warfare
with the establishment, in 1938, of only two airborne companies totalling
approximately three hundred men.[42] These were subsequently disbanded
when the war began.

The Americans and the British demonstrated even less interest. As
late as 1937, the British Secretary of State for War, after receiving a report

29

on German paratroop activity, refused a scheme to use parachutes for troops.[43] Their actions, or lack thereof, implied a belief that airborne forces had limited utility. The increasing frequency of reports of large-scale parachute and air-landing organizations in Europe by American army intelligence officers to the army's Chief of Staff, General George C. Marshall, prompted him to explore the issue further. As a result, he directed his Chief of Infantry, General G.E. Lynch, to conduct a study on the uses of "air infantry." Specifically, Marshall wanted Lynch to determine "the desirability of organizing, training, and conducting tests of a small detachment of air-infantry with a view to ascertaining whether or not our Army should contain a unit or units of this nature." Marshall visualized the role of the subject troops to be one of small detachments parachuting into vitally important areas, namely airfields, to seize and hold the objectives for the follow-up of air-landed reinforcements.[44]

The resultant report, delivered five days later, fell far short of the vision shared by the earlier Soviet airborne pioneers or the current German practitioners. Initially, General Lynch included employing air infantry in "suicide" missions. Although this was rethought it is a clear indication of the limited view that existed in regards to the employment of parachute troops. Nonetheless, his final report outlined the following practical uses for airborne forces:

1. To deposit small combat groups within enemy territory for special specific missions such as demolition of vital communications, factories, munitions. [These missions were seen as suicide in nature.]
2. To deposit small raiding parties for special reconnaissance missions to gain information not otherwise obtainable.
3. To deposit small combat groups, possibly as large as a battalion or regiment with artillery to hold a key point, area or bridge-head until slower moving elements of the army arrive.
4. To work in conjunction with a mechanized force at considerable distance from the main body.[45]

General Lynch recommended lengthy study and experimentation to determine such issues as the size of units to be formed, missions to be assigned, and equipment and weapons to be carried. In addition, matters such as command and control within the army and design characteristics of troop-carrying aircraft would also have to be worked out. Despite the quick response, it took another seven months until any further action was taken in regard to "air infantry." This should not be surprising in light of the attitude that prevailed. In fact, the U.S. Army initially held the general assumption that parachute troops would be employed principally in small detachments for demolition work in enemy rear areas. Slowly it evolved to the idea that these troops would be used as assault units to seize and hold airheads for air-landing troops.[46] This limited application in the minds of senior military commanders was responsible for their hesitant acceptance of what would become a key ingredient of modern war.

Their introduction to this lesson was forcibly made. Daring German airborne operations in Norway and the Low Countries in the spring of 1940, which in the words of their architect, General Kurt Student, "caused the world to gasp," shattered any remaining lethargy that existed in the West.[47] Skeptics and non-believers were forced to re-examine their outlook. The German aerial onslaught became the catalyst for action.

And action was quickly taken. The Americans established their test platoon on June 26. Its inaugural jump was made on August 16, and a month later General Marshall ordered the activation at the earliest practical date of the 1st Parachute Battalion.[48] The British, relative latecomers, reacted even quicker than the Americans. By June 6, 1940, British Prime Minister Winston Churchill directed that Britain also develop an airborne capability. "I very well remember the day in June 1940," Air Chief Marshal Sir John C. Slessor wrote, "when we received one of Mr. Churchill's characteristic minutes: 'Let there be at least 5,000 parachute troops. Pray let me know what is being done' or about the same number of words to that general effect, crowned with the well-known tab 'Action this day.'"[49] Several weeks later he sent a memorandum to the Chiefs of Staff urging them to establish a corps "of parachute troops on a scale of equal to five thousand."[50] Churchill, himself an accomplished adventurer, journalist, and soldier, held "an almost abstract attachment to the offensive."[51] He believed that audacity and willpower constituted the only sound approach to the conduct of war.[52] Paratroopers clearly encapsulated the warrior spirit so close to Churchill's heart. Accordingly, the combative British Prime Minister became the stimulus for the establishment of airborne forces in the British Army.

This proved, however, to be a daunting task, even for the Prime Minister. Conservatism, as well as a degree of concern for more pressing matters, such as the defence of the island itself, prompted vehement resistance from his military commanders, who felt that the utility of airborne troops did not warrant the investment of scarce resources, particularly some of its best soldiers. "There are very real difficulties in this parachute business," wrote one senior Royal Air Force officer. "We are trying to do what we have never been able to do hitherto, namely to introduce a completely new arm into the Service at about five minutes' notice, and with totally inadequate resources and personnel." He pointed out that "little, if any, practical experience is possessed in England of any of these problems" and concluded that "it will be necessary to cover in six months what the Germans have covered in six years."[53]

Not surprisingly, the RAF was especially resistant to establishing a parachute force because of its potential impact on their strategic bombing campaign. "There can be no question," asserted the Air Ministry, "at the moment of forming special units for dropping parachute troops. We have neither the aircraft nor the crews available, nor are we likely in the near future."[54] They went so far as to discount the requirement. A report three months later in September 1940 insisted, "There is reason to believe that the tactics we have witnessed hitherto in the employment of parachutists and airborne troops probably represent past history. They were applicable in unprepared, small neutral states." However, the Air Ministry concluded that airborne operations were "unlikely to be applicable against Germany."[55]

It was this perceived impedance from the RAF, as well as the opposition from senior Army commanders charged with defending England and rebuilding a modern army, that raised the ire of Churchill and the other supporters of airborne forces. "Very early we came to certain definite conclusions," recalled Lieutenant-General F.A.M. Browning, another strong advocate for paratroopers, "which we have kept before us ever since and for which we may rightly say we have fought many a stout battle against the doubters and unbelievers: it is always the same with anything new and there is nothing curious about that."[56] The enmity was initially so entrenched that it required Churchill to continually prod his military commanders for progress reports to ensure some movement was underway.

His frustration was so great at one point that he suggested to Anthony Eden, British Secretary of State for War, that an example should be made of "one or two" of the reluctant officers to set an example for the others.[57] Notwithstanding Churchill's commitment, exigencies at the time, as well as the institutional resistance, combined to convince the Prime Minister to be satisfied, initially in any case, with a parachute corps of five hundred men instead of the five thousand he wanted.[58]

And so, rather hesitantly, if not reluctantly, the Allies set out, albeit in a decentralized manner, to establish an airborne capability of their own. The stunning tactical victories by the German Fallschirmjäger had spread fear throughout unoccupied Europe and even across the channel to England itself.[59] More importantly, they introduced the public to a new element of warfare. Universally, paratroopers embodied offensive spirit and the epitome of the modern fighting man. It seemed that no nation could ignore this advancement in modern warfare.

CHAPTER TWO

Joining the Club — Establishing a
Canadian Airborne Capability

Man is the only creative animal on earth, though paradoxically his resistance to change sometimes can be almost heroically obstinate. He builds institutions in order to preserve past innovations, but in that very act often fails to promote the environment for the growth of new ones.

Robert S. McNamara[60]

The observation of Robert McNamara, a former American secretary of defense, seems to be timeless. It is certainly pertinent to the Allied, including Canada's, experience in regard to establishing an airborne capability. As already noted, the Allied nations, although aware of the advancements in parachute warfare during the inter-war years, chose for a number of reasons to ignore them. However, the stunning German victories in the spring of 1940, particularly those by the daring Fallschirmjäger, transformed the way people thought of modern war.

Canada, like England, its role model and protector, was caught completely unprepared for the conflict that now engulfed the world. Not surprisingly, the Canadian record is similar to that of the British. That is to say, no effort was made in Canada prior to the commencement of hostilities either conceptually or in practice to develop an airborne capability. In fact, Canada did little during this period to ensure that its military in general was capable of participating in a modern war. The economic desperation of the Depression and the vacuum of peace were barriers too great for the military leadership to overcome in their attempts to convince the government of the day to allocate scarce dollars to military spending. The consistent and destructive infighting between the different services only exacerbated the problem. In the end, it took the collapse of Europe and the imminent invasion of England in the dark spring of 1940 to focus attention on the necessity for military renewal. But it was the Germans who now set the template of how a modern army was defined. And their paradigm included paratroopers.

Despite this new reality, the idea of developing a Canadian parachute force was not an immediate reaction. Far from it — the concept was not even raised until August 1940, when Colonel E.L.M. Burns returned to Canada from Europe. Burns's experiences overseas, both on the Continent and in England, were instrumental in convincing him of the importance of establishing a Canadian airborne capability. He was, however, alone in this belief.

Colonel Burns was once described as "the brain that marches like a soldier."[61] Although he was recognized as an officer of great ability and intellect, he was also one virtually without personality.[62] Nonetheless, he was a firm believer that "war is not a static science." He lectured consistently that it was "a dynamic art; [and] improvements in attack and defence succeed each other continuously." He explained, "Unless we are constantly thinking how we can overcome the enemy's latest technique, we will never win battles." Burns concluded that it was "the duty of all of us to think about these things, and contribute what we can."[63]

Burns's perspective was born from his experience in the First World War. It ingrained in him a lasting memory of the "will-sapping effect of struggling through mud, living in mud, for days on end."[64] No one who struggled through it, he later recalled, would ever forget it. According to Burns, the mud and the effect of bad weather negated the ability to effectively execute offensive operations. Put simply, nothing could move. Surprise and decisiveness of action were nearly impossible to achieve. And so, Burns's wartime service entrenched in his thinking a belief in the necessity for mobility and speed as the key to modern warfare.

Initially, for Burns, this took the form of mechanization. During the inter-war years he was a prolific writer and actively participated in the academic debate on mechanization and the character of modern war. Despite his progressive ideas, Burns never contemplated the employment of paratroopers, or the use of air power to transport infantry tactically.[65] He did, however, fully embrace the concept of "motor guerillas," expounded by the leading British military theorist at the time, Major-

General J.F.C. Fuller. This idea, quite simply, called for the use of motorized forces to conduct raids deep into the enemy's rear lines to attack the
antagonist's headquarters and lines of communications, which Fuller
dubbed the "brains and nerves" of the opponent's army.[66] What is
important here is Burns's early appreciation for Deep Battle and tactics
that would emphasize mobility and speed, and thus offensive power.
This would prove important to his later support of parachute troops.

Clearly, he realized the importance of mobility and speed to the offensive. Conceptually, he grasped the importance and utility of striking deep
behind the enemy's lines to attack their command structures and lines of
communication. The successful utilization of German paratroopers in
April and May 1940 now revealed a viable tool to accomplish this aim.
"The successes obtained by the Germans with air-borne troops," asserted
Burns, "seem to show that this will become a regular method of warfare."[67]

Of equal significance to Burns in the formulation of his thinking on airborne forces was the subsequent parachute scare that erupted in the
aftermath of the German aerial onslaught. The German Fallschirmjäger,
by virtue of their stunning accomplishments, were quickly perceived by
the military and general public as invincible. This created a wave of
paranoia that infected the still unoccupied territories in Europe, as well
the population in Britain. As the remnants of the British Expeditionary
Force and the 1st Canadian Division hastily retreated to England, the
threat of an imminent invasion was inescapable. "Invasion," conceded
Burns in his memoirs, "seemed fearfully close in those days."[68] Inherent
in that menace was the imminent spectre of German Fallschirmjäger
descending from the clouds throughout England.

The perception of an airborne invasion even struck at the heart of the
ever fiery and optimistic British Prime Minister, who estimated the
expected scale of airborne attack at approximately thirty thousand paratroopers.[69] As a result, by November 1940, troop dispositions in England,
in the order of fourteen divisions, were tailored to counter the envisioned
airborne invasion and vast amounts of scarce material were invested to
this aim.[70] Furthermore, the government adopted a policy to safeguard
the country by ordering all open spaces (meaning virtually every park and
playing field) all over Britain to be seeded with long spiked poles, concrete
blocks, and other obstacles that would impede paratroopers.[71]

Colonel Burns, as part of the Canadian Expeditionary Force (CEF)
in England, now tasked with the defence of the British Isles, was

very conscious of the parachute menace. Their role was now to guard against it. Canada's overseas commander, Lieutenant-General A.G.L. McNaughton, stated that "invasion was a real threat," and the Canadians were in essence, "a mobile reserve with a 360 degree front."[72] He affirmed that they might have to operate anywhere in Great Britain to meet seaborne or airborne attacks.

This abject and bleak environment deeply influenced Colonel Burns when, in July 1940, he returned to Canada. Major-General H.D.G. Crerar, who himself was recalled to take over the position of Chief of the General Staff (CGS) in Ottawa, decided he wanted the intellectually gifted Burns, whom he appointed Assistant Deputy CGS, with him at National Defence Headquarters (NDHQ). Burns was now tasked with the organization and development of Canada's army, in essence to assist in its transformation to a modern force. An all-out effort now commenced. "With the fall of France," recounted Burns in his memoirs, "the limits which had been imposed by the previous cautious policy of Mr. Mackenzie King's government were set aside, and the question now was: how much could we do within the limits of Canada's manpower and political situation to build up and train and equip those formations needed for the task?"[73]

Colonel Burns wasted little time. With his entrenched belief in mobility and speed as critical components of offensive power, combined with his recent experience in Europe, he now set to the task of organizing Canada's army for the new methods of warfare. Significantly, he saw airborne forces as an integral requirement. On August 13, 1940, he submitted his first proposal for the establishment of a Canadian airborne capability, in the form of a battalion of specially selected parachute troops, to Colonel J.C. Murchie, the director of military operations in National Defence Headquarters. "We hope to turn to the offensive against Germany some day," emphasized Burns, "and it appears that full advantage must be taken of all forms of mobility in carrying out such operations."[74] It was not lost on Burns that the possession of airborne troops obliged the Germans to maintain much larger garrisons than they otherwise would because of the threat of a landing anywhere, anytime.

Predictably, Murchie dismissed the idea. "Although the value of the parachute troops in certain situations was very great," he replied, "the provision of such troops by Canada would be a project of doubtful value to the combined Empire war effort in view of the expenditure of time, money and equipment which would be involved."[75] Colonel Murchie further explained that any Canadian parachute units, because of their unique nature and the numbers involved, would likely be part of a British para-chute corps, and as a result, they would be difficult to administer and, more importantly, largely out of Canadian control during operations. "If any additional commitments are accepted," he counselled, "these should be limited to the formation of units to which Canadians are particularly adapted by reason of the nature of this country."[76]

His objection was understandable to a point. First, the Canadian military, after decades of political and military neglect, was struggling to modernize, a formidable task at the best of times, much less during a war in the face of a powerful enemy. Second, the issue of national command remained an important one for Canadians, and one that Lieutenant-General McNaughton fought fiercely for throughout his tenure as the overseas commander. "We had to keep the command in our own hands," he insisted, "otherwise we would have had a succession of people coming in and the order and counter-order would have been similar to what we'd been through on Salisbury Plain in 1914."[77] McNaughton recalled the struggle to claim national control over the Canadian Expeditionary Force during the Great War. Those successful efforts transformed the CEF into a distinct national entity. Its achievements fuelled national pride and a sense of collective accomplishment. As a direct result, over time the Canadian Corps became enshrined in the minds of Canadians. McNaughton was intent on applying that hard-learned lesson to the present conflict.[78]

The initial rejection failed to dissuade Colonel Burns. He quickly submitted a second memorandum to the CGS a mere six days later. This time, however, he wisely reverted to a venerable Canadian approach when discussing a suggested increase to the nation's military capability. He cloaked his proposal in the mantle of home defence. "In the defence of Canada against raids or a serious attempt at invasion," Burns argued, "they [paratroops] would be the quickest means of building up a front against an attacker, and also could harass his communications." He further elaborated, "We have often thought of the problem of preventing an enemy from establishing a base for supplying submarines in remote sections of the coast which could not easily be reached by land. If we had even a battalion of Paratroops who could be landed to counter-attack such bases, it would make their establishment very much more difficult for an enemy; it would probably be necessary for him to send about a brigade of troops for land defences." He went so far as to sug-

gest that they "might also provide a highly mobile force for internal
security duties." But in the end, his true motives surfaced. "Above all," he
argued, "I would stress the moral advantage to our troops in knowing
that we are preparing for all forms of offensive action."[79]

Tenaciously, two weeks later, on August 28, 1940, he forwarded a
third memorandum. "Parachute troops," he insisted, "are no longer just
a stunt." He emphasized, "All armies, including the Americans, are to
have them." He explained that "airborne troops are merely the most
mobile form of land forces, and the fact that some of them land by parachute is due to the characteristics of the aeroplane." Once again he linked
his scheme to a distinctly national orientation and theme in an attempt
to win support. "Canada is often claimed to be a country essentially
adapted to air transport — witness development of the Northland."
Therefore, "training air-borne troops," he argued, "would be a development in line with the emphasis on air training generally." Again, he
emphasized their ability to assist with internal security by being able to
"reach centres of disaffection in remote areas very quickly." Similarly,
Burns reiterated the psychological value of establishing an airborne
capability. "To begin training parachute troops," he affirmed, "would be
valuable in stimulating the morale, both of the service and the public. It
would be a step towards a 'quality' army, and would show that we were
actually doing something to create a force with offensive capabilities, and
that the General staff had a modern outlook."[80]

His attempt at appealing to the military and public perception was
significant. The year 1940 was a low point in the Allied war effort.
Defeats, retreats, and withdrawals were the order of the day. Worse yet,
England was bracing for invasion. Within this context, Burns recognized the importance of establishing and training a corps of aggressive
and inherently offensive-minded paratroopers. Correctly, he surmised
that this would provide a boost to public and military morale.

But Burns was quite alone in his thinking. Although in philosophical terms the CGS appeared in concert with the utility of airborne forces,
he was not prepared to take any concrete action. "It is," Crerar responded, "not a project of importance to the winning of the war just now."[81] He
directed that the matter be set aside and brought forward to his attention
in three months' time. On November 12, 1940, Colonel Burns diligently
staffed his fourth and final paper to the Chief of the General Staff.
Although it was largely a cut and paste of his three earlier memorandums, the one key component that was central to understanding the airborne concept was once again stressed. "We hope to turn to the offensive

against Germany some day," reiterated Burns, "and it appears that full advantage must be taken of all forms of mobility in carrying out operations." Unquestionably, to Burns, paratroopers represented mobility and offensive power. They also personified a modern army.

The issue was adroitly sidestepped. Crerar had the idea forwarded to the Canadian Military Headquarters (CMHQ) in London, England to ascertain the views of both the War Office and Canadian Overseas Commander McNaughton. The War Office promptly reported that parachute troops were in fact being organized and that one "special service battalion" was undergoing active training. The British concept of employment was explained as filling the role of light cavalry to "seize bridge crossings, defiles and aerodromes well in advance of the slower-moving main body of the army."[82]

In essence, at this early stage of development, particularly in light of the internal resistance to the idea of airborne forces, neither the British nor the Americans had fully appreciated the potential of paratroopers. At this juncture the role of airborne forces was still largely limited to raids of three types: first, a raid on a selected position, to be followed by the evacuation of the raiding force by air; second, a raid to be followed by evacuation by sea; and third, the dropping of parachutists simply as saboteurs.[83] Critics, particularly in the Air Ministry, continued to argue that "dropping troops from the air by parachute is a clumsy and obsolescent method" and that the German use of paratroopers in the Low Countries "may be the last time that parachute troops are used on a serious scale in major operations."[84]

Of note was the impression left by Lieutenant-General Andrew G.L. McNaughton in response to the CGS's query. "It is understood," wrote one of his staff officers, "that General McNaughton favours the idea that Canada should commence the organization and training of both parachute and glider-borne troops, and that one battalion should be raised in the first instance, later perhaps, expanding to one brigade."[85] However, Major-General Crerar was of a different mind. During a meeting on December 20, 1940, at the Canadian Military Headquarters, he proclaimed that he was "agreeable to a proportion (say a platoon) in each infantry battalion being trained in this work [parachuting], [but] he is not in favour of training special airborne units unless the War Office make specific requests for them, which is unlikely."[86] McNaughton, although stating that "the use of air-borne troops has distinct possibilities" quickly acquiesced to the views of the CGS and was not prepared to press his views.[87] As a consequence, no further action was undertaken. In the end, not even a "proportion" of infantry, as Crerar indicated he would be agreeable to, were trained as paratroopers.

Colonel Burns's efforts were noteworthy, yet, as history has shown, largely futile. Despite his rationalization of airborne forces in a home defence/security role, or as the harbinger of a modern offensive army, his prescience was lost on his military superiors. They failed to see the importance or relevance of such forces, particularly in the Canadian context. In all fairness, they were also preoccupied with creating a mechanized army from scratch. Nonetheless, Burns's persistent exertions at establishing a Canadian airborne capability arguably earn him the title of "father" of Canada's airborne forces.

And so, by late 1940, the concept of an airborne force slipped into obscurity. It was not until the early part of August 1941, after Colonel Burns was promoted and sent overseas, that the idea resurfaced in the faceless tomb of NDHQ. But the re-emergence of the debate was not the result of in-depth analysis or a change in direction by the Canadian military leadership. Rather, it was inevitably linked to an Allied change of heart.

The startling success of the German Fallschirmjäger in their conquest of the Mediterranean island of Crete in May 1941 prompted the British to adopt a more ambitious program for airborne forces. This was driven by Prime Minister Churchill himself. "This is a sad story," he lamented in the aftermath of the invasion, "and I feel myself greatly to blame for allowing myself to be overborne by the resistances which were offered." He concluded, "We are always found behind-hand by the enemy."[88] But this was to change. On May 27, 1941, Churchill declared, "We ought to have 5,000 parachutists and an Air-borne Division on the German model, with any improvements which might suggest themselves from experience." This time he was not to be deterred. "A whole year has been lost," he warned, "and I now invite the Chiefs of the Staff to make proposals for trying, so far as is possible, to repair the misfortune."[89] Four days later, the British general and air staffs agreed to press forward as quickly as possible with the airborne program. A brigade of 2,500 fully trained parachutists was to be formed by July 1, 1941. Even before this was achieved, army staff began to plan for a division-sized organization.[90]

Despite the renewed effort in the British camp, initially Canadian non-interest remained prevalent. Notwithstanding the dramatic seizure of Crete and Churchill's fear that Cyprus and Syria would be next, the Canadian commanders still failed to see any reason for raising specialized troops who were perceived as lacking a credible role in the Canadian context. Nonetheless, the British flurry of activity did prompt queries from the CGS.[91] But the latent enmity towards going down the airborne path was clearly evident in General McNaughton, the Canadian overseas commander. Although he left an impression at a meeting in December 1940 that he supported the idea of airborne forces, he now showed his true colours. In response to the latest Canadian query on what the War Office was doing in regard to paratroopers, he bluntly declared, "I do not advocate the establishment of any separate parachute troops in the Canadian Forces."[92] He explained that he had watched "with interest the organization here [England] of such special units as Commandos, Ski Battalions and Para Tps." The cycle was always the same, he insisted. "Initial enthusiasm very high," he wrote, "and draws good officers and men from regular units distracting and unsettling others and upsetting the unit's organization." However, he concluded, "with prolonged period awaiting appropriate opportunity for employment enthusiasm evaporates [and] officers and men ask [for] re-transfer and return to former units disappointed."[93] In McNaughton's view there were only two reasons that justified the creation of a special airborne force. The first was the probability of early and continued employment in a special role, and the second was the need for specialized training on lines greatly different from regular units.[94]

Despite the perfunctory rejection by the Canadian overseas commander, the renewed airborne effort lingered. Paradoxically, the reason for the continued interest was not driven by the Army but rather by the Royal Canadian Air Force. In October 1941, the RCAF began to press NDHQ in Ottawa in regard to the policy being considered in respect to the establishment of parachute troops. Furthermore, Air Force staff officers relayed an offer from the Royal Air Force to provide instructors and equipment to assist the army in the event they wished to proceed with training airborne forces.[95]

As no definitive answer was forthcoming, the RCAF continued to forward a stream of messages requesting an update on the Army's airborne policy. This bothersome attention prompted Vice Chief of the General Staff Major-General Maurice Pope to direct in January 1942 that the effort be indefinitely deferred because the home army provided no scope for the employment of parachute troops.[96] An Appreciation on Air Landing Troops conducted the same month reinforced Pope's assertion. "Parachute troops," it clearly explained, "will not be considered except in passing. Our operations at home are largely static (coast defence), and, as a consequence, do not provide scope for the employment of parachute troops."[97]

This belief was institutionally entrenched. The earliest military appreciations completed during the war emphasized "the requirement for Home Defence" since the "situation in the 'Old World' is bound to be precarious at best."[98] But in the discussion of forces required for the defence of Canada, absolutely no reference was ever made to the employment of, or the requirement for, paratroopers.[99] Furthermore, the annual Army Programmes, for the period 1940 to 1944, never included even a mention of airborne troops.

Despite the repetitive assertions by senior military commanders that parachute troops were of limited relevance to the Canadian Army, a letter from CMHQ in mid-February 1942 stated, "The policy to be adopted by the Canadian Army with regard to paratroop training is [still] under consideration by NDHQ at the moment. According to our latest information no decision was to be given until this matter had been thoroughly discussed with Lt.-General McNaughton."[100]

Apparently, some senior staff officers were still watching the British expansion with interest. In addition, the continued efforts of the Royal Canadian Air Force kept the issue of airborne troops alive. Although the matter continued to simmer, little evident headway was made. Even editorials in the *Globe and Mail* on April 6 and 7, 1942 respectively, failed to ignite the issue. "If the Canadian Corps is really the point of a dagger aimed at the heart of Berlin," questioned an anonymous critic, "why is it not being trained as a modern air-borne assault force here in Canada, where space and climatic conditions favour such training?"[101] A follow-up article the next day hammered at that same theme. "The public," asserted the editorial, "might be pardoned for asking when the new Canadian Army, which is to be the spearhead of the attack, ... 'the point of a dagger aimed at the heart of Berlin,' is going to start training the necessary parachute and air-borne troops without which it cannot land on the Continent without a terrible sacrifice of life."[102]

The latest resurgence, however, seemed to have little effect. In fact, the continuing resistance by the military hierarchy to establishing a distinct

Canadian airborne capability was reinforced by none other than the Minister of National Defence (MND) several weeks later. The Honourable J.L. Ralston explained in the House of Commons that "the formation of an actual paratroop unit is not being gone ahead with at the present moment, but rather the training of men so that they can be used as paratroops when the time comes, with additional training to be done with aircraft."[103] The policy seemed consistent. So too was the continuing failure to begin the much-heralded "training of men" for paratroop employment.

But the continued indifference shown by the Canadians was not shared by their Allies. On March 10, 1942, the British War Cabinet Chiefs of Staff Committee declared, "airborne forces have come to stay and ... they must in future be as much a part of the Army as are armoured forces."[104] In consonance with this policy was an increasing liaison and cooperation between the British and the Americans on the subject of airborne forces. In May, Churchill appealed directly to the President of the United States for additional transport aircraft to expedite the training and operational readiness of his paratroopers.[105] Shortly thereafter, General George C. Marshall, the Chief of Staff of the United States Army, visited England to view first-hand the British airborne forces. That same month, shortly after Marshall's visit, it was announced that an American parachute battalion would be dispatched to England as a result of a personal invitation from Prime Minister Churchill to President Franklin Delano Roosevelt.[106] Furthermore, in June, the War Office established a new Air Directorate to deal specifically with airborne forces. It was to act as a special link between the War Office and the Air Ministry on all air matters.

Clearly, Canada had been left behind. Investigation into the matter proved just that. In early June, Lieutenant-Colonel R.H. Keefler, from the Directorate of Military Training, NDHQ, was sent to Fort Benning, Georgia, to report on the state of parachute training in the United States. Coincident with the submission of his final report were discussions with Air Vice Marshal Ernest Walter Steadman of the RCAF, who had just returned from a visit with the 6th British Airborne Division. Once the scope of ongoing activity was realized, a change of heart occurred. The Chief of the General Staff now reversed his earlier position and forwarded a proposal to the Minister of National Defence for nothing less than the organization of a parachute battalion.[107]

Approval was not long in coming. The Canadian War Cabinet Committee gave its blessing on Canada Day 1942. Ironically, the purpose of the unit was described as home defence, specifically, "to provide a means of recapture of aerodromes or re-enforcements of remote localities by air-borne troops."[108] The Minister's proposal for the organization, training, and equipment of a parachute battalion clearly stated "for employment in Canada."

The glaring inconsistency went unchallenged. For years the idea of establishing a parachute force had been rejected by the military and political leadership because the airborne capability was dismissed as irrelevant to the Home Army. Yet, almost ludicrously, concomitant with an improvement in the general strategic situation for the Allies, the military was now arguing that airborne forces were necessary for national security. In fact, it declared, "The Army has a definite requirement to train one battalion of 600 paratroops by 1st January 1943."[109] A mere month later, an assessment on the Army requirement for gliders stated that a demand did exist for paratroopers, but only one company in strength.[110] Astoundingly, by early December 1942, the demand changed again. Now the Directorate of Military Operations and Plans envisioned a need for approximately one thousand personnel for airborne operations in Canada, exclusive of the newly designated 1st Canadian Parachute Battalion.[111] But this flew in the face of a previous DMO & P report to the CGS stemming from a November 10, 1942 conference, which stated:

> Under the present forms and scales of attack against Canada, a raid of comparatively short duration only is envisaged. On this basis, our airborne troops would be used either to re-inforce a garrison against a threatened raid or to drive out an enemy in temporary possession as a result of a raid. In the first case especially, most areas which might be threatened are at least reasonably close to aerodromes, landing fields or seaplane bases where air landing troops would suffice; in many of the other places — particularly in British Columbia and Newfoundland — where an enemy raid might be made, the topography is such that the landing of parachute troops could not be attempted.

> Parachute troops are generally not well suited for these kinds of operations, particularly for dropping whilst operations are in progress.[112]

The situation seems perplexing. However, the key to understanding this seeming contradiction is not found in the "officially" stated role. One must look beyond the rhetoric and words. Quite simply, the senior Canadian leadership now wanted a parachute capability. To ensure they received the necessary approval they cloaked their proposal in the mantle of home defence, since this rationale was the surest means of gaining acquiescence from their political masters. Lieutenant-Colonel Fraser Eadie, the last commanding officer of the 1st Canadian Parachute Battalion, acknowledged that the Minister of National Defence finally agreed to the concept on the basis that the force was designated for home defence.[113]

The stratagem became evident once the parachute battalion was approved. Now that it was authorized its ultimate employment created a degree of consternation for Canada's military commanders. As late as December 1942, six months after approval, the Canadian military attache in the United States commented on the absence of any policy having been "formulated indicating for what service the Battalion was to be used."[114] At the same time, the Deputy CGS passed a note to his superior, counselling, "I do not consider that it is feasible at present to decide the ultimate role of the 1st Parachute B[attalio]n."[115] Instead, he suggested that the unit continue its training, which was not expected to be completed prior to the end of March 1943, at the earliest. Not surprisingly, even before the newly formed parachute unit was deemed fit for active service, overtures were made to the War Office for its inclusion in a British airborne formation. Fraser Eadie, the former paratroop commander, recalled a telephone conversation during this period with Major Jeff Nicklin, the Battalion's deputy commanding officer. Nicklin confided that neither the Canadian government nor the field commanders in England had any idea what to do with the paratroopers, and as a result, they were being offered up to the British.[116] On March 18, 1943, General Sir Bernard Paget, Commander-in-Chief of home forces (UK), welcomed the offer and stated the battalion could be included in the establishment of a second British airborne division that was forming.[117]

It became apparent that the issues of national control of Canadian forces outside of the country and relevance to home defence, the key reasons for inhibiting the establishment of paratroopers since the initial rejection of Colonel Burns's proposal in 1940, were not, after all, important. But the latest turn in events underscored another theme. Namely, in Canada, the ultimate aim was never to develop the airborne capability for use in the country's defence. That was merely a manoeuvre to placate the critics. The senior military leadership and airborne advocates wanted to use it in the active theatres of Europe. Indeed, they had finally absorbed the fact that to their Allies, airborne forces had become a symbol of a modern army. Moreover, they represented the cutting edge of offensive action. The British, as a result of their study of German Fallschirmjäger, viewed parachute troops as "a highly mobile force of shock troops which can be projected at short notice into an enemy area which might otherwise consider itself immune from attack." They saw the airborne weapon solely in terms of the offense.[118] "I am convinced," wrote the Chief of the Imperial General Staff, "that an Airborne Division ... is a necessary component of any major military force."[119] Not surprisingly, they authorized the establishment of an Airborne Division as early as November 1941.

The American doctrinal and philosophical development was similar. The Americans converted the 82nd Motorized Infantry Division to the airborne role on June 26, 1942.[120] Furthermore, their change in thinking was clearly reflected in the U.S. War Department's 1942 Strategy Book, which stated:

> The Use of Parachutists ... Nowadays one cannot possibly hope to succeed in landing operations unless one can be assured of the cooperation of parachutists on a scale hitherto undreamed of. In fact, only the parachutist will be able to take enemy territory from the rear, thus preventing destruction of the attacking forces by artillery fire and enabling them to get a foothold on the coast.... 25,000 men set down in advance at every important point of attack should be able to do the work, especially if it proves possible to get them assembled. They must obviously be regarded as the pivot of success of the entire operation.[121]

In addition, airborne forces, as Burns had suggested two years earlier, were devoured by a public hungry for indications that the tide of war would soon shift irrevocably against the Germans. The aggressive, fearless paratroopers provided this perception. Not surprisingly, an element of the Canadian military wanted to ensure they were part of the neophyte club. "We members of the 1st Canadian Parachute Battalion," wrote the unit's chronicler in the War Diary, "are well aware of our unique position as a newly born unit in a new phase of warfare. We are therefore, confident of our success and trust that we well be given the opportunity to prove our value."[122] Lieutenant-Colonel G.F.P. Bradbrooke, the first commanding officer of the unit, clearly explained his understanding of his battalion's purpose. "The paratroopers," he declared, "are the tip of the spear. They must expect to go in first, to penetrate behind enemy lines and to fight in isolated positions."[123]

Not the media, the senior military commanders, nor those who flocked to the new parachute unit left any doubt as to the role of the new paratroopers. They were to be Canada's premier combat unit. When Brigadier E.G. Weeks, Deputy Chief of the General Staff, announced that the 1st Canadian Parachute Battalion was to be formed, he pointed out, "The Dominion's aim was to develop such a hard striking unit that it would have an efficiency excelled by no other such group in the world."[124] To the military community, being a modern, offensive-minded army meant, rightly or wrongly, the possession of paratroops. Canada had now joined the club.

CHAPTER THREE

Canada's Hardy, Tanned Sons — Developing a Canadian Military Elite

Three officers and 10 men are action-hungry and impatient to fill their role as the sharp, hardened tip of the Canadian army's "dagger pointed at the heart of Berlin." The army picked them out of thousands of fit young Canadian soldiers who sought berths in the Canadian army's newest and already its elite corps, the first parachute battalion.

Robert Taylor, the *Toronto Daily Star*, August 12, 1942[125]

Canada's military leadership was undoubtably hesitant and certainly relatively late in deciding to establish a distinct Canadian airborne capability. However, once this decision was made, no effort was spared. The nation's paratroopers were to represent nothing less than the country's fighting elite.[126]

The dramatic shift in attitude by Canada's military commanders was largely driven by events. By the summer of 1942, the war had dragged on for almost three years — years filled with few victories. Defeat, humiliation, and an inability to strike back at the Reich permeated the minds of soldiers and citizens alike. For much of this time Britain and the Commonwealth were pinned to the wall. Survival was tenuous at best, and the Axis juggernaut seemed unstoppable. It was a time when the public had a need for heroes, which tough, fearless, highly publicized paratroopers aptly filled. "It builds our morale, it stiffens the spine and braces the backbone of the public," explained American Lieutenant-General E.M. Flanagan, "to hear talk about the independent type airborne operation."[127] As Colonel E.L.M. Burns had argued as early as the summer of 1940, the public hungered for a sign of offensive capability or, as Flanagan elaborated, a force able "to deal a lethal blow to the enemy, deep in his backyard."[128]

The public appeal of the paratrooper was directly linked to the symbolism that was attached to the image of the parachute soldier. The use of airborne forces, as exemplified by the stunning German victories in the Low Countries in 1940, represented a revolutionary new form of warfare. It was a weapon that was perceived as transcending the stifling death, futility, and lethargy of the trench warfare of the previous war experience. As a result, airborne forces quickly framed the public's conception of modern war. The paratrooper was portrayed as the leading edge, the "tip of the spear." Airborne forces were deigned as special troops with a highly dangerous and extremely hazardous mission to fulfill. The embryonic British Parachute Corps was described by the senior military leadership as elite and as fulfilling the toughest job in the British Army. Moreover, the senior military officers described paratroopers as "super-soldiers."[129] Their task was defined as nothing short of facilitating the general advance of the army by seizing key installations and terrain on the enemy's flanks and in his rear. Furthermore, the paratroopers were given the responsibility of creating "alarm and despondency"and complete confusion in the antagonist's safe areas at the most critical moments of attack. Justified or not, they became associated with the necessary prerequisites for military success.[130] To the public, airborne forces became synonymous with offensive spirit and capability. They represented, in the layman's perception, the sword that could slay the enemy in his deepest redoubt.

Canada's military commanders very quickly exploited their decision to establish a national airborne capability. They realized that it would enhance public morale and provide the impression that Canada was developing a modern offensive force that would soon strike back at the enemy. The media assisted with the delivery of this message. It painted the country's neophyte paratroopers in a transcendent light. Newspapers described the first volunteers as "action-hungry and impatient to fill their role as the sharp, hardened tip of the Canadian army's 'dagger pointed at the heart of Berlin.'"[131] With unanimity, newspapers invariably described the parachute volunteers as "hard as nails," representing the toughest and smartest in soldiers in the Canadian Army.[132] One journalist wrote, "They are good, possibly great soldiers, hard, keen, fast-thinking and eager for battle," while another asserted that they were "Canada's most daring and rugged soldiers ... daring because they'll be training as paratroops: rugged because paratroops do the toughest jobs in hornet nests behind enemy lines."[133]

Others painted a picture of virtual super-men. "Picture men with muscles of iron," depicted one writer, "dropping in parachutes, hanging precariously from slender ropes, braced for any kind of action ... these toughest men who ever wore khaki."[134] Another simply explained, "Your Canadian paratrooper is an utterly fearless, level thinking, calculating killer possessive of all the qualities of a delayed-action time bomb."[135]

In early August 1942, mere weeks after the announcement of the decision to create a parachute battalion, senior military officials were already boasting of their vision for this force. The new unit, which was not even formed yet, was quickly described by the military establishment as a "new shock troop unit" and as an elite.[136] Ironically, although little interest, if not complete apathy, had been shown by Canada's senior officers in regard to the establishment or utility of an airborne capability, they now had the zealousness of the newly converted. "Canada hopes," extolled Deputy Chief of the General Staff Brigadier F.G. Weeks, "to combine the best features of the U.S. and British paratroop technique, to experiment themselves and produce 'the finest air-borne troops in the world.'"[137] He elaborated that "the Dominion's aim was to develop such a hard striking unit that it would have an efficiency excelled by no other such group in the world."[138]

Possession of paratroopers worthy of taking their place in the vanguard of any future offensive action, however, required a solid commitment and special people. The Army, despite the initial reticence about the idea of airborne soldiers, now undertook an all-out effort. The parachute battalion became a select unit worthy of the title of elite and was placed in a position of pre-eminence.[139] As early as July 29, 1942, the DCGS declared, "The formation and individual training of the 1st Canadian Parachute Bn is an urgent matter and [I must] stress the importance of eliminating any delays in this regard."[140] In fact, 1 Cdn Para Bn was now granted "the highest priority."[141]

Army commanders intuitively knew that "only the best men will do."[142] The limited experience of the British clearly demonstrated that paratroopers needed characteristics such as resourcefulness, courage, endurance, and discipline.[143] The *Canadian Army Training Memorandum* (*CATM*) explained, "Parachute training is tough — even in training. It needs young men, alert and clever young men, who can exploit a chance and who have the guts necessary to fight against over-whelming odds and win."[144] But it was evident to the leadership that the airborne soldier also required a level of intelligence above the normal infantry requirement. "Only physically perfect men of high intelligence and good education were admitted," explained Captain F.O. Miksche, a renowned military writer of the time.[145] In addition, the Army leader-ship also decided that all volunteers should be of the rank of private, and they made it mandatory for all volunteers to revert prior acting or substantive rank to that of private before proceeding for training.[146] The conceptual model was such that one journalist quipped, "You've practically got to be Superman's 2IC [second-in-command] in order to get in."[147] And so the theoretical requirement was well articulated.

But these were uncharted waters. Although the general idea of what was required was understood, the actual mechanics of selecting this new elite posed real challenges. A very complex and discerning screening process was undertaken to ensure that only the finest candidates were selected for further training. Army psychiatrist Dr. A.E. Moll developed a rating system that was used to grade volunteers during selection boards. His system ranked an individual from a range of A to E, accord-ing to the following scale:

"A" — Outstanding
"B" — Superior
"C" — Average
"D"— Inferior but acceptable
"E" — Rejected[148]

Only those who achieved an "A" score were kept for airborne train-ing. Moll was certain that the "A" candidates were clearly the best mate-rial. He was equally sure that the "E" personnel should not be consid-ered. However, he conceded some uncertainty in regards to the 80 per-cent who fell into the grey area in between. But Moll and his staff decid-ed that as long as the supply of volunteers remained strong they would continue to accept only the best.[149]

The requirements imposed on the volunteers demanded an excep-tionally high standard of mental, physical, and psychological fitness. Criteria were quickly developed and promulgated. As of July 10, 1942, the initial physical requirements for paratroops were:

Alert, active, supple, with firm muscles and sound limbs: capable of development into aggressive individual fighter with great endurance.

Age: officers — not over 32 years of age for Captains and Lieutenants and not over 35 years for Majors; Other Ranks (ORs) 18–32 inclusive.

Physically qualified as follows:

Weight — maximum, not to exceed 185 pounds.

Height — maximum, not to exceed 72 inches.

Vision — Distant vision uncorrected must be 20/40 each eye.

Feet — Greater than a non-symptomatic 2nd degree pes planus to disqualify.

Genito-urinary System — Recent venereal disease to disqualify.

Nervous System — Evidence of highly labile nervous system to disqualify.

Bones, Joints and Muscles — Lack of normal mobility in every joint, poor or unequally developed musculature, poor coordination, asthemic habitus, or lack of at least average athletic ability to disqualify.

Medical History — History of painful arches, recurrent knees or ankle injuries, recent fracture, old fractures with deformity, pain or limitation of motion, recurrent dislocation, recent severe illness, operation or chronic disease to disqualify.

Other than listed above, the physical standards to be the same as Army Standard "A.1."[150]

Initially, soldiers were required to be fully trained before they could qualify to apply for parachute training. However, within three months this restriction was lifted and volunteers needed only to be "basically trained." This ensured that there was a larger pool of talent to draw from.[151]

The recruiting plan for 1 Cdn Para Bn was based on the rate of intake at Fort Benning, Georgia, where the recruits would be trained until Canadian facilities could be constructed in Camp Shilo, Manitoba. This meant that volunteers were concentrated in Canada in sufficient numbers to ensure that a weekly quota of fifty-five aspiring paratroopers could be sent to the United States for training as basic parachutists. Initially, attracting recruits was not problematic. The publicity surrounding the new unit had a magnetic effect. "I thought it would be a good unit with lots of excitement and action," stated Sergeant Arnie Appleton.[152] Similarly Sergeant Herb Peppard explained, "I guess we all want to get some action."[153] Brigadier James Hill later conceded that the Canadians on the whole were men who were "spoiling for a fight."[154] Another common reason was the desire to belong to an elite unit. Private T.E. Gavinski volunteered because he "wanted to see how far I could go so I picked the best there was."[155] Private Jan de Vries simply commented, "I wanted to be with the best."[156]

However, acceptance depended on more than just willingness or a desire to see action. First, all volunteers were required to pass a very discerning selection process. Not surprisingly, the procedure was based largely on the British system in place. Once an individual volunteered for parachute training he was then put through a personality appraisal that comprised a review of the individual's service record and qualification card data, the completion of a questionnaire, and the administration of a word association test and a self-description test. Finally, there was a psychiatric interview to overcome. The examiners deemed the psychiatric interview essential to determine not only if the volunteer would "take the jumps" but also whether or not he would "become an efficient paratrooper in every sense of the word."[157]

Early on in the process military commanders and examiners agreed, "Only those whose suitability is beyond reasonable doubt are to be recommended."[158] A rigorous application of the selection criteria was imposed despite the understanding that this would make it difficult to meet the quota requirement. Examiners reported that the chief non-physical causes for rejection were lack of enthusiasm for parachute work, which often became evident once individuals learned in more

detail what they had volunteered for, and evidence of emotional instability, which was defined as:

Sociability: unfriendly, reclusive, lacking in social skills.

Adjustment to Army life: discontented, complaining.

Occupational History: frequent changes, little responsibility or pay in relation to ability.

School History: poor progress, truancy, bad conduct.

Family History: home broken by death or divorce, foster parents, alcoholism, juvenile delinquency or crime,
nervous disorders in relatives.

Personal Health and History: tremors, sweating
extremities, stammering, nightmares, pounding heart,
cold sweats, dizzy or fainting spells, nail-biting, alcoholism, vague stomach or nervous ailments, fear of
dark or high places, sex problems, drug addiction, juvenile delinquency or crime, frequent visits to Medical
Inspection Room (MIR).[159]

By December 1942, a report from the director of personnel selection indicated that approximately 50 percent of those volunteering were
rejected.[160] An independent assessment of 613 personnel appraisals provides additional detail. Of the cases examined, 322 of the 613, or 52.5
percent, were accepted.[161] The profile of those chosen for parachute
service became quite apparent and similar. A few examples provide the
formula to success for aspiring volunteers. "Family history civilian and
Army Records are good," wrote Army examiners. "He is well motivated,
alert, keen and confident," they continued, "and should succeed in para
training." Another successful assessment stated, "His hands are steady
and dry and there are no signs of instability. He is very well motivated,
confident and enthusiastic. He appears to be an excellent para prospect."
Yet another positive endorsement read, "He is well motivated, capable,
mentally alert, calm and a gunnery Sgt. instructor at A-8 and A-28. His
hands are steady and dry and there are no signs of instability. He looks
like a first rate para prospect."[162]

Nonetheless, not all made the cut. The other 297 volunteers, or 47.5 percent, were rejected. The most prevalent reason for rejection (29 percent) was for nervousness or "tremulous hands." Any sign of this manifestation by medical examiners meant the individual was automatically sent to the psychiatrists for a consult. The other major categories for rejection were "instability," accounting for 13 percent, "family background" (broken home, parental or spousal disagreement with joining paratroops, family health history) for 12 percent, and "lack of aggressiveness" for 11 percent.[163] A sampling of the actual personnel assessments graphically depicts the mindset of the examiners. It also displays the at times glaringly subjective nature of the process. "He is a quiet, precise, individual rather opposite to what one would expect to see in a paratrooper," concluded one assessment that resulted in a rejection. Another negative appraisal stated, "He appears to be shy and hesitant and altogether too mild for Paratroops training." One examiner opined, "He is not impressive and is shifty and poorly motivated." The presence of a stereotype for paratroopers that centred on an aggressive, overly confident, extroverted individual was clearly present. "He is quiet, shy, even dreamy, unaggressive and very youthful in appearance. He is not a good para risk," concluded one examiner. Another candidate was rejected because he spoke quietly and did not "seem to possess 'combativeness.'"

Nervousness and instability were other key criteria that were consistently cited in assessments that led to rejection. "This man shows very tremulous hands; the palms are quite damp," recorded one report. The examiner concluded, "There seems to be something about this man which I cannot put into words. He certainly does not impress me favourably." Another volunteer assessment revealed, "I feel there is too much evidence of instability in childhood and that enuresis carried on to too late an age to expect him to be good material for Para Bn." In a final example, "a man who as a boy was frequently in trouble and who has certain evidences of instability" was deemed unsuitable for acceptance.[164]

But the Army and medical examiners, as well as the psychiatrists, were but the first hurdles an aspiring paratrooper had to deal with. There were certain truths that seemed insurmountable. Those who demonstrated fear of heights, water, or closed places were automatic rejections. So was any sign of such symptoms as palpitation, nocturnal dyspnea, stomach disorders, frequent headaches, low back pains, and urinary frequency, as well as psychotic or psychopathic tendencies. It addition, reports noted, "the seclusive, lonely type of individual appears to do poorly with this unit."[165] And the list went on. "We know," wrote one specialist, "that men recently married are poor prospects." Furthermore, if parents or spouses disagreed with an individual's choice of joining the paratroops, it was universally agreed by the selection committee that "this domestic set-up will almost surely ruin his chances of succeeding." Moreover, even if an individual passed the initial stages of the selection process, namely convincing the examiners and psychiatrist that at a minimum he should be given the chance to attempt the basic parachutist course, he still had to pass the veto power of the officer commanding (OC) of the parachute battalion. Often, it took mere appearances to dash the hopes of a volunteer. "This soldier is young," assessed the OC Parachute Battalion, "slight in build and does not appear rugged enough to be a paratrooper." In the end, he had the last word — and his veto ended a candidate's career in the paratroops.[166]

The rigorous selection process, not surprisingly, left certain impressions in those veterans who successfully made the grade. One veteran believed that the Army examiners were focused on people who were more mature, motivated, and particularly experienced. Lance-Corporal H.R. Holloway remembered that the examiners "watched your reaction to everything." He stated that any sweating whatsoever was an automatic ticket back to an individual's original unit.[167] To test for steadiness, volunteers often had to stretch their arms to their full extension and then had small pieces of paper placed on the backs of the hand to see if they shook or jiggled.[168]

Much of the process, particularly the questions posed by examiners, left doubts in the minds of many in regards to the sanity of those empowered with selection. Some questions were innocuous, such as "Do you like sports," "Have you ever broken any bones," "Why do you think you would make a good paratrooper," and "Could you use a bayonet to kill someone?" Others, however, were far more personal and, to the young volunteers, bizarre. "I went into his [the psychiatrist's] office," recalled Major John Simpson, "and the first thing he did was jump up on the table and he said, 'Did you wet the bed when you were a little boy?'"[169] Simpson conceded that he was so surprised he just sat there dumbfounded. Others had similar experiences. Questions included whether they had ever thought of having sex with their mother, sexual fantasies, bed wetting tendencies, and nightmares.[170] Lieutenant-Colonel Fraser Eadie recalled the word association test. The first word he was given was "mouse," which made him reflect immediately upon the type of individual he would be soldiering with. On his arrival to the unit, he could not help but reflect on his experience and exclaim to his new Deputy Commanding Officer (DCO), "Strange bloody lot this is!"[171]

Other elements of the selection were clearer to the volunteers, although no part of the selection process was ever explained. Individuals simply completed tests and interviews. One test required squads of ten men of all ranks to solve a series of problems. One was the traversing of a broken bridge. The candidates were required to find a means of crossing the obstacle. Another practical problem placed individuals within a heavily fenced-in prisoner of war compound. Individuals were required to get out, but they could not climb over the fence because it was "electrified." The solution, it appeared, lay in going under the wire. However, those who ventured around the edge of the compound to do a reconnaissance quickly found that there was a hollow recess under a dead tree, which camouflaged an escape tunnel.[172] The examiners were looking for those who were alert, thoughtful, and resourceful. Private Jan de Vries recalled pages of questions to be answered, diagrams that required solutions, and a battery of examinations and tests by doctors and psychologists. But in the end, "I thought the process quite orderly," he insisted, "and considered it made me 'wanting in' more desirable."[173]

The screening procedure was quite severe. As indicated earlier, it averaged a rejection rate of 50 percent. And this was just the beginning. A further 35 percent of successful volunteers were lost due to the normal parachute training wastage rates.[174] It became obvious very quickly that it was necessary to have a large pool of volunteers to draw from if the Army was to maintain the quotas required to fill the weekly training drafts sent to Fort Benning. But just as rapidly, problems developed. Qualified candidates were not found in the numbers required. Moreover, a recruiting crisis reared its ugly head. On August 10, 1942, the Adjutant-General, Major-General H.F.G. Letson, issued a directive that stated that Home Defence (HD) personnel, conscripts raised under the National Resources Mobilization Act (NRMA), would be eligible for the new parachute unit. Furthermore, his order clarified that "it will not be necessary that they go Active in order to be accepted."[175] This innocuous missive had far-reaching undertones. Apparently, Canada's military commanders forgot the offensive capability of the paratroopers and what type of individuals were attracted to this manner of unit. It appears they neglected to read their own press. Less than two months later, on October 1, 1942, the VCGS, Major-General Murchie, confided to the Chief of the General Staff that "response to fill weekly quotas for training is disappointing." He further asserted that the "situation is attributed to the unit being labelled for the HD role."[176] The solution was clear. He proposed to eliminate Home Defence personnel. The CGS, however, was reluctant to change the policy due the "manpower situation."[177]

But there was no hiding the negative effect the NRMA personnel were having on recruiting or the morale within the unit. A report filed by Flight Lieutenant Killick to NDHQ on October 28, 1942, revealed that "it would appear ... that the morale of the Canadian troops at Fort Benning is not as high as we would like to see it. Apparently, the root of the trouble lies in the fact that H.D. personnel are included and that the Battalion is NOT for overseas service." Killick went on to note that "the present H.D. personnel has led the better type of men, and the officers to feel that this is a Home Defence Battalion."[178] Five days later, the DCGS, Brigadier E.G. Weeks, made another appeal to CGS Major-General Ken Stuart. "There is a definite feeling," he argued, "that the inclusion of HD personnel in 1 Cdn Para Bn is having an undesirable effect in respect to the type of man who has volunteered to serve in this unit." The inference, he elaborated, "is that this unit would be used for employment in Canada only, whereas the type of soldier required for parachute training is the aggressive individual who is anxious to serve overseas."[179] The submission seems to have had the necessary effect. The CGS was ready to restrict the participation of NRMA personnel. However, this did run afoul of the government's, albeit not the military's, originally stated intention for the parachute unit, namely home defence. As a result, on November 10, the DCGS sought advice from the Judge Advocate General (JAG). "Experience has shown," he wrote, "that the inclusion of H.D. personnel has had a retarding affect on the flow of volunteers. It is not the intention to announce that the 1st Canadian Parachute Battalion, is for service anywhere, but rather that members, H.D. will not be permitted to volunteer, unless of course they go Active."[180] Once again, the Army was masking its true intention. At this stage in the war, paratroops were universally defined as an inherently offensive force whose true purpose lay in piercing the Reich — overseas.

The JAG responded the same day and confirmed that "the proposed restriction on the transfer of H.D. personnel ... seems to be unobjectionable."[181] Nine days later, an instruction was promulgated that announced, commencing with the November 30 quota, all parachute volunteers for 1 Cdn Para Bn were required to be "Active" personnel. Quite simply, NRMA personnel were required to transfer to active status prior to their dispatch from their home districts if they desired to become paratroopers.[182]

In the end, this lengthy process solved one of the manning problems. Another fix was the amendment of the medical criteria for screening. The initial drafts of volunteers provided some feedback on which individuals succeeded and which failed. As a result, new criteria were produced in an effort to provide candidates that were more likely to succeed. The new selection standards were promulgated in January 1943 (italics indicate amendments):

Alert, active, supple, with firm muscles and sound limbs: capable of development into aggressive individual fighter with *GREAT* endurance.

Age: *18-32, both inclusive.* (In June 1943, the lower end was amended to 18 1/2).

Physically qualified as follows:
Weight — maximum not to exceed *190* pounds.

Height — maximum not to exceed 72 inches.

Vision — Distant vision uncorrected must be 20/40 each eye.

Feet and Lower Limbs — Flat feet not acceptable. Better than average bone structure and muscular development of lower limbs.

Genito-urinary System — Recent venereal disease to disqualify.

Nervous System — Evidence of highly labile nervous system to disqualify. *History of nervous complaints to disqualify.*

Bones, Joints and Muscles — Lack of normal mobility in every joint, poor or unequally developed musculature, poor coordination, asthemic habitus, or lack of *better than average* athletic ability to disqualify.

Hearing — W.V.-10 ft. both ears, i.e. a man standing with his back to the examiner and using both ears must be able to hear a forced whisper 10 ft. away. Must have patent Eustachian Tubes.

Dental — Men must not drop with false teeth; consequently there must be eight sound or reparable teeth (including 2 molars) in the upper jaw, in good functional opposition to corresponding teeth in lower jaw.

Medical History — History of painful arches, recurrent knees or ankle injuries, recent fracture, old fractures with deformity, pain or limitation of motion, recurrent dislocation, recent severe illness, operation or chronic disease to disqualify, *(unless recurring, properly healed fractures not to disqualify).*

Mental and Intelligence Standard — It was agreed that men with alert minds are required for this type of training and that men with doubtful intelligence should be eliminated by intelligence test.

Other than listed above, the physical standards to be the same as Army Standard "A.1."[183]

As the war progressed, however, the rigorous selection process became an impediment, particularly to those who were concerned with quantity instead of quality. Operations overseas and the inevitable casualties they entailed exacerbated the manpower shortage. Therefore, by May 1944, the criteria were severely relaxed. The new standards for "Parachutists (Operational)" were very forgiving:

1.Physical
   1. PULHEMS: 1112111.[184]
   2. Age: 18 1/2 - 32 years inclusive.
   3. Max Height 6'2" max wt. 220 lbs. A proper correlation of height and weight will be required.
   4. Teeth: Must have a sufficient number of second teeth to masticate food reasonably well if dentures should be broken or lost.

5. Must be in good physical condition. A history of participation in rugged sports, or in a civilian occupation or hobby demanding sustained exertion, is very desirable.

2.Other Qualifications
   1. Should be emotionally stable, well-motivated, self-reliant, and relatively aggressive.
   2. Must be General Service prior to despatch for paratroop training.
   3. Must have completed Basic Training.
   4. If non-English speaking, must be sufficiently bilingual to take all instruction in English.
   5. Must have at lest the equivalent of Gr. VI Education.
   6. Must be genuinely interested in paratroop training after having been thoroughly informed concerning the strenuous physical requirements and the emphasis on Infantry training.[185]

But the loosening of the criteria was not enough. The Director of Personnel Selection stressed to his examiners that a psychiatric examination was no longer required at the time of initial nomination. Furthermore, he reminded them that any personnel who met the minimum PULHEMS requirement, and who were otherwise suitable, would be eligible for paratroop service. In fact, Army examiners were prodded to ensure that whenever a suitable recruit was encountered he should be immediately briefed on paratroop service. Moreover, if the recruit displayed any interest, his file was to be specially earmarked. Additionally, the examiners were also instructed to make every effort to stimulate interest in the paratroop corps with a view to securing volunteers.[186] Not surprisingly, the manpower crisis in 1944 necessitated even further allowances. The Director also clarified that those who expressed a "natural concern" over the opposition of their family or intimate acquaintances should no longer be regarded unsuitable "unless there is reason to believe that they could not adjust satisfactorily." He also explained that "undue weight should not be given to minor infractions of conduct as long as such infractions do not appear inconsistent with successful paratroop service."[187]

The dramatic change was not startling when one considers the escalating manpower conundrum that had a tumultuous impact on Canadian society, leading to yet another national conscription crisis. Nonetheless, despite the evolving screening criteria and the easing of rigorous selection standards, the volunteers that were selected reflected in the main the cream of Canada's combat soldiers. Senior commanders acknowledged that paratroopers would require "greater stamina and powers of endurance than is generally asked of an infantry soldier." The Director of Military Training succinctly asserted that "'guts' all along the line" was a necessity.[188] As a result of the strenuous selection and subsequent training the paratroops faced, the Army hierarchy decided that the "Parachute Corps must be considered an elite Corps in every sense."[189] The *Canadian Army Training Memorandum* aptly summarized, "Canada's paratroop units are attracting to their ranks the finest of the Dominion's fighting men ... these recruits are making the paratroops a 'corps elite.'"[190]

And so Canada was now in the club. But more than a new airborne capability, it now also had a bona fide military elite. All that remained was to take the raw material and turn it into trained paratroopers worthy of inclusion in a new, universally recognized warrior fraternity.

CHAPTER FOUR

Making Up for Lost Time — Creating a Canadian Paratrooper

... to produce a formidable fighting man like an expert hunter — always alert and seeking an opportunity of striking its quarry or watching his movements with a view to future opportunities, confident and expert in the use of his weapons, skilled in the use of ground and able to stand fatigue without undue loss of efficiency. He must be determined, inquisitive and self-dependent, but must always remember that he is acting as one of a team.

Canadian Parachute Training Centre —
Standard Syllabus, 1944.[191]

By the late summer of 1942, the efforts of the Canadian Army to create an elite airborne force were laudable. The Army devised and implemented elaborate selection criteria and testing to ensure that only the cream of Canada's soldiers were accepted. But this was not enough. Once the necessary raw material was selected, it still had to be processed. Parachute volunteers now had to be turned into aggressive, resilient, and tough paratroopers.

The necessary transformation was not an easy one. Nonetheless, Canada's military leaders did derive some benefit from their initial hesitation. While they dithered on the question of creating a national airborne capability, the Americans and British had already moved forward with the establishment of their airborne forces. This would be of great help. But, Canada now had to make up for lost time.

"Paratrooper," by George Pepper.

Courtesy of the Canadian War Museum

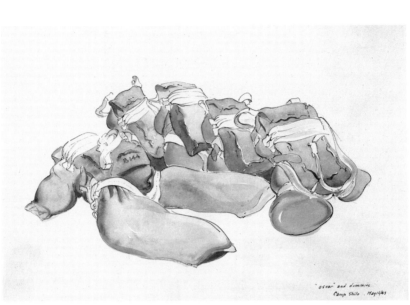

"Oscar," by George Pepper, depicting test dummies used at Camp Shilo,
May 1943. Courtesy of the Canadian War Museum

"Dropping Zone," by Captain G.C. Tinning.
1 Cdn Para Bn in England, January 1944.
Courtesy of the Canadian War Museum

"Canadian Paratroopers at Herne Airport," by Captain G.C. Tinning, depicting paratroopers during a training exercise with the 6th British Airborne Division at Salisbury Plain, February 1944.

Courtesy of the Canadian War Museum

"Parachute Troops Preparing to Board a Dropping Plane," by Captain G.C. Tinning, depicting members of 1 Cdn Para Bn preparing to board an Albermarle aircraft for a practice jump, February 1944.

Courtesy of the Canadian War Museum

"Preparing to Take Off," by Captain G.C. Tinning, depicting 1 Cdn Para Bn
on a training exercise in England, February 1944.
Courtesy of the Canadian War Museum

"Drifting Down," by Captain G.C. Tinning. 1 Cdn Para Bn in England.
Courtesy of the Canadian War Museum

"Brigade Tactical Exercise," by Captain G.C. Tinning, depicting 1 Cdn Para Bn
on exercise at Folly Farm, New South Newton, February 7, 1944.
Courtesy of the Canadian War Museum

"Overnight Scheme," by Captain G.C. Tinning, depicting preparations for D-
Day at Folly Wood, Wilts, England, February 1944.
Courtesy of the Canadian War Museum

"Sand Table Lecture," by Captain G.C. Tinning, depicting preparations for the D-Day invasion.

Courtesy of the Canadian War Museum

A most irrevocable step. Paratroopers exiting a C-47 Dakota aircraft. Pencil sketch by Canadian war artist Ted Zuber.

Courtesy of Ted Zuber

"Flight," by Ted Zuber.
Courtesy of Ted Zuber

A lone paratrooper attempting to collapse his parachute in the wind.
Pencil sketch by Ted Zuber.
Courtesy of Ted Zuber

"Tenacious into Battle," by Ted Zuber.
Courtesy of Ted Zuber

Brigadier E.G. Weeks, Deputy Chief of the General Staff, was responsible for the establishment of Canada's embryonic airborne capability. He did not consider Canada's late entry into this new type of warfare as a disadvantage. "Canada hopes to combine the best features of the U.S. and British paratroop technique," acknowledged a confident Weeks, "to experiment ... and produce the finest air-borne troops in the world."[192] Although lagging behind its allies, the Canadian Army gained a substantial advantage from its ability to use the training methods, techniques, and equipment that had already been developed, tested, and used by their counterparts during the past two years.

By the summer of 1942, the British airborne program was well underway. However, this had not always been the case. Army commanders, and particularly the Air Ministry, reluctantly answered Churchill's initial call for paratroopers in early June 1940. There were very few resources and scant manpower available to initiate a new project of this magnitude. Even the Prime Minister's personal urging was not enough to galvanize the necessary effort. Nevertheless, some important initial steps were taken. The Central Landing School (CLS) was quickly established in Ringway, near Manchester, on June 21. The skeletal staff was directed to prepare a parachute training syllabus and qualify personnel as quickly as possible.

Although the first parachute jumps were conducted on July 13, it took a further two years to set up an efficient parachute training facility.[193] The continued institutional resistance, coupled with the lack of policy as to how to train and use these new troops, had an adverse effect on the development of the school. Many commanders and strategists considered that airborne troops would never be more than a nuisance to the enemy and of marginal value to their own side.[194] This attitude hampered the school's efforts to secure equipment and to locate suitable aircraft and aircrews. Equally, it frustrated their ability to formulate a parachute training syllabus, due to the continuing lack of information and expertise available.[195]

The negative outlook of the rest of the armed forces in regards to parachute operations only compounded the CLS's frustration. "Conceived in haste and born of mental confusion, always lacking sufficient staff, accommodation and equipment," lamented a staff officer at the school, "it soon learnt the art of making shift."[196] Churchill's continuing demands, as well as a series of ongoing disagreements between the Air Ministry and the War Office as to who would do what, only complicated the matter for the CLS staff.

Nonetheless, slow progress was made. The School was reorganized and redesignated the Central Landing Establishment (CLE), RAF, on September 19, 1940. This and later reorganizations were implemented to set up new training sections to further expand, study, experiment, and test the different glider, air transportability, air portability, and parachute training concepts, as well as airborne aircraft requirements. The Air Ministry was ordered to develop "the flying side," while the Army Staff, under the command of Lieutenant-Colonel John F. Rock, who reported directly to the War Office, was given the responsibility of developing the Army (Airborne) operational doctrine and training program.[197]

While readily undertaking this new challenge, Rock quickly realized that it was impossible to obtain "any information as to policy or task."[198] It became evident that training this new force required a great deal of patience and experimentation. The lack of forthcoming direction, information, or policy made it clear to Group Captain L.G. Harvey, the CLE Commanding Officer, that he had no other recourse than to proceed with the development of parachute training on a trial and error basis.[199]

Progress though it was, it was too slow for an impatient Prime Minister Churchill, who visited the CLE on April 26, 1941, to observe a glider-parachute demonstration. By this time, eight hundred paratroopers had been trained, but due to lack of aircraft only seventy-two could be dropped at a time.[200] Upon his return to London, an angry Churchill lashed out that a full year had been wasted and very little had been accomplished in developing an airborne capability. In a memo sent to his Chiefs of Staff, he demanded a complete overhaul of the parachute training program, the elaboration of a training timetable, and a report outlining the current status with regards to his request to train five thousand paratroopers.[201]

From the outset, the Air Ministry planning staff regarded the Prime Minister's airborne program as unrealistic. However, by May 31, 1941, with the recent fall of the Mediterranean island of Crete to German Fallschirmjäger on Churchill's mind, they could no longer delay. A joint memorandum on the status of Britain's airborne forces was quickly submitted to the Prime Minister by the Chiefs of Staff. The report presented an encouraging overview of the progress made and outlined future parachute training initiatives. Furthermore, to complement the small parachute force, they recommended that serious consideration be given to the development of a large glider force and the training of air-landing units. They argued that this would allow selected infantry units to be converted and trained in a relatively short time frame, significantly increasing the country's airborne capability. Churchill agreed, but insisted that this new glider force be raised to complement a parachute force, and that parachute training continue forthwith.[202]

Churchill's frustration with the failure of the British airborne program in the wake of the fall of Crete to German paratroopers, combined with his subsequent visit to the CLE and his upbraiding of the Chiefs of Staff, provided the necessary spark to advance the development of parachute and now glider training. This led to the appointment of Squadron Leader Maurice Newnham as commanding officer of the Parachute Training School in July 1941. He quickly noted that the school's staff had to be upgraded and the training approach refined. "We're not a School at all — in the proper sense —," observed Newnham "we haven't any trained teachers.[203]

Furthermore, he believed it was imperative to instill a new mental approach. "We've got to provide," he insisted, "the right atmosphere, to inculcate the *will* to jump as a natural drill."[204] The addition of new instructors the development, of a higher calibre of parachute training, and the introduction of a new approach yielded immediate results. Prior to Newnham's arrival only forty parachutists were qualified on a weekly basis. His improvements caused the number to soar to one hundred per week.[205] This encouraging turn of events led to the expansion of the CLE.

New training sections were created and the CLE was redesignated as the Airborne Forces Establishment (AFE) on September 1, 1941. Their mandate included responsibility for technical developments "to establish the principles of glider and parachute training and to form the first units carrying out this training."[206] More importantly the AFE's RAF and Army staff developed and refined their respective doctrine in regard to airborne training. This expansion of parachute training, and the recommendations of the Chiefs of Staff in their May 1941 joint memorandum, led to the formation of brigade-size formations such as the 1st Parachute Brigade in September 1941, and the 1st Air-Landing Brigade Group a month later.[207]

To further facilitate the airborne forces command and control process, a separate airborne headquarters was established. Commander-in-Chief of Home Forces, General Sir Allan Brooke, recommended that the new airborne forces, "for reasons of morale, to impress the enemy, and for convenience," be led by a divisional commander rather than a "Force" commander.[208] Therefore, on October 29, 1941, the War Office appointed Brigadier F.A.M Browning as Commander Para-Troops and Airborne Troops. He was now directly responsible for the development of Britain's expanding airborne capability.[209]

Browning immediately implemented a series of changes. First, additional RAF instructors replaced Army personnel at Ringway. They were now solely responsible for parachute training. Next, new training schools and units were set up to concentrate on specific components of collective and individual airborne and glider instruction. As the training problems were being addressed, an airborne doctrine was also being developed. Two schools of thought existed regarding the tactical deployment of airborne forces. The first preferred using paratroopers in small, independent groups or with a main force to disrupt communications and operate behind the enemy's front lines. Browning, however, adopted the alternate concept. He believed, "Their [paratroops] greatest importance lay in their power to attack the enemy in force on his open flank — over the top and they considered that the first and most important requirement was a well-balanced force of all arms concentrated on vital objectives which land or sea-borne forces could not reach."[210]

To further enhance the success of future airborne operations, Browning recommended the creation of an air unit that was to train closely with the Airborne Division. As such, on January 15, 1942, the headquarters of 38 Wing was established. Staff of this new Wing immediately set forth to work, train, and provide the much-needed air and glider support to the 1st Airborne Division. The Wing was also responsible for training their aircrews specifically for parachute and airborne/glider operations. The technical expertise developed by these aircrews increased the operational effectiveness of the British airborne forces during the war.[211] Additional organizational changes were implemented, leading to the closure of the Airborne Forces Establishment on February 15, 1942.[212] Its personnel and resources were reallocated to form the No.1 Parachute Training School and the Airborne Forces Experimental Establishment.

Despite this progress there still existed one weakness — the availability of sufficient aircraft required to drop large numbers of parachute troops. Browning attempted to ensure that his airborne personnel and training staff did not let this temporary problem dampen their spirits or efforts. "All ranks have a great deal to do in order to perfect themselves in their airborne role apart from actual flying training," extolled Browning, "therefore, in spite of early disappointment we must arrive and attain that high standard of military efficiency which is essential to the Division." Browning concluded, "Great and important tasks lie ahead and it is my firm belief that both in the final victory and after, British Airborne Forces will play an outstanding part."[213] This positive attitude was vital to galvanizing RAF and Army collaboration and teamwork, which remained evident in airborne operations throughout the war.

The Air Ministry now seemed committed to its part in parachute training. Notwithstanding its numerous operational responsibilities, it nevertheless succeeded in locating Whitley and Albemarle, as well as a limited number of Stirling and Halifax, bombers for parachute and glider operations.[214] But even with these additions, there were still insufficient aircraft. As a result, in May 1942, a desperate Churchill turned to President Roosevelt, asking for early shipment of previously ordered transport aircraft.[215] At that time the Americans were also building up their transport carrier commands, and no airplanes could be provided. Nonetheless, Roosevelt reassured Churchill that four transport groups would be dispatched shortly to the United Kingdom. Six months later, in November 1942, a total of 416 American aircraft and crews were made available to assist the British with their airborne training and operations.[216] And so, despite a hesitant start, by the fall of 1942, a solid foundation for the British airborne capability had been laid. It was now a question of constant refinement. Its acceptance and importance was clearly evident from the number of British Parachute and Air-Landings units that were now steadily expanding.[217]

The British efforts, however, did not represent the only Allied foray into the development of a potent airborne capability. The Americans also ramped up their program in the aftermath of the collapse of Europe in the spring of 1940. Similarly, the development and training of American parachute and glider forces also experienced a series of growing pains due to a lack of resources and a chain of command that believed that there was no clear operational role for such specialized troops. By January 1940, Chief of Staff General George Marshall ordered the American air infantry project to the forefront.[218] The project was given high priority status. Nonetheless, prior to the invasion of the Low Countries in May 1940, little of substance was done. However, as with Britain, this became the catalyst for renewed action. But whereas the RAF had taken the lead in airborne training in the U.K., it was the Infantry

Branch of the United States Army that was assigned the mission of developing and training paratroopers. Major-General George A. Lynch, the Chief of Infantry for the U.S. Army, argued that the aircraft and parachute were only means of delivery. "Once on the ground," he explained, "the parachutist becomes an infantryman and fights as an infantryman." The argument was logical, and the Airborne Development project became the responsibility of the Chief of Infantry at Fort Benning.[219] It was, however, strongly recommended by Lynch that the Air Corps be included as a key contributor.[220] Pooling their resources, the Infantry Branch and the Air Corps prepared the groundwork for what became referred to as the "Airborne Effort." Lynch appointed Major William C. Lee to head this project.

Following a series of discussions, the Fort Benning Infantry Board, led by Lee, analyzed the training requirements. From these, three recommendations were submitted to Major-General Lynch. Their adoption was vital to the implementation of the air infantry project in February 1940. The first was to drop the air transport training phase and focus all available resources on the development of parachute training. The second recommendation was the development of a troop-type parachute "to allow an armed infantryman to debark from an airplane at altitudes ranging between three to five hundred feet."[221] The last proposition argued for the creation of a test platoon under the command of the Infantry Board.[222]

Lynch approved all three recommendations. He believed that sufficient progress had been made in the air transport training phase. He now judged that all available resources should be shifted to the development of a parachute training program. Furthermore, he asked the Air Corps to design a new parachute. By May 1940, the T-4 parachute and reserve had been designed and tested.[223] As well, by July 1, the Parachute Test Platoon was formed and placed under the command of Lieutenant William T. Ryder. All training and testing was conducted at the U.S. Army Infantry School at Fort Benning.[224]

Within a few weeks the first U.S. airborne units were formed and the "mass production" of paratroopers began. The rapid expansion of the American airborne forces necessitated the creation of the Provisional Parachute Group on March 10, 1941. The Group, headed by now Lieutenant-Colonel William C. Lee, was responsible for developing training cadres, drafting training manuals, establishing tactical doctrine, and qualifying the members of all newly created parachute units as basic parachutists.[225]

The Provisional Parachute Group was further expanded on March 21, 1942, and redesignated the Airborne Command. On April 9, it was relocated from Fort Benning to Fort Bragg, North Carolina. Lee, now promoted to the rank of colonel, operated directly under the Army Ground Forces Headquarters. His responsibilities were: to establish and train airborne ground units; to control allocation and training of such Air Corps transport airplane or glider units as might be available by Army Air Forces; to coordinate training with the Army Air Force combat units; to determine operating procedures for airborne operations and supply large forces; and, in coordination with the Navy, to determine procedures for joint airborne-seaborne operations.[226]

These responsibilities were later expanded to include the training of the air-landing battalions and future glider units. By spring 1942, the American parachute training establishments were well on the way to operating at full capacity.[227] During a visit of the U.S. parachute training facilities, Vice-Admiral Lord Louis Mountbatten, Chief of Combined Operations, described the American parachute training system as "a most perfect machine of mass production of paratroops."[228] By mid-1942, both the British and the Americans were well on their way to fielding large airborne formations.

It was these advancements that Canada's military commanders quickly tapped into once they decided that they too wanted to join the "airborne club," a seeming prerequisite to being defined as a modern army. As a result, the War Cabinet authorized the creation of the 1st Canadian Parachute Battalion on July 1, 1942.[229] The CGS quickly appointed Brigadier A.G. Weeks, his DCGS, to oversee the development of the Canadian parachute training. Weeks now had to make up for lost time.

The DCGS quickly explained to journalists why it had taken so much time to join their allies in this new venture. "The Canadian army is expanding very rapidly," he stated, "but you don't run before you walk. That's why we haven't previously started to train parachute troops."[230] He added that many officers had traveled to England and to the United States to observe, assess, and report on existing parachute training techniques. They would now put this acquired knowledge to good use.

Although Canada was a latecomer into the game, Brigadier Weeks and the Minister of National Defence showed great faith in their first parachute volunteers. "The Department of National Defence feels that the last war has proven Canadian officers and men," insisted Weeks, "have the guts and initiative and that Canadian paratroopers will be second to none."[231] Colonel Ralston, the MND, visited the selected volunteers before they left for Fort Benning and offered them words of encouragement. "It is a great satisfaction to us, the way the men in the Canadian Army snap to it when there is a job to be done. ... Bring back everything you can in the way of training, information and experience," emphasized Ralston, "so that this first parachute battalion be the best that Canada can produce. If it is that, it will be second to none in the world."[232]

The selected volunteers were quickly sent to the respective American and British parachute training programs. Those in Canada went to The Parachute School in Fort Benning, Georgia, while those volunteers selected overseas in England attended the Parachute Training School, Royal Air Force Station, Ringway.[233] Concurrently, arrangements were underway to build a Canadian parachute training facility in Camp Shilo, Manitoba.[234]

Both groups underwent rigorous physical training. The American course was particularly harsh. Corporal Darrel Harris described the U.S. parachute instructors as having "a real sadistic streak which formed a part of the composition of those American instructors." He recalled, "They really gave it to us, and I think they were doing their best to see that we caved in." Harris added, "We suffered plenty at first, but we didn't bring the disgrace of quitting onto our heads."[235] Even though the British physical training regimen was demanding, the technique used by the RAF instructors was dramatically different. "They were encouraging, very demanding but respectful, and wanted the candidates to succeed," reminisced Private George Wright, a member of the first Ringway group. "They trained us well," he added, "and we had a lot of faith in our instructors."[236]

The Canadian candidates displayed great stamina and enthusiasm in their respective courses. The Benning group underwent a one-month program that was broken into four distinct phases. The first phase focused on physical fitness and parachute packing classes. The second phase concentrated on apparatus training, specifically in-flight, exiting, and landing drills, while the third portion of the course centred on controlled parachute descents and shock harness training, which was conducted on the 250-foot High Tower. The final phase required each candidate to complete five parachute qualification jumps from an aircraft.[237]

The Ringway group underwent a shorter sixteen-day course that encompassed preparatory ground training and jump training. The parachute training required candidates to master proper in-flight and landing techniques by using various training apparatus. The candidates then made a total of seven parachute descents, two from balloons and five from aircraft.[238] In the end, the entire Benning group qualified as basic parachutists, as opposed to the Ringway group, which had six failures.[239]

Regardless of location, the parachute training proved to be challenging and exciting. However, it always harboured an element of danger. The Canadian initiation to airborne training was marred by the tragic death of Major Hilton D. Proctor, the Battalion's designated commanding officer. As the group's senior ranking officer, Proctor insisted on being the lead jumper. Upon the given signal he exited the airplane. As his parachute opened, his lines were sheared by a following aircraft, causing Proctor to plunge to his death. From the outset, all those who volunteered to become paratroopers were advised that "the new force ... demands the utmost in resourcefulness and acceptance of risk even beyond those of other branches of the Service."[240] Despite this tragedy, the candidates of the Benning group focused their energies on completing their training.

The attitude, interest, and zealousness displayed by these first two groups did not go unnoticed. "It is thrilling to know that so fine a body of men is an ally of ours in this struggle against tyranny," praised Brigadier-General Walter S. Fulton, the commanding general at Fort Benning. His British counterpart, RAF Wing Commander M.A. Newnham, observed, "Their enthusiasm and high spirits required tactful supervision on the part of the instructors."[241] And so, a pattern became evident early on.

Following the Benning group's return to Ottawa, Lieutenant-Colonel R.H. Keefler, the Director of Military Training, told the nation's new paratroopers what was expected of them. "Your real job is just starting now," he explained. "You are the pioneers of this formation. You have to pass on the knowledge you have obtained to others." Keefler elaborated, "There will be differences of opinion but I hope you will be open-minded." He explained, "We have to use the best ideas of both the British and American systems."[242] With these words of encouragement they headed to Camp Shilo, Manitoba, the new home of the Canadian parachute school, where they were to await the arrival of the Ringway group.

But what started out as a fast-paced invigorating adventure suddenly lost its impetus and momentum. Upon their arrival in Shilo, the parachute instructors discovered that the training facilities were not ready. The most optimistic estimates called for the Canadian parachute school to be operational sometime during the spring of 1943.[243] Furthermore, the construction of the proposed landing strip for Camp Shilo was canceled. Moreover, to further complicate the situation they were informed that no aircraft were forecasted to be available for parachute training or airborne exercises in the near future.[244] The school's Quartermaster facilities had been completed, but the shelves were empty and no decisions as to the type of equipment, uniforms, and weapons had yet been made. Upon learning of this setback, a furious Brigadier Weeks complained that the "training plans will have to be completely altered to meet this serious situation and it puts the army in an embarrassing position with the Air Force who have been pressed to provide aircraft on certain dates."[245] As the parachute instructors awaited further orders, NDHQ studied various parachute training options and came up with a temporary but very suitable alternative.[246]

The American and Canadian governments reached an agreement during the first week of October 1942 that solved the immediate problem. American troops were sent to Camp Shilo to conduct winter training and testing of cold weather equipment. In exchange, Canadian parachute volunteers were dispatched to the Parachute School in Fort Benning to undergo their basic parachute training.[247] This was opportune as it allowed the 1st Canadian Parachute Battalion to achieve its goal of qualifying its personnel between October 1942 and March 1943. As a result, the first group of fifty-five volunteers commenced their training right on time.[248] Subsequent groups of fifty-five were then dispatched on a weekly basis up until the Battalion attained its projected War Established Strength of 616 all ranks.[249]

All Canadian volunteers underwent the standard American parachute course. As briefly mentioned earlier, it was divided into four one-week phases, labeled, simply enough, "A", "B", "C," and "D" stages.[250] "A" Stage featured grueling physical and endurance training, running, Jiu-Jitsu, and hand-to-hand combat classes. The American instructors ran the candidates into the ground. "They wore you down until you had nothing left," recalled Corporal Dan Hartigan. "It was during times like this," he added, that "they offered you the opportunity to quit ... it was tough."[251] Private Tom Gavinski agreed. "They always tried to see how far you could go, to keep you on edge," he recalled. "We were losing a man a month because he didn't have that extra step."[252] The objective of "A" Stage was to weed out the weak, the timid, and the unfit. "The instructors drove and drove you to uncanny limits," recollected Private Albert Kemshead. "Everything you did was on the double," he stated, "so our wind and physical being was in good shape."[253]

Rank held no privilege at the Parachute School. All candidates, regardless of rank, underwent the same training regimen. Officers and Other Ranks (ORs) were treated equally — like dirt. The ORs, however, enjoyed this unique egalitarian system. "It was nice to team up for judo with an officer," explained Kemshead, "and throw him hard to the ground in the saw dust pits. It gave one a feeling of satisfaction to knock an officer around for awhile."[254] Those who survived the first phase "felt like they could take on the world," remembered a proud Private E.J. Scott.[255]

Next was "B" Stage. This segment of training focused on learning ground landing techniques, oscillation drills, landing and collapsing parachutes, and exiting drills from dummy fuselage and the dreaded Mock Tower. This tower was a thirty-two-foot-high structure used to practise aircraft exit drills. It was feared by all. When the candidate stepped up and stood alone at the tower's door, this was the first time that he was actually exposed to high elevations. Not surprisingly, "B" Stage was nicknamed "the man breaker" because it had the highest number of failures.[256] Lieutenant-Colonel W.B. Wedd, the military attaché with the Canadian Legation in Washington, reported, "The total average wastage in any class going through the school ranges about 25 percent, but 15 percent is due to accidents and 10 percent to refusals. These refusals nearly all take place when the volunteer is faced with the apparatus [mock tower] from which he must throw himself into space."[257]

By the end of November, Lieutenant-Colonel G.F.P. Bradbrooke, the Battalion's new CO, reported that over forty-five candidates had been disqualified and returned to Canada.[258] At this rate, he projected that 126 candidates would fail the course, translating into a 17 percent wastage rate. This had serious consequences. It would adversely affect the Battalion's parachute training schedule and its ability to achieve its projected War Establishment before returning to Canada.[259] To compensate for this unforseen failure rate Bradbrooke requested the dispatch of an additional five serials of fifty-five parachute candidates.[260]

Bradbrooke believed, however, that the high failure rate could be curtailed. He felt that part of the problem lay in the motivation of the candidates. It became evident that many volunteers had not been presented with a realistic picture of airborne training. "It is strongly recommended," he angrily wrote, "that any personnel desiring to volunteer for parachute work should have it strongly described to them in true facts, in view of the fact that the training is severe and the personnel undergo a great deal of physical and mental strain."[261] The Directorate of Military Training agreed with Bradbrooke's assessment. It was very possible, in an effort to increase the number of volunteers, that the wrong image may have been conveyed during the recruiting drives. "Parachute jumping itself," suggested Keefler, "must be deglamorized and more emphasis put on the hard body breaking task ahead and the hazards confronting them in their ultimate operational role." He stressed that "every effort be made to discourage the faint hearted and those who wish to 'try something new.' The more difficult the job is made to appear, the greater chance we have of appealing to the right type of volunteer."[262] Keefler strongly supported the idea that the Parachute Corps be considered an elite corps in every sense. "Parachute jumping is only a small part of the training of Parachutists," he asserted. "To produce a completely trained paratrooper, many hours of the hardest type of training will have to be endured such as body toughening, force marches, field craft, demolitions, specialized weapon training, all requiring greater stamina and powers of endurance," he emphasized, "than is generally asked of an Infantry soldier, in other words 'guts' all along the line is required."[263]

The Directorate of Personnel Selection investigated the situation further. The staff discovered that many volunteers just wanted to transfer out of their current unit and had no "real interest in parachute work ... others volunteered in good faith but with little understanding of the nature of the job they were undertaking." In either case the result was the same. "When they reach the concentration point they learn of the difficulties and dangers of the work," the report explained, "they lose all enthusiasm. And mere willingness 'to go through with it', is not enough."[264] They quickly realized that it was imperative that a clear picture be provided in regard to the type of training a volunteer was to expect. As a result, the Director of Personnel Selection immediately drafted a letter explaining:

> The advanced training of parachutists is reported to be about 2% jumping and 98% rigorous commando training requiring great physical stamina and courage of a high order. Parachute troops have about 60 lbs. of equipment to carry, including a Tommy or Sten gun, hand grenades, high explosives, radio, ammunition, respirator, rations, etc. They frequently have to travel for

long periods on foot with a full pack and almost at a run. As part of their training they take forced marches of 35 miles a day.[265]

As this issue was being corrected parachute training progressed and the candidates proceeded to their third stage. "C" Stage involved various training exercises on a 250-foot apparatus called the High Tower. The first task consisted of mastering the shock harness, a device used to test a paratrooper's concentration by forcing him to count out loud while falling. This activity had a critical real-life implication. If by the given count the candidate did not feel the sudden shock generated by the opening of the canopy, he knew that he had to immediately activate his reserve parachute because his main assembly had malfunctioned.[266] The second exercise involved undergoing three controlled parachute descents that allowed the candidates to practise their in-flight drills. The last and most important activity consisted of adopting the correct body posture prior to landing.

During the first three weeks, the candidates also underwent parachute packing courses. The rule was that each candidate jumped with the parachute he packed. But the climax of the course and the final test for each paratrooper was the successful completion of five descents from an aircraft in flight. The qualifying jumps were conducted during the fourth and final week. During "D" Stage, drops were conducted at a rate of one per day, usually in the morning. The afternoons were spent repacking parachutes and undergoing further physical training.

For the great majority of the candidates, this was the first time they boarded an aircraft. With three weeks of grueling training behind them, those who remained were now ready to carry out their qualifying jumps. However, all quickly realized that regardless of the hours of training, the first jump was an unnerving experience. "The three things that surprised me on my first jump," recounted Corporal Boyd Anderson, "were the tremendous propeller blast that hit me as soon as I went out the door ... and that we got to the ground so quickly and that I hit so hard."[267] The parachute course quickly became regarded as one of the toughest courses in the Canadian Army.

Of the first quota of fifty-four candidates sent to Fort Benning on October 10, 1942, only thirty-four graduated.[268] Each new paratrooper was presented with a Parachute Qualification Badge and an American parachute certificate. More importantly, they were now authorized to wear the distinctive blood-ox-coloured paratrooper boots with bloused trousers. Their qualification also entitled them to parachute pay and a weekend pass to celebrate their accomplishment.[269]

Having repeatedly faced and conquered their individual fear, the young volunteers were transformed into a new breed of Canadian warriors. A new attitude quickly prevailed amongst the newly qualified paratroopers. "The average young parachutist upon graduation from the four-week course in the U.S. Parachute School," recorded the Battalion's War Diary, "can aptly be described as a 'Bull in a China Shop.'" The entry further noted, "The psychological transformation of the mind of the most introvert to the extrovert is apparent in most of our young chutists after completing their qualifying jumps and course of Judo. They become fearless and to a degree reckless. They feel as though they have been given the key to all physical success and conquered all phases of fear." The chronicler continued, "It seems to be a trademark of American trained parachute troops to highly estimate their prowess, because of the type of training received, and our Canadian parachutists have acquired a similar frame of mind." The diarist concluded, "This spirit should forge a well-knit, hard hitting force."[270]

Those who passed this grueling course felt an unparalleled sense of pride and had a premonition that they would soon be part of a distinctive unit. Following his wings parade, a very boastful Private Joe Nigh, a member of the Signal Platoon, wrote home, "Today I am a parachutist ... and my chest is sticking out."[271] Private Lloyd Ford, another successful volunteer, boasted, "We qualified ... boy, we were proud guys ... can hardly wait to get back home to show off our wings, especially to buddies who said I was crazy."[272] Sergeant Laurence Heal recalled that he "was proud to wear the wings and the maroon beret; we were different we were the elite ... that shared experience produced the closeness we had with one another."[273] The parachute course, due to its danger and toughness, was instrumental in forging the paratrooper's character. In addition, the shared hardship and sense of accomplishment developed a unique sense of camaraderie amongst all ranks that was instrumental for the success of future airborne missions.

Nonetheless, after the completion of the parachute course the initial exuberance of the successful volunteers quickly wore off. No follow-up training designed to challenge the neophyte paratroopers had been developed. This, coupled with the ongoing problem of obtaining parachutist pay, the unavailability of unit insignia and distinct items of dress, and the numerous administrative problems and increasing questions raised as to the Battalion's operational role, thwarted the development of the unit's esprit de corps and lowered morale. Some disheartened paratroopers even requested to be posted back to their previous units.

The development and implementation of the Battalion's subsequent basic and advanced training program for qualified Canadian parachutists had been a constant source of frustration for Lieutenant-Colonel Bradbrooke since his appointment as the unit's commanding officer in October 1942.[274] During the subsequent months of November and December, Bradbrooke and his staff developed a parachute training directive modeled on the existing Canadian Army Basic and Advanced Infantry Training Syllabuses.

Beginning on November 7, and each subsequent week thereafter, qualified Canadian parachutists were taken onto unit strength. This "trickling in" effect further complicated the establishment of a cohesive basic training schedule devised to review and test all facets of basic training.[275] Furthermore, the absence of training directives from NDHQ and the lack of equipment and weapons further restricted the type of activities that could be conducted.[276] Additionally, there was a shortage of qualified instructors because they also had to undergo parachute training.[277] Consequently, until the end of December 1942, the only training carried out by the unit was the continuation of physical fitness activities and the very unpopular foot drill. This dull training regimen paved the way for an unforeseen crisis.

On December 1, 1942, Captain R.W. Becket of the 2nd Canadian Parachute Battalion (2 Cdn Para Bn) arrived in Fort Benning with specific orders from NDHQ to recruit qualified paratroopers for this newly formed unit.[278] During his address Becket guaranteed that "this unit [2 Cdn Para Bn] will see action before this one [1 Cdn Para Bn] does."[279] Consequently, Sergeant Herb Peppard, who had been with the Battalion since its very beginning, and ninety-six other paratroopers requested an immediate transfer. They saw this as a unique and welcomed opportunity to get out of Fort Benning and the dull regimen that was in place. "We had nothing to do so we spent hours marching singly, or in pairs, saluting fenceposts," said Peppard. "We felt," he added, "that we were making jackasses of ourselves in front of the Americans and that we had been put on indefinite hold."[280]

Disheartened by this terrible setback, Bradbrooke immediately expressed his concerns to the Directorate of Military Training requesting urgent clarification in regard to the Battalion's operational status.[281] The Battalion's War Diary captured the state of frustration and uncertainty that prevailed. "The personnel," it revealed, "began to feel as though they were lost souls of a lost Battalion."[282] Lieutenant-Colonel W.B. Wedd, the military attaché with the Canadian Legation in Washington, who closely monitored the Battalion's training, urged the Adjutant-General to send "at least a minimum of training equipment to ... the 1st Battalion without delay." He further remarked that the Canadian paratroopers were "keen, fine soldiers, but it is difficult to keep up their interest without some equipment."[283] A portion of the requested equipment and weapons finally arrived in late December.

In an attempt to stem any further loss of manpower, Bradbrooke took it upon himself to implement numerous initiatives during the months of December 1942 to February 1943. These efforts proved crucial in developing and maintaining unit morale while providing new challenges to bored paratroopers. Personnel were organized into Battalion sub-units, specifically, Headquarters (HQ), "A", "B", "C", and Training companies. This established a much-needed administrative and operational infrastructure. In addition, it instilled a competitive spirit and unit identity.[284] These changes enhanced the motivation of the paratroopers. "Operation of the Battalion is becoming more efficient every day," revealed the War Diary, "morale has improved tremendously."[285]

Eventually, the Battalion was assigned its own training area, and personnel began to build an obstacle course. Moreover, selected qualified paratroopers were sent to the U.S. Parachute School to attend rigging, jump master, communication, and parachute instructor courses.[286] The commanding officer also explored the possibility of conducting collective training at the platoon and company level with American units.[287]

Bradbrooke also implemented a policy that ensured every paratrooper was given the opportunity to jump once every three or four weeks to maintain his parachuting skills. "This is claimed to be sufficient," explained the CO, "in order to keep men in practice and likelihood of injuries causing loss of personnel reduced."[288] Additional training options were also being considered. Colonel R. Gaither, a staff officer at U.S. Army Ground Force Headquarters, proposed that, upon completion of parachute training, the Battalion be relocated to the Glider and Parachute Training Center in Alliance, Nebraska.[289] This was seen as a unique training opportunity in the event that the Canadian

Army considered organizing glider-borne infantry units. However, the lack of aircraft forced the cancellation of the program.

Despite the setback suffered by the loss of personnel, progress continued. Company-level training plans were further developed and implemented upon the arrival of much-needed training equipment and weapons.[290] By the second week of January 1943, sub-unit training was expanded to include basic weapons drill and handling. This was followed by intensive range work to qualify all personnel as First or Second Class shots by the end of February.[291] During the first days of range work, instructors noted that certain men were "gun shy." To correct this problem, .22-calibre rifles were borrowed from the Fort Benning stores for individual weapons coaching and training.[292]

The overall quality of training had clearly improved. "We have accomplished much notwithstanding the multiplicity of obstacles," acknowledged an entry in the unit's War Diary. "Much credit," it continued, "should go to Lieut.-Col. Bradbrooke and Captain Wilkinson for their untiring efforts during our formation stage."[293] Unquestionably, Bradbrooke was instrumental in keeping his paratroopers active and focused. In short, he held the unit together at its most vulnerable stage of development.

By the time the Battalion prepared to relocate to its home base in Camp Shilo, Manitoba, in March 1943, it had achieved its main training objective. A total of 34 officers and 575 men were parachute qualified and had undergone rigorous physical training.[294] Other objectives, however, had not been fully attained. All officers had completed the review of their basic training, whereas only 50 percent of the Other Ranks had completed this phase. The major portion of the training in Fort Benning had been devoted to individual training such as weapons handling and range work, leaving little time to undertake section, platoon, and company collective training.[295] This requirement was scheduled for completion once the Battalion had settled into its new home in Camp Shilo.[296]

The Battalion left Fort Benning on March 22, 1943, for a well-deserved twenty-day leave. Personnel were ordered to reassemble on April 15. Significantly, the Battalion's training schedule was modified due to ongoing talks between senior British and Canadian officers.[297] On April 7, 1943, Canada agreed to contribute the 1st Canadian Parachute Battalion to a second British airborne division that was being formed.[298] As a result, it became imperative that all individual training be quickly completed so that collective training at section, platoon, and company level could be initiated. In addition, physical fitness, continuation parachute training (set at one jump per month), and demolition training for 25 percent of the non-commissioned personnel in the rifle companies were now added to the Battalion's training plan.

But there was more. Army headquarters also directed that special attention be given to a new type of training called "Battle Drill."[299] The objective of the new Battle Drill was to train junior leaders to evaluate circumstances during operations as they developed and to use initiative during combat so as to maintain momentum. The Army considered this "an essential type of training for Parachute troops and this will be carried out by all ranks during collective training on section and Platoon level before Coy. training is commenced."[300] The unit had an ambitious schedule of training. Time now became the critical factor.

With the Battalion's imminent departure, Army Headquarters stipulated that henceforth, the parachute training phase would be the responsibility of the officer commanding the Parachute School. This directive permitted Bradbrooke to concentrate all his energies on preparing his unit. Much of this preparation fell to the Battalion's training officer, the newly promoted Major Jeff Nicklin. He was responsible for the implementation of the Unit's new training syllabus.

Training began in earnest following the arrival of personnel from leave, as well as officers and senior NCOs who returned from the Battle Drill School in Vernon, British Columbia, and the Mortar School in Long Branch, Ontario. In the next two months paratroopers yet again underwent weapons refresher courses, physical training, and route marches.[301] Added to this regimen was a series of new courses from the Battle Drill curriculum.[302] Emphasis was also placed on platoon-level battle drills, map reading and compass courses, long route marches, range practices, and day and night exercises.

To further accentuate the training tempo, Nicklin instilled a new sense of urgency and professionalism. He constantly tested and pushed all members of the Battalion, including company commanders. Attention to detail was essential and mistakes were not tolerated. "Battle Drill definitely requires advanced weapons handling," stressed Nicklin, "and company instructors are hereby advised to jump on every little mistake and not just the most obvious mistakes. It is too late to correct errors on the battle field."[303] The new Battle Drill training quickly became the most demanding part of the Battalion's training program. Simply put, Battle Drill "is the toughest part of our course — and one of the most important," explained Private W.R. Keely. "We can come down fancy as a picture but once we hit the ground we're specialized infantry and we'd better know our job — or else."[304]

As training progressed, Nicklin criticized the intensity levels displayed by both the instructors and the soldiers during the various training phases. Each week, he drafted and posted the upcoming training schedule. In addition, he promulgated recommendations to the unit's leadership. Nicklin was unforgiving. All personnel who were not tasked to regimental garrison duties were ordered to participate in the training. Even sports days failed to meet his expectations. "This is not a holiday for certain personnel to be sitting around, lolling in the sun," declared Nicklin. "This time was to be used," he asserted, "with the view and in mind at all times of developing personnel of companies into able physical condition, which is one of the two prime requisites of our training."[305]

Each week new faults were uncovered. Since this was an operational unit, proper dress and the wearing of webbing by all members was imperative. Nicklin tolerated no exceptions. When Battle Drill training was conducted, all personnel, including the instructors, were to wear full battle order.[306] By the beginning of May, Nicklin noted that the level of intensity was once again dropping off. "Training," he declared, "has been carried on in a very desultory manner and this must cease, especially under the present situation." As a result, he directed, "Training will be really intensified at once, emphasis being laid on junior officers and NCOs."[307]

Parachute continuation jumps were, for the first time, being conducted in Canada. Not surprisingly, the demanding Nicklin was not impressed by the unit's in-flight and landing drills. "Manipulation of parachutes by personnel of this unit is very poor," observed Nicklin, "and for this reason three hours have been allotted to companies for further and very necessary training."[308] Time allotted to routes marches was also increased from 4 hours to 7.5 hours weekly, and now averaged between 20 and 22 miles. Nicklin quickly observed the effect of the intensified training regimen. "The condition of the feet of personnel of this unit," he complained, "seems to be in a very soft state."[309] No one escaped Nicklin's scrutiny, not even the company commanders. He advised them to improve their planning, "instead of waiting for the last mad bustle."[310]

And the tempo was continually augmented. By June, training was further modified and intensified. Weekly training was increased from 41 to 53 hours. The additional training was carried out at night and involved map reading and gas warfare. Morning fitness runs were added, and one extra hour was allotted to weapons training and route marches. Nicklin also recommended that tumbling and landing training be carried out during part of the recreational training period. Furthermore, during this training, companies were directed to organize cross-country runs that were mandatory for all personnel.

The quality of training was also continually improved. For instance, the method of instruction used in map reading classes was deemed below standard. "These periods must be properly supervised," counseled Nicklin, "as it has been pointed out that Officer Instructors are proceeding much to rapidly for personnel to grasp."[311] The training was also increased in complexity with the aim of making the paratroopers more self-reliant. They were now required to cook their own meals (mess tin cooking) while in the field. As well, the route marches evolved to include ambushes, response to enemy fire, gas drills, and live grenade practices. Night training was expanded to encompass night stalking techniques and patrols. Moreover, to keep all personnel active and engaged, Nicklin encouraged the use of competitive methods to keep the interest levels high.[312]

The specialist platoons were particularly challenged. The Signal, Anti-tank, Mortar, and Vickers platoons had to undergo the regular training regimen, as well as become expert in their own respective disciplines. The men of Mortar Platoon had completed their theoretical training and were honing their skills on the firing ranges. The Battalion Demolition School was finally established. Although the objective was to train 25 percent of the personnel in minor demolition work, the Battalion wanted all its members to attend these courses.[313] Interestingly, despite many hours of weapons training and range work, the results were not very encouraging.

Since in Canada, Battalion personnel, many of whom were not originally infantry, encountered difficulties in attaining the required proficiency with personal small arms and battalion weapons. Nicklin was frustrated by the lack of progress and the high failure rate.[314] He had anticipated that by the end of June, 80 percent of Battalion personnel would have qualified and classified as First and Second Class Shots on the rifle and Bren gun. After all, "every man," explained Nicklin, "must be able to fight with every weapon in the field that is on the unit establishment."[315]

As June was drawing to an end, Nicklin instructed the company commanders to ensure that each section was brought up to the required level of proficiency in anticipation of the upcoming platoon training. Battle Drill was taking up 40 percent of the Battalion weekly training schedule.[316] Following an inspection carried out during the last week of June, Nicklin reported "that not one coy. is ready to proceed to higher training such as collective platoon training." Company commanders were advised to ensure that realistic training was conducted to motivate the paratroopers. And Nicklin continued to criticize their training exercise preparations. "It is not good enough," he extolled, "to take men out and make schemes up on arrival."[317]

But Nicklin's constant protestations and exhortations were justified. Despite the increased training regimen and the hard work, a Directorate of Military Training report revealed that the Battalion was still only at the individual or "trained soldier" level. As a result, they recommended that training be accelerated, "as it [this unit] was felt to be below Parachute Battalion standard."[318] As a result, Bradbrooke and his staff diligently carried on with training right up until the moment they left for the United Kingdom.

Prior to departure, during the first week of July 1943, the Battalion was inspected one last time by Major-General J.P. Mackenzie, Inspector-General of Western Canada. Mackenzie observed that Colonel Bradbrooke was "a very efficient officer — energetic with plenty of imagination" and he assessed Major Nicklin as "a good leader and, as a Training Officer, thoroughly satisfactory." The Inspector-General provided an interesting insight regarding the ORs. He noted that overall the discipline was good. However, he also reported, "Due to the youth of the men they are sometimes hard to control." He added, "The men came in with a little Paratroop complex in their soul, which will be ironed out when they get along side other paratroop battalions."[319]

Despite not having started their collective training and although they were under strength with only 30 officers and 543 Other Ranks, for a total of 573 men, NDHQ ordered the Battalion to deploy to the United Kingdom.[320] The nation's paratroopers were dispatched for overseas duty to take their place in the upcoming offensive against Germany. They departed Canada's shores on July 23, 1943, to begin the next phase of their adventure.

CHAPTER FIVE

Sharpening the Spear — Training in England, August 1943–June 1944

I inspected the 1st Canadian Parachute Battalion today. Any man with two eyes in his head could not fail to see that here is a fine battalion — with all the makings of something good — something magnificent.

Major-General R.N. Gale, Commander, 6th Airborne Division.[321]

In July 1943, the Battalion sailed to England for overseas duty. But it was still not ready. Despite the emphasis and effort placed on individual training in both Fort Benning and Camp Shilo, the Canadian airborne soldiers had not fully completed this necessary requirement. However, this shortcoming would soon be overcome. The young Canadian paratroopers were about to benefit from the experience and knowledge acquired by battle-hardened British airborne veterans who had seen service in North Africa. Under the tutelage of instructors from the 6th Airborne Division (6 AB Div) the Canadians would learn their individual skills and advance to collective training at the sub-unit, unit, and formation level. Once in England, the 1st Canadian Parachute Battalion began to focus all its effort and energy on raising the individual strengths of its members and transforming them into a collective whole. Within the next few months the unit would be fashioned into an effective fighting force capable of taking its place at the forefront of battle.

But there were still hurdles to overcome. As the Battalion traversed the dangerous North Atlantic, the Canadian Military Headquarters and the British War Office worked feverishly to finalize numerous legal details relating to the unit's future with the British 6 AB Div.[322] When the Canadians landed in Greenock, Scotland, on July 28, 1943, they had to spend a few days in a nearby holding area while their quarters in Bulford, Whiltshire, were being prepared.

The Battalion's arrival also prompted CMHQ to establish a Canadian liaison section. As such, two Canadian officers were attached to 6 AB Div Headquarters. Their role was to keep the General Staff of the First Canadian Army informed of 6 AB Div developments pertaining to organization, equipment, and airborne tactics. One officer acted as liaison between General McNaughton and Major-General R.N. Gale, the general officer commanding 6th Airborne Division. The second officer provided a direct link between the unit and CMHQ on matters relating to Canadian administration, disciplinary procedures, and the application of Canadian military law.[323] Furthermore, Major-General P.J. Montague, the senior officer at CMHQ, forwarded a directive to Lieutenant-Colonel Bradbrooke notifying the Commanding Officer that his unit was placed "in-combination" with the newly formed 6 AB Div. This meant that Bradbrooke was obligated to comply with all training and operational directives issued by his new commander, Major-General Gale. However, Montague ordered Bradbrooke to continue to report to CMHQ on all other matters affecting his unit's administration and any issues relating to discipline.[324]

Notwithstanding the litany of bureaucratic restrictions, Major-General Gale was overjoyed with the infusion of the 1st Canadian Parachute Battalion in his division.[325] He decided to attach the Canadians to the 3rd Parachute Brigade (3 Para Bde) commanded by airborne veteran Brigadier S. James L. Hill, the former commanding officer of the British 1st Parachute Battalion, which had seen action in North Africa.[326]

Brigadier Hill wasted no time meeting with the Battalion's officers and men. Hill realized immediately that the unit contained the right type of personnel for airborne operations. They were "soldiers," he observed, "who wanted to fight and the sooner the better."[327] But attitude was not enough. Hill explained to his Canadians that there would be a lot of hard training to undergo to get them up to 6 AB Div and 3 Para Bde standards. Nonetheless, Hill was confident that they would successfully endure the rigours of airborne training.

The Brigadier's professionalism and personality made an immediate and lasting impression on the young Canadian paratroopers. "As he welcomed us and sincerely told us he was proud to command a brigade with a Canadian Battalion in it," recalled Corporal Dan Hartigan, "he also informed us that he would brook no nonsense and had great expectation from us, as he had from his other two superb battalions already partially trained to the high standards he had set."[328] The Battalion officers were inspired by the Brigadier's initial greeting, as well as the confidence, efficiency, and professionalism displayed by 6 AB Div personnel. "Their organization was very fine; they knew what they were doing," observed Captain John Madden. "They could teach us," he added, "and they were convinced of their own worth."[329]

From the outset Brigadier Hill stressed that all facets of training were to be based on the two most important cornerstones of the airborne training doctrine — discipline and physical fitness.[330] Moreover, he ordered that all officers, NCOs, and men apply the airborne governing principles of speed in thought and action, simplicity, control, and firepower during every stage of the planning and training phase.[331] In August 1943, with these simple guidelines, the Battalion embarked on a fast-paced and severe training regimen that would last for the next ten months.

The tone was set early on. The Canadians were intent on proving that they could match or even surpass their British counterparts. "We had the incentive to be better than the other Battalions," explained Lieutenant-Colonel Fraser Eadie. "After all," he added, "we had to measure up — we were strangers in a brigade and division."[332] The commander of 3 Para Bde devised a challenging two-part airborne training programme for the Battalion. The first part was to be carried out from August to October 1943 and necessitated all members of 1 Cdn Para Bn to complete their British parachute conversion course.

Concurrently, the unit was to train and qualify selected personnel as heavy machine gunners, mortar and anti-tank teams, wireless operators, and intelligence staff. Furthermore, all personnel were to classify on all weapons and undergo physical training to increase their level of fitness. Additionally, selected personnel underwent qualification jumps with the leg kit bag, which was a new type of individual airborne equipment container. It was devised to enable the paratroopers to jump into battle with their heavy weapons, extra ammunition, and other required equipment.[333]

Hill also ordered that special attention be given to the development of officers. "It is vital for officers of every rank," he emphasized, "to have regular practice in exercising their command."[334] The Brigadier insisted that the development of all junior leaders, particularly lieutenants, be closely monitored. Hill warned that he would personally test them on various subjects and skills relating to their profession.[335] He believed that due to the hazardous nature of airborne operations, it was imperative that the young officers be thoroughly prepared in commanding their soldiers under adverse conditions. Quite simply, Hill demanded that they be capable of completing a mission without hesitation in the event that their superiors were dropped off course, wounded, or killed.[336]

The second part of the unit's training was conducted during the months of November and December. During this period the Battalion commenced advanced training and participated in a series of day and night unit and formation exercises. The requirements were continually increased. Brigadier Hill directed that each paratrooper be capable of performing the duties of a bangalore torpedo assault detachment. In addition, all ranks were to be trained to neutralize common German anti-tank and anti-personnel mines, as well as booby traps.[337]

Moreover, Brigadier Hill exhorted that special attention be taken during this phase of training to increase the stamina and further develop the resistance to physical hardships of the airborne soldiers.[338] Notwithstanding those expectations, the Battalion was also expected to continue with its company and specialized platoon training programmes. As a result, all sub-units trained from Monday to Saturday noon. When exercises were conducted training was extended to the full seven days. The program started at 0615 hours with a run and never finished before 1730 hours.[339] Within the first days, all ranks noted that the tempo prescribed by Brigadier Hill was very demanding. "It wasn't fun," recollected Lieutenant-Colonel Eadie. "It was a lot of work."[340]

Despite the fact that a high percentage of the Battalion was already parachute qualified, inclusion in a British airborne division required that all personnel, regardless of rank, as well as the future parachute reinforcements arriving from Canada, be sent to Hardwick Hall and Ringway for the British parachute conversion course.[341] Many of the Fort Benning graduates approached this course with a "been there, done that" attitude. "We were cocky, we had our American wings and brown boots and we also had our Canadian wings," stated Corporal Boyd Anderson. "Most of our guys didn't take the British instructors seriously. Many of us were going to the nearby British pubs into Manchester every night ... On the first two jumps, some of our guys came down with their legs apart," in accordance with the way they had been taught by the Americans. Anderson recalled, "The British instructors were very upset after our second jump." He added, "We were told very firmly that we must shape up or we would be shipped out." He also remembered that they threatened to "disqualify us."[342] Very quickly, it became clear to all that attitudes toward training had to change. Fearing a "return to unit" (RTU), the young Canadian paratroopers promptly rectified their behaviour.

Interestingly, despite their previous parachute training, or maybe because of it, the Canadians were initially apprehensive when they first saw the British parachute equipment and aircraft. Compared to those used in the American training, these seemed archaic. Furthermore, the prospect of jumping with only one parachute initially raised numerous concerns. In Fort Benning and subsequently in Camp Shilo, the paratroopers had always trained and jumped with a main parachute and a reserve. In England, they jumped only with a main parachute, because of the British doctrine that emphasized a low-dropping altitude. Jumping below one thousand feet simply did not provide a paratrooper who experienced difficulties with his main chute with the required time to activate his reserve. Furthermore, the Whitley aircraft's very narrow fuselage and its small floor-exiting aperture could not accommodate paratroopers wearing this extra parachute. Nonetheless, their concerns were quickly dispelled by the superior quality of instruction received at the No.1 Parachute Training School.[343]

This confidence, which increased daily, enabled them to jump without apprehension at lower altitudes, as well as through the floor apertures of both the barrage balloon and the Whitley/Albemarle converted bombers. In Fort Benning, the candidates did their initial parachute jump training from the 250-foot high tower. Qualifying jumps were then conducted from aircraft that dropped the parachutists from between 1200 and 1500 feet. In Ringway, the initial jumps were performed from a barrage balloon that was elevated to 800 feet. The subsequent qualifying jumps were conducted from altitudes ranging between 800 and 1000 feet.[344] The candidates also found that they preferred the design of the British "X"-type parachute to that of the American assembly. The opening shock generated by the "X"-type canopy deployment was far less violent than that of the American T-4 and later T-5 systems. Additionally, once on the ground it was easier and quicker to unfasten.

This was an important feature, especially when landing directly on objectives in the face of the enemy.

The Canadians also preferred the British landing drill compared to the American method. The Americans taught aspiring paratroopers to land with their feet shoulder-width apart. In Ringway the candidates were instructed to keep their feet and knees together, legs slightly bent and toes pointed toward the rapidly approaching ground. Upon impact, they immediately rolled onto their side, thereby dissipating the shock evenly throughout the entire body. This drill significantly reduced the number of injuries incurred during training. This would prove critical later on in the training when it became imperative to keep personnel healthy because of manpower shortages and upcoming operations.

By the end of October, the great majority of the Battalion members had successfully completed their British parachute conversion training.[345] In the end, the efficiency and professionalism of the British instructors, as well as their superior training methodology, impressed the Canadians. Each group of Canadian airborne soldiers that completed their conversion training agreed that the British course was superior to the American one. Company-Sergeant Major John Kemp explained:

> The training in Benning was very tough and I think their method of training was inferior to the British because it was drilled into you. If you didn't shape up you were a "wash out" and if someone froze and couldn't jump he was given a bucket of water to run around the air field shouting "I'm a wash out." The British brought a man down if he couldn't force himself to jump and he was given some counselling and taken up again, (a little more humane).[346]

Concurrently throughout this period those who had completed the conversion course or were waiting to go to Ringway conducted Battle Drill and specialized training such as night training, map reading courses, physical training, and range work. The training regimen prescribed by Brigadier Hill quickly revealed the Battalion's weaknesses. The most glaring problem remained the low level of marksmanship within the unit. "The firing in this unit is not approaching the standard for qualification as required in this Brigade," wrote a very unsatisfied Bradbrooke. "Weapons training," he ordered, "<u>MUST</u> be concentrated in the short time allotted to it. Mistakes must be corrected and checked on the spot."[347]

But there were other problems as well. The lack of experience of the officers and NCOs in the planning of courses, training, and exercises was also sorely felt.[348] "Company and platoon commanders will make sure," emphasised Bradbrooke, "that reconnaissances are made and plans laid prior to the day the platoon does the training. All ranks will have explained what they are going to do and be taught prior to doing the training."[349] Lastly, the commanding officer observed that map reading skills had regressed. As a result, he ordered that more time be allotted to its instruction.

The CO was also displeased with his paratroopers' comportment and dress. Since they were the only Canadian unit in Bulford, he did not want the Battalion's appearance or conduct to reflect negatively on the Canadian Army. "Smartness and bearing of all ranks are deteriorating," lamented an angry Bradbrooke. "Check up at once and make sure the 1/2 hour morning smartening up MEANS something."[350] Bradbrooke's focus on dress was not a personal quiff. The commanding officer of the 1st Canadian Parachute Battalion was well aware of Brigadier Hill's position on these principles. Regardless of the intensity of the training and the hardships undertaken, these were to be maintained at a very high level at all times. Hill believed that they would invariably reinforce the paratroopers' efficiency in battle. Brigadier Hill explained:

> In battle a unit is either good or bad: there is no halfway house. The discipline in a good unit is invariably good and in a bad fighting unit always bad. You must ask yourself: "Are my men smart, happy, alert? Is their turn out and bearing first class ..." If you ask yourself those questions, you will have a very good idea as how they will fight when you lead them in battle ... Good discipline and contentment walk hand-in-hand.[351]

As a result, Lieutenant-Colonel Bradbrooke and his 2IC, Major Nicklin, made it a point to constantly reinforce to all Battalion officers and NCOs the importance of good discipline and proper dress. They demanded that special attention be paid to these requirements at all times. They were not the only ones. Not surprisingly, throughout the Battalion's stay with the 6 AB Div, Brigadier Hill never relaxed his attention on these two fundamental principles.[352]

Training intensified during October. Brigadier Hill visited the Battalion regularly, and his continued advice proved invaluable to Bradbrooke and Nicklin. Hill's guidance in turn was reflected in the unit's weekly training schedules. For example, added to the already busy daily activities was a two-mile reveille run. He also suggested that the instructors create more imaginative scenarios to enhance the paratroopers' intensity and competitive instincts during the Battle Drill exercises involving individual stalking and section attacks.[353] He believed that developing an aggressive competitive spirit throughout the airborne forces was an indispensable element in keeping the men alert and interested. Moreover, it fostered teamwork.

The inclusion of this new training technique paid off immediate dividends. "There was a fierce competition to be the best Battalion in the Brigade," recollected Corporal Anderson, "then the best company, the best platoon, and finally the best section. Good military organization and good morale and discipline was built on competition. Always the will to be the best had to be there."[354] As the outsiders in 3 Para Bde, the Canadians felt that they constantly had to put out the extra effort. Thus the development and implementation of this new competitive spirit had a beneficial impact on honing their basic infantry skills. They were now on their way to attaining the Brigade's exacting standards.

The Brigadier was encouraged by the Battalion's new competitive spirit and esprit de corps. He felt that these elements were essential for successful night fighting operations. Hill was a strong proponent of this type of warfare. He ordered that all battalion commanders allocate at least six nights per month solely for this purpose.[355] While in North Africa, he and his paratroopers had perfected and used night operations with a great deal of success. "The Germans and the Italians fear the night as much as they fear our Parachute troops," asserted Hill. "They hate it when you creep up to their positions in the darkness unseen and unheard and go in with bomb and bayonet." Hill elaborated, "Darkness does for the parachutists what the supporting artillery and air force do for infantry. It neutralises the effect of the enemy's artillery and heavy supporting weapons."[356]

Lieutenant-Colonel Bradbrooke heartily endorsed the directive. "We must become night minded," he asserted, "and instead of just route marching down the road, night training will consist of compass marches, night patrol, stalking, etc."[357] During these night manoeuvres personnel, regardless of rank, were randomly selected and pulled aside by

British airborne instructors who accompanied Brigadier Hill to observe the training. The selected individuals were quizzed and tested on various subjects, as well as on the object of their mission.

Physical training and forced road marches were also increased to prepare all personnel for their upcoming 3 Para Bde mandatory qualification forced marches. The physical standards were set at:

One 15 mile cross country and road march in physical training kit and boots, to be completed in 3 hours; a 65 mile road march carrying full equipment, less anti-tank rifles, PIAT projectors, 3 inch mortar, to be completed in 60 hours. Swim 100 yards in swimming kit and 50 yards in physical training kits and boots, to be completed in 4 hours. A 100 mile road march carrying full equipment, less anti-tank rifles, PIAT projectors and 3 inch mortars, to be completed in 84 hours; and a 100 yard swim in swimming kits and 50 yards with clothing on.[358]

Hill insisted that a minimum of three marches in excess of fifteen miles on hard roads be conducted monthly. The ultimate aim was to move fully armed troops across country at high speeds. The commander of 3 Para Bde wanted all his paratroopers to be "pre-eminent in physique ... mobile and tireless, tremendous marchers, and of an undefeated spirit."[359] The road marches were grueling and took a physical toll, but nevertheless, the great majority of Canadians passed. It did, however, leave a lasting impression. Lance-Corporal Alec Flexer wrote:

We marched, or perhaps, staggered 50 miles yesterday, in 17 hours flat. I still don't fully understand how, why or when it was done, though I can honestly say, never did I feel as miserable or sick as I did then. We marched the last 20 miles in a howling rain storm and were consequently drenched to the marrow. Today, one and a half days after the ordeal, I still can't point my toes straight. I managed to get a blister diagonally across my left arch — how it ever blistered there is beyond me, unless they sagged so much that I was walking on them. If I ever am as incautious as to sit down, I find myself unable to straighten either knee for a few minutes, then

with a crunch and a squeak I manage to set them in
action. There are rumours that immediately after our
leave we will do 100 mile march.[360]

Even though much had been achieved in the initial months, the
Battalion still experienced difficulties attaining the Division's weapon
classification standards. "Recent range work has definitely proved that
personnel of this Battalion have slipped backwards instead of improving," remarked a frustrated Major Nicklin. "Repetition repeat repetition
is the only answer," he insisted, "coaching by NCOs has been very lack-
adaisical and this will cease." He directed that the companies run sup-
plemental night classes on coaching for NCOs and officers. In closing he
extolled that there was "lots of work to be done here, get busy."[361]

But the lack of improvement was becoming a concern, not only for
the Battalion, but also for the Brigade. Efficient weapons handling and
marksmanship were critical to the survival of the paratrooper on the
battlefield. "As a parachutist," insisted Hill, "you have the minimum of
ammunition to accomplish the stiffest task. You must therefore ensure
that the maximum effect is obtained from every round, whether it be
revolver, rifle, Sten, Bren or grenade that your men fire." He added that
paratroops "must be artists in the use of their weapons and you [offi-
cers] in their direction."[362] Furthermore, the Brigadier demanded that
every parachutist had to be "the master of his weapons" and that "every
shot must be fired to kill."[363]

The marksmanship problem was so grave that by the second week of
October, a staff sergeant from the Small Arms School at Bisely Camp was
invited to assess the Canadian paratroopers' weapons skills. He identified
the weaknesses and discussed his observations with the Battalion's
instructors. The importance of his visit was not lost on the unit. "It is
necessary for all ranks 'to pick his brains' to the utmost," emphasized
Bradbrooke, "in order that we may derive the greatest possible benefit
from a well-qualified NCO, who, no doubt, knows his job."[364] To correct
the continuing problems, additional range work was inserted into the
upcoming second phase of training that commenced the next month.

In November, the Battalion was ready to begin collective training. The
unit's effectiveness was now to be tested and evaluated in a series of bat-
talion- and brigade-level exercises. Brigadier Hill, in keeping with his
previous themes, ordered all his commanding officers to focus on prac-

tising and perfecting day and night movements, manning defensive positions, attacking strongly defended objectives, and perfecting day cross-country movements in the face of enemy opposition.[365] The men were pushed to their limits. The frequent forced marches, the long hours, and the numerous night manoeuvres began to take their toll. Not surprisingly, it was during this month, as well as in December 1943, that the Battalion sustained its highest rates of training-related injuries and illnesses. Between 10 and 15 percent of the personnel were admitted to the base hospital or the unit's medical inspection room. Many others were relegated to light or excused duties.[366]

Despite the injuries the pace of activity attained the desired effect. The Battalion's overall level of individual stamina and physical fitness definitely increased. So too did the experience and knowledge levels of the officers and senior NCOs in regards to leadership and organizational planning.[367] Battalion officers attended continual professional development sessions, such as regular Tactical Exercises Without Troops (TEWT), to practise battle procedure and enhance their tactical acumen. In addition, during this period many officers and NCOs returned to the Battalion after having attended specialized courses. Their absence had somewhat hindered the progression of the individual and sub-unit training. However, their newly acquired expertise and knowledge greatly enhanced the Battalion's pool of instructors for the upcoming activities.[368]

For the first time since taking over command of the unit, Bradbrooke finally felt that he was surrounded by qualified personnel who could provide effective training at the collective level. All were eager to show what they had learned and all were enthusiastic in developing the Battalion into a first-rate cohesive airborne unit. An impatient Bradbrooke commenced the collective training cycle with a short, yet clear, directive. "Lots of work," he extolled, "leave is over, get going!"[369]

The first major change that was implemented was the dissemination of orders to all personnel prior to collective training exercises. Hill insisted, due to the nature of airborne operations (which was to fight isolated from the main army group behind enemy lines) that every paratrooper be "in the picture and know the minds of his commanders."[370] Ultimately, the success of a mission could depend solely on the initiative and resolve of a solitary private. Therefore, to stress the necessity of passing orders to everyone, the Battalion had to alter its normal battle procedure. Instead of briefing a select group of officers, Bradbrooke now gave orders to the entire unit prior to battalion or formation exercises. The implementation of this new methodology was a major departure from the norm. "Lt-Col Bradbrooke, briefed the entire Battalion in the upper gym," recorded the War Diary chronicler, "this being a procedure which in the future will be common to all exercises and operations."[371]

The same briefing methods were used at the company and platoon levels to ensure a standardized format. Additionally, post-exercise, after-action reviews were also implemented to ensure that maximum efficiency could be derived from all activities. The after-action review enabled officers to gather a wide range of information from all of their paratroopers on what equipment and techniques worked and what did not. Commanders realized that the observations and comments of everyone could prove useful in the planning of future exercises, as well as the modification of equipment, doctrine, and tactics. Thus, from this moment on, all ranks were expected to fully understand the Battalion's overall mission, as well the tasks and objectives of their sub-unit and of other units. "The main thing was that everyone in the Battalion had to know what everybody else was doing," recalled Major John Simpson. "If you came on a job that was supposed to be done by people that hadn't showed up," he explained, "you had to figure out how to do it."[372]

The Battalion conducted its first collective exercise during a night brigade-level manouevre, entitled Exercise Schemozzle, on November 9 and 10, 1943. The exercise was designed to test the efficiency of sub-units that were separated from the main body following a simulated drop. The Canadians were tasked to capture and occupy a designated objective.[373] Overall, the Battalion performed well. However, the Brigade Commander noted mistakes in regards to fieldcraft and tactics such as concealment and movement by night. These were subsequently analyzed and explained at the new unit-level post-exercise debrief.[374] "The individual soldier is being thoroughly 'put in the picture,'" noted the War Diary, "before and after each exercise so as to make most certain of his being able to act independently should the situation arise."[375] Hill reiterated the importance of passing pertinent information to all ranks at these unit-level debriefing sessions. "You MUST repeat and exaggerate and repeat and exaggerate and repeat and exaggerate important principles," explained Hill in his Brigade training directive, "if you want your men to remember and act automatically upon them when in battle."[376]

The collective exercises showed improvement in the unit's effectiveness. Weapons skills too were slowly improving, but were still not up to the Brigade standard. As a result, all personnel were ordered to undergo a further six to eight hours of supplementary weekly weapons training.[377] On November 11, 1943, a very concerned Bradbrooke wrote, "It may seem boring to officers and NCOs instructing, but it is only practice and repetition in any subject matter that acquires skill and efficiency, and in the paratroops both skill and efficiency in handling of all weapons must reach and will reach a higher standard than any other arms of the services."[378]

Other issues of continuing concern were map reading and communications procedures using field radios. Map reading skills had not improved since they had been identified as a serious problem earlier in the fall. To remedy this, four one-hour periods were now added to the weekly syllabus.[379] Moreover, Hill ordered that communications courses be developed for all personnel. Officers and NCOs down to the rank of sergeant were expected to become expert radio operators. "The power to command," proclaimed the Brigadier, "depends on good communications."[380] He insisted that all Battalion COs foster a "wireless atmosphere" within their respective battalions. As such, one forty-eight-hour period per month was designated when all Brigade telephones were switched off and all communication were carried out exclusively using the No. 38 radio set and correct transmission procedures.[381]

Since the Battalion's arrival in England, Lieutenant-Colonel Bradbrooke and Major Nicklin had learned a great deal from Brigadier Hill with regards to devising and conducting specialized airborne courses, manoeuvres, and training. Their increasing knowledge was evident in the information that was passed along in the unit training directives. These were particularly important because they summed up the standards that had to be attained, observations, lessons learned, and comments from Battalion instructors, as well as those of other units of the Division that had taken place during the previous week. Major Nicklin continually reinforced their importance to the officers. He directed that they be "continually looked into and checked ... by Company Commanders and Officers, so that they are brought out to full advantage." Nicklin believed that the information brought forward in these weekly directives would "produce the required paratrooper."[382]

The effectiveness of the unit's training plan quickly became evident. Exercises became more complex and demanding. "Gradually we were being moulded into a first class unit of fighting soldiers," recalled Corporal Anderson. "Week after week, month after month," he explained, "we trained."[383] As training progressed, everyone, regardless of rank, felt the pressure to constantly improve performance. Furthermore, they did not want to be transferred out of the unit. "One good aspect of having several eager replacements in the Training Battalion," recalled Private Alcide Carignan, "was that it kept those in the Battalion itself on their toes. Slackers were shipped out and quickly replaced."[384]

While it was imperative to master all facets of field training, Brigadier Hill did not want operational efficiency to be achieved at the detriment of the Battalion's administrative daily tasks and responsibilities. Hill wanted to train and field a complete soldier — a superior fighting man as well as a disciplined garrison soldier. Even though Hill recognized that the members of 1st Canadian Parachute Battalion "were spoiling for a fight," he also knew that "they had to be very well disciplined."[385] As such, on December 6, 1943, Brigadier Hill carried out a detailed inspection of the unit to assess their progress. His reaction was mixed. He noted that physical training instruction was excellent; however, not surprisingly, weapons training still had to be improved. In addition, he assessed the overall instruction, particularly the Test of Elementary Training (TOET) classes given by junior NCOs, as weak. He also found the Battalion's vehicle maintenance wanting. On the positive side, he rated the specialist training in the Signal, Mortar, Anti-tank, and Machine Gun Platoons, as well as the Intelligence Section, as very good.

Hill was also impressed with a demonstration of a platoon attack conducted by "C" Company. "The standard of field craft and enthusiasm," observed a pleased Hill, "shown by all ranks was excellent."[386] In sum, overall improvements were evident, but there were numerous administrative deficiencies to be overcome.[387]

While these deficiencies were being addressed, Battalion personnel busily prepared for the upcoming brigade activity called Exercise Procedure, on December 8 and 9, 1943. Its primary aim was to conduct a mass drop and correct the mistakes noted during previous manoeuvres.[388] Bad weather led to the cancellation of the Battalion's jump. Nevertheless, the exercise was carried out and many valuable lessons were learned in regard to the preparation of a battalion-level drop. These included: moving large numbers of paratroopers quickly from a base camp to an airfield, packing and loading containers onto aircraft, adjusting and verifying parachutes, rigging personal equipment, and practising "stick" emplaning drills.[389]

The Battalion's hard work and performance had not gone unnoticed. During a visit to Bulford, Lieutenant-General A.G.L. McNaughton, Commander of the First Canadian Army, was impressed by the Battalion's progress. A proud McNaughton confided to Major-General Gale, "That Canadian battalion works in your division like a hand in a well-fitting glove."[390]

As the year was coming to a close, the unit had just enough time to conduct one last battalion-level exercise. Exercise Shilo commenced on December 19 and was designed to test the unit in the defence of a position for a twenty-four-hour period using heavy machine guns and mortars. The troops were also assessed on their mine-laying and scouting capabilities.[391] Brigadier Hill watched his Canadian paratroopers with great interest. He later shared his observations with the commanding officer. "The siting of the positions and slit trenches taken up by night was, I thought, good," he wrote, "although one platoon of 'A' Company was rather out in the blue ... I am afraid that a large number of the men in the Battalion would have become corpses as a result of wandering about their own locality." He elaborated, "It must be pointed out to the men that this is just not on." Hill warned that "you will be doing another exercise of this nature at a future date and they must rectify this movement by then."[392]

But the Brigadier also noted some positive points. "Morale of the men was quite first-class," stated Hill, "the men, I thought, played extraordinarily well."[393] Hill fully understood the difficulties his Canadians faced as the only non-British unit in the Division. As a result he made it a point to attend all Battalion exercises, and he even jumped with them from time to time. In addition, he regularly visited unit activities such as courses and range work. "They were the only Canadian troops, entirely cut off from their own army," reminisced Hill many years after the war. "I felt responsible for their lives and welfare and they were a long way from home." He added, "I took that very seriously, particularly in the fighting. It was very important that I looked after them and it paid marvellous dividends."[394] In spite of the Brigadier's encouraging words following Exercise Shilo, all knew that there was still a lot of work to be done.

Despite a challenging training schedule, all knew that time was running out. The tide of the war had shifted, and it was just a matter of time until the Allies would return to the continent. On January 5, 1944, with the impending invasion of Europe looming, the War Office issued an urgent memorandum informing the 6th Airborne Division that they were to be mobilized for overseas service by 0001 hours, February 1, 1944, under the supervision of HQ, Southern Command.[395] CMHQ reacted immediately to this order. They reviewed their previously issued Order of Detail No. 13, of October 11, 1943, which specified that the 1st Canadian Parachute Battalion was "in combination with 6 AB Div for training in the U.K. only."[396] As a result, on February 23, 1944, CMHQ issued Mobilization Order No. 98, authorizing the Battalion to mobilize for operations in Europe by February 29, 1944.[397]

The CMHQ mobilization order confirmed what the members of 1 Cdn Para Bn had suspected for some time. Finally, they would see action. The unit's activities in January 1944 focused on assaults against heavily defended objectives, as well as daylight attacks in open country. Additional training on the laying, clearing, and handling of mines and the breaching of minefields was also included. Range work for all ranks, on all weapons, was compulsory, with special attention given to weapons handling. Special emphasis was still placed on improving radio transmissions, wireless procedures, and map reading. The Battalion's effectiveness regarding these important skills was still disappointing. Major Nicklin rated these as "low."[398]

The priority placed on parachute training was also increased. Monthly continuation parachute descents were conducted from balloons and from American and British aircraft. The Battalion's monthly parachute training plan also incorporated kit bag jumps and container packing courses. On top of all this additional instruction, the emphasis on physical conditioning continued. In addition, a half day per week was still set aside for sporting activities. Nicklin made sure that they were "entertaining and vigorous afternoons." This translated into five-mile cross-country runs for all ranks. Furthermore, all personnel who had failed their 3 Para Bde physical fitness tests and forced marches were retested. Those who had passed went on to the next level of even more demanding physical requirements.[399] This training, as well as a series of specialized platoon, company, battalion, and brigade night jump and ground exercises were carried out until mid-May 1944.

Concurrent to the specialized unit training were numerous exercises imposed by higher headquarters during the January to May 1944 period.

These were designed to practise specific skills. For instance, Exercise P.A.D. Boomer aimed to heighten the ability of personnel to operate during an enemy air raid.[400] More significantly, during Exercise Manitoba, on January 20, 1944, the entire Battalion jumped as a unit for the first time since its inception. The aim of this exercise was threefold: to practise cooperation between 38 Group, RAF, and a parachute battalion; to drop an entire battalion in five minutes; and to clear the unit from the drop zone in fifteen minutes from the time the first paratrooper landed.

Exercise Manitoba was a great success. The drop went smoothly, and after reaching their rendezvous (RV) point, all companies raced to their designated area, dug in, and adopted a defensive posture.[401] Lieutenant G.C. Tinning, a war artist attached to the Battalion during the exercise, recounted:

> The men came out like clock work with no pause between them, there was an undistinguishable blob, the opening twisting larger blob of the chute, till it opened. It seemed enormous in the sky, the blue shadowed, wide-winged plane, the golden arches of the chutes. As the plane roared overhead the first who had jumped were nearer the ground and further back the last so perspective made a diminishing V shape of the parachutes as two planes close together dropped their men ... On landing the men rushed to their containers, took out packs and Bren guns, and ran under cover as much as possible, to the agreed rendezvous. At no time were more than a few men discernable on the field although 500 or more were dropped that afternoon.[402]

With the passing of each day Major Nicklin was encouraged by the progress and teamwork displayed by all ranks of the 1st Canadian Parachute Battalion. "At this period of training the general feeling of confidence held by officers," wrote the Deputy Commanding Officer, "in their men and by the men in their officers is becoming daily more apparent." He explained, "A great feeling of mutual dependence in para work is evident and teamwork develops naturally from this." As a result, he insisted, "All ranks are more confident in themselves, physically and mentally, as fighting men.[403]

His sentiments were correct. Even though the exercises became increasingly demanding, the majority of the paratroopers nevertheless found them challenging and motivating. "I enjoyed those make believe battles when we stayed out in the country for three or four days at a time," recalled Corporal Boyd Anderson. The tough, demanding training and physical fitness regime had greatly enhanced the paratroopers' endurance and stamina. "It was evident," stated one veteran, "that we were healthy when after three days of being soaking wet, not one soldier out of five hundred came down with a cold."[404]

Nonetheless, being pushed to the physical limit inevitably caused many injuries. Members of the 1st Canadian Parachute Battalion dreaded the thought of sustaining an injury that would require a long convalescence period. This invariably signalled the end of their career within the unit. Both the brigade and division commanders agreed that it was important to have well-trained paratroopers. However, if the individual was not in top physical shape to carry out in battle what he had learned, then he was a liability to his unit. If a paratrooper was unable to recover quickly from his injury and keep up with the group, the commanding officer had no other option but to remove the individual from the battalion. This policy was enforced regardless of rank.[405]

As weeks passed, exercises became more complex, putting additional pressure on all 3 Para Bde battalion commanders and company commanders. Exercise Co-operation, on February 7 and 8, 1944, was a dramatic step forward in the preparation for the upcoming invasion of *Festung Europa*. The aim of this twenty-four-hour exercise was to practise cooperation between a parachute brigade group, air landing units, 38 Group, RAF, and the 435 Group Troop Carrier Command, U.S. Army. Of primary importance was the necessity to confirm if 1,370 paratroopers could be dropped on one drop zone in ten minutes, and if all personnel could be cleared from the DZ thirty minutes after the first paratrooper landed.[406]

During this and other exercises, Brigadier Hill made unannounced day and night visits to see how the Canadian paratroopers were performing. During a very rainy and windy night he caught a number of officers and NCOs set up in a barn. Hill was irate. He felt this was unacceptable and detrimental to the concept of airborne teamwork. "He gathered all the sergeants and officers together," stated Anderson, "and told them that in the future he wanted to see them outdoors with the men and not in the barns or other sheltered areas."[407] Hill explained that in order to instill efficient airborne leadership, "You must always lead from the front."[408]

The Brigadier noted that during his visits the paratroopers reacted positively to seeing him in their midst. As time passed Brigadier Hill made a lasting impact on all his Canadian paratroopers. "He was the most marvellous leader you could ever have," asserted Major Richard Hilborn.[409] Hill earned the paratroopers' trust and respect both in England while training and later during the various operational deployments. "In the line of attack," added Sergeant R.F. (Andy) Anderson, "you could always find the Brigadier at your elbow." He added, "I can hardly think of any general that the men could feel any affection for except Hill." Andy Anderson explained, "He was always in front ... he was totally without fear." To Anderson, the Brigadier represented "what I always imagined as a great leader."[410] Regardless of rank, Hill spoke to everyone. "He was visible all the time," explained Sergeant John Feduck. "He was the type of officer that if you wanted to see him, you could talk to him."[411]

Not surprisingly, every time the Brigadier dropped by, the paratroopers' level of activity and intensity invariably increased. This reaction would prove particularly important during the Normandy campaign. Overall, Hill was pleased with the Battalion's progress. "I feel I must write and congratulate you on the excellent show your battalion put up from the Albermarles on Exercise Co-operation," he wrote to Bradbrooke. "If they continue to make progress in this connection at this rate, they will soon be the best jumping exponents in our airborne corps and I should very much like to see them achieve this end for themselves. Well done."[412]

Despite his praise, he still emphasized improvement. Time was running out. As such, he prepared a detailed report addressing the exercise's principal mistakes. His message was clear and to the point. Learning from mistakes and paying attention to detail were of the utmost importance when operating behind enemy lines. "Time is getting short," he asserted, "the big day is approaching; we therefore have to direct all our energies and enthusiasm into correcting that which is wrong." Hill extolled, "I do not expect you to spare yourself in any way in achieving this aim."[413]

The months of March and April 1944 featured a series of platoon- and company-level exercises, continuation jumps from balloons and C-47 Dakota aircraft, range work, and forced marches.[414] The unit War Diary reflected the sense of urgency. In April the training tempo, it recorded, "was speeded up in preparation for the operation that everyone felt was not far away."[415] During that month Brigadier Hill completed a very detailed operational appreciation of the Brigade's invasion role and tasks to be conducted in the Normandy sector.[416] In the light of new information provided by 6 AB Div's intelligence section, Hill immediately ordered that street fighting, demolition, and swimming courses be added to the training schedule. For instance, sub-unit-level street fighting instruction was conducted in bombed-out areas in Southampton.[417] The aim was to teach paratroopers advanced combat skills and tactics required for fighting in built-up areas. Various demolition drills and techniques devised to neutralize and flush out enemy troops entrenched in an urban setting were also taught in preparation for the invasion.

Brigadier Hill's study also took into account that the German forces could possibly flood large areas of Normandy to counter possible Allied parachute and air-landing operations.[418] Therefore, he realized that it was imperative that paratroopers attend swimming classes and pass the necessary tests.[419] Additionally, he believed this training would also be useful in the event that an aircraft was disabled and crashed into the sea or large bodies of water.[420]

By spring 1944, the paratroopers' proficiency in their various individual and collective skills was increasing daily. These were put to the test one last time in Exercise Mush. This two-day, corps-level airborne exercise was conducted on April 29, 1944, under the watchful eye of Lieutenant-General F.A.M. "Boy" Browning, the commander of the 1st British Airborne Corps.[421] The aim was to rehearse the 6th Airborne Division in its invasion role. The 1st Airborne Division acted as the enemy force. "It helped me enormously," remarked Major-General Gale, "to clarify in my own mind on many points, and left us all confident that our plan would work."[422] The Battalion's leadership was satisfied with the professionalism and vigour of its soldiers. "The Battalion," affirmed a War Diary entry, "performed very credibly on this exercise."[423] Everyone felt comfortable with their levels of skill, and they were now ready, if not eager, to take on the Germans. The only concern now was the loss of personnel due to training injuries.[424] By mid-May, all 1st Canadian Parachute Battalion training was purposely toned down. Moreover, all continuation parachute jumps and training had been temporarily suspended in order not to expose paratroopers to unnecessary injuries.

By this stage the Battalion could not afford to lose personnel to injuries. Furthermore, since the Battalion's arrival in England, the question of obtaining parachute-qualified reinforcements to replace the injured or those who left the unit became a pressing concern for both the CMHQ and the 6 AB Div Headquarters. As a front-line parachute fighting unit, the 1st Canadian Parachute Battalion had finally reached its War Establishment strength in May 1944. All positions within the unit had to be filled in order to retain its operational ready status designation. To address the continued availability of parachute-qualified reinforcements, NDHQ, on December 9, 1943, authorized the raising and formation of No.1 Canadian Parachute Training Company (later redesignated the 1st Canadian Parachute Training Battalion).[425] The Company's role was to train all parachute-qualified volunteers arriving from A-35 CPTC, Camp Shilo, Manitoba, as well as personnel recruited from various Canadian units posted in the U.K., to 3 Para Bde standards. The men would continue training with the Training Company until they were called upon to replace injured Battalion personnel.[426]

With the impending deployment of the Battalion in sight, Headquarters officers projected that the unit's casualty rate would probably be very high. Therefore, to ensure that sufficient reinforcements were readily available, a recruitment program was devised to select additional personnel from Canadian Army units in England. Battalion officers noted that Canadian Army personnel recruited in the U.K. were a different breed of soldier from those who came from Canada. Most of the individuals were older, highly motivated, and had considerable military experience. But while some provided the Battalion with maturity, others brought with them some problems.[427] Major Donald Wilkins, a company commander in the Battalion, described the type of parachute volunteer that was recruited in the UK. He explained:

> It was my impression during this selection period that the inflow of officers and soldiers was divided into roughly half. The first half would be good officers or soldiers, people who would be a delight to interview and who we were more than pleased to accept for the parachute training. The other half of the recruits flow seemed to me to consist of soldiers who were "difficult" to discipline, for the lack of a better description ... their previous commanding officers seemed to feel that these men were "independent" types, they might conceivably make good parachutists. Most of them did, although perhaps the elements of discipline required to be more forcibly applied to the latter group.[428]

As these new reinforcements were being trained, the members of the 1st Canadian Parachute Battalion were starting to get impatient and wanted to take the fight to the enemy. "They were motivated," stated a proud Hill. "They became parachute soldiers ... half of these what I call highly strung fighting chaps, and half of them thought it was their duty to do so."[429] Nonetheless, the commander of 3 Para Bde was confident that the paratroopers of his three battalions would get the job done.

Nevertheless, the Brigadier did realize that each of his three battalions had distinct personalities. Even though they had all experienced the same training program, each one of the Brigade's units developed its own distinctive operational character. Hill knew his men well and used their strengths to the fullest during the course of the war. He felt that in the field, the men of 8th Parachute Battalion were rugged and relentless in achieving their objectives. They were very tough and not too concerned about detail. On the other hand, the men of 9th Parachute Battalion were masters at planning and organizing. They approached all tasks and resolved all situations through careful preparation, precision, and professionalism. The 1st Canadian Parachute Battalion, noted Hill, "displayed all the characteristics of a troop of cavalry ... a touch of *élan* and elegance in carrying out its assigned tasks; a sparkle and dash that her sister battalions lacked."[430]

Hill was rightfully proud of his Brigade. And he now had the opportunity to share his pride. The month of May 1944 provided a welcome distraction. The King and Queen, dignitaries, and senior British and Canadian officers inspected the 6th Airborne Division. All were impressed by the paratroopers' professionalism and the endurance displayed during the various demonstrations. Shortly after, General Sir Bernard Montgomery, Ground Forces Commander of the 21st Army Group, also made a trip to Bulford and inspected the Division. "As Colonel of the Parachute Regiment," explained Gale, "his [Montgomery's] interest in them is now very personal." Gale added, "To us all this inspection meant a great deal: for we were to be scrutinized by a practised and very relentless eye."[431] Montgomery left confident that the Division would perform well in Operation Overlord. As such, he congratulated Lieutenant-General F.A.M. "Boy" Browning, the commander of the 1st British Airborne Corps. Browning, in turn, sent a letter to Gale remarking how impressed the visitors had been and how proud he was of his parachute and airborne forces. "To confirm our conversation last night," he wrote, "I should like to congratulate you on the very fine appearance of your division ... It showed a standard which I have always hoped airborne forces would attain and maintain; whatever anyone else thought, I, at any rate, was fully satisfied."[432]

Throughout the month of May, Lieutenant-Colonel Bradbrooke and his company commanders attended numerous meetings at which the D-Day objectives were unveiled and explained.[433] By this time, 1 Cdn Para Bn Intelligence Section had already left Bulford and relocated in a secluded transit camp. There, they analyzed and studied intelligence reports and aerial photographs. They then went on to prepare models and dioramas of the terrain where the Battalion was to be dropped to execute its D-Day missions.[434]

The remainder of the Battalion left Bulford on May 24 and set up their quarters in a transit camp in the vicinity of Down Ampney. Once the last truck entered the camp, the gates were closed. Under no circumstances was anyone authorized to leave its confines. To emphasize the seriousness of this forced isolation, a British regimental sergeant-major (RSM) pointed to the single strand of barbed wire that surrounded the entire camp. "You are now in a place called a security transit camp," he bellowed. "Here you are going to learn the best-kept secrets in the world." The RSM warned, "Anyone who places a foot beyond that single strand of barb wire will be shot without being challenged." He counselled the troops, "Your best bet is not to go within a hundred feet of it."[435]

The move to the transit camp signalled the end of the Battalion's collective training. The relative safety of the training exercises was now left behind. From this point forward, errors and mistakes would lead to fatal consequences. Nonetheless, during the past ten months, the Battalion had trained hard. They had been moulded into Canada's first airborne combat unit. Now the Battalion underwent its final preparations to take up its role as the tip of the spear, ready to penetrate the outer crust of Hitler's Fortress Europa.

PART II

Into the Fire —
Canadian Paratroopers at War

CHAPTER SIX

Every Man an Emperor — The Airborne Battlefield

When the maroon beret is seen on the battlefield it at once inspires confidence, as it is well known that its wearers are good men and true and have the highest standards in all things.
                    Field-Marshal Bernard Montgomery[436]

By the spring of 1944, Canada's specially selected and superbly trained paratroopers were ready to be blooded. However, even though they had solid leadership and completed lengthy preparations for battle, they were still somewhat apprehensive. Lectures, training, and field exercises could go only so far. It was only in the furnace of battle that they would be fully tested. What made their initiation to battle so different from that of other combat soldiers was the unique nature of the airborne battlefield. Airborne detractors have always stated that parachuting is just another way to the battlefield. But they are wrong. The circumstances and environment that paratroopers find themselves in are very distinct from those of their brethren in the infantry or other combat arms. It is for this reason that airborne soldiers were specially selected for mental and physical stamina, as well as resiliency.[437]

The special nature of the airborne battlefield is derived directly from the mission and roles that were assigned to airborne forces.[438] Not surprisingly, the Allies, relative latecomers to this new type of warfare, demonstrated an evolution in doctrine. As late as 1941, official thought on the subject was somewhat rudimentary and simplistic. Airborne

operations were visualized in two forms: major operations that pertained to "the employment of airborne troops at one point for the capture of an objective of the first importance," and minor operations that
entailed the employment of small numbers of airborne troops "against
headquarters, dumps, convoys etc., and for sabotage."[439] The failure to
realize the strategic value of airborne forces was evident in the early
thinking. Their employment centred on small tactical objectives. This
was reinforced by doctrinal publications. Drawing lessons from the
employment of parachutists up to 1942, the *Canadian Army Training
Memorandum* listed the objectives of paratroops as: "the destruction of
bridges; cutting and tapping of telephone wires; incendiarism and the
destruction of public utility enterprises; firing on troops, supply
columns and refugees to create confusion and panic; indication of
bombing targets; spreading false news; seizing and holding certain main
objectives, e.g. an aerodrome; and sabotage generally."[440]

A maturation of thought quickly developed with experience. By
1943, strategic planners and doctrine writers began to see the potential
of airborne forces. Their use was now described as fulfilling three major
functions. The first was in close cooperation with large forces in conjunction with an attack of all arms operating by land, sea, or air, or a
combination of all three. In this capacity airborne forces were expected
to attack the enemy rear and thus assist with the breakthrough of the
main forces. In addition, they were also expected to delay enemy
reserves by holding defiles between them and the battlefield, or conversely to delay a retreating enemy until the main force arrived to ensure
the complete destruction of the withdrawing hostile force. In addition,
paratroops were also deemed capable of capturing enemy airfields to
assist with the air superiority battle, creating diversions and capturing
or destroying belligerent headquarters, which would lead to the para-
lyzation of the enemy's capability of providing a cohesive defence.

The second major function of airborne forces was working independently as units or formations. Strategists envisioned paratroopers
capturing islands or areas not strongly defended or capable of being
reinforced, as well as positions that could seriously embarrass the enemy
and prevent their reserves from being used elsewhere. In addition, the
seizure of vital installations, such as oil refineries, was also seen as viable
for independent action, as was seizing centres of government — the loss
of which would cause severe confusion. Planners also visualized the use
of paratroops to assist guerilla forces by providing a nucleus of trained
soldiers. Overall, within this function airborne forces were seen as ful-

filling the role of an economy of effort force by pinning belligerent resources down or creating a situation by which the enemy would be required to invest a large amount of equipment and manpower to ensure the security of his rear areas.

The third and final function was a harassing role, operating in small numbers and often at a distance from the area of major operations. Paratroops employed in this role were responsible for disrupting communications and destroying aircraft, transport, signal stations, railway trains, locks, bridges, and factories. In addition, they would also be tasked with the destruction of enemy fuel reserves, supplies, and equipment, as well causing panic among the civil population by the dissemination of false information.[441]

That was the theory. But as always, it is the front-line soldier who most accurately describes his actual mission. "The paratroops," asserted Lieutenant-Colonel G.F.P. Bradbrooke, commanding officer of the 1st Canadian Parachute Battalion, "are the tip of the spear." He explained, "They must expect to go in first, to penetrate behind enemy lines and to fight in isolated positions."[442] Major-General Richard Gale, commander of 1st British Airborne Corps, summed up the role of his formation to his officers in a similarly simple fashion. "In almost every case," he extolled, "Airborne Forces will lead the way and be the spearhead of the attack." He further elaborated, "The sort of tasks you may have to do are: capture a position in the rear of the enemy, cut his communications, and isolate him from his reinforcements; attack the enemy in the rear, while our main forces attack his front; capture airfields in enemy country; assist sea or river crossings by making a bridgehead; [and/or] raid special objectives."[443]

The aforementioned missions and tasks of airborne forces paint a formidable picture, namely one of shock troops that are first into battle and often alone to absorb the enemy's retaliatory strikes. More ominously, there are major limitations that detract from the ability of airborne forces to achieve success and that make their battleground that much more difficult. The first glaring weakness was the vulnerability of the aerial armada in flight. The lumbering transport planes and the aircraft towing gliders behind them were slow and inviting targets to both anti-aircraft fire and enemy fighters. As a result, control of the entire "air corridor" was crucial and demanded air supremacy or, at a minimum, local air superiority along the entire route.

But this was only the first requirement. The next challenge lay in the accuracy of the drop itself. Even if the laden aircraft reached their destination, the ability to drop their troops on target was another hurdle that was never easily surmounted. There were just too many factors against an accurate release. Inexperienced and poorly trained aircrews were often unable to maintain aircraft formation, or would release paratroopers at too high an altitude or at too great a speed. During the invasion of Sicily in July 1943, the Allied paratroopers were to be dropped from six hundred feet with the C-47 Dakota aircraft slowing down to almost stalling speed — one hundred miles per hour. But this is where theory and practice diverged. Instead, the troopers were flung out at fifteen hundred feet with the aircraft racing along at nearly their top speed of two hundred miles per hour. This, added to navigational problems and heavy winds, resulted in 3,405 American paratroopers being scattered over a width of 60 miles in southeast Sicily.[444] For the first few hours of the landing, Colonel James Gavin, a regimental commander in the U.S. 82nd Airborne Division, found himself in enemy territory with a force of only nineteen of his soldiers.[445] He later estimated that only 12 percent, or about 425 of the 3,405 men, actually landed somewhere in front of the beachhead as planned.[446] Similarly, of the 144 aircraft that left Africa carrying the 504th Parachute Infantry Regiment, 23 never returned, 37 had major damage, and half the planes required major repairs before they could fly again. Twenty-four hours after the drop, Colonel Reuben Tucker, the regimental commander, could account for only a quarter of the two thousand men who had left Africa.[447] In addition, during the same operation, only 27 of an intended force of 200 British paratroopers (or 14 percent) landed close enough to reach their objective and fight for the Ponte Grande.[448] Almost a year later in Normandy, of the 6,600 men of the American 101st Airborne Division who dropped in the early hours of D-Day, 3,500 were still missing by the end of the day.[449] Moreover, on August 15, 1944, five thousand Allied paratroopers of the 1st Airborne Task Force were dropped in the area of Le Muy, in southern France, as part of Operation Dragoon. Once again accuracy of insertion was lacking. Approximately 60 percent of the American and 40 percent of the British paratroopers landed too far from their drop zones to be considered by Army analysts as constituting a successful drop.[450]

Inexperienced or poorly trained aircrews were not the only challenge. Flak and enemy air activity often caused pilots to take evasive action that created enormous difficulties for airborne soldiers and resulted in missed drop zones. "As we approached the DZ the aircraft took violent evasive moves," recalled nineteen-year-old paratrooper Private Bill Lovatt. "As I approached the door I was flung back violently to the opposite side of the aircraft in a tangle of arms and legs."[451] Simple navigation errors compounded problems, as did high winds or poor weather. When any of these factors, or worse yet, any combination of factors, was present the likelihood of a successful parachute assault was severely taxed. On the evening of September 24, 1943, during the Russian Dnieper River offensive, Soviet pilots panicked when they reached the front lines and began to receive heavy anti-aircraft fire. As a result, the drops were widely dispersed and off target. Of the 4,575 paratroopers and 666 cargo containers dropped, a total of 2,017 men (or 44 percent) and 590 cargo containers (89 percent) failed to reach their intended DZ. German reports accounted for downing only three aircraft and one glider from a total of 296 sorties flown. This low kill rate strongly indicates that Soviet pilots overreacted and failed to push onto their objectives.[452] But it was not only Soviet pilots who reacted in such a manner. American Captain Richard Todd conceded that on D-Day "we lost a number of people over the sea from evasive action who fell out."[453] Canadian Sergeant John Feduck was slightly more fortunate. "Before the light changed the plane suddenly lurched," he remembered, "I couldn't hang on because there was nothing to hang on to so out I went — there was no getting back in."[454] Luckily, he was over the coast of France when the pilot's actions caused his early descent. Similarly, the disastrous drop of twelve hundred German paratroopers under the command of Baron von der Heydte in December 1944 also occurred because of inexperienced pilots and aircrew who were unable to maintain course or formation due to enemy fire. They released their Fallschirmjäger over such a large area that only a tiny fraction of the force was able to regroup. The resultant team was too small to effect its mission of cutting off American reinforcements who had been sent south from Belgium to relieve the pressure created by the surprise German offensive in the Ardennes.[455]

Despite the daunting challenges of flight, there were further impediments to the efficacy of airborne soldiers once they were on the ground. Initially, paratroops are extremely vulnerable on landing. Individual soldiers, weapon systems, radios, and other mission-essential equipment must all be brought together at a rendezvous point so that the proper concentration of force and command and control can be exercised. This takes time — how much time depends on the success, specifically the accuracy, of the drop itself.[456] The greater the dispersion, the greater the time to regroup and assemble combat power. Obviously, there is a direct correlation between time needed to assemble and the degree of surprise and shock action achieved. "The hardest part of the job wasn't the fighting, although that was hard enough at times," conceded Lieutenant-Colonel Bradbrooke, "but getting ourselves organized after we hit the DZ."[457] The location of the drop in relation to the enemy's position also had a dramatic effect. A British Royal Artillery officer serving at Heraklion in Crete in May 1941 observed:

> Those [Fallschirmjäger] dropped on the central sector fell right on top of my gun position, with the result that my small party of 25 men had to deal with vastly superior numbers of parachutists. However, they did more than deal with them; they almost completely destroyed them. If an immediate attack can be made on parachute troops the second they leave the plane and touch the ground, they are almost powerless to resist.[458]

Up until the end of the war, Army planners accepted that one-third of the force that set out would fail to intervene effectively in operations.[459]

The vulnerability of airborne soldiers on landing was further exacerbated by their lack of mobility. Once on the ground, paratroopers were limited to how far and how fast they could move with what they had. This limited the objectives and missions that could be assigned, and failure to recognize this had dire consequences. The failure to quickly capture the bridge at Arnhem in September 1944 was in part due to the fact that drops were made too far from the actual objective. This criticism was substantiated by the German defenders, who acknowledged that they had time to mobilize their defences and respond to the threat.[460]

Yet another major limitation faced by paratroopers was their lack of firepower. Since they normally dropped behind enemy lines, they were often beyond the range of friendly fire support assets such as artillery or naval gunfire. Therefore, all they could depend on was that what they themselves could successfully bring. As a result, sheer logistics negated many heavy weapons. Losses and damages due to bad drops increased the problem. "With the planes not slowing up below 125 or 135 miles an hour," complained one veteran of the Tagaytay Ridge mission in the Phillippines in February 1945, "most of us experienced the hardest physical opening shock in our lives. The result of the shock was that most of us lost helmets, packs broke free from web belts, suspenders broke, and in the wind, which was 20 to 30 miles an hour ... many had hard landings."[461] But, bruises and scrapes aside, it was the loss of equipment that was most sorely felt. Not surprisingly, Canadian paratroopers lamented "the difficult weeks that followed D Day [June 6, 1944], when attacks by enemy infantry and sometimes tanks and self-propelled guns had to be met with an inferior weight of fire power."[462] A little more than three months later at Arnhem, the U.S. 82nd Airborne Division was unable to communicate with their headquarters fifteen miles away because both of their large radio sets were damaged in the drop.[463]

Finally, the last major limitation to airborne operations was that of sustainment and maintaining combat power. All airborne operations depended on an eventual link-up with ground forces, and it was generally recognized that this should occur within forty-eight to seventy-two hours.[464] Normally, air drops were used if link-up between airborne and ground forces could not be achieved. However, resupply drops suffered from the same limitations already noted, and an inherent requirement for accuracy. Nonetheless, airborne elements have been able to hold out for great lengths of time even when surrounded by superior forces. Large Soviet airborne formations operated behind German lines for periods of four to six months during the winter of 1940–41 as part of the battle of Moscow. Furthermore, the Allies held out for a period of eight days in Holland during Operation Market Garden in September 1944 — four times longer than expected. Both cases involved vicious close-quarter combat, including battle against armoured units. Equally, at the end of both engagements, the respective parachute units were severely mauled and virtually ceased to exist.[465]

The myriad of limitations, however, is offset by the array of capabilities inherent in airborne forces. These strengths eclipse the weaknesses and make the use of paratroopers inescapable. They also provide the airborne soldiers with an edge in their fight for survival in their distinctive battlefield. The greatest advantage paratroops have is their strategic mobility. Army planners described them as "highly mobile shock troops which can be projected at short notice into an enemy area which might otherwise consider itself immune from attack." Quite simply, a large number of paratroopers and equipment can be deployed quickly over large distances and over difficult terrain and obstacles. Moreover, they are the only ones who are capable of, on short notice, engaging in combat operations without the prerequisite of secure airfields, ports, beaches, or other points of entry.

Strategically employed, they can seize ground and fortifications critical to manoeuvre, which were hitherto thought impregnable. On May 10, 1940, a mere fifty-five German parachute engineers rendered the key Belgian fortress of Eban Emael, which guarded the strategic Albert Canal with a twelve-hundred-man garrison, ineffective.[466] Additionally, a group of 129 Fallschirmjäger landed near Vroenhoven to capture that key bridge. Within minutes the Belgian garrison was overwhelmed and the bridge disarmed of explosives. In a matter of thirty minutes the bridge was open to German panzers.[467] Approximately a year later, Fallschirmjäger seized the Corinth Canal in Greece, thus capturing approximately 10,000 Allied soldiers at a cost of 63 killed and 174 wounded.[468]

The strategic mobility inherent in airborne operations in turn creates yet another set of capabilities that create tangible combat multipliers, namely surprise and psychological dislocation. Surprise creates confusion, fear, and panic in both the military and the public at large. Moreover, the mere threat of attack by airborne forces necessitates costly countermeasures. More importantly still, it nurtures fear in the minds of the besieged — a comprehension that even rear areas are no longer safe. Examples abound. The German landings in Holland in 1940 caused a wave of panic throughout Europe, as well as in England. "One thing is certain," wrote Captain F.O. Miksche, "there was a parachute obsession everywhere. Everybody saw them being dropped. Everybody was suspect, and even Allied officers and men, sometimes bearing important orders, were arrested by the French military authorities."[469] In Britain, troop dispositions were tailored to counter a perceived airborne invasion, and vast amounts of scarce material were invested to this end. The government adopted a policy in 1940 to safeguard the country by ordering all open spaces (meaning virtually every park and playing field) throughout Britain to be seeded with long spiked poles, concrete blocks, and other obstacles that would impede paratroopers.[470]

The threat of an airborne invasion later reversed itself, and the Axis forces felt the resultant insecurity. The attack on the Tragino aqueduct in Italy on February 10, 1942, by a small group of parachutists caused minimal physical damage or dislocation. Nonetheless, it had far-reaching implications. The Italians had been so unnerved by this operation that they diverted valuable manpower and resources in its aftermath for the protection of every vital point in the country.[471] The Bruneval Raid on the coast of France a little more than two weeks later, also conducted by British paratroopers, was more significant. This raiding force secured elements of the German Wurzburg Radar that proved significant for British radar development and electronic countermeasures.[472] But on a larger tactical level, the threat and actual execution of large-scale airborne assaults created great problems for the German high command. During the invasion of Sicily in 1943, the German 6th Army Headquarters received panicky reports that paratroopers were dropping all over the southern part of the island. This paralyzed their ability to respond in a coherent and decisive manner. The scale of confusion was evident by the Radio Rome broadcast that reported that 60,000 to 120,000 paratroopers had jumped into Sicily, instead of the approximate 7,300 Allied parachutists and glidermen that assaulted over a two-day period.[473] And finally, less than a year later, in the spring of 1944, Field Marshal Erwin Rommel specifically adapted his plan for the defence of the Normandy coast to allow for defence against airborne soldiers. As a result, valuable troops were siphoned away from front-line duty and positioned in the Contentin Peninsula, primarily to provide protection against airborne assault.[474]

Remarkably, the ability of airborne operations to inflict surprise and psychological disruption was so great that even small-scale drops or drops by a nearly vanquished enemy still caused consternation and panic. In December of 1944, the ill-executed German parachute operation during the Ardennes offensive set off a parachutist scare that was felt all the way to Paris. Supreme Allied Commander General Eisenhower became a virtual prisoner in his own headquarters.[475] It is the fear engendered by the sudden appearance of enemy troops in one's rear area and the inability to fully define their objectives that creates a decisive advantage for the invading force. Often, as already shown, inaccurate reports delivered by alarmed commanders, particularly when describing widely dispersed drops, create an impression of massive, wide-scale airborne operations threatening large areas of territory. This in turn paralyzes enemy response because of an attempt by the enemy leadership to determine where the major threat lies before committing forces. In September 1944, during Operation Market Garden, Colonel-General Kurt Student acknowledged, "I could not tell what was happening or where these airborne units were going."[476]

In sum, despite severe limitations, it is the promise of overwhelming success due to the enormous capabilities of the third dimension of war that make paratroopers such a valuable asset to any fighting force. However, their use, although promising high-value payoff, is also high risk. And so within this context, the individual airborne soldier must go to battle. His challenges are great. For him, parachuting is more than just another means of getting to the battlefield. His struggle starts long before he closes with the enemy. Paratroopers normally arrived tired and exhausted. They endured the process of dressing and waiting fully kitted for long periods of time. It was not uncommon for individuals to be weighted down with one hundred pounds of equipment, not including their parachute assembly. American aircrewman Martin Wolfe recalled pushing paratroopers with up to 125 pounds of gear into his aircraft. "With our gear," asserted Colonel Ivan Hershner, "the average man weighed about 300 pounds that night [June 6, 1944]."[477] The exhausting weight was not the only hurdle to overcome. Its effect on the actual jump was enormous. "I got a good opening, tore a few sections in my chute, which was not unusual when you were loaded up with equipment," recalled Edward J. Cole of his drop onto Tagaytay Ridge in February 1945. "[I] reached up to grab my risers and hit the ground," he explained. "I didn't have a chance to release my jump rope ... we had jumped at about 450 feet with full equipment."[478] With the enormous weight and low jump altitude, the descent was rather quick. This was common.

However, once dressed, the salvation of shedding the uncomfortable parachute harness and heavy equipment on the drop zone was but a glimmer in the distant future. First, the ordeal of flight to the destination had to be overcome. Bucking, lurching aircraft that were tossed about in the wash of previous airplanes, as well as the attempts to avoid flak, created additional stress for the paratrooper. Research has shown that airsickness due to turbulent flying conditions in itself creates fatigue. Compounded by anxiety and tension, as well as the heavy loads carried by each airborne soldier, the state of enervation on landing was substantial.[479]

But the exhaustion, as well as the numerous abrasions and bruises, if not more serious injuries such as sprains or fractures, had to be quickly put aside. The battle on the ground now began, and ordinarily, the paratrooper was the first to fight. His mission behind enemy lines placed him in direct contact with the enemy before he was often fully prepared. The airborne insertion of the Poles at Arnhem in September 1944 resulted in them being dropped directly into a raging battle. As a result, they were fired on by both sides.[480] General Matthew Ridgway recounted the "very special dangers that are a combat paratrooper's particular lot — the quick leap out of the plane into the buffeting prop wash, the slow float down, hanging helpless in the harness, the drop into the darkness where armed enemies wait behind every bush and tree."[481] To exacerbate the airborne soldiers' plight, once the drone of the aircraft engines disappeared the paratroopers were normally on their own. They had no rear, no sanctuary to return to, and no pipeline connected to ships or friendly lines. "A parachutist fights a lonely battle," insisted British Lieutenant-General Sir Michael Gray. "He has no real front or rear," he explained. "He often feels he is fighting the battle on his own." Brigadier James Hill, commander of the British 3rd Parachute Brigade during the Normandy invasion, understood the potential confusion that his paratroopers would face. "Gentlemen, in spite of your excellent training and orders," he proclaimed, "do not be daunted if chaos reigns. It undoubtably will." His words were prophetic. Drops were widely dispersed and scattered and units were faced with the task of completing their missions under strength and lacking important equipment.

Within this demanding and unforgiving airborne battlefield it is not surprising that airborne soldiers suffered a higher ratio of casualties than other combat troops. "Jumping out of airplanes was romantic as hell," critiqued one detractor, "but also dangerous and wasteful of lives; what it did was put a very high premium on bravery of a certain kind."[482] The requirement for courage was no understatement. Casualty statistics tell a tale all their own. Of 2,000 German airborne troops (22nd Infantry Division — airlanding) assigned to the capture of the Hague in the Netherlands on May 10, 1940, 40 percent of the officers and 28 percent of the men were killed.[483] Similarly, that same day, the Fallschirmjäger that attacked the Belgian fortress of Eban Emael suffered 30 percent casualties.[484] Almost a year later, German paratroopers suffered 58 percent casualties during their invasion of Crete, a full 25 percent of the participants being killed.[485] "We paid dearly for our victory," Adolf Strauch concluded. "Every third man killed, every second man wounded. Our victory was no victory."[486]

And the bloody trend continued. The British parachute commando action at Tragino, Italy, cost them the loss of 100 percent of the raiding force.[487] The Soviet paratroopers suffered 71 percent casualties during their desperate battles around Vyazma and Moscow during the winter of January to March 1942. The German Waffen SS Paratroop Battalion suffered 62 percent casualties in its raid on Tito's headquarters in Yugoslavia in May 1944,[488] and approximately 80 percent of the British 1st Airborne Division was lost during Operation Market Garden in September of that same year.[489] Finally, the American 82nd Airborne Division incurred 27 percent casualties in Sicily and 46 percent in Normandy.[490] In November 1944, Major-General M.B. Ridgway, then Commander XVIII Corps (Airborne), conceded in a letter to General George C. Marshall, Chief of

Staff of the United States Army, "At the moment of entry into action, an airborne division has already suffered losses far in excess of those of an infantry division at a similar time, through misplaced drops and crash injuries, both of which are in addition to normal battle casualties."[491] In the overall American experience of the Second World War, over 30 percent of all airborne personnel became casualties. This compares to only 10 percent among regular infantry formations.[492]

It is easy to understand why the airborne battlefield exacts a higher price. It is a unique battleground, one where the situation is never clear, where a paratrooper has no distinct starting position and often finds himself, at least initially, totally alone, deep in enemy territory. It is an environment where one is never fully sure who or how many will actually arrive at the objective in time to assist in the battle. To survive in these ambiguous, hostile surroundings requires a special character — an exceptional type of combat soldier. Neither rank nor position hold privilege, as all must share the hardships and dangers of flight and a parachute descent onto an unknown DZ. During the assault on Sicily, many gliders crashed into the Mediterranean Sea. One survivor, clinging to the wreckage of his stricken aircraft, was British Major-General Hoppy Hopkinson, commander of the 1st Airborne Division.[493] During the invasion of Normandy, the First Battalion, 501st Parachute Infantry Regiment, was not only badly scattered but it also had its commanding officer killed, the battalion second in command captured, and all four company commanders missing.[494] "The scattering had an operating influence on the whole battle," disclosed paratroop veteran Corporal Dan Hartigan. "We lost over 50 percent of our officers on D-Day," he revealed, "15 of 27 I believe."[495] The potential loss of leadership necessitated all airborne soldiers to be prepared to carry on the mission themselves. "When its [the airborne division] people hit the ground," declared General Matthew Ridgway, a wartime commander of the 82nd Airborne Division, "they are individuals, and a two-star general and a Pfc. [private] are on exactly the same basis." He further explained, "You have no communications whatsoever for some little time, particularly when you have jumped at night. You don't know where you are. You don't know who's around you, friend or foe."[496]

Without question the airborne battlefield was an arena that required an aggressive individual with courage, initiative, and tenacity, as well as mental alertness and exemplary combat skills. Paratroopers had to be capable of adapting to unforseen situations, and above all else they had to be self-reliant. It is for this reason that special selection processes and tough, rigorous training were implemented. In the end, the formidable entrance requirements and the grueling training, designed to weed out all but the fittest and most aggressive, combined with their unrivalled battlefield performance, created a distinct airborne mentality and philosophy — no mission too daunting, no challenge too great.

The public image of the paratrooper also added to the mystique. The complex and dangerous nature of the operations required what was described as an "elite" type of soldier. Most people, both civilian and military, believed that airborne soldiers had nerves of steel and that they were in superb physical condition so that they could withstand the shock of the jump and the hard landings.[497] "In the first place, they [parachutists] are perfect specimens," wrote Larry Gough from the American *Liberty* magazine. "They have to be," he explained, "because their work is rough tough and full of excellent opportunities to get hurt. Mentally they're quick on the trigger, again because their job demands it, because split seconds can make the difference between instant death or a successfully completed job."[498] A Canadian account was equally dramatic. "Picture men with muscles of iron dropping in parachutes, hanging precariously from slender ropes, braced for any kind of action, bullets whistling about them from below and above," described one journalist. He elaborated further:

> They congregate or scatter. Some are shot. But the others go on with the job. Perhaps they're to dynamite an objective. Perhaps they're to infiltrate through enemy lines and bring about the disorder necessary to break up the foe's defence, where-upon their comrades out in front can break through. Or perhaps they're to do reconnoitering and get back the best way they can. But whatever they're sent out to do, they'll do it, these toughest men who ever wore khaki.[499]

Quite frankly, the public, as well as military commanders, believed that airborne soldiers were the cutting edge of operations — tough, intelligent, and self-reliant shock troops dropping from the sky to paralyze and demoralize the enemy. "It builds our morale, it stiffens the spine and braces the backbone of the public," insisted American Lieutenant-General E.M. Flanagan, "to hear talk about the independent type airborne operation." He elaborated that this was born from the image of an airborne army storming in "to deal a lethal blow to the enemy, deep in his backyard."[500] Brigadier James Hill simply described parachute troops as the best fighting material in the world. He felt that "the parachutists have shown themselves magnificent infantry, pre-eminent in physique and steadiness of nerve, born guerilla fighters, mobile and tireless, tremendous marchers, and of an undefeated spirit."[501] It for this reason that Colonel James Gavin, wartime commander of the 82nd Airborne Division, later wrote, "The term American parachutist has become synonymous with courage of the highest order."[502] Even General Marshall declared, "The courage and dash of airborne troops has become a by-word and is a great inspiration to all others."[503]

But these accolades were well earned. Paratroopers proved themselves aggressive, resilient, and tenacious fighters capable of overcoming adversity. "When tracer bullets began ripping through his canopy, Private Edwin C. Raub became so enraged that he deliberately side slipped his chute so as to land next to the anti-aircraft gun. Without removing his harness, and dragging his parachute behind him, Raub rushed the Germans with his Tommy gun. He killed one, captured the others and then, with plastic explosives destroyed the flak-gun barrels."[504] In another example of tenacity over adversity, Sergeant Bullock, from the British 9th Parachute Battalion, and a handful of others were dropped almost thirty miles inland. They reported to their units four days later with evidence to show that they had killed numerous enemy, including twenty senior German generals of brigadier rank or higher. Another paratrooper swam twenty miles down the Orne River to reach Pegasus Bridge. Yet another example of the airborne spirit that has since entered into legend is the infamous incident of British Captain Eric Mackay relaying his CO's refusal at Arnhem to surrender despite the fact they were cut off, completely surrounded, and had suffered horrendous casualties. "Get the hell out of here," he yelled at the German Waffen SS soldier who had come forward to offer terms. "We're not taking any prisoners."[505]

In the final summation, the prowess of airborne forces lay in their ability to transcend the brutality and unforgiving nature of the airborne battlefield. "The mainspring of these forces," insisted the renowned American soldier and military historian S.L.A. Marshall, "lay in the spirit of the men. They moved and hit like light infantry and what they achieved in surprise more than compensated for what they lacked in fire power."[506] An observer from the American Army War College reported, "My observation of the individual parachute soldier in combat is that he is completely self-reliant and able to operate on his own. He is a killer and imbued with a desire to close with the enemy and destroy him."[507] Major-General Richard Gale, commander of the British 6th Airborne Division, concurred. "In the end," he extolled, "it all boils down to the individual and it is he that counts. Be alert, be vigilant and be resourceful. What you get by stealth and by guts you must hold with skill and determination."[508] It was their ability to overcome their daunting environment that set them apart. "Their duty lies in the van of the battle; they are proud of this honour and have never failed in any task," wrote Field Marshal Bernard Law Montgomery. "They have the highest standards in all things ... [and] they have shown themselves to be as tenacious and determined in defence as they are courageous in attack." They are, he concluded, "men apart — every man an Emperor."[509]

And so, in June 1944, almost two years after their creation, Canada's intrepid airborne soldiers were poised to enter their first battle. During that period the nation's paratroopers conducted challenging and demanding training. They participated in numerous jumps and exercises. They were as ready for the unforgiving airborne battlefield as they could be — or so they believed. Their mettle would soon be tested. It was time to crack open Hitler's *Festung Europa*.

CHAPTER SEVEN

Baptism of Fire —
The Normandy Campaign

Gentlemen, in spite of your excellent training and your detailed briefing do not be daunted if chaos reigns for it certainly will!
Brigadier S.J.L. Hill, Commander
3rd Parachute Brigade, June 5, 1944.[510]

By the spring of 1944, Germany's offensive operations had been successfully halted on all fronts. German ground troops were now desperately trying to contain massive Russian and Allied attacks on both the eastern and Italian fronts. In the Atlantic, the once dreaded U-Boats were now being systematically hunted down and sunk. More importantly, the once mighty Luftwaffe no longer controlled the skies.[511] Day after day, Allied bombers targeted military-industrial areas and railway systems within the Reich. This intensive bombing strategy severely crippled Germany's war effort. The well co-ordinated war of attrition paved the way to the opening of the much anticipated "second front." By the beginning of June 1944, more than 2 million Allied airmen, sailors, and soldiers were ready to return to the European continent as part of Operation Overlord — the invasion of Normandy.[512]

Allied planners determined that their best landing option lay in assaulting the Normandy coast. Although at a greater distance from England than Calais, and lacking port facilities for unloading the substantial stores they would require, the planners nevertheless felt that the element of surprise would enable them to quickly secure and maintain a large bridgehead. General Dwight D. "Ike" Eisenhower, Supreme Commander of the Allied Expeditionary Forces, assigned this monumental task to Field Marshal Bernard Montgomery and his 21st Army Group. Monty's Army Group consisted of two armies: the U.S. 1st Army, commanded by Lieutenant-General Omar N. Bradley, and the British 2nd Army, commanded by Lieutenant-General Sir Miles Dempsey.[513]

Years of painstaking planning had been completed to prepare for arguably the greatest military operation in history. A total of 171 fighter squadrons were tasked to provide the necessary air cover for a formidable armada, which numbered more than 5,000 ships and 4,000 landing craft.[514] Crammed aboard these vessels were 176,475 men and 20,111 vehicles. The sheer mass of the invasion fleet necessitated that all vessels closely adhere to the established timetable. It was critical that ships and craft be in their assigned landing positions in order to take full advantage of the first three tides during the designated invasion period. These tides would enable the vessels to navigate closer to the shoreline and offload troops and vehicles quickly. Once ashore, the Allied soldiers would then storm the five separate and distinct designated beaches that represented more than fifty miles of the Normandy coastline between Dune de Varreville and Ouistreham.[515]

The invading armies were to push inland as rapidly as possible to enable the subsequent unloading and deployment of reinforcements and much-needed stores. As part of the invasion's Eastern Task Force, Dempsey's British 2nd Army was given the responsibility of assaulting three beaches: Gold, Juno, and Sword, located between the coastal towns of Manvieux and Ouistreham. The troops were to move inland and establish a bridgehead south of St.-Lô-Caen and southeast of Caen. Dempsey was ordered to seize and hold designated airfields and to protect the 1st U.S. Army's eastern flank while the Americans were fighting their way to Cherbourg.[516]

In support of Montgomery's plan, one British and two American airborne divisions were tasked to assist the ground forces. The western flank of the invasion force was to be guarded by the U.S. 82nd and 101st Airborne Divisions. The American paratroopers were to hold and defend this flank until the elements of the U.S. 7th Corps landed on Utah Beach and deployed inland. Concurrently, the British 6th Airborne Division was to be dropped on the eastern flank, which was designated the Orne sector. The 6 AB Div was tasked to secure, establish, and hold a bridgehead on the high ground between the Caen Canal and the Orne and Dives Rivers. The defence of this important terrain would enable units of the British 1st Corps, commanded by Lieutenant-General John Crocker, to land and move out quickly from Sword Beach, seize Caen, and consolidate a bridgehead south of the Orne.[517]

As the invasion day approached, the 1st Canadian Parachute Battalion's collective training increasingly focused on larger and larger formation exercises. The emphasis of these manoeuvres was placed on dropping and air-landing the maximum number of troops in the shortest period of time in the smallest possible area. Concurrently, the 6 AB Div, the 3 Para Bde, and the 1 Can Para Bn intelligence staffs were building a detailed picture of the Normandy invasion area. More than ever, Hill insisted that all his paratroopers be thoroughly put in the picture. Meticulous dioramas and models were constructed based on a myriad of air photographs and intelligence reports. Clearly, the paratroopers were to be given every possible advantage.

On the evening of May 31, 1944, Lieutenant-Colonel Bradbrooke unveiled, for the first time to the entire Battalion, a huge map of Normandy's Orne sector. He then proceeded to give the introductory overview of the 6 AB Div's invasion mission. The Division, with the 1st Special Service Brigade (1 SS Bde) under its command, was assigned to protect the left flank of British 1st Corps. Paratroopers and glider infantry would seize and defend the area between the rivers Orne and Dives, north of the Troarn road, Sannerville, and Colombelles. Furthermore, the Division was to engage and delay enemy reserves and reinforcements that attempted to move toward Caen from the east and southeast.[518] "You're going to be surprised and happy when you learn all the things you are going to do on this operation," concluded an upbeat Bradbrooke. "Believe me, there will be a part for every individual soldier here."[519]

The detailed briefings began next morning. To begin this process, the Battalion's intelligence officer gave an overview of the 8th and 9th Parachute Battalion tasks. Under the command of Lieutenant-Colonel A.S. Pearson, 8 Para Bn was to destroy bridges at Troarn and Bures, defend the roadways in these sectors, and mount patrols with the object of deceiving and confusing the enemy.[520] 9 Para Bn, commanded by Lieutenant-Colonel T.B.H. Otway, was tasked to destroy the Merville Battery, destroy an enemy headquarters at Sallanelles, deny the enemy the use of the roads in their area, and finally seize and hold a high ground feature at Le Plein until relieved by the 1 SS Bde.[521]

The 1st Canadian Parachute Battalion was tasked to secure and protect 3 Para Bde's Drop Zone "V," as well as neutralize an enemy headquarters, a communications centre, and defensive positions located in the DZ's immediate vicinity. Furthermore, it was to support the airborne Royal Engineers in the demolition of bridges at Varaville and Robehomme. Moreover, they were to deny the enemy the use of all roads in the Battalion's sector. Upon completion of all these tasks, the companies were to regroup and defend the area in the Le Mesnil, Varaville, Bois de Bavent, and Bréville area.[522]

During the first hours of the invasion each company within 1 Cdn Para Bn was to operate independently from one another. Furthermore, "C" Company would be detached from the Battalion and flown in as part the 3 Para Bde's advance party so as to be inserted ahead of the Brigade to secure Drop Zone "V," located between the Merville Battery and the Varaville Bridge.[523] Once secured, the Brigade's pathfinders were to set up signal beacons to guide the aircraft of the main group to the DZ. Subsequent "C" Company tasks included the destruction of communication headquarters and defensive positions in Varaville. Furthermore, the Company was to provide support for the airborne engineers who were assigned the mission of destroying the bridge at Varaville. Following the demolition of this structure, the paratroopers were tasked to defend the road going through that town. When relieved by elements of the 1 SS Bde, the Company was directed to fall back and regroup at the Le Mesnil crossroads.[524]

"A" Company was designated to jump with the main group. Its mission consisted of protecting 9 Para Bn's move from the drop zone, its subsequent assault on the Merville Battery, and its withdrawal from the area after the objective was destroyed. Additionally, the Company was to lay waste to the enemy in the nearby Gonneville sur Merville area. Upon completion of these tasks, the Company was to link up with 3 Para Bde HQ and regroup at the Le Mesnil crossroads.[525]

"B" Company also jumped with the main group and was ordered to destroy bridges at Robehomme and occupy road and track junctions in the vicinity. Upon the destruction of the bridges, the Company was to withdraw and occupy the high ground in the Robehomme area and protect the return of the airborne engineers to their post-mission rendezvous.[526] Upon completion of all tasks the Company was directed to fall back to Le Mesnil.

Once the Battalion assembled at Le Mesnil, all Mortar, Machine Gun, and Anti-tank Platoon personnel who had been attached to the companies for their initial tasks were directed to report to Battalion Headquarters. The machine gun and anti-tank platoons would then be dispersed throughout the rifle companies to provide additional fire support. The mortar platoon was directed to set up behind the Battalion Headquarters to provide defensive fire anywhere along the unit's perimeter.[527]

Brigadier Hill visited his battalions regularly and made it a point to attend as many briefings as possible. He rated 1 Cdn Para Bn's briefings as "the best in the Division."[528] Although time was getting short, the paratroopers still conducted company-level rehearsals to practise the more complex parts of the missions. There was no room for error. Failure was simply not an option. "There was no question in anyone's mind that the objective not being taken was unthinkable," affirmed Corporal Dan Hartigan. "That just wasn't an option."[529]

While the Canadian paratroopers were finalizing their preparations for the invasion, the German units under the direction of Field Marshal Erwin Rommel, commander of Army Group "B" in Normandy, were busily improving their defensive positions and finalizing details of their own.[530] The German units that were responsible for the defence of the Normandy sector into which the 6 AB Div was preparing to assault were the 21st Panzer Division, the 711th and 716th Infantry Divisions, and elements of the 346th Infantry Division.[531] These formations, however, were not considered front-line combat troops, and many of their units were not at full strength.[532] They were raised primarily as anti-invasion forces and were identified on the German Order of Battle as Static and Reserve Divisions.

The personnel within the formation consisted mainly of older men.[533] Furthermore, to rapidly augment their depleted strength, additional men were drafted from the occupied territories such as Poland and Russia.[534] Having soldiers forced to serve against their will in the German Army further diluted the effectiveness, cohesiveness, and morale of the different units. Furthermore, the infantry divisions were equipped with very little transport, particularly fighting vehicles. They relied mainly on horse-drawn transport. While a high percentage of newly manufactured German weapons and vehicles were sent to the Russian front, the divisions in France were equipped with an assortment of captured armoured and wheeled vehicles, artillery, and heavy weapons.

The only armoured division training in the 6 AB Div designated area was the 21st Panzer Division. Following the division's repatriation from North Africa, it was re-formed in Rennes in July 1943. Joining the survivors were undesirable personnel who had been transferred from a variety of German Seventh Army units posted throughout Normandy and Brittany. This division was mainly equipped with captured French Hotchkiss and Somua tanks and armoured vehicles.[535] However, with the looming threat of invasion, the Division was allocated 127 Mark IV tanks and 40 assault guns in late May 1944.[536] This welcome influx of armour, however, would prove insufficient against the seemingly bottomless supply of Allied tanks chaperoned by an endless number of infantry and rocket-equipped fighter aircraft.[537]

As the German units worked feverishly on expanding their motor pools and their artillery and armoured elements, they also participated during the course of spring 1944 in an increasing number of manoeuvres and anti-airborne exercises. In February 1944, Rommel issued a number of directives on anti-airborne operations and the construction of obstacles to thwart the landing of paratroopers and gliders. Lieutenant-General Joseph Reichert, commander of the 711th Infantry Division, worked diligently to defend his area (Troarn, Varaville, Honfleur, and Dozulé) against paratroopers and air-landing units.[538] He deployed his troops regularly and formed special groups to monitor the skies. To further complicate Allied operations in his sector, all areas that could be used as potential dropping and landing sites were mined or flooded. Reichert explained:

> Against possible air landings, a constant observation service extending over the entire sector of this division is being organized. A second position, ten to twenty kilometres off the coast, was established in the form of strong points in a field type way. Minefields and dummy minefields were being laid in depth, and mine obstacles being prepared on the roads. The Dives and Divette were dammed up and the whole Dives valley was flooded as far as into the hinterland. [539]

The German commanders in France were still unsure as to the exact location of the Allied coastal landing. Rommel and his immediate superior, Field Marshal Gerd von Rundstedt, Commander-in-Chief (West), constantly argued about the disposition of their armoured units. Rundstedt insisted that these divisions be positioned as far as possible from the beachheads. Therefore, when the exact location of the landing was confirmed, a strong sustained counterattack could be organized and launched to crush the invading force. Conversely, Rommel wanted to deploy these armoured divisions as close as possible to the coastline. Hence, within the first hour of the invasion, they could be immediately organized into small battle groups and attack the leading enemy elements before they could establish a foothold.[540] Eventually, Hitler dictated a compromise. Three armoured divisions were deployed in the coastal area while the two SS armoured divisions and the Panzer Lehr Division were positioned between fifty and one hundred miles from the coast.[541] While the defenders were preparing for the worst, the tense Canadian paratroopers used their last hours to verify their equipment and parachutes one last time.

As the anticipated jump approached and the magnitude of the upcoming operation started to sink in, the paratroopers nervously reflected on the possibility of being separated from their comrades. Being stranded alone behind enemy lines was not a pleasant prospect. Despite having to jump with an already very heavy load, which consisted of their personal kit, a weapon, ammunition, and certain components of their section's or platoon's equipment or weapons, many nevertheless asked for extra ammunition. However, all available storage space had already been stuffed with all sorts of supplies. Many sewed extra pockets on their Denison Smocks to circumvent this new problem. These were quickly jammed with extra rounds and grenades. For now the paratroopers did not mind this extra weight. Actually, in many ways it proved to be a source of comfort.[542]

Preoccupied with their preparations, the airborne soldiers had not noticed that Brigadier Hill had decided to spend his last days in their bivouac area. As the Brigadier walked through their camp he was impressed by the stamina displayed by his young Canadians. He recalled:

> All day long the Canadians, with whom I'd pitched my tent, were playing games, throwing a ball about, and I thought what tremendous vitality these Canadians have got. Then in the afternoon I would visit my English battalions and find half a dozen chaps desultorily kicking a football, and the rest asleep. I though to myself, here is the difference between the Old World and the New; the

élan and joie de vivre of the New World of Canadians, and the maturity and the not worrying, not bothering and having a good nap while we can, of the British.[543]

The last preparatory activities were the all-important parachute fittings carried out on June 3. Due to the additional equipment carried by each paratrooper, special attention was required to readjust and check the rigging of equipment and the parachute assembly. The next day the paratroopers were visited by the RAF crews responsible for their flight across the Channel. "Their calm," recorded the War Diary, "greatly reassured the men."[544] That afternoon Major-General Gale visited the troops and gave them a pep talk. "Chaps," extolled Gale with good humour, "as you can see there are a lot of medals on my chest. There are still a few missing and I expect you lads to help fill in the empty spaces." He continued, "Our job is so difficult that no one but a bloody fool would attempt this task, but I, Richard Gale, am fool enough to attempt this job and with your help we will succeed."[545]

The paratroopers made the most of their time off. Some rested or attended concerts. Others preferred to let off steam and participated in various sport activities. Many chose to write one last letter to their loved ones. Private Morris Ellefson's letter to his mother provided a unique insight into the Canadian paratrooper's pre-D-Day psyche:

> This is the jump I have long been waiting for, the one which I have been trained and also looked forward to, but now that it is here, mother, I am scared. This is the last letter I will write before I go into France. And in it I wish to thank you for everything you have done for me, the way you have taken my misgivings and brought me up. Mom, please don't cry, fret or worry.... Your loving son, Morris.[546]

The paratroopers were becoming increasingly impatient. Everyone wanted to get on with the job at hand. "We all felt prepared," acknowledged Private Doug Morrison. "We were itching at the bit to get going."[547] But even Mother Nature tested the paratroopers' nerves. Everything was set for the evening of June 4, but a terrible midday storm the day prior and subsequent bad weather postponed the invasion.[548]

Finally, on June 5, 1944, at 1930 hours, the Battalion paraded one last time. First to depart was "C" Company. The men quickly departed for Harwell Airport.[549] It was an emotional moment for many paratroopers. Despite the joking and the pleasantries unit members knew deep down that many would never return. Lieutenant J.R. Madden of "C" Company was one of the last to leave the transit camp. As his truck stopped at the gate, Lieutenant-Colonel Bradbrooke came up to him, shook his hand, and simply said, "Good-bye John." Being a junior officer, this type of familiarity caught Madden completely off guard. "I distinctly remember that," recalled Madden, "because it was the first time ever he called me by my Christian name."[550] At 2230 hours, "C" Company and the other elements of the 3 Para Bde advance group emplaned in Albemarles. They departed soon after. The other three companies remained behind and were later convoyed to Down Ampney Airport.[551] They then boarded C-47 Dakotas at 2245 hours and lifted off 15 minutes later.[552] And so, in the dead of night on June 5, 1944, the 541 paratroopers of the 1st Canadian Parachute Battalion embarked on the greatest adventure yet. Finally, they would be able to test their skills.[553]

Using the cloud cover and smoke generated by the numerous fires caused by ongoing RAF bombing runs, the Albemarles transporting "C" Company approached the French coast.[554] As the aircraft flew over the German defences, the transport aircraft pilots encountered increasing flak and inland small arms fire. Navigators scrutinized the Normandy countryside to locate landmarks to confirm their flight path. Simultaneously, the pilots dropped altitude and prepared for their final approach. As the aircraft converged toward the DZ, the floor doors were opened, providing restless paratroopers with much-needed cool, fresh air.

The restrictive confines of these British converted bombers were unbearable. "Everybody began to stretch and shift positions in their futile effort to rid themselves of muscle cramps," recalled Corporal Hartigan. "For an hour and twenty-three minutes they had squatted on the floor of a fuselage too low to stand up, while controlling about a hundred pounds of equipment." He added, "Their legs and backs cried out for relief, but they knew that wouldn't come until their parachutes opened up."[555]

Then finally, the green light indicating that the paratroopers could now exit the aircraft was switched on. The paratroopers exited rapidly. Between 0020 hours and 0029 hours on June 6, 1944, members of 1 Cdn Para Bn were some of the first Allied soldiers to invade Occupied Europe. While most of the men of the first aircraft landed on or near DZ

"V," northwest of Varaville, those in the following aircraft were dropped between eight and ten kilometres from the intended point.[556]

Shortly after landing on DZ "V" the 3 Para Bde pathfinder team experienced serious difficulties.[557] Many of their "Eureka" beacons, required to guide the main body to the drop zone, had been either damaged or lost.[558] This would have dramatic consequences. The paratroopers of "C" Company also experienced their fair share of problems. Less than fifty had reached the RV point.[559] Regardless, an impatient company commander, Major H.M. McLeod, refused to wait. With the impending arrival of the main body of 3 Para Bde, including the remainder of 1 Cdn Para Bn, it was imperative that "C" Company accomplish its initial task — securing the DZ.

Once the area was secured, McLeod split up his small force and dispatched one group to seize and hold the Varaville bridge. These paratroopers were instructed to defend the structure at all costs until the arrival of the airborne engineers who were tasked to destroy it. Then McLeod and the remaining men proceeded to their next objective — the capture of a series of defensive positions located on the grounds of Le Grand Château in Varaville. McLeod knew that speed under the cover of darkness, combined with bold aggressive action and surprise, would offset the temporary lack of manpower. Upon arrival they located, captured, and disabled a German communication centre. McLeod then organized his men into small groups to seize the remaining positions, consisting of a bunker, a series of trenches, and an anti-tank gun position. However, as the paratroopers deployed and inched their way toward these positions, the defenders opened up with a withering fire.

Throughout the next few hours, the ongoing battle at the Varaville Château and surrounding area attracted small groups of paratroopers who had been dropped off course. All moved to the sound of battle. These welcomed reinforcements were immediately fed into the battle. One British airborne captain, who landed in the outskirts of Varaville, described the intense fighting. "Complete chaos seemed to reign in the village," he reported. "Against a background of Brens, Spandaus and grenades could be heard shouts in British and Canadian, German and Russian."[560]

The German defenders pinned down the paratroopers with heavy-machine gun and anti-tank fire. However, once the enemy's range and positions were confirmed, the paratroopers replied with well-directed anti-tank, mortar, and Bren gun fire of their own. Around 0300 hours, a German anti-tank shell crashed through the Château's gatehouse, where Major MacLeod and six other paratroopers had set up their anti-tank gun. Upon impact, the projectile ignited the paratroopers' anti-tank shells. A terrible explosion ripped through the group and resulted in the death of four paratroopers. Of the original six-man group, only Privates H.B. Swim and G.A. Thompson survived, but even they sustained serious injury.[561]

Despite this terrible blow, the battle raged on. By 1030 hours that morning, the German garrison of Varaville surrendered. A total of eighty prisoners and walking wounded were corralled. As the prisoners were marched off, the airborne soldiers were surprised by the number of defenders captured. "Two enemy soldiers," tallied Hartigan, "for every Canadian paratrooper who fought in Varaville."[562] "C" Company was then ordered to pull out, regroup, and take up a series of defensive positions to guard the roads going through Varaville.[563] By 1500 hours, the first elements of the British 6th Commando Cycle Troop arrived and relieved the Company.[564] The Canadian paratroopers now commenced the final phase of their D-Day mission. They marched to the Le Mesnil crossroads and took up new defensive positions within the Battalion perimeter.

The occupation and defence of the vital road junction was of great strategic importance. The Le Mesnil crossroads were on the ridge of the highest geographical feature between the Dives and the Orne rivers. The paratroopers were ordered to hold it at all cost. Its successful defence assured that the two bridges spanning the Caen Canal and the Orne River, seized earlier by British Air Landing units, remained in Allied hands.[565] These bridges would prove crucial for the rapid deployment of reinforcements that were fighting their way from Sword Beach and heading toward the 6th Airborne Division sector. Additionally, the occupation of this high ground would deny the use of roads by the enemy leading to and from Caen. German armour and other combat vehicles were now forced to use alternate routes. This resulted in lengthy, frustrating delays, as well as additional fuel consumption. Furthermore, it negated the use of the high ground and hindered the enemy's deployment of forward artillery observers who would be critical in directing artillery fire against the Allied troops and vehicles massed on the overcrowded beaches.

"C" Company had performed admirably despite the scattered jump and the loss of most of their heavy weapons. The use of the leg-kit bags had proved disappointing. When released from a paratrooper's leg, the shock caused by the sudden full extension of the twenty-foot rope was such that the bottom of the bag ripped open, thereby emptying its contents. Paratroopers watched helplessly as their heavy weapons, equipment, and much-needed extra ammunition fell, scattered, and disappeared into the cold, dark water of the flooded areas. More than 70 percent of the Battalion's heavy equipment and support weaponry was lost before a single shot had been fired. Despite these unforseen difficulties, the efficiency and tenacity of the airborne soldiers enabled the remainder of the 3 Para Bde to land safely and unopposed.

The first elements of the 3 Para Bde touched down on French soil shortly before 0100 hours. Their drop also did not go according to plan. Numerous factors caused a very dispersed drop. The most important one was the lack of operating "Eureka" homing beacons required to guide the pilots of the main force to the DZ. This, coupled with the pilots' evasive actions due to flak, inevitably altered the flight path of numerous aircraft. Furthermore, the difficulties experienced by the navigators in identifying and confirming landmarks added to the confusion. The combinations of all these elements and the heavy enemy anti-aircraft fire contributed to the Battalion's unanticipated scattered drop.[566]

This extraordinary night jump would forever be etched in the young paratroopers' minds and souls. "When I left the aircraft it was pitching," wrote Company Sergeant-Major John Kemp. "I was standing in the door," he recalled. "There were 20 of us in the aircraft. I had 19 men behind me pushing. They wanted to get the hell out. The flak was hitting the wings."[567] Private Percy Liggins also experienced a nerve-wracking jump:

> The soles of my feet felt as if they were tickled but I realized it was flak hitting the belly of our plane ... As I tumbled out head first my rifle went sailing past me. At the same time, the plane seemed to increase rather than decrease in power for speed and the speed from the props slammed me tight against the tail section ... I landed in an orchard and as I slid my way down I tried for all my worth to get the straps of my parachute harness off my two-inch mortar. A machine gun stitched holes in my parachute canopy above me and it seemed as if the firing was following me down the tree.[568]

While many endured tumultuous exits, others experienced difficult landings. Several paratroopers crashed into trees or slammed onto buildings, resulting in serious injuries and deaths.[569] However, these landings paled in comparison with those who descended into the dreaded flooded and marshy areas. "Looking out of the plane it looked like pasture below us, but when I jumped I landed in water," recollected Private Doug Morrison. "The Germans had flooded the area a while back and there was a green algae on the water so it actually looked like pasture at night from the air."[570] Many Canadian paratroopers drowned because they were so heavily laden with equipment and ammunition.[571] Sergeant W.R. Kelly was one of the lucky paratroopers who cheated this watery grave.

> One man found Sergeant Kelly hanging upside down, with his head in the water, from a huge deadwood tree. His parachute suspension lines were knotted around his legs and feet. The canopy had caught on a limb and suspended Kelly so he was submerged from the top of his head to his neck ... His sixty pounds to eighty pounds of equipment, which normally hung on his body gravitating toward his feet during the parachute descent, was now bundled up around his chest. It took a massive effort to keep lifting his face above the water for gulps of air. He was nearly exhausted when the soldier found him, cut him loose and assisted him to dry land.[572]

Although this wide dispersal complicated the paratroopers' initial missions, it also confused the German forces. Unable to confirm the exact area of the drop zones, German commanders delayed the deployment of their reserve units. Landing in the town of Varaville, Major Nicklin witnessed this confusion first hand. "The Germans were really windy in Varaville," he observed. "They ran around that town like crazy men and shot at anything that moved. Even a moving cow would get a blast of machine-gun fire. They were so jumpy [that] they ran around in twos and threes to give themselves moral support."[573]

However, the dispersal of Battalion Headquarters personnel severely limited Bradbrooke's command and control capabilities, as well as his communications with Brigade and Divisional headquarters during the first twenty-four hours.[574] "I personally was dropped a couple of miles away from the drop zone," related Bradbrooke, "in a marsh near the

River Dives and arrived at the rendezvous about one and a half hours late and completely soaked."[575]

"The problems of getting organized," explained the frustrated CO, "into effective fighting units are immense, there is considerable confusion in getting order out of chaos."[576] However, on the bright side, he added, "We were not troubled by the enemy at this time [during and immediately after the drop], I suppose he was just as confused as we were."[577]

The detailed briefings received in England, coupled with the initiative of the airborne soldiers, now paid off. All paratroopers, regardless of rank, carried on in small groups or at the sub-unit level to accomplish their tasks. Throughout the night they quickly adapted to the bedlam that existed. Once again Brigadier Hill's prescience came through. "Do not be daunted if chaos reigns," he warned them, "for it certainly will!"[578] The Brigadier's words provided some degree of reassurance to the paratroopers. "I think most of us anticipated that we could go into battle by dropping right onto our objective — right into battle," confessed Private de Vries. "Nonetheless, Brigadier Hill warned us that chaos would reign."[579] Those who had landed away from the drop zone adapted to whatever unplanned situation unfolded. "Going down I was surprised at the quietness and the darkness," recalled Corporal Anderson, "I had expected to hear sounds of shooting or at least some activity ... when I landed flat on my back ... I was in such agony that I cared very little whether I lived or died." But "then the training took over," he explained. He recalled:

> I immediately pulled out my rifle and at the same time hit the release on my parachute. I placed my pack on my back and with the rifle in my arms I started to crawl towards a clump of trees which I could see very dimly. At this time I heard nothing, not an aircraft, not a bomb, not a shot. It was about 1:30 A.M. and the night creatures were all asleep. A strange war.[580]

During the next few hours following the jump, those who had been dropped off course experienced difficulties in identifying their location. "Airplanes dropped us all over hell's half acre," chided Lance-Corporal H.R. Holloway. [581] Some paratroopers were lucky and would eventually rejoin their units. Others did not. "I tried to find out where I was, but could not," reminisced Sergeant John Feduck. "I wandered for an hour or so with no success. I laid down in a bomb crater and tried to get my bearings. Finally, I spotted two English Chaps, we moved out to find our respective units."[582]

Sergeant Denis Flynn felt that the dispersal "changed the whole attitude — once on the ground we all wondered, 'where are we?'" He explained, "Because of the dispersal of the drop I was separated from my group. Things were a little strange. I wondered, 'Where am I? How do I meet up with the others?'" He confessed, "There were a lot of anxious moments."[583] As dawn pierced through the heavy smoke and clouds, the increasing natural light helped numerous paratroopers find their way to the objectives. However, the early morning sunlight proved more of a hindrance to many airborne soldiers who found themselves in the midst of German positions and troops.

But it was not only the Germans who posed a threat. Brigadier Hill gathered a group of forty paratroopers and led them toward Le Mesnil. Suddenly, they were attacked by overzealous Allied fighter pilots. The results of the friendly fire were harrowing. Hill explained:

> We got into the middle of the pattern bombing by fighter aircraft, which was anti-personnel bombs. We were on a little narrow track with no ditches, water on each side ... I threw myself down on the mortar officer of the 9th Battalion, Peters ... Everything was covered in dust and the smell of cordite and death. It was ghastly ... I got on to my arms ... and I thought 'Oh! My God, that's my leg.' I took another look at it. This brown boot belonged to Lieutenant Peters whom I was laying on top of. He was killed and I was alive ... I had lost much of my backside, but it didn't immobilize one.[584]

That day all paratroopers, regardless of rank, fought for their lives while attempting to overcome a myriad of unforseen problems. Eventually, they formed up into larger groups and took the fight to the enemy. Others, however, were not so lucky. The main disadvantage of being isolated was that the individual paratrooper did not have the ability to fight for long against larger numbers. As a result, many British and Canadian paratroopers were captured or killed. In the initial hours following the drop, the German 711th Infantry Division had their best success against the isolated airborne interlopers. "Probably the prisoners' statements were correct — that some elements [aircraft] had lost their route and become lost owing to the lack of flight commanders," concluded Lieutenant-General Joseph Reichert, the Division's commander. "This is also probably the reason," he added, "why the fighting qualities of the troops ... had such little effect." He explained, "Most of them kept in hiding and surrendered, offering no resistance."[585] In the end, the dispersed drop resulted in the capture of eighty-two Canadian paratroopers.[586] Nevertheless, under the cover of darkness many more eventually linked up with the Battalion.

By 0600 hours, only two officers and twenty paratroopers from "A" Company, as well as a handful of airborne soldiers from other units, had reached the RV. Severely undermanned and behind schedule, Lieutenant J.A. Clancy assembled his small group and headed to the Merville Battery to join 9 Para Bn. The drop had also severely hampered 9 Para Bn, who had been give the critical task of destroying the battery. Of the 650 paratroopers earmarked for the assault, only 150 had managed to reach the RV.[587] Nevertheless, anxious to get on with this important task, Lieutenant-Colonel T.H. Otway, the commanding officer, organized his men into two assault teams. They quickly cleared two paths across the minefield surrounding the battery. As they painstakingly inched their way toward their final objective, the German defenders positioned in adjoining casemates opened fire with three heavy machine guns. It quickly turned into a bloodbath.[588] Seventy British paratroopers were killed in the short, savage battle. Notwithstanding these heavy losses, Otway and his men succeeded in capturing the battery by approximately 0500 hours.[589] Yellow signal flares were sent up shortly after to confirm that the battery had been captured and, more importantly, to cancel a naval bombardment from the HMS *Arethusa* that was planned for that morning.[590]

Upon entering the main structure, the British paratroopers were surprised by the type and calibre of the guns positioned at Merville Battery. Due to the size of battery's outer structure, Allied planners assumed that it could possibly contain four 150-mm guns capable of firing 96-pound shells every 15 to 20 seconds, with a maximum 8-mile range.[591] They concluded that if this battery opened fire it could cause great mayhem on the beaches. Therefore, it was important that it be neutralized at all costs before the troops disembarked on the beachhead. But instead of the anticipated 150-mm guns, the paratroopers only found four 100-mm 1916 Skoda Works Czechoslovakian howitzers. Regardless, these had to be destroyed in the event that the Germans mounted a counterattack and recaptured the battery. But since the airborne engineers attached to the Battalion had been dropped off course, it was now up to the paratroopers to neutralize these guns themselves. Gathering their Gammon bombs, they proceeded to destroy two guns and disable the others.[592]

Lieutenant Clancy's group finally reached the battery as Otway's men were in the process of securing the perimeter, tending to the wounded, and assembling the prisoners. Their trek had been delayed at Gonneville-sur-Merville because of heavy RAF bombardments. As the British paratroopers assembled and prepared to move out, Clancy briefed his men. They were to lead the way and protect Otway's march to their final assembly point, the high ground of Le Plein in Amfréville. As the survivors and walking wounded of 9 Para Bn headed toward Le Plein, they suddenly came under fire from a heavy German machine gun located in a nearby château. The Canadians quickly spread out and neutralized this enemy position. Following this short engagement, Clancy reorganized his group so that they formed an all around protective shield for the members of 9 Para Bn during their withdrawal to their new positions in Le Plein.[593] Despite being severely undermanned, the members of "A" Company had nevertheless successfully completed all their D-Day missions. By 0900 hours they left their British comrades and rejoined the Battalion at the Le Mesnil crossroads.

"B" Company's personnel fared no better than the other companies. A total of only thirty all ranks had managed to regroup at the designated RV. Lieutenant Normand Toseland moved the group toward their objective, the Robehomme bridge. During their advance they unexpectedly came across a young French girl who volunteered to guide them. Once at the bridge, they met up with two other Battalion officers, Major C.E. Fuller and Captain Peter Griffin, and a mixed group of British and Canadian paratroopers. The small force took up a defensive posture and waited patiently until 0300 hours for the arrival of a team of British airborne engineers.[594]

Growing restless and unsure if the engineers would actually arrive, the group decided to blow up the bridge themselves. Toseland collected all the available high explosives. A charge was prepared and subsequently detonated. Regrettably, it proved insufficient. Even though the structure had been weakened, it could still be used by enemy infantry. Knowing that this blast would surely attract the enemy's attention, Major Fuller ordered his group to form a defensive perimeter once again to repel any German patrols. As the paratroopers were digging in, a small group of British airborne engineers led by

Lieutenant Jack Inman finally arrived. They proceeded to rig a second charge. It was successfully detonated and sent the structure crashing into the river.[595] With the mission accomplished the group moved off to the Le Mesnil crossroads.

The route to the Battalion's position, however, was now active with enemy troops. Without any means of communications, and uncertain as to the fate of the other companies, Major Fuller preferred to use patience and caution. He opted to travel by night and use the terrain to the fullest to cover his movements. During the next day and a half, Major Fuller's group increased to 150 Canadian and British paratroopers. While pleased at assembling such a large force it nevertheless complicated his mobility behind enemy lines. He ordered that all contacts with the enemy be avoided so as not to compromise their position. If contact could not be averted, they were to attack and pull out quickly. The ad hoc company group finally reached Le Mesnil at 0330 hours on June 8.[596]

Notwithstanding the numerous unforseen complications and the loss of most of their heavy support weaponry during and immediately following the dispersed drop, the stamina and composure of the paratroopers enabled the Battalion to successfully accomplish all its assigned D-Day tasks.[597] The enemy was fully aware that they were not facing a conventional ground force. The commander of the 711th Infantry Division was impressed by the fighting qualities of the 6 AB Div paratroopers. "The portion which were employed in the bridgehead to the east of the Orne," observed Lieutenant-General Joseph Reichert, "fought in an excellent manner both during the attack and the defense."[598]

This is high praise; after all, the strain due to the bad drops, fatigue, stress, and combat were immense. However, their rigorous training and physical conditioning enabled the Canadian paratroopers to endure and, more importantly, to overcome the great physical and mental hardships encountered during D-Day, as well as the remainder of the Normandy Campaign. In hindsight, Lieutenant-Colonel Bradbrooke attested that the Battalion's D-Day successes could not have been achieved if the unit had not undergone such a demanding airborne training regimen. "Dropping at night, several hours before the seaborne assault, in strange and hostile territory, all added up to confusion and an appreciation of the reasons why prior training of such severity was necessary," remarked Bradbrooke.[599]

Brigadier Hill agreed. "All this training," he later acknowledged, "gave us an invaluable asset — Endurance." Hill added, "I think after D-Day without it we would have had difficulty in producing the stamina required to stick to our ridge for ten whole days of intensive fighting at close range after a tough initial parachute operation and with the casualties suffered." Hill underlined, "Physical fitness saves lives in battle and enables men to better survive their wounds."[600]

Nevertheless, the Battalion's initiation to airborne operations was achieved at a very heavy price. After the first 24 hours, a total of 116 all ranks of the 541 paratroopers who had jumped into Normandy were killed, wounded, or taken prisoner.[601] And a great number of paratroopers were still missing. During the course of the following days, the lucky ones eventually made their way back to Le Mesnil. Others were hunted down and captured. Those who had landed far from the DZ and sustained serious injuries during their landings, or who had been wounded in subsequent firefights, died alone.

The Battalion now prepared for the defence of the Le Mesnil crossroads. The undermanned companies, which included the "walking wounded," hurriedly dug their trenches and consolidated the few heavy weapons they had. "We settled into the cross roads and set up the Bren guns," explained Feduck. "There was a great big ditch along there," recollected the ex-Bren gunner, "and that is where we dug our fox holes." The tired paratroopers now waited patiently, expecting the enemy to attack. "From then on, it was mostly patrols, with no intention of attacking anybody. We did not have the strength," he explained, "we were pretty thinned out. Many times, I wished the hell I was back home."[602] Collectively, the various parachute and airborne units of 6 AB Div made up a continuous defensive perimeter. Luckily, their positions were protected by the thickly wooded high grounds and rugged terrain. To the Battalion's immediate left and right were its sister battalions, the 9th and 8th respectively.[603]

As the paratroopers familiarized themselves with their new surroundings, sentries were ordered to remain vigilant and to report enemy activities. It was only a matter of time before the Germans regrouped and launched their counterattacks.[604] These commenced the next day, on June 7, 1944. Having recovered from the initial surprise, the Germans conducted numerous probing attacks to assess and confirm the dispositions of 6 AB Div. Once this information was gathered the paratroopers were subjected to incessant deadly artillery and mortar bombardments.[605]

But it was imperative that the Le Mesnil crossroads be held at all cost. The protection of the left flank of the invasion force still rested squarely on the shoulders of 6 AB Div. Despite the critical nature of its role, the divisional leadership was worried about the effect of a lengthy static operation on the morale of the paratroopers. "Great attention had to be paid to maintaining an aggressive spirit," conceded one airborne staff officer, particularly because "this [defensive] role, an unexpected one for Airborne troops was bound to lead to a sense of disappointment and frustration." Therefore, to maintain the offensive spirit all unit commanders were ordered to carry out extensive "sniping, patrolling, a few minor raids and by training whenever troops could be taken out of the line."[606]

Hill endorsed this directive wholeheartedly. During 3 Para Bde's deployment in Normandy, an active patrolling and raiding program had been implemented. "If there was no fighting going on," recalled Lieutenant-Colonel Fraser Eadie, "Brigadier Hill made sure there was patrolling. He wanted to impart the superiority of our troops — he never wanted the enemy to rest."[607] Moreover, the patrols were necessary to dominate the difficult terrain. This segment of Normandy was referred to as "bocage" country. The roads had three- to four-foot-high embankments on which had been planted thick bramble and blackthorn hedges. The adjacent fields were also surrounded by these compact hedgerows. The bocage forced the vehicles to be constricted to the roads. Quite simply, if a convoy was ambushed it was impossible to manouevre the vehicles off the roads.[608]

During the planning phase of the invasion the strategic possibilities of this terrain had attracted Montgomery's attention. If used efficiently, the bocage would greatly enhance the effectiveness of the airborne soldiers. "Ideal infantry country," observed Monty. "There was excellent concealment for snipers and patrols, while defensive positions dug into the banks were well protected from tanks and artillery."[609] But this was not lost on the Germans either, and they equally made best possible use of the inhospitable surroundings.

Nonetheless, the fact that the Battalion counted in its ranks aboriginals and a good number of men who had spent their youth growing up in Canada's wilderness paid great dividends. They adapted instantly to this hostile environment. "You would stop somewhere," explained John Madden, a battalion officer, "and he [Bowland] would stop somewhere and he would kind of disappear into the background." An amazed Madden continued, "And you would think you were all alone, and then you'd move to go forward and suddenly he would appear from behind a tree or from some other ways where he had been hiding, observing, ready to go forward with you."[610]

The approaches leading to the Battalion's defensive positions were also enhanced by the steep embankments and the flooded surrounding area of the Dives River. This combination restricted the movement of enemy armour and large infantry units. As a result, "the battle around Le Mesnil developed into a type of guerilla warfare," explained Sergeant Bill Dunnett, "with men hunting through the woods and narrow lanes."[611]

To compound these natural obstacles, the Germans added their own devilish tactics to harass, isolate, and demoralize the invaders. Shortly after first light on June 6, and for the duration of the campaign, the enemy deployed snipers. As soon as the first paratroopers of the Battalion's HQ Company reached Le Mesnil that morning, they immediately came under accurate and deadly fire. In a very short time, the marksmanship of the German snipers resulted in several casualties, including one officer.[612]

The efficiency of the German snipers was such that there was no secure area within the Battalion's perimeter. "When we arrived at Le Mesnil," recalled Company Sergeant-Major G.W. Embree, "Bradbrooke ordered Sergeant Green and some men to take out some German snipers that were firing at him."[613] The number of officers and NCOs who were injured by sniper fire was particularly high during the first few days. "I was the fifth to take over as the Company Sergeant-Major," recalled John Kemp. "It was mostly snipers picking them off." The German snipers obviously understood the significance of the paratroopers' rank insignia. "It got so we didn't wear ranks anymore," explained Kemp. "All our men knew us — officers and NCOs."[614]

The German sharpshooters operated with remarkable effectiveness and successfully restricted the movement of the airborne soldiers. "The snipers kept us under cover most of the day," recalled Private Harold Croft.[615] Throughout the duration of the Normandy Campaign, this invisible and elusive adversary wounded and killed many Canadian paratroopers. Those who lost friends to a sniper's bullet were not in a forgiving mood. "As is always the case with sniper activity, a man here and a man there has one or more close calls or almost silently drops stone dead," asserted Corporal Hartigan. "When someone dies from sniper fire," he explained, "anger builds up rapidly in the minds of his fellow soldiers and an increasing toll of revenge is exacted upon the snipers."[616]

To minimize casualties and negate the snipers' deadly accuracy, it became imperative to take the fight to the enemy. The best method to neutralize the snipers was to send out small patrols around the clock. As such, the Canadians conducted numerous day and night ambush, combat, standing, and reconnaissance patrols. Not all yielded successful results. Nevertheless, these bold sorties forced the German marksmen to withdraw and occupy new positions at a safer distance.

The patrol tasks fell to all companies. "I was on some night patrols," reminisced Harold Croft "which was not my favorite pastime."[617] Some, however, enjoyed the challenge and proceeded with reckless abandon. Impressed by the paratroopers' zeal, Brigadier Hill nevertheless intervened, instructing the men to use caution, patience, and stealth so as to limit unnecessary casualties and return with information that could prove useful in future operations.[618]

It did not take long for the paratroopers to learn from their initial mistakes and become experienced combatants. "Once they had been in battle, they are battle trained and they are going to be a better soldier for you on the first few or five days of the next action," explained Company Sergeant-Major George Green. "They know what to do and they have a better idea," he added. "They know they can get hurt, and that is very important because until someone does get hurt, you don't realize that people can get hurt."[619] While on a reconnaissance patrol, Private de Vries came across one of his comrades who had been shot earlier in the forehead by a sniper. "I tell you," he confessed, "[after that] I ran a lot faster and lower than before."[620]

This dangerous battleground provided the young paratroopers with many important survival lessons regarding protection against artillery and mortar bombardments as well. Private Mervin F. Jones recalled:

> In our basic training, we were led to believe that when a shell hit, the shrapnel raised on an angle. We had blankets out to dry after it rained at Le Mesnil and the Germans put in a few shells. Some of the blankets were badly cut where the shrapnel had speared right along the ground. We had been dropping to the ground under fire. But after that, we took off for a trench.[621]

The incessant shelling also forced the paratroopers to modify their trenches. "Up to this time many of the paratroopers were green, untried and somewhat naive infantry soldiers who had not dug deep enough," explained Hartigan. "Also, none of their L-shaped trenches had half-roofs covering one arm of the "L" to make them more shrapnel proof. So several men were needlessly lost ... hard lessons quickly remedied by experience."[622] However, those who survived the first days now knew how to react to mortar fire. "It got to the point," explained Private Morrsion, "where you could tell by the whistle if it [the mortar round] would land or go past you."[623]

From June 7 to 17, the paratroopers defended the Le Mesnil cross-roads tenaciously. They monitored German troop movements and disrupted the enemy as he formed up to attack. They also harassed forward artillery observation posts and hunted down the despised snipers.[624] The Battalion also conducted a number of attacks. On June 8, platoons from "B"and "HQ" Companies commanded by Captain Peter R. Griffin assaulted German troops and their supporting amour located in the Bavent area, a mere two hundred yards from the Battalion's front lines. Although successful, these captured objectives could not be occupied. "Jerry [Germans] had every inch of it," explained Griffin, "registered with his mortars and artillery."[625] Nonetheless, the paratroopers inflicted heavy casualties on the enemy and forced him to withdraw.[626] The many tedious hours spent on the Bulford ranges now paid off great dividends. Throughout the attack, Privates R.A. Geddes and W. Noval, armed with a Bren gun and a sniper's rifle, accounted for approximately twenty-five Germans killed.[627]

Taking into account that this was their first exposure to combat, the paratroopers had performed remarkably well. However, despite their youth and conditioning, fatigue was fast becoming their most formidable foe. Many had not slept since their departure from England on June 5, 1944. Notwithstanding their combat spirit, after three solid days of fighting, exhaustion was setting in. Brigadier Hill noted this worrisome condition, but regardless was impressed by their continuing willingness to fight. "The Canadians were very tired," observed Hill, "it didn't make the slightest difference, but they were tired."[628] The inevitable soon occurred. "Many of our people became beat ... really beat," explained Lieutenant John Madden. "I remember shaking sentries awake I don't know how many times. You go around at night to check and make sure everybody was alert."[629] Corporal Hartigan concurred. "We learned," he stated, "that the lack of sleep was the worst of all deprivations, far worse than hunger or thirst."[630] Hartigan explained:

> Hour after hour the paratroopers peered into the darkness in an attempt to differentiate between fact or fiction, as conditions for mirage activity set in ... seem-

ingly buildings or villages which in fact were outlines of clumps of trees. Tired eyes made fields appear like lakes and lowering animals like advancing enemy boats. As the buildings moved up close and the water faded away, the animals became enemy vehicles or groups of enemy soldiers. Imaginary towns moved away, the lakes re-appeared, and the forming dew made the grass begin to flow so the lake was now a river alongside which a cow became a parked scout car.[631]

Their first opportunity to get some rest finally came on June 9, when there was a lull in German attacks.[632] The paratroopers quickly learned that it was important to pace themselves and rest whenever possible.

The Battalion's next major action took place in the nearby town of Bréville on June 12. Located to the left of 1 Cdn Para Bn's position, it had been under constant attack since June 7. Additional artillery support was requested from the Divisional artillery of 3rd British Infantry Division to break up large German infantry and armour attacks. Nonetheless, the situation remained critical. On June 10, a squadron of the 13/18 Royal Hussars consisting of Sherman tanks and the 5th Battalion, 51st Highland Division, were sent to strengthen this part of the 6 AB Div's sector. For the next two days, these, as well as 6 AB Div air-landing units, launched a series of unsuccessful attacks to push the well-entrenched enemy from Bréville. However, all that was achieved was heavy losses. Destroyed Sherman tanks and the bodies of British infantrymen and paratroopers lay everywhere.

Buoyed by success, German artillery and mortar fire rained unmercifully on the British entrenchments. These barrages were then immediately followed by massive infantry attacks supported by tanks and self-propelled guns. By late afternoon on June 12, the situation had deteriorated and an enemy breakthrough in the Bréville area was imminent. If successful, it would seriously compromise the weakened 6th Airborne Division's positions and their ability to contain future German attacks.[633] But the Division's personnel were stretched to the limit.

Brigadier Hill, who was recuperating from a serious injury sustained on D-Day, decided to take matters into his own hands and respond to the crisis.[634] He rushed over to the 1st Canadian Parachute Battalion Headquarters to gather all available personnel. Bradbrooke, whose own positions were also under heavy attack, did his best to accommodate the Brigadier's request. Captain John P. Hanson and approximately forty paratroopers from "C" and "HQ" Companies were given to the Brigadier. "Come along Chaps, nothing to worry about," encouraged Brigadier Hill as he led his ad hoc force to the rescue.[635]

Hanson recalled the urgency of the situation and Hill's hasty briefing. "Hanson, old man, the Scots on our left are having some heavy going and we will have to go in to help them out."[636] Within seconds the small group raced off to Bréville. This was the most intense German offensive in the Division's area since the D-Day drop. The Canadians arrived amidst a raging battle. The terrain was cluttered with smouldering vehicles and exploding ammunition. Bodies were strewn everywhere. The small band of paratroopers immediately deployed in the woods located east of the Château St-Côme. There they dug in at the edge of the tree lines and occupied some of the hastily abandoned positions of the Highland Battalion. The paratroopers' sense of survival and scavenger instinct kicked in. Within minutes, they found three Vickers medium machine guns and plenty of ammunition.[637] With this newly found firepower, the paratroopers were eagerly looking for potential targets. Then "three Sherman tanks pulled up on our right and stopped in front of our positions," recalled de Vries. "Suddenly," stated the paratrooper, "they were brewed up by German self-propelled guns." This unexpected turn of events "now blocked our field of fire," explained the frustrated airborne soldier.[638]

As some of the paratroopers moved out under heavy enemy fire to find alternate positions, a calm Hill hobbled from one position to another encouraging his young paratroopers. As the Brigadier approached a trench occupied by Private Michael Ball and his sergeant, an enemy shell exploded over their position. "My Sergeant got killed," remembered Ball, "he got a piece of shrapnel in the head ... Brigadier Hill, however, never backed down at all."[639] The battle raged on for hours, until finally naval and artillery fire was called in to silence the enemy's self-propelled guns. However, enemy troops succeeded in penetrating certain areas of the paratroopers' perimeter. This led in many instances to hand-to-hand fighting.[640] The Canadians fought aggressively, stood their ground, and forced larger groups of German infantry to fall back. The pugnacious leadership of Hill and Hanson, coupled with the arrival and tenacious defence of the paratroopers, lifted the spirits of the other British defenders and thwarted the Germans' advance. "The Black Watch Battalion was completely disorganized," wrote Hanson, "and I can safely say that 'C' Company saved a complete route and a split in our left flank."[641] By nine o'clock that evening, only twenty Canadian paratroopers returned to the Battalion's headquarters. The remaining British defenders and some reinforcements fought on until the next evening.[642] Bréville was now secure.

Those six days, from June 7 to 12, were the most grueling of the Battalion's Normandy campaign. Nevertheless, casualties due to mortar and sniper fire mounted daily, leaving those who were still fit to fight with increasing duties and responsibilities. The combat in the close, confined bocage country was intense. Canadian war correspondent Ross Munro wrote, "It was savage, chaotic fighting in closely wooded country which the Canadians called 'squirt gun' territory."[643]

The physical hardships and psychological strain continued to severely test the Battalion. "One day we were shelled for 12 hours straight," recalled Private Mervin Jones. "No one was hurt," he added, "but it was sure hard on the nerves."[644]

"It seemed they knew exactly where we were and that during every meal they opened up on us with artillery," recalled Private King. "This was really hard on morale."[645] Private de Vries conceded, "After a barrage let up I use to feel guilty that during a barrage I prayed that the shells would fall somewhere else, knowing that it meant on someone else."[646]

However, despite the enemy's best efforts, they failed to dislodge the paratroopers from their positions. A drained Lieutenant-Colonel Bradbrooke was proud of his unit's performance. He explained:

> The country around Le Mesnil was very close with its ditches and hedges, and it was a perfect position for determined boys like ours. We were just one little pocket out on the end of nowhere. After three days we had 300 men and we held for days against many attacks. The Germans were methodical as the devil but our mortars and machine guns knocked the hell out of them. Between 200 and 300 hundred dead Germans piled up in the fields in front of us and for days we could not even get out to bury them because of incessant sniping.[647]

Brigadier Hill later referred to Le Mesnil as "one of the great battles of the war ... In the first eight days I lost over a thousand chaps and I think 58 officers ... It was very, very tough."[648] The Battalion losses incurred during the twelve days at the Le Mesnil crossroads were 10 dead and 109 wounded.[649]

But the enemy was not the only challenge. The warmer than usual weather conditions in Normandy for that time of year further tested the endurance of the airborne soldiers. "There was a pungent odor that constantly hovered over both sides of this clustered area like a black ominous cloud of death." Worse still, Private J.A. Collins remembered, "There was no where to turn to get away from the constant smell of decomposing flesh."[650]

Although these were very difficult times, neither the enemy nor the severe living conditions could destroy the resolve and comradeship of the paratroopers. "Even the wounded couldn't wait to get back to the unit," asserted Private de Vries. "The desire to belong to a good outfit and be with buddies" grew stronger by the day. "It [the Battalion] became family," extolled de Vries, "and you felt uncomfortable anywhere else."[651]

On June 17, the remaining 312 exhausted paratroopers of the 1st Canadian Parachute Battalion were relieved by the 5th Parachute Battalion and sent to a rest area.[652] The revitalized Canadian paratroopers returned to their front-line positions eight days later on June 25. Bradbrooke now changed his defensive posture. Instead of deploying all three of his rifle companies in the forward edge of the defensive perimeter, as had been done previously, he now opted to position two companies in the front lines and hold one back in reserve. This gave him a force to react to any unforeseen developments. Equally important, his paratroopers could be rotated in and out of the perimeter, thus enabling them to rest up, wash, and get warm meals.

The Germans had also altered their tactics. They now realized that they could not push the invaders back into the sea.[653] Moreover, having sustained heavy losses during the course of the previous weeks, the Germans could no longer carry out large frontal infantry attacks on positions defended by Canadian and British troops. Furthermore, increased Allied daylight air strikes against German ground forces further complicated the assembling of large forces for offensive operations. The paratroopers also noted that the Germans had withdrawn their units back to a safer distance.[654] Frontal assaults were now replaced by increased sniping and patrolling. But even these patrols "had become unusually cautious about opening fire."[655] The shelling had also somewhat decreased because the German mortar groups and artillery were forced to frequently shift their positions so as to escape counterartillery bombardments.

Nonetheless, the enemy's continued shelling still forced the Battalion to set up a vigorous patrolling program to locate and confirm the exact whereabouts of the enemy.[656] The enemy's agile dispositions, coupled with the cover offered by the hedgerows, necessitated new techniques for locating the enemy's firing positions. "As the country does not allow long vision observation posts," recorded the War Diary, "its difficult to observe fire with the results that ranging must now be done by sound and map reference."[657]

The enemy's constant movement and the paratroopers' inability to quickly confirm their new locations frustrated Brigadier Hill. On June 27, Hill visited Bradbrooke's headquarters and expressed his dissatisfaction with the Battalion's ability to obtain information regarding the location of the enemy's positions in the unit's area of responsibility.[658] Later that evening "A" and "B" Companies were sent out to provide supporting fire to elements of the 8th Parachute Battalion, who were tasked with attacking a suspected enemy headquarters. The assault was successful and important information was gained.[659]

The enemy maintained this "hide and seek" strategy until the Battalion was once again pulled out on July 4 for a rest and recuperation period. This time, its positions were taken over by the 13th Parachute Battalion. The unit moved to the divisional rest area by the Orne River until July 20. During this period the Battalion was reinforced with seven officers and one hundred Other Ranks from an infantry reinforcement depot.[660] At that time, it was decided not to send the members of the 1st Canadian Parachute Training Battalion because they would be needed to reinforce the unit for future airborne operations. The current operation was now simply a ground war.

The Battalion returned to the front on July 21. Amidst heavy rains, it relieved the 12th Battalion Devonshire Regiment and occupied new positions in the Bois de Bavent until July 27. Living conditions during the next six days were terrible. Heavy rains forced the airborne soldiers to vacate their trenches, which now became mud baths. Soaked paratroopers wore the same wet clothes for days on end. The rain and the mud tested the morale of the airborne soldiers. More importantly, it complicated the daily weapons maintenance and cleaning. After three days the rain finally let up. However, the excessive humidity unleashed swarms of huge mosquitoes that continually plagued all combatants.[661] Regardless of these difficult conditions, the Battalion sent out an increasing number of patrols.

To hinder the movements of the paratroopers, the Germans now laid numerous booby traps leading to their front lines. As a result, many paratroops were wounded or killed. Private Harold Croft was one of the lucky ones to have escaped unharmed. He recalled:

> We did some patrols at night and one morning we found that the Germans had pulled out at night. So we took off after them. We had to cross a minefield, which was fun, and after we got through it we stopped for a rest. I was half lying down when I moved my foot and noticed that it was caught on a cord. There was a grenade attached to the other end but the string just stretched so it didn't go off. [662]

On July 27, after seven days of braving both the elements and the enemy, the Battalion was pulled out. On July 31 they returned from their short leave and replaced the Argyll and Sutherland Highlanders of the 51st Highland Division. From August 1 to 16, the Battalion endured regular shelling and mortar fire. All companies were tasked to organize patrols to dominate the terrain around the clock. However, despite the increased patrolling very little information was collected regarding the enemy's positions and intentions. This was largely due to constant contact with large roving German patrols. But the tedious static warfare soon gave way to offensive operations.

On August 7, Lieutenant-General Sir John Crocker, commander of 1st Corps, informed Major-General Gale that the Germans were preparing to withdraw their troops from Normandy. Crocker ordered the 6th Airborne Division to prepare to pursue the retreating German troops up to the Seine River. During their advance they were to apply constant pressure on the enemy's rearguard and limit their demolition work intended to delay the Allies.[663] The paratroopers were to harass and occupy the right flank of the retreating German forces. Their actions would enable the 1st Canadian Army to move southeast from Caen toward Falaise and then turn eastwards toward the Seine River.[664]

On August 16, Canadian paratroopers received their warning order. Operation Paddle was launched the next day at 0300 hours. The initial advance was carried out by the 8th and 9th Parachute Battalions of 3rd Parachute Brigade while 1 Cdn Para Bn was held in reserve. By 0800 hours, the Battalion was given its first mission. It was ordered to enter and clear the Bois de Bures. "B" Company's aggressive advance was soon curbed by the devious actions of the enemy. "We lost six men from booby-traps and mines ... They were "S" Mines, or jumping mines," affirmed Company Sergeant-Major Kemp. "There were three prongs that stuck out of the ground," he explained. "It was in a casing. When you stepped on it, it was activated. When you took your foot off, it jumped up about three feet and exploded." The results were devastating. "It was full of ball bearing shot," asserted Kemp, "and could kill or wound anyone within a radius of fifty yards."[665]

Nevertheless, the Battalion pushed on and crossed the Dives River using bridges constructed by 3 Para Sqn, Royal Engineers. By nightfall, "A" Company, the Battalion's lead element, had started to engage enemy rear parties. In the event that there was no resistance, the lightly armed airborne troops were ordered to advance as quickly as possible. They were to maintain contact with the retreating enemy columns and prevent them from establishing proper defences.

While the young paratroopers eagerly pursued the offensive, some Battalion officers felt that they did not have the required training for such operations. "We appear to be committed as Infantry of the line indefinitely," explained Captain Griffin, "worse luck as we're not trained as such and haven't got the transport."[666] Griffin also noted during this pursuit that the weeks of static warfare and eating tin rations had weakened the paratroopers' endurance. He conceded:

> We're all tuckered out with sore feet, bad stomachs, etc. I firmly believe I lost over 10 pounds. We've been on tin food since June 6 and for over two months sat in trenches pursuing a "what we have we hold" role with a consequent rapid drop in our physical fitness. Our training has always been strenuous and fitted us for those first 15 to 20 days (hectic), but we're not suited to doing relatively nothing, so when we leaped out and started after Ludwig two weeks ago it took about one 6 mile pursuit march to put most of us on our knees.[667]

Regardless the 1st Canadian Parachute Battalion forged ahead. Two days later, on August 18, at 2300 hours, the Battalion took part in Operation Paddle II. The 1st Canadian Parachute Battalion was tasked to capture four bridges that spanned over the St-Samson-Dives-sur-mer-Canal. "A" Company captured their bridge intact. "Our Battalion had only one really good show and that was a set piece attack on 4 bridges," wrote Griffin. "My Company captured ours intact, the only one of four and we duly named it 'Canada Bridge' with a Canadian parachute badge drawn on it."[668]

The paratroopers were pleased with their accomplishments and thankful that the retreating Germans, despite being well armed, seemed to have tired of fighting. "We collected 35 prisoners," stated Griffin, "11 machine guns, 2 field phones, an anti-mine detecting instrument, 20 Lugers and any amount of other weapons. Since then we've been fortunate with his rearguard — each time we've passed through to make contact he's withdrawn."[669] The paratroopers had once again attained their objectives. And, as always, the Battalion now set up defensive positions and defended the four bridges throughout the night.[670]

For the next few days, the airborne troops continued advancing, averaging between two to three miles a day. The enemy's tactics did not change. Upon seeing the paratroops the German rearguard fired a few shots and withdrew. When the Battalion encountered strong resistance, the paratroopers were ordered to dig in and let the artillery shell the defenders. By August 19, the area between the Dives Rives and the St-Samson-Dives-sur-Mer Canal were controlled by 3 Para Bde. The German units who operated in this location, the 744th Grenadier Regiment of the 711th Infantry Division, had ceased to exist as a fighting force.[671] A few days later, on August 21, the Battalion took the lead and advanced from Dozulé to Annebault under heavy rain and shelling. During a lull in the fighting, on August 23, the Battalion was visited by CMHQ Chief of Staff Lieutenant-General Ken Stuart. The same day, Lieutenant-Colonel G.F.P Bradbrooke was appointed to a position with the General Staff at the Canadian Military Headquarters in London.

Major G. Fraser Eadie, acting as the unit's deputy commanding officer due to Major Nicklin's medical evacuation, was ordered to assume temporary command of the Battalion. During the next eight days the Battalion advanced slowly through Vauville, Tourgeville, Bonneville sur Touques, St-Gatien, St-Benoît-d'Hébertot, and La Moderie. Organized German resistance all but ceased by August 25. 6 AB Div personnel had liberated more than four hundred square miles of French territory and captured over one thousand German prisoners.[672] The Battalion's losses during this pursuit were fourteen Other Ranks killed and twenty-four wounded.[673]

The next day, on August 26, 1944, Major-General Gale drafted a "Special Order Of The Day" thanking his troops for their great work. "I congratulate you on your greatest achievements, on your stamina, on your skill and on your grim determination," praised Gale. "The motto of the 6th British Airborne Division is 'Go To It,'" he continued. "You have gone to it and right splendidly, you have done it."[674] For the first time since June 6, 1944, the Division's personnel could finally relax.

Battalion members were authorized to visit in the nearby town of Beuzeville. It did not take long for the paratroopers to celebrate their victories. "It was like any city on New Year's Eve, except more so," described Griffin, "I never saw such hilarious celebrations and so much to drink."[675] The energy, efficiency, and professionalism of the paratroopers displayed during the pursuit had not gone unnoticed. Lieutenant-General H.D.G. Crerar, commander of the 1st Canadian Army, sent a congratulatory note to Crocker, who forwarded it immediately Major-General Gale. "The determination and speed with which his [Gale's] troops have pressed on in spite of all enemy efforts to the contrary," he wrote, "have been impressive and of greatest assistance to Army as a whole."[676] The same day, a delighted Gale replied, "It was a great day for us when the Canadian government deemed it fit to place the 1st Canadian Parachute Battalion under my command." Gale continued, "You know how magnificently that Battalion has done. It was a great day for us when we found ourselves an integral part of the 1st Canadian Army."[677]

For the young men who had survived the Normandy Campaign, they earned the enviable distinction of now being referred to as veterans. "I am proud and very glad I was part of the 1st Canadian Parachute Battalion airborne invasion of France," confided Private Mervin Jones, "but I would never, never do it again ... jumping out of an airplane into black space towards a land full of the enemy ... There are no front lines at a time like this; there were Germans all over the place ... you could be among any number of them."[678] His sentiments are understandable. They had jumped in the dead of night into chaotic conditions. Separated from their comrades, they formed small groups and successfully attained their assigned objectives. By the end of the campaign, they had mastered and perfected new defensive skills required to counter a devious and tenacious enemy, as well as the hostile terrain. They enhanced their patrolling capabilities, and, in the final phase of their deployment, they vigorously pursued and engaged the enemy's rearguard until all organized resistance ceased. Their operational record was commendable. They had never retreated, abandoned, nor lost the ground that they defended.

The Battalion had also earned its share of military decorations during the Normandy Campaign. Of the sixty officers and men of 6 AB Div decorated for bravery under fire, eight individuals belonged to 1 Cdn Para Bn, specifically two officers and six Other Ranks.[679] Brigadier Hill was very pleased with "his Canadians" and their first exposure to combat. They performed remarkably for a unit that had never "seen a battle or had seen a shot fired in anger before," recalled Hill. Captain Peter Griffin had also witnessed first-hand the transformation of these young men into tough, seasoned, reliable veterans. "Don't think the men in our Battalion aren't the best in the world," wrote Griffin, "but they're young (19, 20, 21) and they've been right in the front line for 22 out of 28 days without being reinforced."[680] After the war, Bradbrooke also reflected on the youthfulness of his paratroopers. Their average age was much younger in comparison to other Canadians who took part in D-Day. "I was," reflected Bradbrooke, "the 'old man' at age 32!"[681]

On September 1, all non-parachute reinforcements attached to the Battalion during the course of the Normandy campaign were taken off strength and returned to the Canadian General Reinforcement Unit.[682] Meanwhile, back at Carter Barracks, Battalion Headquarters personnel were already busily attempting to bring the Battalion back to full strength. Orders finally arrived on September 2 for the 1 Cdn Para Bn to return to England. The surviving members of the Battalion marched to a concentration area and waited to board a vessel. On September 6, the unit sailed to England. Of the original 547 paratroopers who had jumped into Normandy, only 197 returned.[683] Unbeknownst to them, the Battalion would be recalled sooner than they thought to fight once again on the European continent.

CHAPTER EIGHT

The Trouble with Heroes —
Problems in England

I went back to England with 22 men left in the company. The problem now became one of reintegrating the old and the new. They all had to be taught to think alike.

Major Richard (Dick) Hilborn.[684]

On September 6, 1944, the survivors of the 1st Canadian Parachute Battalion returned to England. The bitter and drawn-out campaign in Normandy was finally over. On August 20, the Allies had closed the Falaise pocket, trapping a large portion of the German Army in the west. Simultaneously, American forces continued their advance toward the Seine River. With France largely in Allied hands, the paratroopers were pulled out of battle and replaced by regular line infantry.

The price of defeat was great for the Germans. More than two hundred thousand soldiers were killed or wounded, and another two hundred thousand had been captured. Scattered throughout France were the destroyed remnants of 1,300 tanks, 20,000 vehicles, 500 assault guns, 5,500 field guns, and 3,545 aircraft.[685] These were losses that the German war industry could no longer replace. Those who had escaped were now desperately attempting to regroup and stabilize the Western Front.

But for the Allies, victory had not been easy. They had also sustained heavy losses.[686] The grueling three-month Normandy Campaign both tested and weakened the Allied field force. For units such as the 1st Canadian Parachute Battalion it was also their baptism of fire. The success achieved by the paratroopers validated their relevancy to Allied commanders. "Airborne forces must now form an essential part of the Army," extolled Montgomery, the commander of the 21st Army Group. "Apart from their participation in the battle, the threat of their use can be turned to important advantage." He believed that "experience has shown that thereby the enemy can be led to make considerable and even vital dispersions of his front line forces." He added, "This is in addition to the need to lock up troops in rear areas for guarding vital zones and installations when the opponent is known to have airborne troops at his disposal."[687] But as already stated, the airborne accomplishments came at great cost. Now the Allies had to rebuild the capability if they were to use it again — and use it they certainly would.

The 1st Canadian Parachute Battalion was no different. The survivors landed in England on September 7 and arrived in Bulford the following day.[688] The general feeling that prevailed, recalled Sergeant R.F. Anderson, was one of "tremendous relief and of great success and of having survived a most harrowing experience."[689] During the next four days activities were mostly administrative in nature, consisting of clothing, pay, and medical parades. While discipline remained high, the officers and the senior NCOs ensured that the tempo of activity was relaxed and that the men were not rushed. Everyone knew that these first few days would prove difficult. Many familiar faces had vanished. "Out of my company's 120 men," recalled John Kemp, "there were 22 of us that returned to Carter Barracks."[690]

The survivors were well treated. The base staff went out of their way to welcome the paratroopers back home, and great care was taken to prepare excellent meals. Furthermore, many day passes were issued, enabling the paratroopers to go out on the town, dance, and have a few pints. For those who preferred to stay in camp, they had the option of taking in a movie or show. On September 11, the paratroopers were given a well-deserved thirteen-day furlough. Prior to heading off to their various destinations, the paratroopers were warned that the day following their return, training would start once again in earnest.[691]

As promised, on September 26, 1944, Acting Lieutenant-Colonel Jeff Nicklin, the Battalion's new commanding officer, had the unit form up for a special parade.[692] His address was short and to the point. He wanted to command the best battalion in the Division. As a result, training would be very demanding.[693] While his previous "in your face," harsh

The airborne invasion of Normandy.
Courtesy of the British Airborne Forces Charities

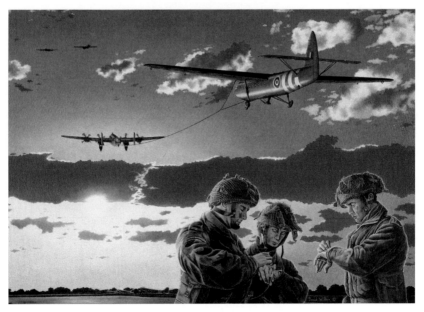

Rendezvous with destiny — gliders depart for Normandy.
Painting by David Walker.
Courtesy of the British Airborne Forces Charities

Many paratroopers landed in the flooded fields of Normandy.
Pencil sketch by Ted Zuber.
Courtesy of Ted Zuber

Coup de main at Pegasus Bridge, Ranville, France, June 6, 1944.
Oil painting by Major Gerald Lacoste.
Courtesy of British Airborne Forces Charities.

Troarn, June 6, 1944. Oil painting by Major Gerald Lacoste.
Courtesy of British Airborne Forces Charities.

Merville Battery, June 6, 1944. Oil painting by Major Gerald Lacoste.
Courtesy of British Airborne Forces Charities.

"Gliders in a Wheatfield," by Captain W.A. Ogilvie, depicting destroyed
gliders near the mouth of the Orne River, July 1944.
Courtesy of the Canadian War Museum

A lone paratrooper works his way back to friendly lines through the
hedgerows of Normandy. Pencil sketch by Ted Zuber.

Courtesy of Ted Zuber

Searching for the enemy that always seemed to vanish, Ardennes, January 1945.
Pencil sketch by Ted Zuber.

Courtesy of Ted Zuber

Under fire in the Ardennes, January 1945.
Pencil sketch by Ted Zuber.
Courtesy of Ted Zuber

Winter patrol, Ardennes, January 1945. Pencil sketch by Ted Zuber.
Courtesy of Ted Zuber

Ardennes Patrol, winter 1944/45. Artwork by Tony Theobald.
Courtesy of the British Airborne Forces Charities

Operation Varsity, Rhine, March 1945.
Courtesy of British Airborne Forces Charities

Dangerous descent. The last combat drop for 1 Cdn Para Bn — Operation
Varsity, March 24, 1945. Pencil sketch by Ted Zuber.
Courtesy of Ted Zuber

Assault crossing of the Rhine, 6th Airborne Division, Operation Varsity,
March 24, 1945. Painting by John F. Sellars.
Courtesy of British Airborne Forces Charities

6th Airborne Division gliders landing during Operation Varsity near
Hamminkeln, March 24, 1945. Oil painting by John F. Sellars
Courtesy of British Airborne Forces Charities

Top and Bottom:
Members of 1 Cdn Para Bn assaulting directly off the Drop Zone in Roger
Chabot's painting "Op Varsity, 24 March 1945."
Courtesy of Roger Chabot

Concentrated mass drop of 1 Cdn Para Bn.
Pencil sketch by Ted Zuber.
Courtesy of Ted Zuber

Crossing the Rhine. Canadian commemorative stamp no. 1544. Reproduced
with permission.
Courtesy of Canada Post Corporation, 1995

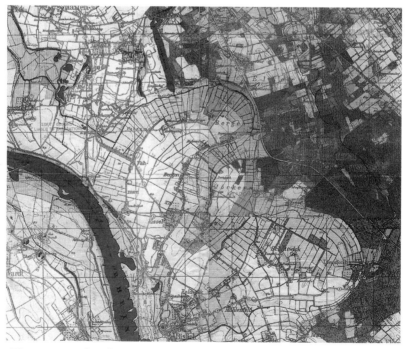

Lieutenant-Colonel Fraser Eadie's silk "escape map" for Operation Varsity.
Courtesy of the Canadian War Museum

"Entangled parachute," by Captain G.C. Tinning.
Courtesy of the Canadian War Museum

Airborne troops in Hamminkeln, 24 March 1945.

Airborne troops in Hamminkeln, March 24, 1945.
Artwork by Tony Theobald.
Courtesy of British Airborne Forces Charities

Paratrooper with Bren gun fighting in village.
Drawing by Peter Miles, Military Bivouacs Northumberland.
Courtesy of British Airborne Forces Charities

Confirming the enemy's location during the pursuit
through northwest Germany.
Courtesy of Ted Zuber

Senseless delay. Members of 1 Cdn Para Bn overcome
another enemy rear guard action.
Courtesy of Ted Zuber

SECONDE GUERRE MONDIALE · 1939-1945 · SECOND WORLD WAR

CANADA

1945

43

VETERANS RETURN HOME · LE RETOUR AU PAYS

Veterans returning home, 1945. Canadian commemorative stamp
no. 1541. Reproduced with permission.
Courtesy of Canada Post Corporation

disciplinary style as the unit's DCO had been tolerated by the untested troops, now it annoyed the "blooded" veterans. However, Nicklin's command approach was fully endorsed by Brigadier Hill, who believed that strong leadership was necessary to ensure that the paratroopers put forth full commitment and effort during training.

Part of the problem also lay in the difference between the old and the new CO. Lieutenant-Colonel Bradbrooke, prior to D-Day, had been judged by most, including his superiors, as acceptable insofar as he commanded a unit that had not seen combat. Brigadier Hill rated Bradbrooke as "a good administrator, a very good CO in peacetime and an intrepid parachutist."[694] However, in Normandy, Bradbrooke's leadership during the defence of the Le Mesnil crossroads and the subsequent pursuit of the retreating German forces was not up to Hill's, nor the unit's, expectations. As the Normandy Campaign progressed, Hill noted that Bradbrooke lacked the aggressive leadership required to lead his men during combat. It was not lost on the soldiers either that the CO was seldom seen on the front lines.

In comparison, the behaviour and demeanour of the Battalion's deputy commanding officer, Major Jeff Nicklin, caught Hill's attention. Nicklin had been very active throughout the entire course of the campaign. The ex-Canadian Football League star regularly visited his soldiers in their forward positions. Furthermore, he enjoyed the action and even took part in reconnaissance patrols. Nicklin was a rugged, physical individual who was feared and could sense fear, recalled Brigadier Hill.[695] In this officer, Hill discerned the leadership qualities that could prove very useful to supervise the Battalion's post-campaign training.

While Hill respected the accomplishments and sacrifices of his Canadian paratroopers, he had nevertheless learned a valuable leadership lesson while commanding soldiers during the Battle of France in 1940 and later paratroopers in North Africa in 1942. The Brigadier had observed that "blooded" veterans who returned from combat duty to resume daily training routine showed an unwillingness to "snap to it" and put up with various aspects of garrison duties and discipline. Therefore, he believed that a strong hand was required to once again motivate, closely supervise, and control battle-hardened troops. Hill was right. Having faced death and survived, many veterans now thought that they were better than their new, untested comrades. Hill identified this type of combatant as "heroes and crooked berets that had to be knocked on the head and have discipline reimposed."[696]

This post-operational mindset was now developing within 1 Cdn Para Bn. "Here we have very tough chaps, heroes," explained Hill. "They had to be disciplined. So, I popped in Jeff Nicklin."[697] In the end, regardless of what the paratroopers had accomplished, Hill would not shy away from his two airborne tenets — discipline and physical fitness. There was still much to accomplish, and the war was far from over.

The brigade and divisional headquarters staff now re-examined all facets of the Normandy Campaign in order to identify the strengths and weaknesses of the 6 AB Div. These could then be applied so as to better prepare the formation for their next operational mission. The staff quickly identified the formation's greatest strength as its organizational makeup, specifically the type of units within the Division and its training program. In addition, in the Normandy Campaign the proficiency of 6 AB Div lay in the exploitation of the initial element of surprise following the jump. This enabled the Division to successfully attain all of its D-Day tasks.

However, there were also points to improve. The coordination of its operational planning with higher formations was assessed as weak. The communications between the various airborne units and the ability to obtain and rapidly deploy reinforcements also needed improvement. Additionally, the coordination of resupply airdrops of sufficient quantities of ammunition for its airborne light artillery batteries had to be improved. Headquarters staff also observed that the Division's personnel needed to improve target identification for air strikes and requests to obtain additional artillery support, as well as the requirement to upgrade their counter-mortar drills. These skills were critical in light of the paratroopers' lack of heavy weaponry. Recommendations were also made to augment the airborne sappers' equipment tables so as to increase their contribution to the Division. Finally, the planners agreed that it was imperative for the survival of the paratroopers that the link-up between ground forces and airborne troops take place within the first forty-eight hours of the operation.[698]

Brigadier Hill studied these recommendations. He also promulgated his own three main lessons learned. The first was that it is better to command in action untried, well-trained, and well-disciplined troops than to command troops with considerable battle experience who may be termed "battle conceited." Untried troops tended to adapt quickly to different situations, used initiative, and were willing to take more risks. This was due to the fact that they had not been previously exposed to the dangers and horrors of war. Secondly, the Brigadier noted that brave men without discipline lasted only two or three days without breaking. However, with discipline they lasted seemingly beyond the bounds of human endurance. Lastly, during the Brigade's initial D-Day tasks and subsequent missions, regardless of the chaos, it was imperative to maintain all efforts on the primary objective and never deviate from the aim of the mission.[699]

Overall, the leadership of 6 AB Div agreed that the individual paratrooper had been well trained for the campaign and that he had performed remarkably well. Therefore they believed that if the Division addressed its weaknesses, it would further enhance its operational effectiveness. Remarkably, the Brigadier felt that at the unit level no major changes were required. As such all three battalions were directed to proceed with their collective training programs.

As the units began their training, Hill convened a conference for the commanding officers on September 26, 1944. The commander of 3 Para Bde unveiled the Brigade's future operations.[700] Hill announced that 3 Parachute Brigade could be called upon to deploy to Burma and that the men were to be informed of this possibility.[701] He then proceeded to outline the Brigade's training objectives for the month of October. Above and beyond each battalion's collective training program, Hill insisted that special attention be given to physical fitness, which was still the Brigade's top priority. He directed that each paratrooper was required to undergo and pass two tests: a ten-mile forced march in full equipment, to be completed in two hours, and a fifteen-mile forced march in P.T. kit and boots, to be completed in three hours.[702]

Hill also demanded that intensive weapons training was to be continued and carefully supervised. The Brigadier demanded that by the end of October all airborne personnel be qualified on personal and support weapons, as well as have completed street fighting and live fire training.[703] Moreover, Hill emphasized that during exercises, special attention was to be directed at getting all weapons into action as quickly as possible. Due to the problems observed by Hill in combat in Normandy, he realized that the Brigade needed to focus specific attention on improving its firepower. He directed his paratroops to put in extra hours to improve their marksmanship on the rifle and Sten gun. Hill understood that part of the Brigade's firepower problem was the inability of the soldiers to properly utilize their current weapon systems.[704] As a result, Hill ordered that one section of each PIAT platoon be sent on a six-pounder anti-tank course. With the possible addition of these guns to the Brigade, personnel were also required to undergo glider training, so as to learn the proper loading, transporting, and unloading of these weapons.[705]

Hill also directed that extra parachute training be incorporated into the program. Each unit was ordered to organize a monthly battalion- or company-level jump. Integrated within the jump training was the testing of a new trial reinforced leg kit bag.[706] The use of the previous model of this personal equipment container had proved disastrous during the D-Day. Each unit was also required to prepare its personnel for a brigade-level mass drop scheduled to take place between October 6 and 8, 1944.

On the tactical side, the Brigadier insisted that during night exercises, paratroopers improve their night movement.[707] In addition, each battalion was to include in seven days for street fighting its October schedule. Allied planners informed 6 AB Div of the likelihood that the ground war in Germany would be a long and grueling campaign that would spill into towns and cities. Taking this into account, Hill ordered each battalion to create four specialist groups to be trained to assault and operate in urban settings. The groups consisted of: a mine and wire group (one platoon per company was to specialize in mine warfare and the use of the bangalore torpedo); covering groups (to provide fire support for both the close break-in party and the main assault group); an assault group, including a Royal Engineer assault group; and a reserve group.[708]

The last item on the agenda dealt with the removal of unsuitable personnel. On this issue Hill was unyielding. Regardless of rank, those who had not performed up to expectation during the Normandy Campaign, or who were unable to maintain the airborne standard, were to be identified by September 28.[709] These individuals would then be immediately posted out of the battalions. During the entire course of the meeting, the commanding officers detected a sense of urgency. This could only mean one thing. The Brigade would once again be deployed in the very near future.

The 1st Canadian Parachute Battalion had its work cut out for it. It was a long way from its pre-D-Day level of operational readiness. Lieutenant-Colonel Jeff Nicklin accepted this challenge without hesitation. The men immediately noted the change in tempo. "The training got more severe," recalled Sergeant John Feduck, "and nothing was let go. Nothing was overlooked." He added, "Nicklin was the type of guy, who did everything strictly by the book, and he had his own way of training, making sure you went for your runs. There was no slacking off." Nicklin's training schedule was very simple. "You trained all the time," stated Feduck. "You had no time for yourself. Leaves were a little shorter and you worked harder."[710]

Physical training under Nicklin "was a hell of a lot tougher," recalled Sergeant Harry Reid. "He wanted us to become linebackers."[711] The new commanding officer's objective was clear. "He wanted to have the best battalion in the Brigade," explained Sergeant Andy Anderson. "Nicklin had us out on the parade square at six o'clock in the morning and worked us till dark." The NCO noted, "Brigadier Hill was thrilled and he did not object to that." Nicklin really enjoyed the physical part of the training. He personally led the bimonthly ten-mile forced march. As the paratroopers arrived at the finish line, "he [Nicklin] and the RSM would stand at the gate with a clipboard," recounted Anderson, "and took down the names of the stragglers." No quarter was given. "If they could not keep up," stated Anderson, "they were gone."[712] Nicklin wanted each platoon to arrive at the finish line as a group.

Nicklin's Normandy experience had confirmed that a well-trained group that worked together skillfully could inflict greater damage than a few isolated paratroopers. Since the Battalion's return from France, Nicklin inculcated the importance of teamwork in all training to both the veterans and to the reinforcements. He had personally experienced the benefits and results of this concept, as well as the close-knit camaraderie that it fostered, during his tenure with the Canadian Football League's Winnipeg Blue Bombers. He realized that teamwork was vital in winning football games. Nicklin knew that it would also enhance the effectiveness of his paratroopers.

Furthermore, Nicklin insisted that all his officers become team players. They were now ordered to take part with their men in all training activities. Under Nicklin there were no exceptions. "He started pushing them hard," recalled Sergeant Roland Larose. "He ordered all the officers to take part in these runs and physical training exercises."[713] This was one of the rare Nicklin training directives that the troops appreciated.

Although the leadership approach to training had changed, the unit's overall training activities were identical to those conducted during the pre-Normandy period.[714] However, inserted throughout the weekly schedule were refresher courses to address the Battalion's perennial weaknesses, specifically, radio communications and map reading. Map reading had been identified as a subject that had to be improved on. Many had experienced various degrees of difficulties using their maps to find their exact locations following the dispersed drop in Normandy. To further enhance the navigational skills of the airborne soldiers, aerial photograph interpretation lectures were added to the training program.

Despite the demanding schedule training went smoothly.[715] This was attributed to the fact that 1 Cdn Para Bn instructors had attended numerous specialized courses and gained valuable experience during the past twelve months in England. Furthermore, the Battalion now had a good nucleus of well-trained veterans in its ranks. During his visits, Hill noted that the overall instruction and training were superior to that given prior to D-Day. The Brigadier was confident that these seasoned officers and NCOs could quickly bring the Battalion to a level that would surpass their pre-D-Day standard. However, time was of the essence. Throughout the fall of 1944, Hill regularly reminded his Battalion COs, "Time is very short" and "training must be simple and restricted to the bare essentials."[716]

Seeing that unit-level training was proceeding efficiently, Hill now wanted to test the three battalions in a Brigade exercise. After only ten days of training, the units received their Warning Order for Exercise Fog, which took place October 9 and 10. The main objective of the exercise was to organize a large-scale parachute operation in conjunction with the United States Army Air Force (9th Troop Carrying Command). Together they would practise the drop of an entire brigade onto one drop zone. Planning and timing were critical. Hill wanted to confirm whether the DZ could be cleared of all personnel twenty minutes after the first man had landed.

The subsequent tactical phase involved practising night movement, securing key road junctions under the cover of darkness, and evacuating casualties.[717] Specifically, 1 Cdn Para Bn was tasked to link up with glider elements and lead them to the Brigade's final objective. Next the Canadian paratroopers were tasked to seize and hold a key terrain feature east of Shrewton and prevent enemy deployments south of their position.[718] The Battalion performed well. The unit attained all its objectives and fought off small enemy attacks until late the next morning. Following the exercise, the paratroopers took part in a two-and-a-half-hour forced march back to Bulford.[719]

Exercise Fog had revealed many valuable lessons. The two most important were the development of DZ fighting drills and the creation of an identification marking system that enabled the paratroopers to quickly reassemble upon landing by sub-units. Hill also directed that the first battalion to land be designated the "DZ battalion." Its primary role consisted of securing the drop zone. Once this was done, the designated paratroopers were responsible for clearing any enemy resistance in the vicinity of the DZ and disrupting any potential counterattacks by directing artillery fire on enemy troop concentrations and by denying them the use of roads leading to the drop zone. This new tactic was designed to enable the follow-on parachute battalions to land safely, vacate the DZ within minutes, and rush to their initial objectives unopposed.[720]

For 1 Cdn Para Bn, the exercise provided the unit with an opportunity to integrate, for the first time, the new reinforcements into the unit in a field setting. The first few weeks had proven difficult for the new men. "That's when the BS [bull shit] started, the attitude of some of veterans was, 'We were there [Normandy] and you weren't,'" explained Major Hilborn.[721] The new men had to prove to the veterans that they could indeed fit in and, more importantly, keep up.

Nicklin had anticipated this situation and told his officers he would not put up with such behaviour. "There was no lording over others," recalled Lieutenant Alf Tucker. Nicklin insisted that all veterans use "their experience to show the replacements how to react and protect themselves or how to act in a manner that was in their best interest."

"I remember," explained Tucker, "that the officers took that to heart."[722]

"The problem," said Hilborn, "now became one of reintegrating the old with the new. They all had to be taught to think alike."[723] A redeeming factor was that the reinforcements were all qualified paratroopers. They had also undergone advanced weapons and fieldcraft training similar to that of the 1st Canadian Parachute Battalion. Thus, the men had a good handle on their basic skills. They just had to be accepted by the veterans. "They were shunned for a while," remarked Sergeant Anderson, "but by the time we went to the Ardennes, they were accepted by the veterans." Despite the haughty attitudes, Private Carignan felt very reassured. "We had NCOs and guys who had combat experience gained in Normandy," he confided. "It raised my level of confidence."[724]

The integration of the new members eventually worked itself out. By mid-October 1944, the Battalion's training program was progressing well and the undesirables had been weeded out. Corporal Richard Creelman commented, "There were quite a few that did not come up to what they were expected to and they were replaced. They [Battalion Headquarters] found out quickly who were the leaders and who weren't." Those who chose to remain knew that they would have to work hard. "We had some experience by now," said Creelman, "and we knew what was expected of us. We knew what it was like getting shot at."[725]

It was also easier to keep the men in line. "All you had to do," explained Sergeant Larose, "was to tell them to smarten up, or they'd be back to the Canadian Army. That was it."[726] Even though the training was difficult, the pride of wearing the distinctive maroon beret and the unique Canadian Parachute Badge, as well as the fact that they were the first to take the fight to the enemy, were reasons enough for the paratroopers to dig deeper and find the energy to keep up with the unrelenting tempo.

Those who remained were extremely professional. They were self-motivated and possessed good leadership skills and initiative. "In the Nicklin regime, we had to be prepared and were expected to take on a lot of initiative," revealed Andy Anderson. "Certain phases during the exercises were especially prepared to evaluate candidates [all ranks] and their use of initiative," he explained. "You would be briefed and once you landed [during an exercise], referees would black arm band [identification system used during an exercise to simulate casualties and wounded personnel] a certain percentage of your stick." A paratrooper would then be designated by the referees to carry on with the unit's task. "You had to know where you were," stated Anderson, "who was missing, what you had to do and what resources were at your disposal. This was a new part of the training that had been derived from our Normandy experience." He concluded, "This training really paid off." Quick thinking and adapting to any situation resulted in the mission's success. It also kept casualties to a minimum.

These qualities would be critical when the unit was required to fight in built-up areas as the Allied planners had warned.[727] "Nicklin took a personal interest in these courses and was a stickler for realism," recalled Andy Anderson. The degree of realism during the house-to-house combat training was extremely dangerous due to the use of live ammunition and explosives. Anderson remembered one such dangerous incident:

> He [Nicklin] wanted me to lay booby traps, explosives and mines. "I don't want any little thunder flashes, I want some real scary explosives," ordered Nicklin. So I rigged a booby-trap in the door way and attached a 27 Detonator to a length of prima cord. This cord came in coils. I cut a length and placed it under a floor board. What I failed to

realize was that the prima cord coiled back on itself and formed a clump. I remember standing at the end of a street observing a platoon carrying out its house-clearing drills. It was Corporal [Roland] Larose's group. He charged into the house, and the door way blew up. Larose and two other guys got blown back into the street. A shocked Captain who was standing beside me suddenly yelled out, "Oh! My God. You've killed them all!" We ran down the street and there was Nicklin, standing there with a big smile. Luckily no one was hurt. He turned to me and said, "Now, that's what I call a good exercise."[728]

Another live fire drill consisted of walking down a street and shooting at pop-up targets. "It was a difficult exercise," explained Roland Larose, "there must have been at least ten pop-up targets. I got in about three quarters of the way down the street and was declared 'killed.'"[729] He added, "It was great training. We also learned how to jump through windows, use toggle ropes to climb walls and I learned how to use a flame thrower."[730]

Despite the challenging training, the paratroopers were becoming increasingly annoyed with certain aspects of their commanding officer's uncompromising level of discipline. Roland Larose recalled one particular case. "Sometimes NCOs, had to give drill exercise to defaulters [paratroopers who had committed infractions or had not performed up to expectation]. He [Nicklin] got them to wear a smock with a big yellow stripe down their back. That really cheesed us off," said Larose. "You can only push a guy so far ... They weren't yellow, that's the part we didn't like."[731]

Even the smallest detail did not escape Nicklin's watchful eye. "We used to have to blanco [colour] our stripes [rank insignia] white," stated Corporal Ernie Jeans. He went on, "I didn't do that because I wasn't on parade much. However, one day, Nicklin noted my stripes and hollered at me from across the parade square. I had to race over and I had a lot of explaining to do."[732] By mid-October, a group of paratroopers decided that they would no longer put up with this excessive discipline and organized a hunger strike.

On October 20, the Battalion War Diary entry reported that the men were formed up for the evening supper parade; however, they refused to eat their meal.[733] This hunger strike was organized by a group of malcontents to protest what Captain Madden described as "a parade square type discipline."[734] Madden explained, "The men saw it as chick-enshit ... They knew that so many of the manifestations of this parade square discipline were unessential to getting the job done in war."[735] Private Jan de Vries added, "Many paratroopers were uncomfortable with this course of action." However, he conceded, "We were put in a position that we had to show solidarity and go with the flow."[736]

Although discipline was an integral element of a military life, Nicklin enforced it with an iron hand on absolutely every facet of the daily lives of his men. "He imposed such requirements," complained Madden, "that when they went to the canteen at night, they couldn't go casually dressed. They had to go with their battledress jacket buttoned up. They couldn't wear their fatigue shoes; they had to wear proper ammunition boots, and that sort of thing."[737] The hunger strike came at an inopportune moment. With the influx of a large number of new paratroopers, NCOs, and officers, the incident could cause irreparable damage to the unit's cohesiveness and morale. Many officers were very concerned by this turn of events. While some backed the CO's actions wholeheartedly, others thought that Nicklin was unnecessarily hard on the men. "It was disconcerting," lamented Madden, "in that you were expected to go back to battle with these guys and here they had, you know, dug in their heels and shown that they weren't prepared to obey orders or do what was required...."[738]

Lieutenant William Jenkins agreed. "It was an unpleasant experience around camp," he stated, "because morale was usually very very high. But, now whose part do you take. You could not condemn them [the men] for what they did. The position that most of us [officers] took, was that it was your business and do whatever you like ... It was a tense peri-od for a while."[739] The strike went on for the next three days and further strained the relations between the men, the NCOs, and the officers.[740]

Brigadier Hill monitored the situation and finally, on October 23, decided to intervene. Hill ordered the entire Battalion to be assembled in the base auditorium. Upon Hill's arrival all officers and warrant offi-cers were asked to leave. The men were then given a few minutes to pres-ent their concerns. The Brigade Commander then interjected, "Look, you are letting the whole party down." He then appealed to their sense of pride. "More importantly," he chided, "you are letting Canada down."[741] The meeting was short and to the point. Deep down, the para-troopers knew that the Brigadier was right. He was a professional sol-dier and would not tolerate such nonsense. Hill ended the meeting abruptly. "Now," he emphatically stated, "I am making it absolutely clear

I am giving you an order, and you are going back to eat your lunch."[742]
A few hours later, Brigadier Hill was informed that the Canadian paratroopers had done as they were told.

The following day, six paratroopers requested to meet with the
Brigadier. They identified themselves as the ringleaders and apologized
for their behaviour. Hill was impressed by this show of character:

> I accepted their apologies and thanked them very much
> for coming in. I always loved those Canadians and that
> made me love them more and more. That couldn't have
> happened to any other battalion except a Canadian bat-
> talion. It was wonderful. Of course, really, that I had the
> grip on them to some extent was that I loved them, lit-
> erally. If you love people you are commanding and,
> lead, they will always reciprocate.[743]

Although the men had given in, Nicklin refused to change his
rules. "Major Eadie, the Battalion's Second in Command," remarked
Sergeant Anderson, "told me after the war that on many occasions he
asked Nicklin to back off on certain issues regarding discipline. But he
refused to do so."[744]

With the hunger strike behind them, everything returned back to
normal at Carter Barracks, and the Battalion started its November
training. Brigadier Hill instructed Nicklin to further enhance the street-
fighting techniques, weapons handling, and demolition training of his
paratroopers. These would be tested during upcoming battalion- and
brigade-level exercises.[745] Additionally, new experimentation and training were to be conducted on the lighter American 60-mm mortar during the first week of November. The Brigade wanted to confirm if it was
indeed easier for the paratroopers to jump with this mortar, instead of
the heavier British three-inch mortar. However, it was stipulated that
the American mortar would be used only during the initial twenty-four
hours of an operation.[746] Mortar personnel would then revert to use
their regular three-inch mortar, which would be brought forward by
their supply personnel the next day.

During the month of November, Hill visited Nicklin and ordered
him to prepare a battalion exercise to evaluate two specific areas. The
first involved the assessment of the Battalion's deputy commanding
officer and his ability to take over command of the unit in a combat situation. In the event that a battalion commander was captured or killed,

Hill wanted to confirm that the DCO could quickly take over command and complete the mission. The second test item was the evaluation of the ability of the paratroops to fight against enemy armour deployed in open country.[747] The Brigadier wanted to affirm that the paratroopers could defend and hold their positions until help arrived regardless of the type of enemy encountered.

As part of the increased training, the paratroopers concentrated on drills and tactics for assaulting enemy pillboxes and fortified positions. Whereas as the Brigadier was confident in the ability of his men to deal with enemy fortifications and armour, he was very concerned about his Brigade's ability to fight in a lengthy winter operation. He knew that the British Army supply system did not have the required equipment to properly outfit the men for prolonged winter deployments. To counter the lack of proper clothing, Hill stressed the importance of maintaining high morale during difficult weather conditions. Furthermore, he ordered his COs to ensure that their men be fit and able to travel in a C-47 aircraft, in low temperatures, for an extended period of time.[748] Hill closely monitored these capabilities during Brigade exercises.

With the Brigadier's numerous objectives in mind, Lieutenant-Colonel Nicklin briefed the entire Battalion on November 17, 1944, in preparation for Exercise Eve. On November 21, the Battalion emplaned at Gosfield airfield and, following a one-hour flight, jumped with various containers and heavy weapons onto the DZ.[749] Companies then assembled at their respective RVs and prepared to assault designated enemy positions.[750] Following their successful attacks, the Canadian paratroopers bolstered their defensive positions and waited for a combined infantry and armour counterattack. To their chagrin, the attack never materialized and the exercise ended by mid-afternoon.[751]

During the course of the last week of November the companies continued their range work, physical fitness, and small sub-unit exercises with renewed vigour, anticipating their first well-deserved long furlough.[752] In this instance, they were not disappointed. The month of December started off with a ten-day privilege leave. This was then followed by a special two-day leave granted by the commander of 6 AB Div. Upon return, the well-rested soldiers resumed their regular company and specialist platoon training until December 19. During this time the paratroopers eagerly looked forward to a peaceful Christmas leave. They would be sorely disappointed.

CHAPTER NINE

Christmas Interlude — The Ardennes

Looking back on the whole Ardennes involvement, one would have to say it was not one of the highlights of the Battalion history in the war ... It was a time that everything seemed to be shrouded in both confusion and mystery ... the Ardennes was not so much covered with glory, as extreme hardship.
Sergeant R.F. Anderson [753]

As the paratroopers busily trained in England, the Allied armies slowly ground their way across occupied Europe toward the German border. Tenacious German resistance made it a painful and costly process. But, much to the surprise of Allied commanders, the Germans were not yet fully committed to the defensive. Unbeknownst to them, Hitler planned one final offensive gamble in the West.

During the first two weeks of December 1944, Hitler ordered that the armoured units, mechanized infantry, and parachute forces of Army Group "B," under the command of Field-Marshal Walter Model, take up positions between the cities of Moncschau and Echternach, located near the German border. [754] Terrible weather conditions enabled the German commanders to move large forces undetected to their front lines. Hitler's plan was both daring and simple. Following an intense artillery barrage along this entire front, tanks accompanied by mechanized infantry would break through the weakly defended Ardennes sector. During this rapid advance both flanks would be secured by infantry while the remainder of the German mechanized force raced west to seize a series of the bridges over the Meuse between Liege and Givet.[755] Once these objectives were secured, the German troops were to continue their advance toward Antwerp.

In theory the plan was simple. But its execution was a different matter. For this reason, Field-Marshal von Rundstedt, Commander-in-Chief of the Western Front, was totally opposed to this operation. "Antwerp!" he lamented. "If we reach the Meuse we should go down on our knees and thank God!"[756] Rundstedt's skepticism was shared by all Army commanders who were involved in the Fuhrer's latest gambit. Even Hitler's loyal general, SS-Obergruppenführer Josef "Sepp" Dietrich, Commander-in-Chief of the 6th SS Panzer Army, was very concerned with the campaign's overall planning. Later, Dietrich confided:

> I had merely to cross a river, capture Brussels and then go on to take the port of Antwerp. And all this in the worst months of the year, December, January, February, through the countryside where snow was waist deep and there wasn't room to deploy four tanks abreast, let alone six armored divisions; when it didn't get light until eight in the morning and it was dark again at four in the afternoon; with divisions that had just been reformed and contained chiefly raw, untried recruits; and at Christmas time.[757]

Nevertheless, at 0530 hours, on December 16, 1944, following a heavy artillery barrage, more than two hundred thousand German troops massed on a forty-five-mile front and started their advance against eighty thousand unprepared American soldiers.[758] This attack caught the defenders completely by surprise. Within hours, complete chaos reigned in the American sector. By December 18, the enemy armour had overrun 28 of the 109 American divisions deployed in the area. The lead elements of the Panzer units had advanced thirty-two kilometres, wreaking havoc and occupying Trois Ponts and Vielsalm. The next day the 5th Panzer Army had reached Hotton, Marche, and Laroche.[759]

Having sustained heavy losses in material and men during the first days of the onslaught, General Dwight D. Eisenhower, Supreme Commander of the Allied Expeditionary Forces, turned to Field Marshal Montgomery on December 20 for assistance. Eisenhower instructed Montgomery to take over the command of the First and Ninth U.S. Armies. His primary mission was to stabilize the front and organize reinforcements. Once this was accomplished, the Allies would then go on the offensive.

That same day, back in England, Major-General Eric L. Bols, the newly appointed commander of the 6th Airborne Division, received an order to prepare his Division for immediate deployment to Belgium.[760] Within the hour, Lieutenant-Colonel Jeff Nicklin ordered all ranks to prepare to deploy to the continent once again. Preparations were carried out in a hasty manner. "It was very sudden," recalled Del Parlee. "Some of us were rooted out of bed. We were the advance party."[761] This small group left without delay to Folkstone, where it oversaw the unit's embarkation preparations. Despite the sudden flurry of activities, no additional details were provided by either the Division or the Brigade. Contrary to their D-Day experience, the Battalion's soldiers and officers received no briefings as to the unit's role or area of operation.[762] To add to the conundrum, all ranks were warned that the Division's move to the seaport was categorized as "secret" and should not be discussed with anyone.[763]

The next afternoon, on December 21, Hill summoned his battalion commanders for a briefing on the impending deployment to the continent. He directed that all paratroopers be placed on six hours' notice to move as of 0600 hours, December 22. The Brigadier also shared what little information he had received from 6 AB Div Headquarters. It appeared that the 3 Para Bde's main focus would be patrolling. Since the units had done very little patrolling following their return from Normandy, the Brigadier ordered his unit COs to instruct their officers and NCOs to review the patrol drills.[764] Hill also insisted that the scale of clothing and equipment "be cut down in everything not absolutely essential except arms and ammunition." These directives only added to the mystery.[765] Regardless, the paratroopers eagerly accepted this latest challenge.

On Christmas Eve, the Canadians embarked on a train and headed for Folkstone. Upon their arrival, the men were treated to a Christmas dinner. Shortly after, at 0400 hours on December 26, the airborne soldiers departed Britain on the S.S. *Canterbury*. It was only when the vessel had left the English coastal waters that the officers were informed that they were to land in Ostend, Belgium.[766] While the Canadians were eager to fight, they were nevertheless very disappointed that they were not parachuted into the combat zone. "We were supposed to be paratroopers," stated Sergeant Harry Reid, "and here we were being loaded on a damn boat."[767] It was by no means a pleasant trip. "We were jammed like sardines," recalled Corporal Ernie Jeans. "Most people slept on the floor. It was quite crisp."[768] As the vessel steamed toward the continent, the temperature continued to drop. The weather conditions in Belgium were still very severe. The heavy cloud cover grounded all Allied aircraft. Furthermore, information as to the Battalion's area of deployment was still unavailable. "No one knew what was going on," recalled a concerned Major Richard Hilborn. "It was great confusion."[769]

The paratroopers docked in Ostend after an uneventful trip. As the men disembarked and the equipment was unloaded, Major Fraser Eadie asked a divisional officer what exactly was going on. The information was still sketchy. However, the officer confided that he "had heard that Jerry cracked through in the Ardennes." The officer figured "we were plugging a hole," stated Eadie.[770] 1 Cdn Para Bn personnel then quickly boarded trucks and headed toward Taintignies, Belgium.[771]

Meanwhile Lieutenant-Colonel Nicklin and his Headquarters personnel joined a group of British officers from 3 Para Bde HQ. Together they left Ostend to reconnoiter the area that was assigned to the Brigade.[772] Despite the great sense of urgency, the paratroopers still did not have a clue as to their next destination. "It was hazy," recollected Sergeant Art Stammers, "I didn't know where we were going."[773] Following this cold, uncomfortable, eight-and-a-half-hour truck ride the paratroopers finally arrived in Taintignies. The men were billeted in a nearby village in groups of two in unheated homes. The next few days were spent preparing and waiting. In the early hours of December 31, the paratroopers were ordered to relocate to Maredet.

This was welcome news. Morale had plummeted during this frustrating waiting period. After six days in Belgium, the Battalion had not yet been deployed to the front lines. Finally, on January 1, 1945, 6 AB Div received its orders. The Division was tasked to deploy and hold the front extending from the towns of Givet to Hargimont located in the southern sector of the front. 3 Para Bde was tasked to occupy defensive positions extending from Rochefort to Aye. The next day, 1 Cdn Para Bn moved into Rochefort while 8 Para Bn took up positions in Boisonville and 9 Para Bn occupied the town of Humain.[774]

The Battalion's first task was to defend all roads leading to Rochefort. For the next sixteen days of this short campaign, 1 Cdn Para Bn's role consisted mainly of reconnaissance and standing patrols, as well as occupying defensive positions and manning observation posts. Attached to the Battalion were four forward observation officers. These specialists were tasked with providing immediate fire support to the paratroopers. At their disposal were numerous batteries of 25-pounder guns located behind the Battalion's positions.[775] However, by this time, the last German attacks on Bastogne, which took place on January 3 and 4, had been contained. The enemy's offensive had ground to a full stop. In the meantime, the American troops, who had felt the brunt of the onslaught, regrouped as fresh troops arrived daily.

Even though the tide had turned, the Canadian paratroopers were nevertheless astounded by the degree of devastation that had been caused by the German offensive. "There were quantities of abandoned American equipment and bodies still on the sides of the roads," recalled Sergeant Anderson. "We were shocked by this disaster. There were overturned and burnt out jeeps, trucks and tanks," he added. "I remember sitting in a shack that we used as a headquarters during an early morning, these horse drawn carts passed by with twenty to thirty dead American bodies. It was endless."[776]

Certain American units had sustained such heavy losses that they were forced to deploy anyone who was available, regardless of their trade. Lieutenant Alf Tucker was surprised by the type of American troops defending the front lines. "A singular memory of the Ardennes was an anti-tank gun manned by clerks," recalled Tucker, "commanding the main road but plunked in the middle of it." He continued, "It was a good indication of the quality of troops being thrown into the battle."[777] Even untrained soldiers were now needed to plug the gap in the weakened Allied defensive line.

The extreme weather conditions further added to the discomfort of the hostile and sombre surroundings. To provide some comfort to the ill-equipped paratroopers, each company set up their headquarters and kitchens in large buildings or barns located at a safe distance from the front lines. These shelters were turned into a form of base camp. This enabled the airborne soldiers to sleep, eat, and be briefed in a safe and warm environment. Once settled in, each section and platoon was given an overview of their patrolling and defensive tasks. The men felt confident in their weapons skills and tactics. However, after the first few days in the Ardennes, all were concerned that the lack of proper winter clothing and footwear would hamper their fighting skills. The elements became the real enemy.

"My prevalent memory of the Ardennes was that it was very cold," shuddered Sergeant Denis Flynn. "It seemed where we were going was always colder than the place we just left."[778] The Brigadier anticipated that frozen feet would be the major problem during this deployment. Regrettably, appropriate winter footwear was in very short supply. In the interim, Hill ordered that great care be taken to ensure proper foot care.[779] Feet of all personnel were to be inspected and rubbed twice daily. "It was a terrible shock for us to be in snow up to our knees with only our regular black boots and Denison Smocks," recollected Sergeant Andy Anderson. The type of footwear worn during this campaign was totally ineffective.

"I brought the issue of lack of proper footwear and clothing," stated Corporal Jeans, "to our medical officer. He told me not too much could be done. We just had to endure."[780] Sergeant Reid observed, "These leather boots were not the thing to wear in the winter — they had steel toe and heel caps and 13 hob nails."[781] Corporal John Ross recalled that his company had some extra blankets. These were quickly put to good use. "We'd cut them up and made booties," explained Ross. "We put them over our boots to sleep in. I was sure happy that we had them."[782] While some devised ways to keep their feet warm, others such as Private Joe King simply refused to take their boots off. "I was afraid I couldn't get them back on," he said.[783] Static defensive duties became the most difficult tasks. Long hours spent sitting in slit trenches resulted in numerous cases of badly frozen feet. To alleviate this terrible problem, paratroopers resorted to wrapping lengths of burlap and tying them to their boots for added warmth.[784]

It did not take long for the resourceful paratroopers to devise other means to keep warm. "Being Canadians," remarked Major Hilborn, "I thought we adjusted to the weather conditions better than anyone else."[785] The ingenuity and scavenger instincts of the paratroopers quickly kicked in. Spare blankets were converted into ponchos and extra woollen socks doubled as gloves. While on patrol, the airborne soldiers entered abandoned homes and brought back any type of fabric that they could find. Some men found a sewing machine, which was quickly put to good use.[786] Blankets were cut up and stitched into the smocks. These makeshift liners were then stuffed with newspapers and magazines.[787] Others made hoods and sewed them onto the collars of the Denison Smocks.

Another important issue of concern was the personal camouflage of the airborne soldiers. While on their first patrols the paratroopers felt extremely vulnerable walking through snow-covered fields wearing their green, brown, and khaki camouflage smocks and their khaki battledress trousers. The Normandy veterans knew the tactical and life-saving importance of camouflage uniforms. Having examined a few captured German reversible winter parkas (white/camouflage), the soldiers decided to make their own. "We found some needles and thread, and we'd tear up white bed sheets. Pretty soon," stated Corporal Richard Creelman, "you'd see more and more of those, they were just stitched together, anything for camouflage."[788]

However, despite Canadian ingenuity and stamina, the cold was an enemy that was not easily defeated. "The Ardennes was a horrible war," acknowledged Private King. "Just terrible weather, much like the Canadian winters. Everything was cold in the Ardennes."[789] Sergeant Anderson recalled, "I was amazed that we did not lose more men to the elements."[790]

"The poor guys suffered more from frost bites and colds rather than wounds," asserted Corporal Jeans, who served as a Battalion medical orderly. The severe conditions started to affect the morale of the paratroopers. "My guys were always cold," recalled Lieutenant Jenkins, "when you are cold your morale is not very high. If any one factor disturbed them, it was the cold."[791]

But there was a war to fight. On January 4, 1945, Division Headquarters ordered 3 Para Bde to dispatch patrols on the Rochefort and Waverville roads. Subsequently, 1 Cdn Para Bn was tasked by Brigade Headquarters to protect artillery batteries that were establishing new positions west of these roads. In addition, the Battalion was to patrol in the region north of the Waverville road.[792] There seemed to be was very little enemy activity in this area, but the threat was always there. The hilly terrain, the thick forests, and the low cloud cover shielded the enemy patrols while severely restricting long-range observation. "You couldn't see anything," recalled Sergeant Stammers.[793] Therefore, countless hours were spent patrolling through the hills and forests, walking through the deep snow to confirm that enemy troops had not returned to operate behind Allied lines.

In actuality, offensive action was the furthest thing from the enemy's mind. The Canadians' eagerness for a fight was curbed by the German withdrawal tactics. "Every day, it seemed, we moved up to attack a village," recalled Private Jan de Vries, "we shelled a bit, then found that the Germans had left."[794] Frustration soon set in. "We spent a lot of time marching. It was very dull — march, march, march," lamented Sergeant Denis Flynn. "We weren't very happy to be wandering around like that, and every time we caught up with the enemy they would withdraw. We had no heavy contact, just a light fire fight and then they would disappear."[795] A dejected Corporal Del Parlee added, "It was always over by the time we got there."[796] An equally disappointed Lieutenant Alex Rossiter stated, "We came over here all pepped up to fight, then we found out, that they don't want to play. It's been something of a jolt all round."[797]

Despite the frustrating tactics carried out by a very elusive and cunning enemy, the paratroopers were repeatedly warned to proceed with caution. One morning, Harry Wright left with his group on a reconnaissance patrol. The sector had been quiet for the past few days. As the patrol headed toward a few abandoned buildings, a concealed German machine gunner opened fire. Within seconds three men lay on the ground severely wounded. One of them was Sergeant Wright. "I was hit in the face," shuddered Wright. "A bullet came in the left side of my face and came out the right. I had lost four teeth."[798] Even though there was very little activity in the 1 Cdn Para Bn sector, such isolated incidents nevertheless kept the stress levels of the paratroopers very high.

Another troubling factor further complicated the tasks of the Canadian paratroopers. They were briefed to be on the lookout for German soldiers dressed in American uniforms, who were operating behind the front lines. These men were part of a group led by SS-Obersturmbannführer Otto Skorzeny, a master in special operations. Skorzeny had been ordered by Hitler to recruit and train English-speaking personnel. They were to operate as a special mobile, long-range penetration force. Their mission, code-named Operation Grief, consisted of capturing one or more bridges on the Meuse River between Liège and Namur. To facilitate their movements behind the American front lines, Skorzeny's volunteers were trained to use American weapons, drive American military vehicles, and adopt the demeanour of the average American soldier.

As the Germans launched their attack on December 16, 1944, Skorzeny's group simultaneously set into motion Operation Grief. Under the cover of a massive artillery barrage they raced ahead and infiltrated American positions. These small groups never reached the bridges over the Meuse River. Nevertheless, during the first days they carried out acts of sabotage, cut telephone lines, disrupted and diverted

American reinforcement columns, and spread rumours that added to the chaos and confusion.

While their tactical accomplishments were very limited, the psychological impact on the Allied soldiers wreaked havoc. American soldiers arrested and detained other American soldiers. General Omar Bradley, commander of the 12th Army Group, was extremely upset by this course of events, which led to "half a million GI's [General Issue, term for American soldiers] playing cat and mouse with each other every time they met."[799] Rumours were circulating that some of these German infiltration groups were on their way to assassinate General Eisenhower and other high-ranking officers. This threat forced Eisenhower to vacate his field headquarters. As a precautionary measure, the Supreme Commander of the Allied Expeditionary Forces was sent back to his Versailles headquarters under armed escort. There, under heavy guard, he was kept as a virtual prisoner for many days. The capture of some of Skorzeny's men deep behind the lines further fueled the paranoia. This resulted in thousands of American soldiers being deployed deep behind the front lines. For many weeks, they manned hundreds of checkpoints and guarded strategic positions.[800]

All new Allied troops entering the Ardennes were briefed on the possibility of encountering these German infiltrators. The Canadian paratroopers had initially been warned of this situation during their sea voyage to Ostend. "We were told," recalled Private Alcide Carignan, "not to trust anyone, even if they were wearing American uniforms. We were also ordered to remove our 'Airborne' stripe that was sewn under our divisional patch." The paratroopers had been instructed, continued Carignan, "that if we saw anybody wearing them [the Airborne stripes], to shoot them."[801]

Danger lurked everywhere. Even deep behind the front lines there was no safe haven. Simple guard duty and road block assignments were now regarded as perilous tasks. "Any time an American vehicle came toward us," explained Lieutenant Tucker, "you did not know whether they were Germans or not."[802] To uncover this devious adversary, the Americans implemented an elaborate quizzing process. Among some of the questions asked were listing a football team's offensive linemen, or naming the current spouse of a Hollywood actor.[803] Lieutenant-Colonel Eadie recalled that on many occasions he was stopped by Americans soldiers and asked, "Who won the World Series?"[804]

The state of paranoia continued to prevail despite the news received on January 8 that the German troops had commenced their withdrawal. The Allies were in the midst of reorganizing their front and were not ready to launch a full-scale pursuit throughout the Ardennes.[805] Nonetheless, it was important to keep constant contact with the retreating enemy to maintain the pressure and monitor their latest positions. However, the continuing poor weather conditions severely limited their ability to observe the enemy's actions and define their intentions. For the moment, the only alternative was sending out numerous night reconnaissance patrols. Such tasks meant plodding long distances through deep snow, in the dark and in sub-zero temperatures. Regardless of the hardships, these patrols were great morale boosters for the men.

Finally, the paratroopers were given an opportunity to unnerve their elusive foe. "Lieutenant Eric Burdon, and two Other Ranks were patrolling for 11 hours," said then Major G.F. Eadie to a journalist. "They covered 14 miles in deep snow [and] found some Jerry minefields." He added that they "went right through the enemy front, and came back with a load of information."[806] Others, like Captain Sam McGowan and his group, enjoyed infiltrating German positions and playing mind games with the nervous defenders. A proud Eadie related McGowan's accomplishments:

> Now Sam really is a hell-damner. The other day, he went out to recce some German positions, and did he recce them. He recce everything but their socks. He and two others — they went right into the Jerry lines and played ducks and drakes with them. Played tag. After a while the Jerries knew some joker was in and among them, and they got the wind up, but they couldn't find Sam. They fired rifles, machine-guns, grenades and mortars but every time they fired Sam and his boys were somewhere else.[807]

While some had the opportunity to torment the enemy, others, such as Sergeant Andy Anderson, encountered tense moments upon returning from their night patrol. "It was a very nervous time," recollected Anderson, "as I was bringing a patrol back through the 8th [Parachute] Battalion lines just before daybreak when we were halted at a forward trench. The call came over 'Password,' and I gave one that was 24 hours old, which then brought us under small arms fire from the Brits." He remembered, "We then started calling names at one another, and some bright Corporal finally asked if we were the Bulford Canadians." Anderson acknowledged "that the Brits were very sorry for shooting at us and by way of apology they offered us a cup of tea."[808]

Even though the patrols confirmed the locations of the German troops and their withdrawal routes toward the Reich's border, the Allied pursuit of the enemy was very slow. The advance of the British and American soldiers had been curbed due to numerous unmarked American and German minefields, poor visibility, bad road conditions, difficult terrain, and the constant threat of ambushes. "We were creeping from village to village," recalled a frustrated Lieutenant Rossiter.[809] By January 8, 1 Cdn Para Bn's sector was far removed from any action, and the paratroopers were ordered to redeploy to a new area.

The next day, the Battalion left Aye and led the 3 Para Bde advance to the town of Marche. The Battalion then moved out and reached Champlon Famenine, where they relieved the 71st Brigade's Highland Light Infantry.[810] Frequent moves during a winter campaign were not favourably looked upon by the troops, especially when they involved relocating somewhere else on the front. This meant leaving the comfort and warmth of their customized shelters. Worse yet, they had no idea if any buildings were left standing in their new area.

On January 10, Brigadier Hill ordered the Battalion to reconnoiter and occupy the town of Roy.[811] As the paratroopers headed toward the town, they came under enemy mortar fire, but luckily sustained no casualties. Once again the enemy was nowhere to be seen. "The Germans retreated faster than we could catch up," observed a disheartened Private de Vries.[812]

Two days later, on January 12, "B" Company personnel entered the town of Bande. There they discovered the bodies of thirty-seven Belgian men and young boys in the cellar of a destroyed building. The paratroopers assisted in the grizzly task of removing of the bodies. "It was quite a shock to me," explained Corporal Jeans, "we had found many men that had been beaten to a pulp."[813] A few villagers told Company Sergeant-Major John Kemp what had happened. "They [German troops] had massacred a bunch of old men and boys from the village," related Kemp, "because they had refused to dig trenches for them. They just shot them and threw them down the basement of a church and then threw grenades in, on them."[814] However, for the Canadian paratroopers this was their first exposure to such heinous war crimes. Nicklin ordered that one man from each platoon be brought to this site "and shown the German cruelty."[815] He then stated that he would not to be too worried about taking prisoners after this. The discovery of these bodies changed the outlook of the paratroopers in regards to their enemy. "The sadist who committed this atrocity," wrote an unidentified paratrooper, "must have been half animal."[816] Sergeant Roland Larose simply commented, "They were real mean bastards."[817]

To counter the horrors of war and the effects of the rigorous weather, Hill decided that his men should be given some time off to relax and have fun. Since there was now very little action in the 3 Para Bde sector, Brigadier Hill thought that this was the opportune moment to organize a winter sports day. As 3 Para Bde prepared for these festivities, the First and Third U.S. Armies, a few miles away, were relentlessly attacking the flanks of the remnants of several stranded German units. The projected link-up of these two American armies was to take place in the next few days in the town of Houffalize, located approximately fifteen miles from the Battalion's current position.[818] Notwithstanding the proximity of the heavy fighting, the Brigade held its sports day on January 14, 1945. "The guys loved it," recalled Major Hilborn. "They made toboggans out of doors and bath tubs."[819] There were many other activities, such as four- and one-man toboggan races, wood chopping, wood sawing, and snow-man building.[820] This was probably the only time that the paratroopers were impervious to the cold and snow.

This short break was very beneficial, and in the following days, 1 Cdn Para Bn continued its mission with renewed vigour. During their patrols the Canadian paratroopers came upon a few abandoned German Panther tanks. "They were huge," said Hilborn. "These were absolutely new shining Panther tanks. They had just run out of gas." He stated that Brigadier Hill was so impressed by these vehicles that he wanted to bring one back to Bulford."[821] Another paratrooper, Private Mike Ball, was amazed by the tanks' main armament. "The part that was the most elab-orate on them was the size of the barrel. The length of it! How did they ever move around in a town I don't know."[822] With such an abundance of enemy equipment and vehicles the Battalion's Intelligence Section spent the next few days looking for new variants and updating their files for future reference.[823] By January 19, the Battalion was informed that the 1st and 3rd U.S. Armies had linked up in Houffalize.

Although firefights and encounters between 1 Cdn Para Bn and German infantry troops had been relatively few, the paratroopers respected their enemy's fighting capabilities. The German troops that were deployed in the southern sector of the Ardennes were elements of the Fifth Panzer Army. Enemy armour and infantry troops who operated in the 1 Cdn Para Bn sector were units of the 47th Panzer Corps under the command of General Graf Heinrich von Lütwitz.[824] Sergeant John Feduck, a Normandy veteran, rated those he encountered as very cunning and well-equipped combatants.[825] "They were full of ginger," recalled Lieutenant Tucker. "They would shout at you as Americans soldiers. If you stuck your head up, they would take a shot at you."[826] Lieutenant Williams Jenkins remembered them as "pretty tough. They were expert soldiers, well equipped, I thought very good."[827]

Now that the front had been secured, company sergeant-majors were ordered to prepare training schedules to keep the men active. As the troops commenced their training, rumours began to circulate to the effect that the Division would be deployed to Holland. As fate would have it, after having endured the bitter cold for twenty-five days, the paratroopers were finally issued rubber boots, clean underwear, socks, and gloves.[828] There was much grumbling about this late issue. Nevertheless, these items proved useful in Holland. The Battalion was pulled from its front-line positions on January 18 and spent the next few days resting in Ponderome, Mortouzin, Neuville, and Pennugan.

It had been a frustrating campaign for the Canadians. However, 1 Cdn Para Bn had nevertheless successfully carried out all its tasks and earned the distinction of being the only Canadian combat unit to have taken part in the Battle of the Bulge.[829] On January 22, 6 AB Div personnel, including the Canadians, were loaded onto lorries and departed the snowy Ardennes for Holland.

Simultaneously, the last remnants of German units trudged through the deep snow and dense forests to reach the safety of their western frontier. In the end, the enemy's bold offensive had paid off very few dividends. "Germany was given a breathing space," stated a dejected General Hasso-Eccard von Manteuffel, commander of the Fifth Panzer Army, "but the cost was so great that the offensive failed to show a profit." Manteuffel conceded that the "time gained was illusory."[830] Germany had once again sustained very heavy losses. More than one hundred thousand soldiers had been killed, wounded, or captured. But the Allies also suffered. The Americans had lost 81,000 killed, wounded, or taken prisoner, and the British lost 1,400 men. Losses in vehicles and equipment had been staggering. The American and German armoured units had each lost approximately eight hundred tanks.[831] The Americans could quickly replace these tanks, but the Germans could not.

Following a long and cold thirteen-hour truck ride, the Canadian para-troopers arrived in Roggel, Holland, on January 22. Just as in the first days of the Ardennes campaign, the paratroopers were billeted in the homes of the civilian population. The Dutch had also suffered terribly during the long German occupation. Lieutenant Eric L. Burdon remembered:

> My platoon slept in a house occupied by a man and his wife and two children ... The house had no heat and the people lived on starvation rations. For example, the husband went to work the first morning we were there after breakfasting on a cup of clear weak tea and a small withered apple. Needless, to say, we shared our food with these fine decent people and when we left after two days we gave them a modest supply of tinned Army food. They gave us the only thing they had ... kindness.[832]

During both these deployments, the Canadian airborne soldiers went out of their way to help the civilians. The men made it a point to bring back from their company kitchens whatever extra fresh and canned rations the cooks could spare. These were distributed to the hungry families. The Battalion medical orderlies and medical officer spent numerous hours tending to the assorted ailments of the population. "English troops are not the most popular in the world, or the Americans," wrote an unidentified Canadian paratrooper. "For some particular reason," he continued, "Canadians appear to be acceptable and are welcomed by civilians."[833]

Nonetheless, the paratroopers had work to do. The 6th Airborne Division was busily fortifying its defensive positions between the towns of Venlo and Roermond on the western shore of the Maas River. The 3rd Parachute Brigade took over positions previously held by the 46th Infantry Brigade, 12th Corps of the Second British Army. This area had been the object of very heavy fighting during the course of the previous weeks. Here, the British 12th Corps, as well as the elements of the Ninth U.S. Army, were still clearing pockets of stubborn enemy resistance.[834] Brigadier Hill ordered 9 Para Bn to dig in near Venlo. 1 Cdn Para Bn Headquarters and "HQ" Company were deployed in the town of Haelen. "A" Company took up positions in Buggenum. "B" Company settled in Berik, and "C" Company occupied the town of Nunhem. 8

Para Bn moved into the area next to 1 Cdn Para Bn and protected the right flank of 6 AB Div.[835] As of January 23, 1945, the Canadian paratroopers were once again called upon to man static defensive positions. Their tasks included observation and listening duties and reconnaissance, standing, and interdicting patrols.

As the paratroopers familiarized themselves with their new surroundings and monitored the enemy shoreline, Brigadier Hill briefed his battalion commanders on their respective tasks. All units were to seal off any bridgeheads established by enemy forces. Furthermore, the units were to hold and defend all roadways in their area of responsibility. Additionally, they were to maintain a series of ten-men standing patrols to observe the enemy's day and night crossing points. Moreover, during the night of January 25, Hill ordered that 1 Cdn Para Bn was to send a reconnaissance patrol across the Buggenum railway bridge and observe enemy activities in that area. Also, during the night of January 26, each battalion was to send two-man patrols into the enemy-held territory. These patrols were to remain behind enemy lines for a twenty-four-hour period. Their missions consisted of observing and recording all enemy activities. Under the cover of darkness, they were to return the following night. Upon their return, the patrol members were to be debriefed by the battalion commanders. From the information gathered, each CO was to select a specific objective. These were to be attacked the next night by fifteen-man fighting patrols.[836]

Following the Brigadier's briefing, the battalion commanders returned to their headquarters and briefed their officers. Compared to the 8 and 9 Para Bn areas, 1 Cdn Para Bn's front was relatively quiet during the first three days. However, due to an increase of reported enemy troop movements, 1 Cdn Para Bn was ordered to keep a very close watch. Personnel manning observation posts were ordered to note the type of activities that were taking place in front of their positions on the other side of the river.[837] Once again, long hours were spent in cold, damp slit trenches observing the eastern shoreline of the Maas River. The weather was just as miserable as it had been in the Ardennes. "The ground was frozen so hard," recalled Kemp, "that we had to use high explosives to break through the crust, so we could get down to dirt we could dig."[838]

Whereas observation post duties and standing and interdicting patrols were the main tasks for the companies for the first few days, these were now supplemented with the more dangerous and demanding reconnaissance patrols. The Battalion sent two such patrols into enemy territory during the last week of January 1945. Andy Anderson provided an insight into his experience on the January 27 patrol:

> Personally, I have lots of patrols, but this is something else again, and I am nervous as hell ... We went through our defense position at the bridge [destroyed railway bridge between Buggenum and Roermond], one of our Company platoons have this point. Lots of hand shaking and good wishes all round. Started across the girders, not too bad on our side, but getting close to mid-river the water is running fast and we are spending too much time looking for foot-holds that will lead to other sections. After about an hour, we finally found a solution to the puzzle, and by climbing and jumping a few feet from girder to girder, we got within fifty feet of the German side. Sam McGowan caught up to me and we agreed to wait fifteen minutes to see if we had been detected, since we have been making some kind of noise. We started to put on our white smocks. Sam got his on OK, but in getting mine untangled with the ropes, it fell out of my hands and into the river below. This is a real mess, but after a quiet discussion with Sam, we decided to push on. We got to the far side just before dawn, we stayed concealed and marked a few German positions, especially a mortar set-up, then we decided to head back and mark our route for future use. We have to move fast since we do not want to be spotted on the bridge when daylight comes. It was a much faster trip back, and I'm afraid we were not as careful about the noise. In any case we reached our positions about daylight, and we were greeted, then we walked back to Headquarters for de-briefing. We had a hot meal and a shot of rum. We have shown the marked route, and the "Old Man" [Brigadier Hill] is happy as hell and he cannot wait to report to the Division.[839]

The second patrol was a twenty-four-hour, three-man patrol led by Lieutenant J. L Davies on January 29–30. The small group traveled undetected behind enemy lines. The men observed German troops and vehicle movements, and noted the emplacements of occupied and abandoned defensive positions. From their observations, it was evident that these were in fact the enemy's forward positions. Their larger contingents and vehicles were kept further back near the Siegfried Line.[840] The majority of the Canadian patrols had been successful. They had provided the Division's Intelligence Section with valuable information. However, all patrol members concurred that the most difficult phase of these mission were the boat trips on the Maas River.

While this fast-flowing river provided a great natural defensive barrier against the Germans, it also proved quite an obstacle to overcome. Initially, the paratroopers experienced difficulties paddling and navigating their light canvas assault boats. To address this problem, selected Battalion personnel were sent to an indoctrination course at a boating school located on the nearby Julian Canal. "We learned to navigate, and control these small [six-man] canvas boats," explained Sergeant Larose.[841] These craft were then used regularly during the Canadians' stay at the front. The efficient manoeuvring of these vessels enabled numerous 1 Cdn Para Bn patrols to cross and land undetected on the enemy shore. However, if the paratroopers were caught in the open, these assault boats provided very little protection. "We were fired on the way back from our first patrol," recalled Lieutenant Burdon, "and our boat was hit and quickly sank." Burdon continued, "Miraculously, no men were hit or drowned, but we lost all our weapons ... I can assure you that the Maas is a very cold swimming pool in February."[842]

Apart from the occasional burst from a machine gun and mortar shelling, there was very little action in the sector held by the Canadian paratroopers. Boredom set in, and the Canadians quickly discovered that the Germans were also listless. "I remember that we were on the west side of the river and the Germans were on the east side, about two hundred yards apart," recalled Lieutenant Jenkins. "Our guys would hold up a helmet and the Germans would take a shot at it." He chuckled. "Then we would wave back signaling if it was a Magpie or Bull's Eye [signals used during range work to indicate where the bullet hit the target]. The Germans would do the same thing." He concluded, "Apparently, it was a universal signal."[843]

While there were some amusing moments, these did not take place when the paratroopers operated behind enemy lines. There were many close calls. Sergeant Feduck recalled one particular mission. "We had to go over the Maas in a folding canvas boat. They'd row us across and drop us off and we would have to try and get some prisoners," stated Feduck. "It was bitterly cold ... We got close to a road and we saw some Germans, so, we went under the bridge and got into the water. The Germans stopped on the bridge and started talking." Feduck shuddered. "They went on and on and finally left." He laughed, "We finally were lucky and captured a German officer." A few hours later Feduck's group signaled for the boat to come and pick them up. The patrol returned safely to base.

The Germans also conducted their fair share of patrols on the Allied side of the river. On February 4, a twenty-five-man enemy patrol crossed over and entered a sector occupied by the 6th Air Landing Brigade. Their efforts resulted in the capture of a British airborne soldier. The day after, pamphlets were distributed to all 6 AB Div informing them of the raid and extolling that all personnel be alert and vigilant. All were reminded, "It is better to finish the war fighting on our side, than in the hands of the enemy."[844] To discourage enemy incursions in the 1 Cdn Para Bn's sector, Lieutenant-Colonel Nicklin ordered that "Section Commanders will use absolute fire control and only see that weapons open fire on enemy 45 feet or less." Nicklin wanted this close range fire to inflict "heavy enemy casualties," and more importantly cause "shock ... consternation and panic in enemy ranks."[845]

Despite the well-entrenched positions, heavy weapons, and aggressive fire policy of the airborne soldiers, the enemy were still successful in sending probing patrols into the Canadian sector. Captain S.W. McGowan described one dangerous encounter with a three-man enemy reconnaissance patrol:

> At approximately 0030 hours, 12 February 1945, I along with CSM Kemp was making a tour of company sentries ... heard sounds of someone moving down the main road. ... We immediately went to the ground and observed. It was very dark but nevertheless we could see what appeared to be three men. ... They melted into the shadows of the trees and remained there for about ten minutes. ... I ordered them to halt — they halted and in fairly good English said 'It's alright Buddy.' I ordered fire and we fired. Both men went to the ground. I threw a #36 grenade. I sent Private Hislop to get a Bren Group to move around to their rear and catch the third Jerry. Hislop was fired at and hit by CSM Kemp who in the

darkness thought he was an enemy — sounds of groaning came from across the road ... 2 inch mortar illuminating flares were used ... nothing was seen ... SHEILA [all patrols were given code names] patrol combed area but nothing was found.[846]

While some enemy patrols were successful in infiltrating 1 Cdn Para Bn's defensive positions, others failed and paid a terrible price. The following day, one of the Canadian observation posts engaged an enemy boat heading toward their position.[847] The paratroopers opened fire and quickly heard screaming in the darkness.[848] And so the relentless war of attrition continued until February 18, 1945.[849]

That same day, an advance party from the 79th U.S. Infantry Division reached the 6 AB Div's positions.[850] The Canadians were happy to meet their replacements. Of all the 1 Cdn Para Bn deployments, the men rated this one as the least challenging. "Holland I thought was a soft war," recalled Private Joseph King. "We never advanced too much — it was a very civilized war."[851] Private Doug Morrison agreed, "It wasn't really that tough of a time."[852] Relieved to vacate these inhospitable surroundings, the Canadian paratroopers boarded transport trucks and were transported to Zeveneecken. From there, the rifle companies left for Ostend on February 21 and returned to England by ship. "HQ" Company and the Battalion HQ boarded aircraft at Nivelles the following day and landed at Neatheravon airport.[853] For the Canadian paratroopers, both the Ardennes and Holland campaigns had proven very frustrating and physically demanding. Nevertheless, for the new airborne soldiers who had joined the Battalion following D-Day, the experience proved to be invaluable.

The two deployments enabled the NCOs to assess the fighting capability of their sections and platoons. "On the plus side of the ledger," commented Sergeant R.F. Anderson, "it did give me a chance to measure the men in my platoon. I expect I will transfer a few before another action." But he disclosed, "Ninety nine percent performed extremely well, and I have a feeling that we have been all brought closer as a fighting unit."[854] They had learned a great deal regarding patrolling, manning observation posts, and operating at night and in frightful winter conditions. Furthermore, the NCOs had had the unique opportunity to further enhance their leadership skills. "We had exceptionally good sergeants," recalled Sergeant Flynn. "They knew how to organize and prepare soldiers." He stressed, "That was their key function — teaching soldiers how to do their job and survive."[855]

More importantly, strong bonds of comradeship had been forged between veterans and the new rookie paratroopers as they shared the hardship of the operations in the Ardennes and Holland. In total, during the course of these two campaigns, the unit sustained twelve casualties as a result of enemy action and accidents due to poor weapon handling.[856] And so the Canadian paratroopers returned to their training regimen in Bulford waiting for their next call to arms. They did not have long to wait.

CHAPTER TEN

Penetrating the Reich — Crossing the Rhine

Speed and initiative is the order of the day. Risks will be taken. The enemy will be attacked and destroyed wherever he is found.

Brigadier S. James L. Hill[857]

A s the Battalion returned from its relatively uneventful sojourn in Belgium and Holland, all were struck with the realization that Hitler's Third Reich was rapidly crumbling. The last real barrier remaining was the Rhine River. But even this was merely temporary, for the Allies were now preparing to pierce the very Reich itself. Once again, Canada's paratroopers would be in the forefront of battle.

Hitler's failed gamble in the Ardennes had exhausted what little reserves the Germans had been able to cobble together. Conversely, by mid-January 1945, the Allies had not only beaten off the desperate German counterattack but had also, despite the heavy losses sustained in the Battle of the Bulge, amassed almost four million men under arms in northwest Europe. As a result, the Allied steamroller once again began its relentless advance. By March 10, 1945, the Germans were forced to withdraw to the east bank of the Rhine River in a last effort to defend the German frontier itself.[858]

Planning for the crossing of the Rhine River had begun as early as October 1944. At this time, Allied planners targeted the Emmerich-Wesel area as a crossing point because of its strategic location close to the vital Ruhr region, as well as the suitability of its terrain for a rapid breakout by mechanized forces once a bridgehead was achieved. In addition, the ground also lent itself to the possibility of large airborne operations in support of the complex river crossing.[859] Field Marshal Montgomery and his 21st Army Group were charged with conducting the portentous assault into Germany, which was given the code name Operation Plunder.

"My intention," declared Montgomery, "was to secure a bridgehead prior to developing operations to isolate the Ruhr and to thrust into the Northern plains of Germany."[860] He planned to cross the Rhine on a front of two armies between Rheinberg and Rees with the Ninth U.S. Army on the right and the Second British Army on the left. He dictated that the bridgehead be sufficiently large to cover Wesel in the south from enemy and ground action, as well as being capable of encompassing bridge sites to the north in Emmerich. Equally important, the bridgehead had to provide enough space to form up large formations for the final drive that would culminate in the complete collapse of German resistance.[861]

Montgomery assigned to Lieutenant-General Sir Miles Dempsey's Second Army the task of thrusting across the Rhine and seizing Wesel. To assist Dempsey in this feat, the Army Group Commander was given the support of the First Allied Airborne Army (FAAA), which was responsible for dropping the American XVIII Airborne Corps, commanded by Major-General Matthew Ridgway, in direct support of the operation. The XVIII Airborne Corps consisted of the U.S. 17th and British 6th Airborne Divisions. Its mission was to "disrupt the hostile defense of the Rhine in the Wesel Sector by the seizure of key terrain by airborne attack, in order to rapidly deepen the bridgehead to be seized in an assault crossing of the Rhine by British ground forces, in order to facilitate the further offensive operations of the Second Army" and its link-up with the U.S. Ninth Army.[862] The airborne component of the assault into Germany was designated Operation Varsity.

The finalized XVIII Airborne Corps plan centred on dropping the two divisions abreast to seize the Diersfordter Wald and high ground three to five miles east of the Rhine River and north of Wesel up to the Issel River. Allied commanders felt that this was critical to the success of the assault river crossing because it would bottle up potential reinforcements and, more significantly, deny enemy artillery observers the ability to call down accurate and devastating fire from the ridge that dominated the Rhine River. Equally important was the necessity to seize control of the eight-by-ten-kilometre tract of woods covering the high ground that could mask camouflaged, well-entrenched enemy infantry and gun positions capable of inflicting punishing casualties and significant delay to the crossing and subsequent break-out operations. As a result, the 17th U.S. Airborne Division was ordered to seize, clear, and secure the high ground east of Diersfordt and a number of bridges over the Issel River to protect the southern flank of the airborne corps and to establish contact with 1st Commando Brigade in Wesel to its right, 6th British Airborne Division to its left, and 12th British Corps to its rear. The 6th British Airborne Division was specifically tasked to seize the high ground east of Bergen in the northwest part of the Diersfordter Wald, the town of Hamminkeln, and a number of bridges over the Issel River. It was also responsible for protecting the northern flank of the airborne corps and for establishing contact with 12th British Corps moving up from its rear and the 17th U.S. Airborne Division on its right.[863]

In turn, the mission assigned to 3rd Parachute Brigade, to which the Canadian paratroopers belonged, was to drop first and secure the drop zone and then clear the northern part of the Diersfordter Wald. More importantly, it was given the daunting mission of seizing the 150-foot-high Schnappenburg ridge that was defended by the well-blooded 7th German Parachute Division. It was essential that all enemy artillery positions and infantry entrenchments in the woods and surrounding farms and villages be silenced.

Within the Brigade, the 8th Parachute Battalion was assigned the task of seizing the northern part of the Brigade's allocated section of the Wald, while the 9th Parachute Battalion was given responsibility for the southern part, including the Schnappenburg ridge. The Canadian paratroopers were responsible for the central part, specifically the western part of the woods, a number of buildings, and a section of the main road that ran north from Wesel to Emmerich.[864]

The overwhelming force available to smother German resistance was not the only component of the outline plan that foreshadowed success. Airborne operations had matured dramatically since the beginning of the war. Allied planners and airborne commanders applied the hard lessons learned to date. As a result, some dramatic departures from established practice were exercised. Most significant was the decision to drop the airborne troops after the actual crossing of the Rhine River by ground forces. FAAA commanders and planners quickly noted that an airborne operation prior to the crossing would "hamstring artillery for the assault crossing." Moreover, they argued that the river crossing was not the most difficult part of the operation, but rather the real challenge lay in "the subsequent expansion of the bridgehead and in particular [the] capture of the [Diersfordter] wood" to ensure that the assaulting division would not be hemmed in on the far bank.[865]

Montgomery endorsed this plan. Both he and his airborne commanders were convinced that a daylight drop would be desirable to avoid the problems experienced in previous airborne operations, such as navigating to the objective, missing drop zones and the resultant dispersion, and the difficulties of assembling the paratroopers in a timely fashion once on the ground and providing them with adequate protective fire. In addition, both divisions were to be dropped directly on their objectives within range of their supporting guns that were sited on the west side of the river. This available fire support would not only provide immediate assistance to the paratroopers but would also facilitate link-up with ground forces on the first day, thus overcoming two fundamental problems experienced on earlier airborne missions.[866]

The hazards of a daytime drop, however, particularly into an area that was easily recognized by the enemy as ideal for an airborne assault and known by the Allies to be inundated with flak positions and machine gun nests, was well understood by airborne commanders such as Ridgway, Gale, Bols, and Hill. Nonetheless, they felt that the risk of a daylight drop directly on the objective would be mitigated by concurrent actions of the ground force, as well as the preparation of the battlefield by the Allied Air Force. They believed that by conducting the river crossing first, the German commanders would react accordingly and be preoccupied with the hordes of Allied forces flowing across the Rhine. "Well, gentlemen, you'll be glad to know," announced Major-General Eric Bols, commander of 6th Airborne Division, "that this time we're not going to be dropped down as a carrot held out for the ground forces." He explained that the "Army and the Navy are going to storm across the Rhine, and just when they've gained Jerry's attention in front — bingo! We drop down behind him."[867]

The airborne commanders also placed faith in the bombing campaigning, which, compounded by artillery support from the friendly bank, would theoretically disorient and destroy German infantry, artillery, and anti-aircraft positions. They also felt that by landing directly on their targets, the paratroopers would avoid a long, drawn-out fight to their objectives and be able to simply overwhelm any enemy force that survived the aerial and artillery bombardment. To that end, it was decided that the airborne force be "put down in the shortest possible time" into a concentrated area.[868] In addition, the glider element of the parachute brigades was increased above the normal allocation to enable the carriage of heavy weapons, jeeps, stores, and reserve ammunition. This also allowed for a margin of safety should attrition en route to and at the objective be excessively high. Finally, of equal importance, as already noted, landing on the objective enabled the airborne force to link up with ground forces on the first day, freeing the lightly armed paratroopers from a lengthy defence such as that experienced at Arnhem, Holland six months earlier.

The overall plan was carefully knit together and the necessary coordination completed. On March 14, 1945, a firm decision was made to conduct both Operations Plunder and Varsity on March 24.[869] Despite the overwhelming force that was amassed to crush German resistance, further steps were taken to guarantee unhindered success. During the three days prior to the operation, the Allies commenced a massive sustained bombing campaign that was designed to suppress the German capacity to fight, hinder defensive preparations, and disrupt communications. In the initial phase, Allied bombers flew over sixteen thousand sorties and dropped nearly fifty thousand tons of bombs.[870] These strikes not only hampered the movement of vital economic traffic from the Ruhr industrial region but also denied the enemy the ability to communicate and facilitate large-scale reinforcement or redeployment of men and material to the targeted Rhine area. In addition, 14 bridges and viaducts were made impassable, enemy headquarter complexes and hutted camps were completely demolished, 160 enemy aircraft were destroyed either on the ground or in the air, and 23 known flak positions in the area of the designated parachute dropping zones and glider landing zones were neutralized.[871] In sum, the overall air effort against Germany during by the Allied Air Forces in the week of March 18–25, 1945, resulted in a total of 44,894 sorties and 38,505 tons of bombs dropped.[872] All told, the Germans suffered colossal damage prior to the first Allied soldier crossing the river.

Although initial planning for Operation Varsity had begun in October 1944, ongoing operations and the crisis in the Ardennes pushed the planning process to the back burner. When it was resurrected in February and March 1945, there was little time to mount the large preparations that were seen prior to Normandy. But there was neither the same interest nor the same sense of significance. Everyone was tired of the war. Moreover, it was apparent that the German army was rapidly crumbling. "There was also some feeling," acknowledged veteran paratrooper Sergeant Andy Anderson, "that the success of the mission, perhaps did in fact mean a rapid end to the war."[873]

And so, when the 1st Canadian Parachute Battalion returned from the seven days' leave awarded after their return from the Ardennes campaign on March 7, 1945, there was little time for much worry or preparation. The Battalion was brought up to full strength. All personnel were once again tested on their weapon TOETs, which was followed up by a field firing exercise and a review of battle drill. However, the need to pre-position and prepare equipment, as well as the necessity of not injuring soldiers prior to the operation, meant that no large-scale exercise or practice parachute drops were conducted. This state of affairs did not sit well with the Canadian paratroop commanders. Their men had not jumped since Exercise Eve in November 1944. And now they were expected to jump onto the objective, into waiting enemy guns, without the ability to rehearse their parachuting drills.

Nevertheless, anxiety was put aside so that all could get on with the realities of a complex operation. On March 19, follow-on equipment in the form of large packs were submitted for transit overseas. The next day the Battalion was confined to Hill Hall Transit Camp in East Anglia in England. For the next three days the paratroopers were briefed on plasticine models and enlarged maps in regard to the entire operation and their part in it. Weapons were repeatedly cleaned and checked. Personal equipment was nervously prepared, and in many cases final letters were written for loved ones back home. The waiting was always the worst. Nonetheless, the Battalion was set. "If ever a fighting unit was ready for anything," extolled one veteran paratrooper, "this had to be it."[874]

At 2100 hours, on March 23, 1945, the guns suddenly lifted their bombardment. Under the cover of darkness British commandos commenced their attack on Wesel. An hour later, the first of a series of assaults that were to continue throughout the night across the Rhine River was conducted by the Second British and Ninth U.S. Armies. By first light, nine small bridgeheads had been secured across the Rhine between Emmerich and Wesel.[875]

As the Allied ground troops swarmed across the Rhine in the eerie darkness, the airborne forces were just beginning to form up in bases in England and France. The aerial armada, numbering 1,696 troop transports and 1,050 tug aircraft towing 1,348 gliders, departed from 26 airfields and met in the crowded airspace over Belgium. In their cramped fuselages were crammed approximately 14,000 American and British airborne soldiers.[876] In support were 889 escorting fighters to ensure the air fleet was not molested by German fighter aircraft. In addition, another 2,153 fighter aircraft maintained an umbrella over the target area or ranged far over Germany hunting for any German plane that would dare to take off.[877]

The Canadians awoke at 0200 hours and emplaned aboard 35 C-47 Dakota aircraft. At 0730 hours they departed from Chipping Ongar airfield, in Essex, for their two hour and ten minute flight to Germany. The aircraft were crewed by airmen of the American IX Troop Carrier Command. "They were the scruffiest-looking guys, with baseball hats and cigars," asserted Major Richard Hilborn, "but they were awfully good."[878] Another veteran opined, "The Yanks radiated matter-of-fact confidence, well suited to the fleeting but vital relationship between parachutists and aircrews."[879] In fact, their skill was one of the primary reasons that Brigadier Hill based his plan on dropping 2,200 fighting men in a comparatively restricted area that measured approximately 800 by 1000 yards in six minutes.[880]

The flight across the English Channel and France was uneventful. The weather was perfect — a clear blue sky and negligible winds. "It was a gorgeous morning," recalled Corporal Dan Hartigan, "one of the most beautiful days I've ever experienced."[881] Private Joe King agreed. "Going across the channel," he said, "seeing all those aircraft in the beautiful morning sky was fantastic."[882] Moreover, not a single German aircraft penetrated the Allied fighter shield. "We met no opposition until we were right over the dropping zone," boasted one airborne commander. "The air cover was wonderful."[883]

The tranquility, however, was somewhat deceiving. The ground told a different story. "When dawn came pilots who flew east of the Rhine and north of the Ruhr," reported one journalist, "they [had] never seen anything like it — whole towns and villages burning in an utter holocaust."[884] The Canadian paratroopers would soon find themselves dropping into this furnace. "Looking out the window briefly before 'Stand Up' my impression is of a very wide lake," wrote Sergeant Anderson. "I have no idea what I expected, but the river was massive, cold and uninviting ... within seconds someone hollered the customary, stand up and hook up."[885] But Anderson's attention, like that of so many others, was soon focused on their battle for survival. The transport planes, flying in nine-aircraft formations, held true to their course and maintained a steady formation despite the heavy flak that now spit up from the earth. "We went out in a tight formation," confirmed Private Jan de Vries, "the pilots took no evasive action."[886] Private Morris Zakaluk reminisced, "It was a ride to enjoy." However, as they neared their objective, "I could see puffs of smoke in the air between hundreds of planes," he recalled, "anti-aircraft shells exploding and tracers arcing their way into the sky," mixed with "balls of fire" screaming down to earth as aircraft were hit.[887] "Lying on the ground, looking up taking off my chute," remembered Lieutenant William Jenkins, "I could see these things [C-47s] blasted all over the sky." He added, "I couldn't help but admire those guys."[888] The deputy commanding officer during the jump, Major Fraser Eadie, noted, "They came in a little higher than we wanted — we wanted 450 feet."[889] Nonetheless, "the Yank aircraft did a hell of a job for us," praised Eadie, "I have never been on a better drop, not training or operational."[890] Major Hilborn concurred. "The pilot," he remarked, "put us down approximately 100 yards from where I wanted to be within a minute of the time I had to be there."[891]

The descent was not quite as accommodating. Neither the aerial bombing nor the artillery bombardment was as effective as the airborne soldiers had been praying for. Private Zakaluk was relieved to feel his parachute open and find himself cascading down to earth. But his relief soon dissipated. "Buzzing all around me!" he recalled. "I can't see them, but I can hear them." Then it hit, "Hey! These guys are shooting at me!"[892] He was not only one.

"I heard bullets going by and looked up to see bullet holes in my chute," reminisced Private de Vries. "It sounds just like being in the rifle butts!" His thoughts, he admitted, "were to get down fast."[893] Major Eadie too became the target of some well-aimed shots that cracked about his ears. He quickly went limp in his harness, feigning death, hoping this would fool his tormentors. It seemed to work, although his landing left a lot to be desired.[894]

On the ground the airborne forces met with varying resistance. In some areas opposition was negligible, but elsewhere troops dropped directly on entrenched enemy positions and dug-in artillery and air defence guns. From Eadie's vantage point, "It was hot!"[895] One paratrooper recalled that he landed "like a rock" and found himself stretched out on the ground, somewhat amazed to find nothing broken, and his kit bag still intact. Like others, he unpacked his gear and started for the RV point at the edge of the woods about two hundred yards away. "Crouched low, running like hell," he recalled, "conscious of fire coming from some-where, and several men lying motionless on the DZ."[896] A paratroop offi-cer later acknowledged, "It was real flat-out fighting until about noon." Another simply said it was "two hours of real killing."[897]

Brigadier James Hill, the imperturbable commander of the 3rd Parachute Brigade, had counseled his NCOs prior to the operation that "if by chance you should happen to meet one of these Huns in person, you will treat him, gentlemen, with extreme disfavour."[898] But evidently, the enemy was given the same type of briefing by their commanders. Although the Third Reich was crumbling, its soldiers were still proving to be formidable foes.

"The Germans we were up against on this operation put up a pretty good fight," acknowledged Company Sergeant-Major John Kemp, "they were as good as us."[899] Even the 6th Airborne Division intelligence staff had to grudgingly agree. Although they reported that the First Parachute Army was severely mauled in the preceding month on the west side of the Rhine River, the "Estimate of the Enemy Situation" prior to Operation Varsity warned that the enemy's fanaticism and level of skill was still such that they would be able to provide fearsome opposition.[900] And they did. Every farm was turned into a stronghold. "Morale was fairly high and this was espe-cially true in the Fallschirm divisions," confirmed Lieutenant-General Gustav Hoehne, commander of the German 2nd Parachute Division, in a post-war interrogation.[901] But many of the Canadian paratroopers already knew this — the contested areas of the drop zone were murderous. "They were young and full of fight," reminisced Corporal Dick Creelman.[902] Another paratrooper recalled, "They fought like tigers."[903]

The German tenacity did not bode well for the paratroopers. As the first Allied parachute serial appeared over the target at 0952 hours, an unexplained eight minutes early, enemy reaction began slowly but quickly gained momentum. The Canadians jumped three minutes later. Dug in on the edge of the woods, the German machine guns and light flak canons now wreaked havoc on the DZ. It was utter chaos. "We were getting pretty badly hammered from some houses on the edge of the field we landed in," recollected Kemp, "we knew we had to attack them right away."[904] Most of the Battalion faced heavy machine gun and sniper fire, which accounted for most of the unit's casualties.[905] "We were fight-ing right on the dropping zone immediately as we landed," lamented Lieutenant Bob Firlotte. "It was pretty bad."[906]

But this was not totally unexpected. "Listen clear now! Pay atten-tion!" bellowed senior NCOs in the different aircraft. "As soon as you hit the bloody deck, and you're out of your parachutes, fix bayonets and go for the goddam woods!"[907] Most followed this advice. The DZ became a hive of activity with small groups of men shedding their parachute harnesses and rushing the wood line, firing from the hip. Officers and NCOs attempted to rally men to form organized assaults wherever possible. But the initiative of the airborne soldier came to the forefront once again. Private James Quigley gathered a number of men who were milling around him on the DZ but were uncertain of the direction to the rendevous point. Despite the intense fire, "by his dash and contempt for the hail of bullets [he] inspired them to follow him" and destroy a company objective.[908]

The Battalion quickly gained the upper hand despite the variance in the quality of the enemy encountered throughout the unit's area of responsibility. "It was individual fighting in the first stages until we got organized," explained Major Hilborn, "and the boys did a terrific job."[909] And once organized, there was no stopping them. "C" Company was once again the first Canadian sub-unit to jump. They raced off the DZ to their RV points, where platoons quickly assaulted their objectives — a series of road junctions, wood lines, and the Hingendahlshof farm. Within thirty minutes they had achieved all of their tasks. This they accomplished without their senior leadership. The company commander, Major John Hanson, broke his shoulder on landing. Furthermore, the second-in-command, Captain John Clancy, as well as a platoon commander, Lieutenant Ken Spicer, failed to even reach the DZ. Their aircraft was hit by flak on the approach and turned into a blazing torch. As the aircrew struggled to keep the airplane aloft, the paratroopers managed to bail out. However, all were dispersed, and Clancy unfortunately landed in enemy territory and was captured. Nonetheless, Sergeants Miles Saunders and Bill Murray quickly organized the available troops and successfully executed the Company's mission. With their objectives secure, they then dug in on the north side of the Battalion perimeter and adopted a defensive posture. But for them the pressure remained. For the next sixteen hours they held off German probing attacks and exchanged direct and indirect fire with an enemy that simply would not quit.

Concurrently, "A" Company landed on the eastern end of the drop zone. They had an extremely accurate drop and within 30 minutes were organized in their RV with approximately 70 percent of their men. The officer commanding, Major Peter Griffin, decided to mount an immediate attack on a group of buildings that were designated for use by Battalion Headquarters. Initially, they met fierce enemy resistance, and the attack seemed to falter. Without hesitation, and under heavy fire, Company Sergeant-Major George Green organized covering fire and then led a PIAT anti-tank weapon detachment up to the first house. Using the weight of fire to his benefit, he then personally led the assault into the building. After vicious close-quarter combat, the structure was rid of its hostile hosts. Green then went on to clear the remainder of the houses in a similar manner. He was awarded the Distinguished Conduct Medal for his "contempt of danger" and "inspiration to the men."[910]

Despite the brief struggle, the Battalion War Diary account stated that overall, "A" Company met "practically no resistance" and collected forty prisoners. The sub-unit reported their objective clear by 1130 hours and subsequently took up their company position at the southern end of the village of Bergerfürth. Later in the day the enemy attempted to recapture the lost territory, but the counterattack was easily beaten off.

"B" Company's reception, much like that of "C" Company, was "hot!" The Company 2IC described the DZ as a "holocaust." "Everyone running in all directions," he wrote, "but finally following NCO's and Officers to the RV." The Company formed up in the rendevous point "with the usual confusion which is attached to a reorganization."[911] The OC, Captain Sam McGowan, showed up late, bleeding heavily and sporting a bullet hole in his helmet that miraculously entered the front, traveled around the inside rim, and then exited through the back. He immediately directed the platoons to assault their objectives. As a result, a group of farm buildings and a wooded area were quickly brought under attack. Under a heavy covering fire from their Bren guns, "B" Company quickly "overran the bunkers and buildings, driving the enemy out with grenades and gunfire."[912] The Bren gun coverage kept "their [the enemy's] heads down," explained one veteran. "We ran in right after the explosion and shot up anyone still there."[913] It was controlled chaos. "We are off and running," confided Sergeant Anderson to his diary, "firing wildly from the hip covered by Bren fire. We overrun bunkers, toss grenades into the houses and barns, generally raise hell and take a few prisoners."[914] In less than thirty minutes they too had secured their objectives.

Once established in his defensive position, the "B" Company commander dispatched a patrol to clear the woods in the immediate vicinity of the sub-unit's perimeter. Shortly thereafter, Sergeant A. Page and his six-man patrol returned with ninety-eight prisoners. Throughout the day the company engaged enemy soldiers who were attempting to flee from the field of battle.

By noon, the Battalion was firmly in control of its area of responsibility. In fact, this was the case for the entire formation. Within 35 minutes of the drop, 85 percent of the Brigade had reported in.[915] Shortly thereafter, the respective objectives began to fall. A pattern now began to emerge. Throughout the day, as the Battalion settled into its defensive position, stragglers continued to report in, many wounded, to their respective organizations. In addition, by 1400 hours it seemed as though direct enemy resistance in the immediate area had ceased. As a result, patrols were dispatched to ensure the DZ and surrounding woods were clear of enemy. The patrols also searched for missing paratroopers who could be wounded and in need of aid. They also attempted to bring in much needed supplies from the damaged gliders that lay strewn around the landing zone.

Throughout the night the enemy made attempts to infiltrate the position or to simply escape the Rhine bridgehead that had been established. The alert paratroopers, with the aid of their Vickers medium machine guns (MMG) and mortars, ably responded to the enemy movements. However, at first light a number of self-propelled (SP) guns began to fire at the Battalion positions from four hundred yards out. The SP guns specifically targeted the Vickers MMGs and the mortars, due to their effectiveness. German infantry then commenced an assault but quickly withdrew as a result of the withering fire that poured into their ranks. One SP gun was destroyed and another pulled back when they were fired on by four PIAT anti-tank weapon teams who responded to the threat along with well-directed mortar fire.[916] The defeat of the latest attack marked the end of the German countermoves. Although the enemy had now largely disappeared, they still maintained harassing mortar and artillery fire, which became more of a nuisance than an actual threat.

The battle was brief but exceptionally bloody. Two and a half hours after the commencement of the airborne assault, all Allied paratroops had been dropped and were in possession of their designated objectives. Moreover, 109 tons of ammunition, 695 vehicles, and 113 artillery pieces had been landed by gliders.[917] But the cost was high. Within the 6th Airborne Division, approximately 45 percent of the vehicles, 29 percent of the 75-mm Pack Howitzers, 50 percent of the 25-pounder artillery pieces, and 56 percent of the 17-pounder anti-tank guns delivered by gliders were damaged or destroyed.[918] The casualty count for the

Division was 1,297 killed, wounded, or missing.[919] The Battalion's share of the butcher's bill was 67 of approximately 475 personnel.[920] One of the dead was Private Andy J.J. McNally. Having been wounded at both Normandy and in the Ardennes, he felt destined to survive the war. "I have had it twice," he told his comrades in Bulford and again at the air-field, "I'm safe this trip."[921] But there are no guarantees in war.

Also included in the casualty count was the commanding officer, Lieutenant-Colonel Jeff Nicklin. When he failed to show up at the RV, Fraser Eadie immediately took command. However, as time went on, concern began to mount. A clearance patrol found Nicklin approximate-ly thirty-six hours after the attack. He was discovered hanging from a tree still in his parachute, his body riddled with bullets. He had dropped into the trees directly above German entrenchments and never had a fighting chance. The news was a bit of a shock to many. He was "one who almost seemed indestructible," remarked Sergeant Anderson, "6'3" tall, football hero back home, a stern disciplinarian, physical fitness his specialty."[922] Ironically, normally Nicklin jumped in the middle of the stick so that he could have half of his headquarters on either side of him upon landing. However, for this operation he wanted to be the number one jumper so that he could lead his troops into battle.[923] That fateful decision cost him his life and the Battalion their commanding officer. Eadie was subse-quently promoted and became the CO for the remainder of the war.

As the members of the Battalion reflected on their accomplishments, as well as their lost comrades, a fatigue and quiet personal rejoicing seeped over the survivors. Harrowing tales of close calls and stories of individual gallantry and heroism now surfaced. One such account revolved around Corporal Frederick Topham, who earned the only Victoria Cross (VC) to be awarded in the 6th Airborne Division during the Second World War. The twenty-seven-year-old Toronto native was the eleventh Canadian to win the British Empire's highest award for bravery in the war.

During the initial battle, while treating casualties on the drop zone, Corporal Topham and several other medical orderlies heard a cry for help emanating from the fire-swept DZ. Two medics moved forward to rescue the wounded soldier. However, they were themselves perfuncto-rily shot and killed. On his own initiative and without hesitation, Topham braved the intense fire to assist the wounded paratrooper even though he saw the other two orderlies killed before his eyes. "I only did," he later modestly stated, "what every last man in my outfit would do."[924] As he treated the wounded soldier he was shot through the nose. Bleeding profusely and in great pain he completed first aid and then carried the wounded man slowly and steadily through the hail of fire to protective cover in the woods.

For the next two hours Topham refused medical attention for his own wound and continued to evacuate casualties from the drop zone with complete disregard for the heavy and accurate enemy fire. "I didn't have time to think about it," he later explained, "I was too busy."[925] It was not until all the wounded paratroopers had been evacuated that he consented to his wound being treated. By now his face had swelled up enormously, and the medical officer ordered his evacuation. He interceded with such vigour that he was allowed to return to duty. On his way back to his company, he came across a Bren gun carrier that had just received a direct hit. It lay burning fiercely amidst falling enemy artillery shells and its own exploding mortar ammunition, which it was carrying. Despite the direction of an experienced officer on the spot who warned everyone not to approach the carrier, Topham immediately went out alone and rescued the three occupants and arranged for their evacuation. Topham's valour was unrivaled. "For six hours," read his commendation, "most of the time in great pain, he performed a series of acts of outstanding bravery, and his magnificent and selfless courage inspired all those who witnessed it."[926]

Bravery and courage by all belligerents aside, it became clear early on that the airborne assault had been a success. "The sight of the massive drop," wrote one Canadian veteran, "descending in an area about ten by ten kilometres square, floored them [the Germans]."[927] The show of force could not but impress even the Allied soldiers. "The very concentrated drop," wrote a medic, "gave an impression of irresistible might."[928] A British infantry captain, voicing the opinion of many, questioned, "How on earth can they [the Germans] go on in face of this?"[929] German prisoners provided the answer. They attested to the hopelessness they felt once they witnessed the overwhelming number of paratroopers that seemed to flow from an endless stream of aircraft. Major-General Fiebig, commander of 84th Infantry Division, confessed he "had been badly surprised by the sudden advent of two complete divisions in his area" and throughout his interrogation reiterated "the shattering effect of such immensely superior forces on his already badly depleted troops."[930]

The effect on the enemy quickly translated itself to events on the ground. By 1500 hours the reconnaissance elements of the 15th Scottish Division linked up with the Battalion. By 0430 hours the next morning the first armoured columns of tanks and Bren gun carriers of the 15th Scottish Division began to pass through the unit's position. The paratroopers welcomed them warmly. They had achieved link-up with the ground force in less than twenty-four hours. But there was little time to celebrate. The final push was now commencing.

The following day, March 26, almost forty-eight hours exactly to the hour of the Battalion's fateful drop into Germany, they were ordered into a brigade assembly area for a hot meal and some rest. "The battalion," boasted Hill, "really put up a most tremendous performance on 'D' day and as a result of their dash and enthusiasm they overcame their objectives, which were very sticky ones, with considerable ease killing a very large number of Germans and capturing many others."[931]

Overall, Allied commanders declared that Operation Varsity was an enormous success. "The airborne drop in depth," explained Major-General Ridgway, "destroyed enemy gun and rear defensive positions in one day — positions it might have taken many days to reduce by ground attack." He added, "The impact of the airborne divisions at one blow shattered hostile defence and permitted the prompt link-up with ground troops. The increased bridgehead materially assisted the build-up essential for subsequent success." The tenacious drive eastward and "rapid seizure of key terrain," he concluded, "were decisive to subsequent developments, permitting Allied armour to debouch into the North German plain at full strength and momentum."[932]

The Canadian paratroopers played an integral part in this success. Once again they achieved all of their missions, earning a Victoria Cross in the process. Despite the fatigue and the realization that casualties were once again heavy, they were buoyed by the realization that the war was coming to a rapid conclusion. All that lay ahead was to roll-up the final vestiges of Hitler's vaunted Third Reich.

CHAPTER ELEVEN

The Beginning of the End — Collapsing the Reich

Again we are mounted on decks of tanks, the pace is very fast. We are running through towns and villages too fast to recollect. Where we are stopped with shooting, the tanks merely level the opposition, in most cases there is no need to dismount the troops. Everything is speed and shoot anything that gets in the way.

Private E.H. Jackson[933]

The *success of Operation Varsity* set in motion the final act of the war — collapsing the very Reich itself. There was little time to reflect on the short but bloody battle that had just been fought. The focus now turned to exploiting the fatal crack in the German defence. Field Marshal Montgomery, commander of the 21st Army Group, wanted to explode across the northern plains of Germany and push for the Elbe River and ultimately the Baltic Sea. However, General Eisenhower pulled the U.S. XVIII Airborne Corps and the U.S. Ninth Army from the 21st Army Group to form the left wing of the American juggernaut to the south. As a result, the 6th Airborne Division was regrouped with the British 2nd Army. The Division, as well as its Canadian paratroopers, now became an integral component of Montgomery's push to the north.

But the race for the Baltic Sea became more than just another military operation to exploit a tactical success. It also took on a larger political overtone. By the end of March 1945, it became clear to many of the Allied leaders, particularly British Prime Minister Winston Churchill, that the Soviets were not living up to the political accords agreed to at Yalta on February 4–11, 1945. Communist rule had since been imposed on Romania, and the same was now feared for Poland. In addition, access to previously agreed bases and airstrips in Russia and the newly occupied territories was excessively restricted and in most cases never even materialized. As the war drew to a close and the Soviets became less dependent on Allied material assistance, their true post-war aspirations began to seep through. Therefore, Churchill argued that the Western armies should advance on Berlin and secure a bargaining position from which to insist that the Soviets honour the political agreements that they had entered into.[934] However, the American president and his military commanders were more concerned with the evolving concept of an Alpine Fortress used by some of Hitler's more fanatical followers to wage a protracted guerilla war to liberate occupied Germany at the end of hostilities. The capture of the German capital, which was on the verge of imminent collapse to the advancing Russian army in any case, became meaningless to the concerned supreme allied commander, General Eisenhower, when compared to the perceived threat that the "National Redoubt" represented.[935]

But not all agreed. Churchill's suspicions of the Soviets, compounded by his frustration with American naïveté and tolerance of Soviet actions, prompted him to take some unilateral action. As such, he decided to beat the Soviets to the Baltic Sea and occupy territory that had been allocated to the Russians.

And so Canada's paratroops were not only engaged in snuffing out the last flames of Hitler's thousand-year Reich but were now also participants in a precursor to the Cold War that would become one of the war's greatest legacies. As part of the 6th Airborne Division, they embarked on a race to Wismar on the Baltic coast on the personal instruction of Churchill himself.[936] "I took the message personally from Brigade headquarters," recalled Lieutenant Alf Tucker, the unit's signals officer, "direct from London, that we were to proceed to the Baltic by any means we could and not to let the Russians overrun us."[937] For an airborne formation, short of transport, this was, by any standard, an enormous demand.

But these larger issues were the furthest things from the minds of the poor paratroopers who found themselves on the pointy end. To them, it was a series of "constant fire fights." One paratroop veteran summed it up as "a rotation of walk, ride on tanks, ride on trucks and then the cycle would start again."[938] The Germans, commented Private Jan de Vries, "would set up at every obstacle for rear-guard action to slow-up our advance."[939] Another veteran recalled, "The boys rode on tanks until they came to an obstacle. If the obstacle happened to be small arms fire, the tank would turn on them and blow it up." He further explained that "if it happened to be heavy arms equipment the boys would get off the tank, do a movement around the gun and knock it out."[940] Resistance was no longer as formidable as it once was. "You knew it was over," affirmed de Vries, "and so did they."[941] But it remained a very dangerous and unforgiving environment nonetheless.

For the 3rd Parachute Brigade and the Canadians, the advance began on March 26. Having just been released from the task as the corps reserve for the U.S. XVIII Airborne Corps, the formation moved forward to Issel. Once the Brigadier discovered that the far bank had been abandoned, he quickly seized the opportunity and established a bridgehead that he was immediately given permission to exploit. The next morning at 0530 hours, the 1st Canadian Parachute Battalion advanced in heavy rain towards its first objective of the day — the village of Burch. Resistance was negligible, and it was quickly captured by "B" Company, which was the lead sub-unit within the Battalion.

The unit then continued to its next objective, which was a piece of dominating terrain along its axis. Although the rain had stopped, a ground fog limited visibility and created a foreboding atmosphere. The paratroopers' unease was shortly realized. The stillness in the air was pierced by the ear-shattering roar of a Tiger tank that suddenly materialized on the constricted roadway. Scattering for cover, the paratroopers quickly returned fire and forced the tank to retreat. The paratroops from "B" Company proceeded to double forward in pursuit but soon came under heavy fire from enemy armoured vehicles in a copse of woods four hundred metres to their front. Lieutenant-Colonel Fraser Eadie, who had been officially appointed the commanding officer following Nicklin's death, quickly moved forward to assess the situation. "B" Company endured the brunt of the shelling as the enemy pounded away in an attempt to thwart further movement. Things would not get better. Eadie realized that the only option available was a frontal assault, across open ground against an unknown enemy with armour hidden in woods. Artillery was unavailable, therefore, his only support was his integral unit weapons — his PIAT teams, his mortars, and his Vickers medium machine guns.

But as often is the case in war, chance played its hand. Just at the cataclysmic moment that the Battalion was about to launch its attack across the exposed ground, a pair of British jeeps from an unknown unit, armed with .50-calibre heavy machine guns mounted both fore and aft, magically appeared and offered assistance. They quickly flanked the German position and provided fire support, as well as a much-needed diversion. Under cover of this fortuitous support, the Battalion conducted its frontal assault and quickly swept through the woods to the village on the far side. The enemy had, as almost always, vanished, leaving behind only death and a burning village. The unit now moved in to the buildings that had not been destroyed and prepared to rest for the night.

A pattern began to emerge early on. "The routine is advance as far as possible for the day, dig in for the night and hold," explained Private E.H. Jackson. "We are making about 15 miles per day, rotating with other companies and platoons for the point."[942] Events to this point also taught some important tactical lessons that would be applied for the remainder of the war. First was the value of encircling the enemy defence, which by this point was focused almost exclusively on defending the roads. Second was the importance of moving at night. And third was the realization "that speed on its own account will often gain surprise, and, following out of this, the importance of keeping up the momentum of the advance, once contact has been made, in order not to allow the enemy to withdraw in an orderly manner to reform his defence elsewhere."[943] Wherever possible these lessons were followed.

The next morning at 0800 hours, the Brigade spearheaded the advance on a divisional axis centred on the towns of Erle, Rhade, and Lembeck. The Brigade quickly ran afoul of a number of well-dug-in anti-aircraft (AA) guns and infantry in a woods outside of Rhade. As the paratroopers approached, the guns fired airburst charges that inflicted casualties on the 8th Parachute Battalion, which was leading the Brigade. Brigadier Hill ordered the Canadians to deal with the threat on the main axis and instructed 8 Para Bn to conduct a right flanking on the town of Lembeck. Eadie quickly ordered an attack by "A" and "C" Companies, which soon silenced the enemy outpost.

The town of Lembeck, however, proved to be a more formidable obstacle. The 8th Parachute Battalion soon ran into some difficulties. "Severe enemy opposition," recorded the 3rd Parachute Brigade War Diary, "3 Bn attack put in."[944] The level of resistance soon prompted Brigadier

Hill to limit the extent of the penetration of 8 Para Bn. He then ordered 1 Cdn Para Bn to conduct a night attack. However, at midnight, two hours before the Canadians were to launch their assault, enemy resistance within the town was overcome by the tenacious efforts and "bitter hand to hand fighting" of 8 Para Bn's lead company. As a result, the Canadians were sent in immediately to assist with the mopping up of any remaining resistance. Concurrently, the 9th Parachute Battalion had successfully executed a left flanking manouevre and closed off Lembeck from the rear. In the end, the Brigade annihilated a Panzer Grenadier Training Battalion that was holding the town.[945]

By 1000 hours the next morning, the Brigade was consolidated in Lembeck. It then spent the remainder of the day resting, having just completed a fifteen-mile advance on foot in twenty-four hours while engaged in continuous combat for eighteen of those hours.[946] On March 30, 1 Cdn Para Bn boarded trucks provided by the Royal Army Service Corps and moved to Coesfeld, where "A" and "B" Companies cross-loaded onto Churchill tanks of the 4th Tank Battalion Grenadier Guards. Each company was assigned to a sister squadron. The lead troop in each squadron carried no infantry so that they could react immediately upon making contact with the enemy. This was the first time that the Canadians had ever ridden on armour. "Riding the tanks was great fun," acknowledged Major Dick Hilborn. "You could put about 10–15 guys on one of those things [Churchill tanks]."[947]

Novelty aside, the Canadians now spearheaded the advance to Greven, approximately sixty kilometres distant, with the aim of seizing the important bridges across the Dortmund-Ems canal that lay just beyond. The combined arms team of infantrymen and tank had just departed Coesfeld when they began to run into roadblocks and small arms fire. Once again a pattern developed. The "speed bumps" were normally a mix of *Hitler Jugend* (Hitler Youth) and *Volkstrum* (Home Guard) troops with small arms and *panzerfaust* personal anti-tank weapons. In this case, the road was barred by felled trees that were also booby-trapped. Although more of a nuisance than an actual threat, they still inflicted casualties and required a swift response. Normally, upon the flash-bang of an anti-tank weapon or the crack of small arms, the lead tanks would respond immediately with fire and the paratroopers would dismount and swiftly sweep through the roadblock. "With the Canadians acting as terriers and the tanks as guns," wrote an armoured corps veteran, "the bazookamen stood no chance."[948]

Sadly, during the early afternoon, an explosion within the advancing column brought it to an immediate standstill. Fears of yet another enemy ambush were, however, unfounded. It soon became evident that the highly respected OC of "B" Company, Captain Sam McGowan, had been virtually torn apart, and five others wounded, when a grenade in his webbing exploded for some unknown reason. He cheated death once on the drop zone during Operation Varsity, but was unable to do so a second time. He was quickly buried at the roadside. War waits for no man.

The mechanized column continued to force its way tenaciously through to Greven. "The tanks," revealed one account, "sped on through one village, then another, dealing on the way with an enemy staff car, fleeing bicyclists, and many other targets which the gunners could not resist."[949] The tanks never stopped until they reached the suburbs. As darkness started to seep into the sky, "A" Company quickly dismounted and seized the bridge as the tanks deployed along the riverbank. However, jubilation was ill founded. As 9 Para Bn pushed its way through 1 Cdn Para Bn into the centre of town they spotted yet another bridge. It erupted in a ball of flame as a reconnaissance party approached. The retreating Germans had once again imposed delay. Unfortunately, "it was an error in map reading," conceded the War Diary, "which caused the Coy to stop on the first bridge as they could have gone on to the second bridge with little trouble."[950]

Nonetheless, the captured portion of town was in "a hell of a mess." Eadie later recounted to a war correspondent that "there was a lot of confusion from shells and smoke and explosions and those guys [Germans] didn't know which were our troops and which were theirs."[951] Added to the pandemonium was the explosion of numerous ammunition dumps in the midst of the paratroopers. Order was finally restored. But the advance was delayed until the engineers could move forward and work their magic.

The pause, however, did not bring any rest or respite to the paratroopers. During the night, inexplicably, a German troop train filled with soldiers arrived at the railway station in Greven, only to be immediately seized and its contents marched into confinement. In addition, the enemy on the far bank shelled the town heavily during the hours of darkness, causing further casualties.

The next morning, under a very sombre and wet sky, engineers from 249th Field Company, Royal Engineers, strengthened an existing bridge in the town, while a sapper company from 8 Corps constructed a Bailey Bridge. The Brigade continued its advance and reached the west bank of the Dortmund-Ems canal by midday, but all bridges spanning the obstacle had also been destroyed. The Battalion took up defensive positions and once again impatiently waited for the engineers. The drudgery of the wait was further exacerbated by constant rain and heavy shelling.

By 1030 hours on April 1, 1945, the crossing of the canal commenced; however, the activity attracted heavy fire from enemy SP guns. The Germans utilized air burst charges, which worked on a timed fuse, causing the shell to explode in the air instead of on contact with the ground. This type of munition was particularly heinous, as it afforded no cover. The paratroopers could protect themselves from a ground burst shell, which exploded once it hit and sent its deadly shrapnel upwards and outwards, by finding a depression in the ground in which to lie. But the air burst shell would explode above the ground and send its lethal splinters downwards. Therefore, only those with some form of overhead cover were safe. The casualties were heavy — losses that the depleted Battalion could ill afford to absorb.

Despite its losses the Battalion crossed the canal on a repaired portion of one of the blown bridges, which was passable only on foot, and advanced on Ladbergen. The town was defended by a platoon of infantry supported by 20-mm flak cannons and two of the dreaded 88-mm guns.[952] "C" Company was given the task of clearing it out. The acting company commander, Lieutenant Don Proulx, sent one platoon under Sergeant Aurelle Bray to execute a left hook into the town while another platoon was ordered to enter by the main road. The enemy was now focused on these developments and failed to react to the third platoon led by Lieutenant Eric Burdon, which swept in from the right and crushed the enemy against the remainder of the company.[953] The German defenders were quickly killed or captured in the brief but vicious street fight. The unit then took up defensive positions within the town and settled in for a thirty-six-hour break.

The struggle was so short that the German headquarters responsible for the area did not even have time to realize that the town had fallen. The next day, April 2, a dispatcher rider arrived with a message for the local commander informing him that no reinforcements would be forthcoming.[954] The rider was quickly snapped, and his correspondence was welcome news for the paratroopers.

The soldiers soon found quarters throughout the town. The brief pause allowed for some attention to hygiene, drying out of clothes, and rest. But a soldier never truly rests. The paratroopers immediately did what they could to improve their lot in life. The Canadian soldier, remarked Eadie, "is a marvelous scrounger and whether needed or not is able to find anything."[955] Rather than rely on the issue rations they immediately set off looking for fresh meals. In very short order, the troops "liberated" foodstuffs such as "chicken, eggs, vegetables, and various preserved fruits."[956] This created some discord as Major Hilborn, the Battalion's deputy commanding officer, and some of his staff from Headquarters Company had doggedly struggled forward over the canal and bad roads with Army rations only to find that their efforts were anything but appreciated or wanted.

In the post-war years a myth began to develop that the race for Wismar outstripped the supply chain and that the troops were forced to live off the land and use German equipment and clothing. This was simply not the case. Although the attraction of using exotic weapons and equipment is always an allure to soldiers of any generation, the commanding officer acknowledged that "we never had to rely on that stuff — what we got off the land, because we didn't need it. There was always an ample supply of food and clothing."[957] Private Del Parlee agreed. "There was no shortage of rations or equipment," he conceded, "but we lived off the land because it was better." He recalled how everyone and everything that moved had cases of eggs with them after a dairy in Greven was liberated, and how the troops would confiscate sides of ham and other foodstuffs from homes. "When the QM came forward with hayboxes packed with food," he laughed, "no-one wanted any."[958] Lieutenant Alf Tucker actually praised the quartermaster staff, stating, "The QM did quite a job getting our equipment and food forward."[959] Lieutenant-Colonel Eadie summed it up. "We didn't want for a hell of a lot," he asserted, "but to go home."[960]

An army on the march is a living, breathing thing that requires care and a degree of latitude to ensure its morale and fighting effectiveness is maintained. But the looting of food and other personal property was actually prohibited. A 21st Army Group directive, "Policy on Relations between Allied Occupying Forces and Inhabitants of Germany," dated September 1944, stated, "Looting and violence to civilians are forbidden."[961] It explained that "any lack of discipline on the part of British troops will weaken the prestige and make more difficult the eventual task of governing the Germans." The Canadian mindset was similar. In fact, the commanding officer issued orders that reminded "<u>ALL RANKS</u> be made to realize that the good reputation of Canada and of this unit is in their hands."[962] The directives, however, had little effect even though they both warned of serious consequences.

The relentless push through Germany called for some extreme measures to be taken. The lack of transport integral to an airborne formation made anything with wheels invaluable. "We went through farms and store houses and literally stole anything that had wheels under it," conceded Lieutenant Alf Tucker.[963] But the march through enemy territory also allowed for opportunists to profit. It became evident that war souvenirs, transport, and foodstuffs were not the only contraband that was collected. "One thing that concerns me a little," confessed Sergeant Anderson, "is the looting of watches and jewelry by some of our men."[964] Reinhard Behrand was one such target. "Our decorations and watches, as well as our rings were taken," he complained. "That wasn't good."[965] A German family lamented the loss of their Leica and Rolleiflex cameras and precious stamp collection.[966] To the victor go the spoils is an age-old adage that is easily adopted in the anarchy of conflict.

Nonetheless, the conveniences of the town were soon left behind. On April 3, the Brigade once again moved out in the pouring rain. Fortuitously, the entire Brigade was to be transported by either tank, armoured personnel carrier, or troop carrying vehicle (TCV). But the going was extremely hard. Roadblocks and ambushes delayed the column. The 9th Parachute Battalion, which was in the lead, finally secured Wissingen in the late afternoon after heavy fighting. They killed approximately fifty enemies and captured another sixty, as well as destroying twenty armoured vehicles, ten AA guns, and fifty horse-drawn transports.[967] "The fleeing boche was scrambling out with all types of transport short of dogs, pulling self-propelled guns," exulted one veteran. "They were merrily shot up," he added, "the more that burned the happier we were."[968] By the time 1 Cdn Para Bn reached the objective at the end of a long sixty-four-kilometre truck ride in the Brigade's rear, the town lay in smoldering ruins.[969]

The next morning the Brigade set off once again with the town of Lubbecke as its immediate goal and Minden as the final objective of the day. The pace of the advance was swift. The lead elements rode on tanks while the remainder followed to the best of their abilities. The 8th Parachute Battalion took the lead and aggressively forced its way through a myriad of small towns and villages, capturing Lubbecke without any casualties. The Brigade pushed through until 8 Para Bn was finally halted at 1600 hours, approximately two kilometres outside of Minden, by a German Panther tank and four SP guns. The formidable enemy force motivated Brigadier Hill to decide on a night attack.[970]

Hill gathered his Orders Group together at 2100 hours. He announced that the Americans would cancel their scheduled aerial bombing of the city the next morning if the Brigade captured the city before dawn. Hill then ordered 1 Cdn Para Bn to clear and secure Minden by first light on April 5.

"Are we going to use the tanks?" queried Lieutenant-Colonel Eadie.

"No, they can't drive at night," replied Hill.

"What about artillery?" questioned Eadie.

"We've outrun the artillery," responded Hill matter-of-factly.

"So, what you're telling me is I have no support," stated the CO rhetorically. "Who's down there?" asked Eadie as he was preparing to leave.

"That's what I want you to find out!" answered the Brigadier, who fondly quipped that he "used the Canadians as our cavalry."[971]

Eadie promptly assembled his own Orders Group and passed on the news. It was suspected that a panzer training regiment and some infantry were holding the town. He then informed his subordinates, "We're on our own."[972] He allocated the support platoons to the rifle companies and gave his last direction. The lead company was told to provide a small reconnaissance patrol that the CO would accompany. "If there is opposition on entry into town," he explained, "spread out for house clearing and street fighting drills." What he didn't share with his subordinates, though, was his belief that it "could be a disastrous night."[973]

At 2330 hours, Eadie moved out with the scouts from "B" Company. Very soon thereafter they met a young German civilian who was coming up the street towards them. He revealed that there were no enemy soldiers anywhere to be found and agreed, "after some persuasion," to guide the party into the town.[974] Amazingly, the enemy had vanished. Lieutenant-Colonel Eadie quickly ordered the remainder of the Battalion to move in.[975] By 0035 hours, on April 5, 1945, 3rd Parachute Brigade reported the town clear and both 1 Cdn Para Bn and 8 Para Bn occupying their objectives.[976] The Battalion itself reported their sector secure at 0230 hours.[977] In the end, "insignificant fighting took place" for Minden.[978]

The taking of Minden in such a compressed period of time was typical of the confusion and pace of activities. "Often times there was no time to fully brief everyone," lamented the CO. "The poor soldiers — they would learn of things at the last minute with normally an 'up on your feet, let's go, we're attacking the town.'"[979] Private de Vries had the same recollection but from a different perspective. "It struck me that having always been 'on point' so to speak very little information reached us," he explained. "I never knew just where Battalion headquarters was or the other Battalion companies. It was always vaguely 'over there somewhere.'"[980] Another veteran added that "you didn't know what was going on — we were just told to do something." Often, he added, "even the officers didn't know."[981]

Fortuitously, all worked out for the best in Minden. The Battalion quickly took up residence in various commercial establishments within the city. Headquarters adopted the luxurious Victoria Hotel, but it was 4 Platoon, "B" Company, that became the envy of the remainder of the unit when it was discovered that the bar they chose as their billet still had beer on tap. This quickly became a closely guarded secret. Unfortunately, there was little time to enjoy the spoils of victory. Although the Brigade had advanced almost sixty kilometres in seventy hours, much of it under contact, and had captured Minden, which was actually an objective of the U.S. Ninth Army, the race to the Baltic demanded great effort.

During the morning of April 5, the Americans took over Minden. This released the 3rd Parachute Brigade to proceed to their next objective, Kutenhausen, which was five kilometres to the north. The Battalion led the way and after a "sharp skirmish" occupied the village. Although the Allied juggernaut was unstoppable, resistance was amazingly still fierce in some areas. "The war with Germany has at times seemed to be within an ace of ending," lamented a 6th Airborne Division intelligence summary on April 6, 1945, "yet tonight there has been further proof to add to what the past fortnight has shown. The German field forces and their NAZI bosses will fight it out until there is no more land to fight in."[982] This futile resistance sometimes wore on the paratroopers. In one instance a four-man detachment returned from a patrol having suffered a senseless casualty to a sniper's bullet. On return to the Battalion position, one of the patrol members, who had just lost his best friend, calmly walked over to a roped-off area holding approximately forty or fifty German prisoners. He then began to spray the PoWs with bullets from his sten gun, changing magazines before other paratroopers subdued him.

The latest combat earned the weary paratroopers a brief respite. Billeted in village homes, the airborne soldiers received their large packs, which now allowed for the provision of some badly needed clothing. More important, though, was the arrival of some desperately needed reinforcements. A total of three officers and one hundred Other Ranks arrived from England to fill out the ranks of the unit.[983]

The next day, the Battalion took the lead and marched across the Weser River to Lahde, where "A" and "B" Companies boarded the lumbering Churchill tanks of the 4th Battalion, Grenadier Guards. The remainder of the unit followed on foot using whatever means possible to transport their equipment and ammunition. The enemy offered little resistance, but nonetheless, it was well after dark before the Battalion arrived at Wolpinghausen for some well-deserved rest.

The advance recommenced early the next day, April 8. Although 1 Cdn Para Bn was still lead battalion, the mounted component was rotated. On this day, both "C" Company and the Vickers and mortar platoons were riding on the tanks. The day began without much incident. They cleared one more of a seemingly endless string of German villages and liberated yet another small prisoner of war camp filled with French PoWs. Wunsdorf was quickly captured; however, the push ground to a halt once the Allied forces continued their advance. The Reconnaissance Regiment of the 6th Guards Tank Brigade had set off in advance to seize a bridge three kilometres away in Luthe. The recce troops captured the bridge but were immediately ambushed by a Panther tank. A two-minute mortar "stonk" was fired to suppress the Germans. In addition, heavy machine gun fire and smoke was thrown at the enemy while one company from 1 Cdn Para Bn conducted a right flanking. The remainder of the Battalion quickly followed up. A few prisoners were captured, but the Panther tank, as well as an unknown number of other enemy, had made a successful getaway.[984]

The belligerents would soon meet again. The advance continued toward Ricklingin but very quickly ran into enemy fire once again. Concern now mounted. At 0900 hours that morning, a reconnaissance unit of the 15th Scottish Division had secured the Brigade's objective for the day — the bridge at Ricklingin. This light force was now caught between the retreating enemy tanks and the advancing Allies.[985] Without hesitation, the Canadians came to the rescue. Under covering fire from their supporting tanks, 1 Cdn Para Bn "advanced quickly along ditches across the open ground and along the bank of the road to the bridge where under their own smoke they crossed just in time to see the

Panther pull out with three other tanks."[986] Unfortunately, their intervention was not wholly successful. "The Recce carriers were found," recorded the Brigade War Diary, "some untouched others blown up, crews were seen to come from neighbouring woods."[987] In total ten crewmen were missing presumed taken prisoner.

The timely rescue by the Canadians did not go unnoticed. "Having marched 20 miles over very bad roads the day before, they marched a further 14 yesterday morning and were then called to put in an assault on a small village," wrote Brigadier Hill to the Canadian Military Headquarters in London. "This they successfully did," he explained. "Meanwhile an S.O.S. had been sent out for them to try and rescue a small reconnaissance detachment which was holding an important bridge just to the south of Hanover, and in order to do this the leading company of the battalion doubled pretty well non-stop for two miles with full equipment and stormed the bridge over an extremely open piece of ground under fire from three or four German S.P. guns without turning a hair." He added, "They got the bridge intact, but the reconnaissance regiment unfortunately had been unable to hold out."[988]

Exhausted, the Canadians turned over the bridge to the Americans of the U.S. Ninth Army and returned to Luthe for a day of rest. The pace of activity dropped dramatically. On April 9, the Battalion boarded trucks and drove through Neustadt to Mettel and then marched to Brelingen. Here they settled in for a three-and-a-half-day rest in billets. This allowed time for baths and a Battalion church parade.

Next, the Battalion marched to the town of Celle, approximately forty kilometres away. The Brigade had already dispatched an advance party, which facilitated the arrival of the battalions on the evening of April 14. During the brief stay several suspected "Werewolves" were captured.[989] The following day the Battalion boarded trucks and completed a long trip that ended at Eschede for the night. The 6th Airlanding Brigade was involved in heavy fighting around Uelzen, which prevented the Canadians from reaching their designated stop point to the southeast.

The continuing delays were lamentable, yet at the same time impressive. How could the German forces manage to keep fighting? "The First Parachute Army," stated a 6th Airborne Division intelligence summary, "has continued its skillful defence with no less than its normal fanaticism but with gradually tiring blows."[990] The Brigade War Diary captured the grim results. "Village on fire — area extremely battle scarred after clash between 15 (S) [Scottish Division] and SS tps," it recorded. "Many tanks and SP guns KO. Heavy toll of Recce, Domestic and Adm vehs of 15 (S) Div."[991] It was not until the next day that the Airlanding Brigade cleared the area and captured Nettlecamp.

The Brigade awoke at 0200 hours on April 17 to continue its drive to the Baltic coast. A mobile radar section accompanied the lead elements to assist with the location of enemy tanks, guns, and mortars. The 1st Canadian Parachute Battalion halted at the village of Hanstedt II five hours later, where it was joined by tanks. It promptly embussed and moved to Ratzlingen. On arrival, the unit discovered that 9 Para Bn was already in town heavily engaged against a battery of 88-mm guns. The immediate intervention of 1 Cdn Para Bn and its supporting tanks forced the enemy to withdraw. However, the Battalion was ordered to pursue the retreating enemy, who had taken up positions in the neighbouring village of Riestedt.

Hugging the covering fire provided by the artillery, and with their supporting tanks moving forward with them, the paratroopers charged over the open ground. The battle was relatively short and was over by early afternoon. The enemy had three SP guns destroyed, a number of soldiers killed, and 117 captured. The Battalion immediately dug in and waited for a counterattack that fortunately never materialized. The enemy did, however, continue a very aggressive program of shelling and mortar fire.[992]

Amazingly, the next night, April 18, Captain J.A. Clancy, who had escaped his captors, returned to the Battalion. He had been dropped into enemy positions on March 24 and since then had undergone interrogation and an endless series of marches to internment camps. He successfully slipped from the column of PoWs he was traveling in and, with two others, made his way back to Allied lines. He eluded German military forces and civilians for three days, partly by luck and partly by the clever use of ground. On more than one occasion his party awoke deep in the woods to the coughing of enemy soldiers nearby or the roar of SP guns opening fire.[993] Clancy's sudden appearance was welcomed by all. He was immediately placed in command of "A" Company.

Clancy's return seemed to be a good omen. Not only had the weather remained stable, but the unit was also withdrawn back to Hanstedt II for a brief rest. Better yet, on April 21, the Battalion was trucked to a rest area at Kolkhagen, where it remained for nine days. The stay, however, was not a rest. Hill quickly issued a directive that clarified that "the present period is NOT to be regarded as a rest period but as an opportunity to prepare for what may be the last hard battle of the War."[994] The relief from combat was filled with inspections by both the commanding officer and the brigade commander, as well as drill, PT, and sporting events. The Brigade also organized a competitive shoot for the Mortar and Vickers Platoons. The respite was also an opportunity to update inoculations and refit the unit and Brigade for the final push.

While the Brigade enjoyed its relatively quiet sojourn, the remainder of the Allied armies were closing in on the Elbe River. In the Second Army's sector the river was three hundred to four hundred metres wide, and although there were a number of ferries in the area, there was only one bridge — a railway bridge at Lauenburg. Not surprisingly, it had been demolished by the enemy. On April 29, the Battalion was ordered to move forward to Lauenburg in preparation for the crossing. The German Army by this stage was in almost complete disintegration, and very little preparation was deemed necessary to cross the last real natural obstacle that existed before extinguishing German resistance once and for all.

The Brigade began its crossing in the late afternoon of April 30, 1945, on a bridge built by the sappers of 8th British Corps. The day was cold and rainy. The Battalion crossed without incident and seized its objective, the key road and rail junction at Boisenberg, without encountering any resistance. That night, by 2330 hours, the Brigade had attained all of its objectives. Aside from a friendly fire incident — the shelling of 1 Cdn Para Bn by the Americans, who were firing from the west bank of the Elbe in support of their bridgehead enlargement operations — no other activity transpired. The shelling, however, did raise great concern. Although there were no casualties, the scope for disaster was huge. In the midst of "C" Company's area was a fully loaded ammunition train sitting exposed on the rail line. This potential problem was alleviated when contact was made with the Americans the next morning at 1000 hours.[995]

The crossing of the Elbe proved to be an important benchmark. Hitler's Reich had finally collapsed. Throughout the pursuit of the German Army across the plains of northern Germany, enemy troops and units surrendered in large numbers and were often dispatched to the rear without disarming them or providing guards. "I was somewhat concerned," confessed Private Alcide Carignan, "with the number of Germans still armed that we passed who would often wave us on."[996] Company Sergeant-Major John Kemp recalled, "As we advanced we were running into German soldiers who were surrendering without a shot — they were glad to give up."[997]

However, now entire formations were surrendering. In addition, the flow of refugees became staggering. The proximity of the advancing Soviet Army clearly created fear and panic in German soldier and civilian alike. Lieutenant Alf Tucker was amazed as they literally drove through a German armoured unit that was coming towards them. "They passed us without doing a thing," he remarked, "because they were retreating from the Russians." He added, "We went through unit after unit as we drove up."[998] Corporal Dick Creelman remembered traveling up the edge of the road as the Germans moved in the opposite direction down the centre and "they would still have their rifles and everything."[999]

But the crumbling resistance just made the day-long delay in Boisenberg, particularly in the heavy rain, that much more frustrating. Clearly, the end was near — Wismar was within reach! "Dawn broke, cold and foggy," recorded the 1st Canadian Parachute Battalion War Diary on May 2, 1945, "on a history-making day."[1000] Brigadier Hill chose his Canadians to lead the final advance. In the eerie predawn darkness at 0500 hours, "B" Company mounted the tanks of the Royal Scots Greys for the final leg of the "race." The remainder of the Battalion embussed in TCVs. Originally, Hill had planned to reach Wittenberg by noon, but opposition had completely crumbled and the lead elements of the Brigade arrived at 0920 hours.[1001] Hill pushed on.

The column forged on until it reached Lutzow. Here a refueling stop for the petrol-guzzling tanks was necessary. But as the reserve fuel was being downloaded from the TCVs, an amazing sight transpired. In the woods just in front of the refueling area, the Canadian paratroopers came across a German workshop detachment that numbered three thousand military personnel plus their families. "The confusion was indescribable in the woods," reported the unit War Diary, "German civilian women, men and children were there with the troops, and when the troops were lined up three deep on the road, many had their wives and children with them, to accompany them on the trek back to P.W. cage." The reason soon became evident. It was rumoured that the Russian Army was only nine miles away. "The civilians and soldiers," recorded the War Diary, "were terrified of the Russians, and wanted only to be taken by us."[1002]

After refueling, the tanks thundered off again at "top speed." Resistance had all but ceased. The Germans now reasoned, albeit rather late, that the more territory occupied by the Western Allies, the less that could be taken over by the dreaded Russians. "Thousands of German troops lined the roads and crowded the villages, some even cheering us on," described the Battalion War Diary, "though most were a despondent-looking mob."[1003]

Upon reaching the outskirts of Wismar, at approximately 0900 hours, the lead tanks bumped a roadblock held by some infantry. The paratroopers quickly swept through the position as the tanks shot their way through. "B" Company was immediately "sent straight through the town to take up position beyond the railway and astride a main road leading into town from the North." In turn, "C" Company was sent to the east edge of the town to cover the bridges and the road leading in from the east. Finally, "A" Company was held in reserve in the centre of town close to Battalion HQ, which had set up in Frundt's Hotel.[1004] Churchill received his wish — the 1st Canadian Parachute Battalion, as the leading edge of the 6th Airborne Division, beat the Soviets to Wismar. The race was over.

Throughout the afternoon and night German refugees and soldiers "by the thousands" poured through the Allied lines. "They constituted a serious traffic problem," revealed the Battalion War Diary, "and finally orders were issued to turn them out into the fields, since it was impossible to cope with them."[1005] For many the situation was clear. "Well, it's over! We ran out of Germans and ran into the Russians," wrote Major Jerry McFadden. "May 2, 1945," he added, "was the last day of the war as far as we were concerned."[1006]

The first encounter with the Russians is difficult to decipher. It seems that almost everyone in uniform was the first to meet them. Nonetheless, the first official contact occurred that evening at 2000 hours, when the lead elements, or the representative, of the Russian 3rd Tank Corps of the 70th Army bumped into the roadblock established by "C" Company on the outskirts of the town.[1007] "A Russian officer arrived in a jeep, with his driver," noted the Battalion War Diary, "it was quite unofficial, since he had no idea that we were in Wismar until he came to our barrier." It added, "He had come far in advance of his own columns, and was quite put out to find us sitting on what was the Russian's ultimate objective."[1008] The "first contact with numbers of troops was by 'B' Company to the North of Wismar."[1009] The task of "handshaking and Vodka-drinking on behalf of the Battalion" fell to Lieutenant P.G. Insole, who quickly discovered that the average Russian "could stow away prodigious quantities of the stuff."[1010]

It quickly became evident why the Germans were so terrified of the Russians. Sergeant "Andy" Anderson was responsible for setting up one of the initial roadblocks on the outskirts of Wismar. "The civilians were fleeing," he recalled, "and they were scared to death of the Russians who were massacring them."[1011] Private Jan de Vries remembers that first night while on guard duty hearing shots in the Russian area and women screaming.[1012] "They would rape," asserted Private Alcide Carignan, "every female between 9 and 90 that they could get their hands on."[1013] Clearly, the Russians did not make a good impression on the Canadians. "They were real hard sacks of shit," spat out veteran paratrooper Sergeant Roland Larose.[1014] Private de Vries commented philosophically that they "were thoughtless of life."[1015] Most agreed. "My first reaction was that they were the hardest looking bunch of toughs I have ever seen," confided Sergeant Anderson to his diary. "On the surface at least, they seem more like an enemy than an ally."[1016] They were a "pretty wild bunch," recalled Private Doug Morrison, while another described them as a "rag-tag outfit."[1017] Overall, the Canadians felt that the Russians were definitely a "rugged" crowd and quite "scruffy."[1018]

The initial euphoria soon wore off. The next day was spent searching for German soldiers hiding within the town and securing "comfortable billets." German prisoners were still being pushed back along the Division axis and refugees were still being diverted into the neighbouring fields. Major Dick Hilborn was assigned the position of chief liaison officer between the Battalion and the Russians. The Battalion actually had a number of Russian-speaking soldiers from the Winnipeg area, and as a result, the Canadians provided the bulk of the Division's interpreters.

Initially, contact with the eastern ally was full of elation and good cheer. However, this soon ceased. By May 5, the Russians had erected a roadblock one hundred metres from that of the Canadians, complete with heavy tanks. "As far as we were concerned the war was over on 2 May when we met up with the Russians," explained Hillborn. "We put our gun muzzles on and pointed them off to the west. The Russians, however, dug-in and kept their artillery facing us."[1019] Access to the Soviet zone of occupation became very restricted. Only the daily jeep courier was allowed through. Notwithstanding the chill in relations, high-level liaison to discuss the occupation of territory continued unabated.

The Russians, on the other hand, were allowed to enter and leave Wismar at will. This was in accordance with the Divisional direction that stated, "Dealings with the Russians will be as far as possible governed by a spirit of friendliness and tolerance, tempered with firmness."[1020] This was easier said than done. Russian access to Wismar created nothing but trouble for the Canadians. They would often appear at the roadblock, "half of them drunk and out of control." Sergeant Anderson remembered that they kept saying, "Women, we want women." He added, "There was no discipline among them at all, nothing."[1021] Major John Simpson remembered that the "biggest problem was controlling them within our own lines."[1022] Not surprisingly, the denizens of Wismar were terrified of them. Sergeant John Feduck recalls:

We patrolled the town because of the inhabitants. They were deadly afraid of the Russians. When we were told to leave, they begged and cried not to leave them with the Russians. They were so scared, believe me I'm telling you and these Russians, they were vicious, they would think nothing of molesting women. I was on night patrol, we heard this screaming ... I go upstairs and this Russian guy is shooting at this girl ... he had most of her clothes off. She was hiding behind a brick chimney and he'd shoot at her if he saw any part of her. So we got him and knocked him out. [1023]

The very evident chill and continuing downward spiral in relations also owed a lot to the level of conflict over ownership of the occupied territory. Much like the demand placed on Major-General Eric Bols, the 6th Airborne Division commander, to seize and hold Wismar, so too did his Russian counterpart have directions to capture Lubeck. Bols remained firm and reminded his counterpart that he had a parachute brigade in possession of the city, supported by divisional artillery and armour. No resolution could be reached, so they agreed to allow the senior echelon to work out a solution to the problem. On May 7, 1945, Soviet Marshal Rokossovsky, the Commander-in-Chief of the Byelo-Russian Army Group, met with Field Marshal Montgomery to discuss the way ahead. In the end, the decision was a political one that defaulted to the Yalta accords. As such, the 6th Airborne Division eventually surrendered Wismar to the Russians.

But the immediate fix was to maintain the status quo. To the paratroopers, May 7 brought more important news. On that morning it was officially announced that the Germans had signed an unconditional surrender. Prime Minister Churchill promptly declared May 8 "Victory in Europe" (VE) day. Celebrations ensued. "And the celebration," recorded the War Diary, "was worth all the waiting. The gin, whiskey, vodka, wine schnapps flowed, and everybody had a grand time acquiring the inevitable hangover."[1024]

With the war over, Brigadier Hill imposed increasing discipline and routine onto his battalions. Lieutenant-Colonel Eadie quickly passed direction that all German military and civilian equipment was no longer to be used. "The men," noted Sergeant Anderson in his diary, "have been ordered to get rid of German clothing, cars, bicycles, and all looting must stop."[1025] "VE" Day celebrations were conducted with British and Russian troops in Wismar on May 9. Two days later a Brigade parade was held in the town square in front of a large German crowd that watched "docilely but sullenly."[1026] On May 13, a memorial service was held at the Nikolaikirche Cathedral. These activities, however, failed to contain the restlessness that permeated the Battalion. The long struggle was over — now everyone wanted to go home.

The first step came sooner than expected. The Battalion was warned that it would soon be returning to England. Preparations began on May 14. Five days later the Canadian paratroopers were trucked to Luneburg where they spent the night in a bivouac four kilometres from the airdrome. The next day they flew to England, finally arriving at Bulford Camp at 2030 hours that night. After a few days of settling in, the Battalion was given a well-deserved nine days' leave.

The war was truly over. The Canadian paratroopers had proved themselves once again. Despite continuous enemy resistance, constant physical discomfort, and adversity, the members of the 1st Canadian Parachute Battalion played an instrumental part in collapsing Hitler's Third Reich. Brigadier Hill praised their role in the "fighting trek on our flat feet across 275 miles of Germany when we more than kept pace with the Armoured Division on our flank which ended with our lead battalion, the Canadians, entering the town of Wismar on the Baltic Sea 3 hours ahead of the Russians, as Sir Winston Churchill had personally demanded."[1027] Lieutenant-General Sir Miles Dempsey, commander of the British 2nd Army, also recognized the accomplishment. "Your spectacular dash to Wismar, and your arrival to time on the shores of the Baltic," he wrote to the Commander of the 6th Airborne Division, "are a great ending to the brilliant successes gained by your division in this campaign."[1028] Brigadier Hill would later write to Lieutenant-Colonel Eadie, "I shall ever remember, with great pride, that I had the honour to have under my command, both in and out of battle, a Canadian Battalion which is regarded by all of us as, as fine a fighting unit as has ever left these shores."[1029]

The accolades were well deserved. But praise was not what the paratroopers wanted. For the members of the 1st Canadian Parachute Battalion, the only important detail that remained was their repatriation home. And that would come sooner than anyone had hoped for.

CONCLUSION

Your unit is young — as the age of our famous Canadian fighting units is measured — but in the few short years of its existence and in the year of its fighting history you have made a gallant and brilliant record.
Major-General A.E. Walford, Adjutant-General[1030]

For the men of the 1st Canadian Parachute Battalion the war had finally ended. The Third Reich was crushed and the defeat of Imperial Japan was imminent. Some thought of volunteering for the Far East theatre of operations. Most, however, just wanted to go home. But then, so did the rest of the Canadian Army overseas. Finding transport would be no easy task. For now, most would just have to sit and wait. With this in mind, on May 24, the Canadian paratroopers left Bulford Camp for a well-deserved nine-day leave. While the men celebrated, Lieutenant-Colonel Fraser Eadie met with Canadian Military Headquarters staff. During their conversations, Eadie discussed the possibilities of the Battalion's early repatriation to Canada. As luck would have it there was space still available on the *Ile de France*, moored in Gourock, Scotland. The ship was scheduled to leave for Canada in the later part of June.[1031]

This was an incredible opportunity. Eadie immediately contacted the British and Canadian Provost Corps, as well as the English and Scottish constabulary authorities. His directive was simple. All 1 Cdn Para Bn personnel were to return immediately to Bulford. Within hours of the directive, which was given on May 27, 1945, all paratroopers seen wearing the 1st Canadian Parachute Battalion shoulder flash were ordered to return without delay to their base.[1032] "Nobody knew what was going on," explained Alcide Carignan. "A Red Cap [military policeman] saw me and said, 'Hey Canada!, you'd better get back to camp.'"[1033] No reasons were given for the recall. The hasty return led to numerous rumours and wild speculation. "We thought we were going to be incorporated in some American unit and go to Japan," stated Alf Tucker.[1034]

Their speculation was not unwarranted. Unbeknownst to the paratroopers, during the month of May, the War Office had unsuccessfully attempted to convince CMHQ to extend 1 Cdn Para Bn's service with the 6 AB Div so that they could deploy to Palestine with the formation.[1035] CMHQ categorically rejected the War Office's request.[1036] CMHQ Chief of Staff Lieutenant-General P.J. Montague informed the Under Secretary of State of the War Office that 1 Cdn Para Bn would be withdrawn from 6 AB Div as soon it returned to the U.K. from Wismar and that it would be placed under the command of the First Canadian Army.[1037]

The sudden interest in 1 Cdn Para Bn was not sparked by operational necessity but rather by a government that was now interested in demobilizing a large and costly wartime army. And the future was not particularly bright for the paratroopers. Beginning in May 1945, no training was conducted at the parachute training centre in Canada, since Army headquarters did not foresee a requirement for airborne troops in the postwar army. Similarly, in the same month the 1st Canadian Parachute Training Battalion was also disbanded.[1038] The Battalion itself was also marked for disbandment, but staff planners decided to keep this quiet for the moment. They decided to prolong the unit's existence so that it would serve as an administrative tool to process the orderly release of those members who did not sign on to stay in the Active Force.[1039]

But for the moment, the future of the unit was the farthest thing from the minds of the Canadian paratroopers. As the airborne soldiers returned to camp they discovered that they were to be the first Canadian unit in its entirety to return to Canada.[1040] This unexpected news led to wild cheering. Pandemonium broke out throughout the ranks for several minutes. Major Richard Hilborn, officer commanding "B"Company, was also both thrilled and relieved by the great news. "Our guys became a nuisance," revealed Hilborn. "They were energetic guys with not much to do to burn up all their energy." But he also realized that their good fortune would not be accepted by everyone. "Our speedy repatriation

didn't make us many friends with other Canadian units," he commented. "I don't think we made too many friends that way."[1041]

The good news was quickly followed by a dose of reality. After that
announcement came a requirement for volunteers to either join the
Canadian Army Pacific Force for possible deployment to the Far East or
sign up with the Canadian Army Occupation Force for service in
Germany. In the end, a total of 11 officers and 169 Other Ranks volunteered to serve with the Canadian Army Pacific Force.[1042]

During the next four days paratroopers worked long hours to clean
their quarters and verify and return their weapons, vehicles, and equipment. No one needed to be prodded to complete their chores. "It was just
like preparing for another invasion," recalled Private Michael Ball.[1043] On
May 31, 1945, the paratroopers of the 1st Canadian Parachute Battalion
left Bulford for the last time.

As the Battalion marched to the camp's train siding, they were greeted by
Major-General E.L. Bols, Brigadier James Hill, and numerous officers
from various airborne units. Both Bols and Hill made sure that the
Battalion was given a proper send-off. Flags and bunting decorated the
railway siding. Amid these were a large Canadian parachute badge and a
gold maple leaf. In the background a band played military marches.
Despite the overcast skies and the intermittent showers nothing could
dampen the paratroopers' spirit. Following a few speeches, Brigadier Hill
walked through the Battalion's ranks and shook every man's hand. "He
had a sincere interest in his men," recalled Sergeant R.F. Anderson.[1044] He
explained that the Brigadier had "become an 'icon' to each and every
man." He described Hill as a "Soldier's soldier."[1045]

It was a bittersweet moment. After the final dismissal, the troops
boarded the train. Hill walked by each compartment window and
wished the men well. At this point the goodbyes became emotional. "He
was pretty upset," recalled Corporal Richard Creelman, "so were an
awful lot of the guys in the train." Creelman remembered, "Brigadier
Hill had tears in his eyes."[1046]

The fondness for Brigadier Hill was not surprising. He took care of
his Canadian paratroopers right to the last moment. He believed that it
was very important that the Canadian people be given the opportunity
to welcome home their paratroopers properly. During the previous
week, Hill had written to Major-General E.G. Weeks at CMHQ, requesting the General to send the Battalion home in substantial groups. "I

know I am voicing the opinion of the General [Bols] and all of us," asserted Hill, "when I say that it would break our hearts and theirs if they were disbanded and dispersed over here."[1047] CMHQ agreed with Hill's request. The entire Battalion, as well as the Training Battalion, was repatriated to Canada together as a unit.[1048]

The train left Bulford and headed to the No.3 Repatriation Depot in Farnborough. The men spent the following days going through various administrative processes to update their personnel files. It was during this time that the Battalion underwent a dramatic change. The men were ordered to break ranks and reform under their military district numerical designation.[1049] The order shocked everyone. In less than one hour the camaraderie and the competitive team spirit that had been developed and nurtured over the course of the past three years was dissolved for administrative expediency. Almost as a precursor of things to come, it seemed as if 1 Cdn Para Bn no longer existed. On June 15, 1945, the *Ile de France* left Scotland for Canada.

On June 20, the *Ile de France* entered Halifax Harbour. As the forty-three-thousand-ton vessel inched its way toward its berth at the Ocean Terminal Pier 21, more than eight thousand veterans rushed to the ship's port side. The soldiers and airmen cheered and showered the dock with coins, cookies, chocolates, and life preservers.[1050] This sudden shift caused the large vessel to tilt. "It was incredible," recalled Sergeant Harry Wright. "The ship's Captain got on the intercom and said, 'I can't dock the ship. Some of you will have to move to the other side.' I don't think a single man moved," laughed Wright.[1051] As order was being re-established, Lieutenant-Colonel Eadie gathered his senior NCOs and briefed them on the day's upcoming activities. Being the first complete unit repatriated to Canada, the Battalion was ordered to take part in a parade and festivities. Realizing that it would be difficult to motivate the men, Eadie insisted that the paratroopers put on a good show.[1052] Most of the paratroopers had been away from home for many years and were in no mood to take part in a parade or any other official activities, such as receiving the keys to the city. They just wanted to go home and be with their families.

But the desires of the soldiers became lost in the good intentions of their fellow countrymen. The citizens of Halifax, as well as the civic and military authorities, joined forces and went to great lengths to prepare this homecoming. The entire parade route was decorated. Citizens were asked to prepare confetti and ticker tape and to shower the troops with these during their march. Furthermore, all civic and provincial offices were closed for a few hours to enable staff to attend the celebrations. Employers who had private businesses were encouraged to follow suit.[1053] As the Battalion formed up on Terminal Road shortly after lunch, on June 20, it started to rain. However, this had very little effect on the onlookers. Prior to the start of the parade, the acting mayor of Halifax, J.E. Ahern, presented Lieutenant-Colonel Eadie with the keys to the city and a scroll. Eadie was then given the flag of Nova Scotia by W.B. MacCoy on behalf of Premier A.S. MacMillan and the Provincial Government.

Following the civic welcoming ceremonies, the paratroopers, along with two military bands and a small air force contingent, marched, in the rain, through the streets of Halifax. "I wasn't too happy," explained Corporal Creelman. "We were soaked. You didn't look your best. The uniforms were rumpled...."[1054] Impervious to the rain, an exuberant crowd lined up six-deep along the entire route. After entering the Garrison Grounds, the Battalion formed up in a hollow square and prepared for inspection.[1055] The paratroopers were then welcomed by Major-General A.E. Walford, the Army's adjutant-general, and other high-ranking officers and dignitaries.

Major-General Walford read messages sent by Prime Minister W.L. Mackenzie King and the Minister of National Defence, General A.G.L. McNaughton. The Prime Minister congratulated the paratroopers on their professionalism. "From the glowing accounts we have received from the senior British officers commanding formations of which your battalion formed a part," praised the Prime Minister, "we know how valiantly and how skillfully you carried out the tasks assigned to you.[1056]

The Minister of Defence also lauded the accomplishments of the airborne soldiers. "You have fulfilled," he stated, "every task entrusted to you. You have made a very great contribution to the victory over Germany and we are indeed all very proud of the valor and the skill at arms and of the effectiveness with which you have carried through your operations in battle." He added, "We are very proud to of the high reputation of discipline which you have established for yourselves."[1057]

Major-General Walford concluded the ceremonies by declaring how proud he was of the men of the 1st Canadian Parachute Battalion. "You showed yourself to be first class infantry as well as airborne troops," extolled Walford, "and I can pay you no greater compliment or honor than to class you with our outstanding infantry regiments."[1058] The troops were then dismissed. Within seconds family and friends rushed onto the field to join their loved ones.

But the closeness of the unit still shone through. Despite the joyous occasion, their lost comrades were not forgotten. Speaking to reporters, Lieutenant Ed Friel stated, "Don't write about us. Write about all the swell guys who aren't coming back." He pointed out, "There are plenty of them and they're the ones who count."[1059] His sentiments were not hard to understand. "It was a brotherhood," explained Private Thomas Gavinski, "the most wonderful thing that ever happened to me."[1060]

After a brief reunion, the paratroopers formed up and marched back to the *Ile de France*. The next day they embarked on special trains and headed off to their respective military districts for a well-deserved thirty-day leave. Upon arrival, each contingent was given a tumultuous welcome. By the beginning of July all the paratroopers had returned home. For many, this was the last time that they would see their comrades.[1061] Personnel who were eligible for immediate discharge were ordered to report to their military district headquarters.[1062]

After the disembarkation leave, the Battalion members who had volunteered for the Pacific Force reported to the No.1 Pacific Infantry Training Brigade. The remainder reported to Camp Niagara-on-the-Lake, Ontario, on July 27, 1945. For the next nine weeks the paratroopers awaited their demobilization.[1063] To keep the men occupied, daily sport activities and other events were organized. Leave passes were issued regularly, enabling the airborne soldiers to visit the Niagara peninsula or cross the border and visit Buffalo and Burlington. Those who wanted to earn extra money were given a six-month industrial leave or the opportunity to pick peaches in nearby farms.[1064]

Suddenly, on August 2, 1945, the remaining paratroopers received astonishing news. The Canadian media reported that Corporal Frederick George Topham, a Battalion medical orderly, had been awarded the Victoria Cross, the highest decoration for valour in the British Commonwealth. Topham had been awarded this prestigious British decoration for his gallant action and bravery under fire during the first hours of Operation Varsity, on March 24, 1945.[1065] To mark this heroic achievement the City of Toronto organized a parade. The twenty-seven-year-old Topham was the eleventh and youngest Canadian to be awarded the VC.

Despite the numerous awards and honours presented to Battalion personnel and their unit's operational accomplishments, on September 4, 1945, the Adjutant-General, Major-General A.E. Walford, officially directed that the unit be disbanded.[1066] "As there no longer exists an operational requirement for No.1 Cdn Para Bn," explained Walford, "this unit will be reduced to Nil Strength effective 30 September 1945."[1067] Two weeks later, on September 17, the paratroopers were given the bad news.[1068] The announcement was greeted with mixed reactions. "I couldn't believe it," lamented Private Hector Allan, "I had no idea that it would happen." He explained, "We were picking peaches in Niagara and the next thing we knew we were told we were being sent back to our original areas of enrolment."[1069] Sergeant Roland Larose commented, "Many weren't happy. It was hard to accept, because when you are Airborne, you are Airborne for life." Others, however, had a more stoic outlook. "I accepted it as a normal thing," recalled Sergeant Art Stammer. "The war was over. They didn't need us any more."[1070] Corporal Ernie Jeans agreed, "The job was done. I had to get on with my life."[1071] In a matter of weeks the last paratrooper left Camp Niagara-on-the-Lake, and the Battalion became a part of history.

In less than thirty-eight months of existence, the 1st Canadian Parachute Battalion had achieved an impressive combat record. The Canadian paratroopers were amongst the first Allied troops to jump into Normandy, and they played a vital role in ensuring the success of the invasion and subsequent breakout. They were the only Canadians to have participated in the Battle of the Bulge in the Ardennes in the winter of 1944–45. In addition, they were an integral component of the massive airborne army that dropped into Germany and in the process advanced deeper into the Reich itself than any other Canadian unit.

In sum, the Battalion never failed to achieve its assigned missions, nor did it ever lose an objective once captured. Throughout their combat experience, the Canadian paratroopers displayed exceptional courage, endurance, fighting skill, and tenacity. Their actions had earned them the respect of their British airborne comrades, as well as the respect of their enemy.

Regrettably, NDHQ did not believe that airborne forces were a necessity in the post-war Canadian Army. A frustrated Lieutenant-Colonel Eadie vehemently argued to the contrary. "Here was a program that developed some of the best soldiers I ever saw," declared Eadie. "Not to take anything away from the other units," he asserted, "but here we had a group that could put the Canadian Army on the map, if we were only given a chance."[1072]

"It was the end of a great adventure," concluded Corporal Jeans.[1073] Now it was up to the future generations of Canadian airborne soldiers to carry on the proud Canadian Airborne tradition that had been established by the intrepid volunteers of the 1st Canadian Parachute Battalion.

APPENDIX 1

Ten Commandments of Canadian Parachute Troops

1. You are the elite of the Canadian Army. For you action shall be fulfilment and you must train yourself to stand every test.

2. Cultivate true comradeship, for together with your comrades you will triumph or die.

3. Be shy of speech and incorruptible. The strong act, the weak chatter; will bring you to the grave.

4. Calmness and caution, thoroughness and determination, valour and a relentless spirit of attack will make you superior when the test comes.

5. Face to face with the enemy, the most precious thing is ammunition. The man who fires aimlessly merely to reassure himself has no guts. He is a weakling and does not deserve the name of "Paratrooper."

6. Never Surrender. Your honour lies in victory or death.

7. Only with good weapons can you achieve success. Look after them therefore, on the principle, "First my weapons, then myself."

8. You must grasp the full meaning of each operation so that, even if your leader should fall, you can carry it out cooly and warily.

9. Fight chivalrously against an honourable foe; fifth columnist and civilian snipers deserve no quarter.

10. With your eyes open, keyed up to the highest pitch, agile as a greyhound, tough as leather, hard as steel, you will be the embodiment of a Canadian Paratrooper.

Originally printed in *Canadian Army Training Memorandum*, No. 24, March 1943.

APPENDIX 2

Honours and Awards Granted to Personnel of the 1st Canadian Parachute Battalion During the Second World War

The Victoria Cross
      Corporal F. G. Topham

The Distinguished Service Order
      Lieutenant-Colonel G. F. Eadie

Officer of the Order of the British Empire
      Lieutenant-Colonel J. A. Nicklin

Military Cross
      Captain P. R. Griffin
      Lieutenant J. P. Hanson
      Captain J. A. Clancy

Distinguished Conduct Medal
      Warrant Officer II J. Kemp
      Sergeant (A/Warrant Officer I) G.W. Green

Military Medal
      Sergeant J.A. Lacasse
      Sergeant G.H. Morgan
      Private W.S. Ducker
      Private R.A. Geddes
      Private W. Noval

Corporal (A/Sgt) W.P. Minard
Sergeant A. Bray
Private J.O. Quigley
Warrant Officer II G.W. Green

Source: DHH, file 1 Cdn Para Bn, List of personnel who received British decorations or medals during World War II. Honours and Awards Section, July 6 ,1949.

APPENDIX 3

Corporal F.G. Topham's Citation for the Victoria Cross

On *March 24, 1945, Cpl.* Topham, a medical orderly, parachuted with his battalion onto a strongly defended area east of the Rhine. At about 11 a.m., whilst treating casualties sustained in the drop, a cry for help came from a wounded man in the open. Two medical orderlies from a field ambulance went out to this man in succession, but both were killed as they knelt beside the casualty. Without hesitation and on his own initiative Cpl. Topham went forward through intense fire to replace the orderlies who had been killed before his eyes. As he worked on the wounded man, he was himself shot through the nose. In spite of severe bleeding and intense pain he never faltered in his task. Having completed immediate first aid he carried the wounded man steadily and slowly back through continuous fire to a shelter of the woods. During the next two hours Cpl. Topham refused all offers of medical help for his own wound. He worked most devotedly throughout this period to bring in wounded, showing complete disregard for the heavy and accurate enemy fire. It was only when all casualties had been cleared that he consented to his own wounded being treated. His immediate evacuation was ordered, but he interceded so earnestly on his own behalf that he was eventually allowed to return to duty. On his way back to his company he came across a carrier which had received a direct hit. Enemy mortar fire was still dropping around, the carrier itself was burning fiercely, and its own mortar ammunition was exploding: an experienced officer on the spot warned all not to approach the carrier. Cpl. Topham, however, immediately went out alone in spite of the blasting ammunition and enemy fire, and rescued the three occupants of the carrier. He brought these men back across the open ground, and although one died almost immediately afterwards, he arranged for the evacuation of the other two, who undoubtedly owe their lives to him. This non-commissioned officer showed sustained gallantry of the highest order, for six hours, most of the time in great pain. He performed a series of acts of outstanding bravery and his magnificent and selfless courage inspired all those who witnessed it.

APPENDIX 4

Maps

D-DAY, 6 June 1944.

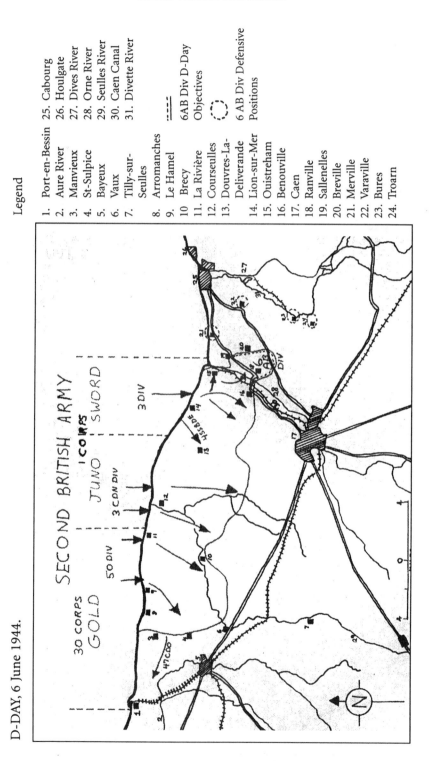

Legend

1. Port-en-Bessin
2. Aure River
3. Manvieux
4. St-Sulpice
5. Bayeux
6. Vaux
7. Tilly-sur-Seulles
8. Arromanches
9. Le Hamel
10. Brecy
11. La Rivière
12. Courseulles
13. Douvres-La-Deliverande
14. Lion-sur-Mer
15. Ouistreham
16. Benouville
17. Caen
18. Ranville
19. Sallenelles
20. Breville
21. Merville
22. Varaville
23. Bures
24. Troarn
25. Cabourg
26. Houlgate
27. Dives River
28. Orne River
29. Seulles River
30. Caen Canal
31. Divette River

---- 6AB Div D-Day Objectives

◌ 6 AB Div Defensive Positions

6 AB Div Landing Zones and Dropping Zones and
1 Cdn Para Bn D-Day Objectives, June, 6 1944.

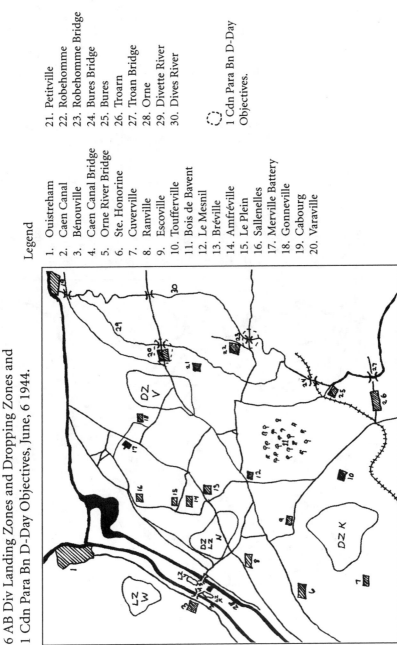

Legend

1. Ouistreham
2. Caen Canal
3. Bénouville
4. Caen Canal Bridge
5. Orne River Bridge
6. Ste. Honorine
7. Cuverville
8. Ranville
9. Escoville
10. Toufferville
11. Bois de Bavent
12. Le Mesnil
13. Bréville
14. Amfréville
15. Le Plein
16. Sallenelles
17. Merville Battery
18. Gonneville
19. Cabourg
20. Varaville

21. Petitville
22. Robehomme
23. Robehomme Bridge
24. Bures Bridge
25. Bures
26. Troarn
27. Troan Bridge
28. Orne
29. Divette River
30. Dives River

 1 Cdn Para Bn D-Day Objectives.

Defence of the Invasion Force's Left Flank by 6 AB Div,
June 6–August 16, 1944.

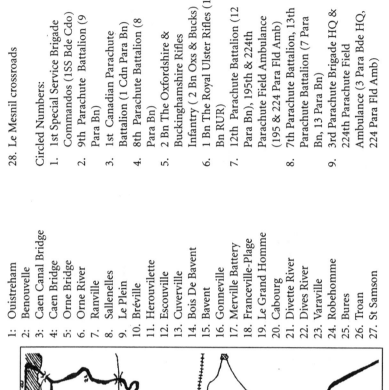

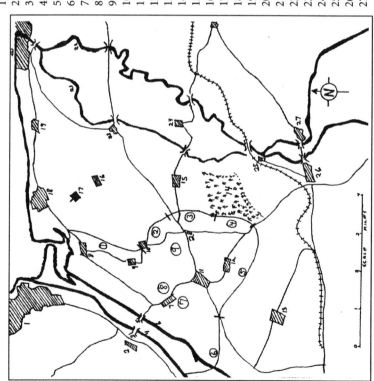

Legend

1: Ouistreham
2: Benouvelle
3: Caen Canal Bridge
4: Caen Bridge
5: Orne Bridge
6: Orne River
7: Ranville
8: Sallenelles
9: Le Plein
10: Bréville
11: Herouvilette
12: Escouville
13: Cuverville
14: Bois De Bavent
15: Bavent
16: Gonneville
17: Merville Battery
18: Franceville-Plage
19: Le Grand Homme
20: Cabourg
21: Divette River
22: Dives River
23: Varaville
24: Robehomme
25: Bures
26: Troan
27: St Samson
28. Le Mesnil crossroads

Circled Numbers:

1. 1st Special Service Brigade Commandos (1SS Bde Cdo)
2. 9th Parachute Battalion (9 Para Bn)
3. 1st Canadian Parachute Battalion (1 Cdn Para Bn)
4. 8th Parachute Battalion (8 Para Bn)
5. 2 Bn The Oxfordshire & Buckinghamshire Rifles Infantry (2 Bn Oxs & Bucks)
6. 1 Bn The Royal Ulster Rifles (1 Bn RUR)
7. 12th Parachute Battalion (12 Para Bn), 195th & 224th Parachute Field Ambulance (195 & 224 Para Fld Amb)
8. 7th Parachute Battalion, 13th Parachute Battalion (7 Para Bn, 13 Para Bn)
9. 3rd Parachute Brigade HQ & 224th Parachute Field Ambulance (3 Para Bde HQ, 224 Para Fld Amb)

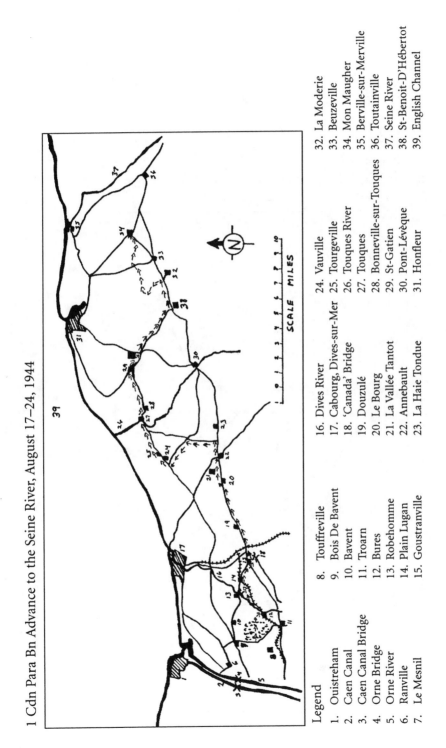

1 Cdn Para Bn Advance to the Seine River, August 17–24, 1944

Legend

1. Ouistreham
2. Caen Canal
3. Caen Canal Bridge
4. Orne Bridge
5. Orne River
6. Ranville
7. Le Mesnil
8. Touffreville
9. Bois De Bavent
10. Bavent
11. Troarn
12. Bures
13. Robehomme
14. Plain Lugan
15. Goustranville
16. Dives River
17. Cabourg, Dives-sur-Mer
18. 'Canada' Bridge
19. Douzulé
20. Le Bourg
21. La Vallée Tantot
22. Annebault
23. La Haie Tondue
24. Vauville
25. Tourgeville
26. Touques River
27. Touques
28. Bonneville-sur-Touques
29. St-Gatien
30. Pont-Lévéque
31. Honfleur
32. La Moderie
33. Beuzeville
34. Mon Maugher
35. Berville-sur-Merville
36. Toutainville
37. Seine River
38. St-Benoit-D'Hébertot
39. English Channel

Ardennes Campaign (Belgium), December 24, 1944–January 21, 1945.

Legend

→→→ 1 Cdn Para Bn Advance

⌐⌐⌐ 1 Cdn Para Bn Defensive Tasks and Patrolling

1. Meuse River
2. Anseremme
3. Givet
4. Celles
5. Ciergnon
6. Beaurang
7. Rochefort
8. Humain
9. Aye
10. March-en-Famenne
11. Hotton
12. Hargimont
13. Nassogne
14. Saint-Hubert
15. Champlon
16. Ortheuville
17. Bastogne
18. Noville
19. Allerborn
20. Bande
21. Waverville

1 Cdn Para Bn Deployment in Holland, January 22–February 21, 1945.

Legend

1. Maas River
2. Railway Bridge
3. Numhem, "C" Coy
4. Haelen, "HQ" Coy, 1 Cdn Para Bn HQ
5. Berik, "B" Coy
6. Buggenum, "A" Coy
7. Leeuwen
8. Overhaelen Station

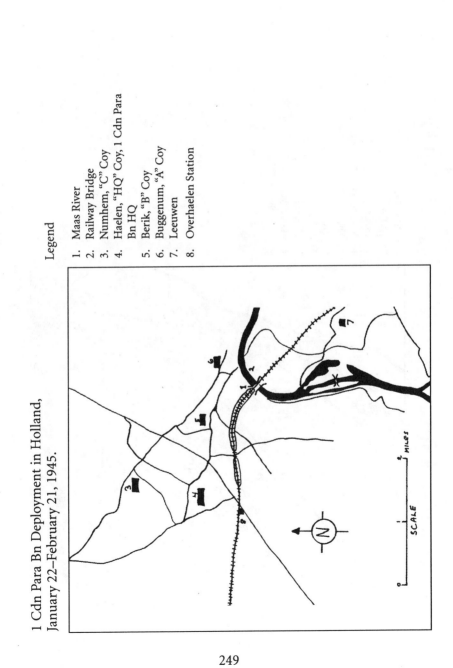

Operation Varsity, March 24, 1945

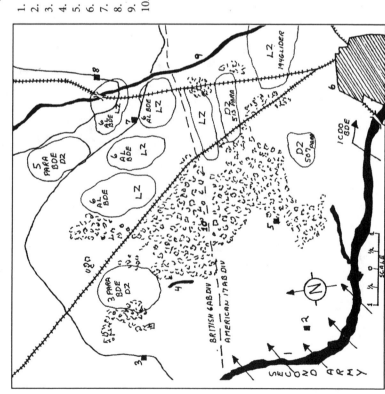

Legend

1. Rhine River
2. Bislich
3. Mehr
4. Schneppenberg Ridge
5. Diersfordt
6. Wesel
7. Hamminkeln
8. Ringenberg
9. Issel River
10. Diersfordter Wald

The Race to Wismar, March 24–May 2, 1945.

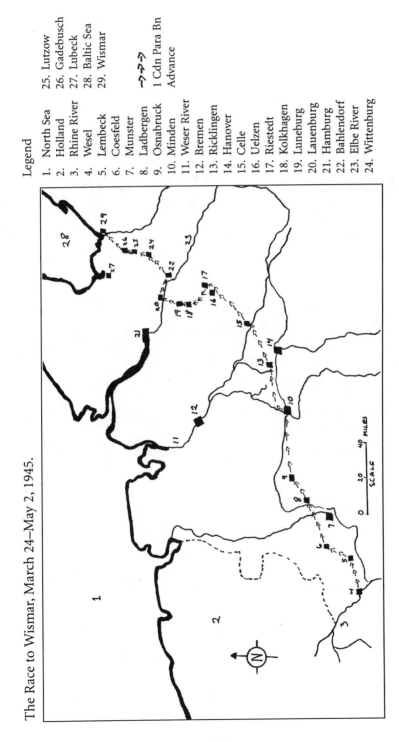

GLOSSARY OF ABBREVIATIONS

AA	Anti-Aircraft
AB	Airborne
AFE	Airborne Forces Establishment
AGL	Above Ground Level
Bde	Brigade
BHQ	Battalion Headquarters
Bn	Battalion
Bty	Battery
C-47	Dakota aircraft
CAFM	Canadian Airborne Forces Museum
CAPF	Canadian Army Pacific Force
CATM	*Canadian Army Training Memorandum*
CAS	Chief of the Air Staff
Cdn	Canadian
CEF	Canadian Expeditionary Force
CGS	Chief of the General Staff
CIBG	Canadian Infantry Brigade Group
CIGS	Chief of the Imperial General Staff
CinC	Commander-in-Chief
CLE	Central Landing Establishment
CLS	Central Landing School
CMHQ	Canadian Military Headquarters
CO	Commanding Officer
Coy	Company

CP	Command Post
CPTC	(A-35) Canadian Parachute Training Centre
CPTS	(S-14) Canadian Parachute Training School
CSM	Company Sergeant-Major
CWAC	Canadian Women's Army Corps
CWM	Canadian War Museum
DCGS	Deputy Chief of the General Staff
DCO	Deputy Commanding Officer
Det	Detachment
DHH	Directorate of History and Heritage (DND)
Div	Division
DLO	Director of Land Operations
DMO & P	Directorate of Military Operations and Plans
DMT	Directorate of Military Training
DND	Department of National Defence
DZ	Drop Zone
Engr	Engineer
Ex	Exercise
FAAA	First Allied Airborne Army
FAC	Forward Air Controller
Fd	Field
FOO	Forward Observation Officer
FSSF	First Special Service Force
Gp	Group
GOC	General Officer Commanding
GS	General Staff
HD	Home Defence
HQ	Headquarters
JAG	Judge Advocate General
JM	Jumpmaster
Km	Kilometre
MG	Machine Gun
MMG	Medium Machine Gun
MHQ	Military Headquarters
MIR	Medical Inspection Room
MND	Minister of National Defence
NA	National Archives of Canada
NCO	Non-Commissioned Officer
NDHQ	National Defence Headquarters
NL	National Library of Canada

NRMA	National Resources Mobilization Act
OC	Officer Commanding (normally a company or commando)
OP	Operation or Observation Post (depending on context)
Ops O	Operations Officer
OR	Other Ranks
Para	Paratrooper
P-Hour	Parachute Hour (time a drop will commence)
PI	Parachute Instructor
PIAT	Project Infantry Anti-Tank
PIR	Parachute Infantry Regiment
PJBD	Permanent Joint Board of Defence
Pl	Platoon
PoW	Prisoner of war
PPCLI	Princess Patricia's Canadian Light Infantry
PRO	Public Record Office (UK)
PT	Physical Training
PTS	Parachute Training School
QM	Quarter Master
RA	Royal Artillery
RAF	Royal Air Force
R22eR	Royal 22nd Regiment
RCA	Royal Canadian Artillery
RCAF	Royal Canadian Air Force
RCAMC	Royal Canadian Army Medical Corps
RCASC	Royal Canadian Army Service Corps
RCD	Royal Canadian Dragoons
RCE	Royal Canadian Engineers
RCHA	Royal Canadian Horse Artillery
RCIC	Royal Canadian Infantry Corps
RCOC	Royal Canadian Ordnance Corps
RCR	Royal Canadian Regiment
Recce	Reconnaissance
Regt	Regiment
RHQ	Regimental Headquarters
RSM	Regimental Sergeant-Major
RTU	Return to Unit
RV	Rendevous Point
SA	*Sturmabteilung* (German)
SS	*Schutzstaffeln* (German)
SAS	Special Air Service (British)

Sect	Section
SOP	Standard Operating Procedure
SP	Self-Propelled
Sqn	Squadron
TCV	Troop Carrying Vehicle
TEWT	Tactical Exercise Without Troops
TOET	Tests of Elementary Training (for weapons)
Tp	Troop
Tpt	Transport
Trg	Training
VC	Victoria Cross
VCGS	Vice Chief of the General Staff
Veh	Vehicle
WO	War Office (UK)

1 Cdn Para Bn	1st Canadian Parachute Battalion
1 Cdn Trg Bn	1st Canadian Parachute Coy / Battalion
1 SS Bde	1st Special Service Brigade (British)
2IC	Second-in-Command
3 Para Bde	3rd Parachute Brigade (British)
6 AB Div	6th Airborne Division (British)
8 Para Bn	8th Parachute Battalion (British)
9 Para Bn	9th Parachute Battalion (British)
82nd AB Div	82nd Airborne Division (US)

ENDNOTES

1. Lieutenant-Colonel Fraser Eadie, interview with Bernd Horn, June 23, 1998. See also Brigadier General Denis Whitaker and Shelagh Whitaker, *Rhineland: The Battle to End the War* (Toronto: Stoddart, 2000), 320.

2. Memorandum, file 1/Para-Tps/1/22-1, National Archives (NA), RG 24, Vol 12260. This is a common sentiment voiced by many of the 1 Cdn Para Bn veterans. Even the liaison officer (rank of major), originally established in July 1943 as a link between 6th Airborne Division and the Canadian Military Headquarters, was terminated after only four months because it was felt that the two entities were well enough established to maintain normal liaison without the need of a specially designated staff officer. However, it must be noted that there is no bitterness or recrimination in these observations. The paratroopers were proud of their origin and equally loyal to their new formation.

3. Address given by Brigadier S.J.L. Hill, June 1, 1997, Bulford Garrison Church, on occasion of the unveiling of a plaque to the memory of the 1st Canadian Parachute Battalion. *Maroon Beret*, Vol 2, No. 2, August 1997, 56-57.

4. Epilogue written by Lieutenant-Colonel Fraser Eadie for John Willes, *Out of the Clouds: The History of the 1st Canadian Parachute Battalion* (Port Perry: private printing, 1981), 195.

5. Casualty figures from Canadian Army Headquarters, Historical Section (G.S.), Report No. 17, "The First Canadian Parachute Battalion in the Low Countries and in Germany. Final Operations 2 January–18 February and 24 March–-5 May 1945," 12, DND Department of History and Heritage (DHH). Quote is from address given by Brigadier S.J.L. Hill, June 1, 1997, Bulford Garrison Church, on occasion of the unveiling of a plaque to the memory of the 1st Canadian Parachute Battalion. *Maroon Beret*, Vol 2, No. 2, August 1997, 56-57. He gave casualty figures as 128 killed, 296 wounded, and 84 taken prisoner.

6. Letter from Field-Marshall Sir Allan Brooke to Lieutenant-General J.C. Murchie, dated June 26, 1945. On display at the Canadian Airborne Forces Museum (CAFM), CFB Petawawa, Ontario.

7. The importance of this quote to the concept of airborne forces is evident in the fact

that almost every book on the history of airborne forces includes it. A sampling of examples includes: War Department (U.S.) *Enemy Air-Borne Forces* (Washington D.C.: War Department, December 2, 1942), 3; Major-General James Gavin, *Airborne Warfare* (Washington D.C.: Infantry Journal Press, 1947), vii; Matthew B. Ridgway, *Soldier: The Memoirs of Matthew B. Ridgway* (New York: Harper & Brothers, 1956), 69; Charles MacDonald, *Airborne* (Ballantine Books, Inc., 1970), 57; Brigadier M.A.J. Tugwell, "Day of the Paratroops," *Military Review* (Vol 57, No. 3, March 1977), 40-41; William B. Breuer, *Geronimo* (New York: St. Martin's Press, 1992), preface; and Tom Clancy, *Airborne* (New York: Berkley Books, 1997), xvii.

8.   See War Department (U.S.) *Enemy Air-Borne Forces,* 3–4; Ridgway, *Soldier,* 69; John Weeks, *The Airborne Soldier* (Dorset: Blandford Press, 1982), 11; and John Lucas, *The Silken Canopy: A History of the Parachute* (Shrewsbury, England: Airlife Publishing, 1997).

9.   War Department (U.S.) *Enemy Air-Borne Forces,* 4.

10. Weeks, *The Airborne Soldier,* 7.

11. Ibid.

12. See Lucas, *The Silken Canopy,* for a comprehensive history of the parachute.

13. Volkmar Kuhn, *German Paratroops in World War II* (London: Ian Allan Ltd, 1978), 7.

14. See John Weeks, *Airborne Equipment: A History of its Development* (London: David & Charles Newton Abbot, 1990), 10–11; and Max Arthur, *Men of the Red Beret: Airborne Forces 1940–1990* (London: Warner Books, 1990), xiii. Interestingly, issuing parachutes to fighter pilots was initially resisted because of the fear that this would encourage individuals to jump as soon as the "going got rough."

15. Although the German pilots' use of parachutes may have galvanized Mitchell's actions, it must be remembered that by this time the use of aircraft and parachutes to deliver individuals and supplies was already established. Within the first two years of the war, the British, for example, landed special agents behind enemy lines. In addition, in 1916, General Sir Charles Townshend's beleaguered force at Kut-al-Amara in Mesopotamia received some supplies by air, until their surrender in April 1916 to Turkish forces. Finally, as early as the spring of 1918, the French had dropped two-man demolition teams to destroy communications.

16. Brigadier-General William Mitchell, *Memoirs of World War I* (New York: Random House, 1928), 268. Mitchell felt "this was a perfectly feasible proposition. The Germans were already using parachutes for their pilots. Many a good man of theirs had been saved from an untimely death by this device."

17. Twenty-six years later, in August 1944, Lieutenant-General Brereton would be appointed commander of the newly formed First Allied Airborne Army.

18. See Lewis H. Brereton, *The Brereton Diaries: The War in the Air in the Pacific, Middle East and Europe, 3 October 1941–8 May 1945* (New York: William Morrow and Company, 1946).

19. See John R. Galvin, *Air Assault: the development of airmobile warfare* (New York: Hawthorn Books Inc, 1969), 3-4; MacDonald, *Airborne,* 57; Weeks, *Airborne Equipment,* 12; Weeks, *Airborne Soldiers,* 18; Michael Hickey, *Out of the Sky: A History of Airborne Warfare* (London: Mills & Boon Ltd, 1979), 14; Maurice Tugwell, *Airborne to Battle* (London: William Kimber, 1971), 23–24. The idea of using aircraft for transporting and air-landing troops over great distances was fairly common in the 1920s and onwards. For example, the British used their Vickers Vernon transport aircraft to deploy infantry to Iraq to subdue dissident tribesmen.

20. Shimon Naveh, *In Pursuit of Military Excellence — The Evolution of Operational*

Theory (London: Frank Cass, 1997), 209. The concept of "desanty" refers to the "operational manoeuvring potential, giving the ability to avoid physical friction and time consumption, caused by the movement of ground forces to the depth."

21.   Richard Simpkin, *Deep Battle: The Brainchild of Marshal Tukhachevskii* (London: Brassey's Defence Publishers, 1987), 34. There are numerous different spellings for Tukhachevsky, including Tukhachevskii and Tuchachevskiy.

22.   Harriet F. Scott and William F. Scott, eds., *The Soviet Art of War — Doctrine, Strategy, and Tactics* (Boulder, Colorado: Westview Press, 1982), 44.

23.   Simpkin, *Deep Battle*, 40. Deep penetration was defined as fifty to sixty kilometres into the opponent's territory to reach the line of the enemy's operational reserves, tactical airfields and army headquarters.

24.   David Glantz, *The History of Soviet Airborne Forces* (Portland: Frank Cas & Company, 1994), 4; and Scott, *The Soviet Art of War*, 64.

25.   Galvin, 4. In August 1933, the Soviets broke the world record for mass jumps when they dropped forty-six paratroopers from two large bombers at an air show in Moscow.

26.   Arthur, xv. See also Alexander Barmine, "I saw Parachute-War Born," *Saturday Night*, June 7, 1941, 9–10.

27.   David Glantz, *The Soviet Airborne Experience* (Fort Leavenworth: U.S. Army Command and General Staff College, 1984), 2; Steven J. Zaloga, *Inside the Blue Berets* (Novato: Presidio Press, 1995), 15; Galvin, 4; and Hickey, 16–17. Several detractions of the force became evident to Wavell. First, it took one and a half hours before the regiment was formed up and ready to fight. Second, they were lightly armed. Third, they had no motor transport. However, a small tank was also dropped during this exercise. Although it landed intact, it failed to start and was towed off the drop zone. See also Lieutenant-Colonel T.B.H. Otway, *Airborne Forces* (London: Imperial War Museum, 1990, reprint), 3–4.

28.   Condoelezza Rice, "The Making of Soviet Strategy," *The Makers of Modern Strategy*, Peter Paret, ed. (Princeton: Princeton University Press, 1986), 665. See also Frederick Kagan, "Army Doctrine and Modern War," *Parameters,* Spring 1997, 137–140.

29.   Simpkin, 181; and Charles Dick, "Soviet Operational Art," *International Defense Review,* (8/1988), 904.

30.   Naveh, 190.

31.   Tugwell, *Airborne to Battle*, 16.

32.   See Rudolf Böhmler and Werner Haupt, *Fallschirmjäger /Paratrooper* (Dorheim: Verlag Hans-Henning Podzun, 1971), 24; Roger J. Bender and George A. Petersen, *"Herman Göring": From Regiment to Fallschirmpanzerkorps* (San Jose, CA: Bender Publishing, 1975), 7; James Lucas, *Storming Eagles: German Airborne Forces in WWII* (London: Cassel & Co., 1988), 17–18; Bruce Quarrie, *German Airborne Troops 1939–45* (London: Osprey Publishing, 1983), 5; Hickey, 18; and Kuhn, 9.

33.   Bender and Petersen, 9.

34.   Kuhn, 15; Tugwell, *Airborne to Battle*, 27; and Hickey, 18.

35.   See Callum MacDonald, *The Lost Battle, Crete 1941* (New York: The Free Press, 1993), 6–7; and General Sir John Hackett, "Student," *Hitler's Generals,* ed. Corelli Barnet (London: Weidenfeld & Nicolson, 1987), 463–78. Hitler regarded airborne troops as one of his secret weapons in the early years of the war.

36.   See Böhmler and Haupt, 24; and Hickey, 19–20. The 7th Air Division had excellent integral aviation support. It consisted of 250 Ju52 transport aircraft, a close air support group with fighters, liaison aircraft, and dive bombers, and gliders.

37. MacDonald, *The Lost Battle*, 14.
38. Kuhn, 16.
39. Ibid. Student later lamented the difficulty of developing the "new weapon" in what he described as "often in the face of the ignorance and indifference of our own arch-conservative military establishment." Roger Edwards, *German Airborne Troops 1936–45* (London: Macdonald and Jane's, 1974), foreword. One of his biographers later wrote, "Kurt Student pursued his goals in an atmosphere of frustration. There was jealousy, lassitude, indecision, and limited vision on the part of many of his military colleagues, and wavering dedication and limited foresight on the part of his dictator, Adolf Hitler." A. H. Farrar-Hockley, *Student* (New York: Ballantine Books Inc., 1973), 6. However, Student did himself later concede that the first employment of parachute forces in war "was truly a leap in the dark in the truest sense of the word." Furthermore, he believed that there "was only a thin line separating defeat from victory" in regards to airborne operations. Böhmler and Haupt, 8, foreword by Kurt Student.
40. Lucas, *Storming Eagles*, 19. See also Otway, 6–16.
41. MacDonald, *The Lost Battle*, 13; and Kuhn, 16. Student's assessment was reinforced by Captain F.O Miksche, a witness to the paratroop scare that swept unoccupied Europe after May 10, 1940. Miksche wrote, "The defence against airborne invasion is necessarily associated with feelings of uncertainty and a sense almost of frustration during the long period of expectation when nothing happens though much is threatened. These feelings and the necessity for being on the constant alert may react unfavourably on the defender's nerves and in time lead to a decrease in his vigilance." Captain F.O. Miksche, *Paratroops — the history, organization and tactical use of airborne formations* (London: Faber and Faber Ltd, 1942), 133.
42. Thierry Vivier, "La Naissance de L'Arme Aéroportée en France," *Revue Historique Des Armées*, No. 4, 1992, 40-51; and Albert Merglen, *Histoire et Avenir des Troupes Aeroportees* (France: B. Arthaud, 1968).
43. Lucas, *Silken Canopy*, 104.
44. Memorandum for the Chief of Infantry from the Assistant Chief of Staff, May 1, 1939, extracted from Gerard Devlin, *Paratrooper* (New York: St. Martin's Press, 1979), 35.
45. Devlin, 36; and Lieutenant-General E.M. Flanagan, *The Angels — A History of the 11th Airborne Division* (Novato: Presidio Press, 1989), 8–9.
46. Martin Blumensen et al., Office of the Chief of Military History, Department of the Army, "Airborne Operations," declassified, no date, 1.
47. Edwards, foreword.
48. Breuer, *Geronimo*, 4–6; Flanagan, *The Angels*, 10–14; and Devlin, 80–81.
49. Air Marshall Sir John C. Slessor, "Some Reflection of Airborne Forces," *Army Quarterly 1948*, DHH.
50. Winston S. Churchill, *The Second World War: Their Finest Hour* (Boston: Houghton Mifflin Company, 1949), 246–247 & 466. There is some discrepancy regarding the actual date. Most sources, based on the seminal work done on the British Parachute Regiment (*The Red Beret*), state that General Ismay, Chief of the Imperial General Staff (CIGS), received instruction to establish a parachute corps on June 22, 1940. See Hilary St. George Saunders, *The Red Beret: The Story of the Parachute Regiment at War 1940–1945* (London: Michael Joseph, 1950), 27.
51. Patrick Cosgrove, *Churchill at War — Alone 1939–1940* (London: William Collins Sons & Co. Ltd., 1974), 95.
52. See Eliot A. Cohen, *Commandos and Politicians* (Cambridge: Center for

International Affairs, Harvard University, 1978), 37–40; Maxwell Schoenfeld, *The War Ministry of Winston Churchill* (Ames: The Iowa State University Press, 1972), 124; and Cosgrove, 95. Churchill was also the catalyst for the formation of the British commandos. His belief in special troops was apparent a letter to his Chief of Staff, General Hasting Ismay, on June 5, 1940, when he wrote, "Enterprises must be prepared, with specially trained troops of the hunter class who can develop a reign of terror down these coasts, first of all on the butcher and bolt policy; but later on, or perhaps as soon as we are organized, we should surprise Calais or Boulogne, kill and capture the Hun garrison and hold the place until all the preparations to reduce it by siege or heavy storm have been made, and then away." Cohen, 37.

53.   Otway, 23.

54.   "Development of Parachute Troops — Air Requirement — Conclusions of a Conference held in the Air Ministry on June 10 1940," Public Records Office (PRO), Air 39 /132, Air Ministry: Army Cooperation Command: Registered Files, AB Forces History, June 1940–1944. See also Otway, 25–26; and General Sir Richard Gale, *Call to Arms, An Autobiography* (London: Hutchison of London, 1968), 124.

55.   "Appendix A, to Agenda for Conference at the Air Ministry on 5 September 1940 — Note on the Employment of Airborne Forces," 3, PRO, Air 29/520, Air Ministry and MND: Operations Record Book, Miscellaneous units. No. 1 Parachute Training School Ringway, Previously Training Squadrons, Training Units.

56.   F.A.M. Browning, "Airborne Forces," *Royal United Services Institute* (*RUSI*), Vol 89, No. 556, November 1944, 351. Browning went on to become the commander of all British airborne troops by the end of the war.

57.   Robert W. Black, *Rangers in World War II* (New York: Ivy Books, 1992), 8.

58.   Churchill, *Their Finest Hour*, 247.

59.   Ibid, 176. A General HQ (GHQ) memo reported, "There were constant rumours and alarms during operations with regard to parachute troops and fifth column activities. It is essential that means to deal with this menace be thought out in detail ... to compete with this menace and to restore public confidence. An efficient 'parashot' organisation is of high importance since it is essential to maintain mobile reserves to deal with the situation in case of enemy break throughs." GHQ Home Forces, "Notes on the Operations in Flanders and Belgium 10th to 31st May with Particular Reference to the Present Problem of Home Defence," June 28, 1940. DHH, file 146.141009 (D2). Even the ever fiery and optimistic British Prime Minister was not immune to the wave of anxiety that swept through England. Churchill estimated the expected scale of airborne attack at approximately thirty thousand paratroopers. Churchill, *Their Finest Hour*, 285. In Britain, troop dispositions were tailored to counter the envisioned airborne invasion, and vast amounts of scarce materials were invested to this aim. The government adopted a policy to safeguard the country by ordering all open spaces (meaning virtually every park and playing field) all over Britain to be seeded with long spiked poles, concrete blocks, and other obstacles that would impede paratroopers. See also G.G. Norton, *The Red Devils* (Hampshire: Leo Cooper, 1971), 254; and Philip Warner, *The Special Forces of World War II* (London: Granada, 1985), 8.

60.   Robert S. McNamara, *The Essence of Security* (New York: Harper & Row Publishers, Inc., 1968), 107.

61.   "Meet 'Tommy' Burns – A Soldier's Soldier," by N. Gregor Guthrie. NA, MG 31, G6, E.L.M. Burns Fond, Vol 1, file — Veterans Affairs — MGen Burns.

62.   J.L. Granatstein, *The Generals: The Canadian Army's Senior Commanders in the Second World War* (Don Mills, Ontario: Stoddart, 1993), 116–117.

63. "Notes for Lecture Delivered to Offrs of CACRUs at Blackdown, 29 Dec 43." NA, MG 31, G6, E.L.M. Burns Fonds, Vol 9, file — Articles, Papers, Speeches, 9.

64. Lieutenant-General E.L.M. Burns, *General Mud: Memoir of World War II* (Toronto: Clarke, Irwin & Company Ltd, 1970), 18 and 25.

65. Burns published the "Mechanization of Cavalry" as early as 1923 in the *Canadian Defence Quarterly (CDQ)* Vol 1, No.3, 1923-1924, 37.

66. Major E.L.M. Burns, "Prize Essay — Protection of the Rearward Services and Headquarters in Modern War," *CDQ*, Vol 10, No. 3, April 1933, 295–313. Burns's notion of "motor-guerillas" raiding enemy rear areas was an extension of Fuller's concept born from his observations during the German "Michael Offensive" of March 21, 1918. The German penetration severed the command and control and logistics between the Allied rear and the front line. This in turn created a state of paralysis in the Allied armies. From this experience Fuller developed the belief that the key was to employ mobility as a psychological weapon to paralyze not only an enemy's command but also his government. See J.F.C. Fuller, *Conduct of War* (London: Eyre & Spottis Woode, 1961), 256–257; A.J. Trythall, *Boney Fuller: The Intellectual General 1878–1966* (London: Cassell, 1977), 60; and Brian Holden Reid, *J.F.C. Fuller Military Thinker* (Basingstoke: Macmillan, 1987), 49–51.

67. Memorandum Burns to CGS, August 13, 1940; DHH, file 112.1 (D32): Airborne Troops, Cdn 1940; and NA, RG 24, CMHQ, Vol 12260, file 1/Para Tps/1 , Memo Burns to CGS, November 12, 1940, 1.

68. Burns, *General Mud*, 100–101.

69. Churchill, *Their Finest Hour*, 285.

70. "Central Landing Establishment Memorandum. Provision of an Airborne Force, Nov: 1st 1940," PRO, AIR 39/132 Air Ministry: Army Cooperation Command: Registered Files, airborne forces history, June 1940–1944.

71. Ibid, 176; Norton, 254; and Warner, *The Special Forces*, 8. To assist in training personnel in countering enemy airborne operations, the British Army promulgated *Airborne Troops — Military Training Pamphlet*, No. 50, Part I — Defence Against Airborne Troops, 1941. National Library of Canada (NL).

72. John Swettenham, *McNaughton, Volume 2* (Toronto: The Ryerson Press Toronto, 1969), 117–119.

73. Burns, *General Mud*, 102.

74. Ibid.

75. Major D.H. Cunningham, "Further Material Relating to the Organization and Training of the 1st Canadian Parachute Battalion," Appendix A, To Historical Section, CMHQ Report No. 138, December 5, 1949, 1. DHH, CMHQ Report No. 138, July 7, 1945; and DHH, file Hist 1B.

76. Ibid., 1.

77. Swettenham, *McNaughton, Vol 2*, 30.

78. C.P. Stacey, *Six Years of War: The Army in Canada, Britain and the Pacific, Volume 1* (Ottawa: Queen's Printer, 1966), 212–221.

79. Memorandum, Burns to CGS, August 19, 1940. DHH, file 112.1 (D32): Airborne Troops, Cdn 1940.

80. Memorandum, Burns to CGS, August 28, 1940. DHH, file 112.1 (D32): Airborne Troops, Cdn 1940.

81. "Further Material Relating to the Organization and Training of the 1st Canadian Parachute Battalion," CMHQ Report 138, July 7, 1945. DHH, file Hist 1B, 2.

82. Message (G.S. 3140) Major-General Crerar, CGS, to H.Q. Cdn Corps, December

16, 1940. NA, RG 24, Vol 12260, file 1/Para Tps/ 1; and CMHQ Report 138, July 7, 1945, 1.

83. "Minutes of a Meeting held at the Air Ministry at 3.30 p.m. on September 5th, 1940, to discuss the provision of Airborne Forces." PRO, AIR 29/520 Air Ministry and Minister of Defence: Operations Record Book, Miscellaneous Units. No. 1 Parachute Training School Ringway, Previous Parachute Training Squadron, Training Units. See also Otway, 22. See also message, Canmilitry to Defensor, no date, DHH, file 112.1 (D32) AB Tps Cdn 1940.

84. "Air Staff Note — Present Situation in Respect of the Development of Parachute Training," September 1940, PRO, PREMIER 3/32/1; and "Churchill at War. The Prime Minister's Office Papers, 1940–45," Unit 1, reel 12, University Publications of America, Bethesda, Maryland.

85. Memorandum by Brigadier M.A. Pope, CMHQ, December 6, 1940. DHH file 112.1 (D32) AB Tps Cdn 1940; and Memo CMHQ, December 6, 1940. NA, RG 24, Vol 12260, CMHQ, file 1/Para Tps/1, 2.

86. "Historical Notes 1942–1945, First Canadian Parachute Battalion," 1. DHH, file 145.4013 (D1); "Historical Reports 1 Cdn Para Bn, 1942-1945." CAFM, Document A 87.002.61, 1; and CMHQ Report 138, 1-2.

87. "Extract from Meeting held at CMHQ London, at 1015 hrs, 20 Dec 40." DHH, file 112.1 (D32) AB Tps Cdn 1940.

88. Prime Minister Personal Minute Serial No. D 169/1 to General Ismay for C.O.S. Committee, May 27, 1941, PRO, PREMIER 3/32/1; and "Churchill at War. The Prime Minister's Office Papers, 1940–45," Unit 1, reel 12, University Publications of America, Bethesda, Maryland.

89. Ibid.

90. D.F. Butler, "The Airborne Forces, 1940–1943," 6–9. PRO, CAB 101/220, War Cabinet and Cabinet Officer: Historical Section: War Histories (Second World War), Military. See also "Minutes — War Office to Air Ministry, 27 August 1941." PRO, AIR, 39/38, Air Ministry: Army Cooperation Command: Registered Files. Airborne Forces Policy, December 1940–1941; "War Cabinet Chiefs of Staff Committee — Training of Parachutists," May 13, 1942. PRO, CAB 120/262; MGen Crerar, CGS, to H.Q. Cdn Corps, 15 Aug 41. NA, RG 24, CMHQ, Vol 12260, file 1/Para Tps/1, Msg (G.S. 0493).

91. Msg (G.S. 0493), Defensor to Canmilitry, August 15, 1941. NA, RG 24, CMHQ, Vol 12260, file 1/Para Tps/1, 22-1.

92. Msg (GS 1647), Canmilitry to Defensor, August 19, 1941. NA, RG 24, CMHQ, Vol 12260, file 1/Para Tps/1, 22-1.

93. Ibid. The original text was written in message form by telegraph and as a result appears choppy, if not grammatically challenged.

94. Msg (G.S. 1647), Canmilitry to Defensor, August 19, 1941, NA, RG 24, CMHQ, Vol 12260, file 1/Para Tps/1, 22-1; Letter, Brigadier B.G.S. G. G. Simonds, B.G.S. Cdn Corps to C.M.H.Q., "Paratroop Training," October 30, 1941. NA, CMHQ, RG 24, Vol 12260, file 1/Para Tps/1; and CMHQ Report 138, 2.

95. Telegram GS No. 2403, Canmilitry to Defensor, November 3, 1941. NA, RG 24, CMHQ, Vol 12260, file 1/Para Tps/1. See the given volume for a series of messages and memorandums asking for updates on the Army's policy on airborne forces. Interestingly, one series of reply correspondence were lost because the ship they were on was sunk by enemy submarines. The RCAF insistence is paradoxical. The paradox lies in the fact that the Air Ministry in England attempted to thwart the Army's expansion of airborne forces at every turn. For them, any

increase in paratroopers or gliders meant the diversion of pilots and aircraft away from the strategic bombing program. Air Marshal Sir Arthur Harris believed the crux of the matter was "whether Bomber Command was to continue its offensive action by bombing Germany or whether it was to be turned into a training and transport command for carrying about a few thousand airborne troops to some undetermined destination for some vague purpose." Butler, "Airborne Forces, 1940–1943," PRO, CAB 101/220, 13.

96.   CMHQ Report 138, 2.

97.   General Staff, "Appreciation Re Air Landing Troops," January 24, 1942. DHH, file 112.3M2 (D232)

98.   "Appreciation — What should be the nature of Canada's military effort during the next year," September 25, 1940. NA, MG 27, III, B11, Ralston Papers, Vol 37, Ralston Papers, 4.

99.   NA, Ralston Papers, MG 27, III, B11, Vol 38 — Army Programmes 1940–1944.

100. CMHQ Report 138, 3.

101. "The Dagger's Point — No. 1," *The Globe and Mail,* Toronto, Vol XCIX, No. 28800, April 6, 1942, 6. NL, microfilm N-20031.

102. "The Dagger's Point — No. II," *The Globe and Mail,* Toronto, Vol XCIX, No. 28801, April 7, 1942, 6. NL, microfilm N-20031.

103. Canada, *House of Common Debates* (hereafter *Debates),* April 22, 1942, 1851.

104. "Army Air Requirements. Memorandum by the Chief of the Imperial General Staff," 10 March 1942. PRO, PREMIER 3/32/2 and "Churchill at War. The Prime Minister's Office Papers, 1940-45," Unit 1, reel 12, University Publications of America, Bethesda, Maryland.

105. Otway, 52.

106. Ibid., 56. On 10 June 1942 General Marshal wrote his counterpart, Sir Alan Brooke (CIGS) and invited Major-General F.A.M. Browning for a visit to the United States "for the purpose of furthering the exchange of these [airborne] ideas on this important activity." Letter, 10 June 1942, *The Papers of George C. Marshall: Selected WWII Correspondence.* Reel 5, file 0773, University Publications of America, Bethesda, Maryland.

107. "Minutes of a Meeting of the Inter-Service Committee on Air Borne Troops, Held at NDHQ, 1000 hours, 25 July 42," July 28, 1942. DHH, file 112.3M2 (D232), 1. A letter from Volfair Safety Chute to Major H.O. Proctor, a staff officer at NDHQ, dated July 25, 1942, captured the precipitateness of the shift. It stated, "The Canadian Army has suddenly expressed an interest in parachutes." DHH, file 314.009 (D321).

108. *Minutes of the War Committee of the Cabinet,* Vols 7-11, 1942. Reel 3, July 1, 1942.

109. "Minutes of a Meeting of the Inter-Service Committee on Air Borne Troops, Held at NDHQ, 1000 hours, 25 July 42," July 28, 1942. DHH, file 112.3M2 (D232), Appendix A.

110. Directorate of Military Operations and Planning (DMO & P), "The Army Use of Gliders," August 5, 1942. DHH, file 112.3M2 (D232).

111. DMO & P, "Policy — Airborne Troops," December 7, 1942. DHH, file 112.3M2 (D232).

112. Minutes (HQS 8846-1, Vol 9), DMO & P to CGS, no date. DHH, file 112.3M2 (D232). Even the looming Japanese threat on the West Coast did not overly concern the military. Even after the Japanese seizure of the islands of Attu, Agatu, and Kiska in the Aleutians in July 1942, the official analysis reaffirmed that "the forms and scales of attack envisioned on the entry of Japan into the war remained unchanged."

The Armed Forces' position rested on the basis that there were no military objectives of sufficient importance to justify anything other than very small scale tip-and-run raids, the effect of which would have little military significance. In addition, the generals emphasized the fact that the Japanese were already over-committed. The Chiefs of Staff Committee clearly professed that an actual attempt at an invasion on this coast by Japanese forces was considered highly remote. See "An Appreciation of the Military World Situation with Particular Regard to its Effect on Canada," (as of July 31, 1942), completed by the General Staff (GS), August 4, 1942, 7, NA, Ralston Papers, MG 27, III, B11, Vol 37; "Brief Appreciation of the Situation as of 24 Feb 1941," GS estimate February 25, 1941, 2; and "Japanese Occupation of the Aleutians Islands," GS estimate July 15, 1942, 3, NA, Ralston Papers, MG 27, III, B11, Vol 37.

113.   Lieutenant-Colonel Fraser Eadie, interview with Bernd Horn, June 23, 1998.

114.   Letter, Canadian Attache to the Adjutant-General, "Transfer of Personnel from 1st to 2nd Canadian Parachute Battalion," February 25, 1943. NA, RG 24, Series C-1, file HQS 8846-1, Reports on Parachute Troops, Vol 1, Reel C-5277.

115.   DCGS (A), "Role of 1st Parachute Bn.," December 6, 1942. DHH, file 112.21009 (D197).

116.   Lieutenant-Colonel Fraser Eadie interview, June 23, 1998.

117.   Message (G.S. 142), CGS, Major-General Stuart to Lieutenant-General McNaughton, March 6, 1943, and (G.S. 583) McNaughton to Stuart, March 18, 1943. NA, RG 24, CMHQ, Vol 12260, file 1/Para Tps/1, 22-1.

118.   War Office (UK), *Army Training Instruction #5. Employment of Parachute Troops, 1941* (London: War Office, August 20, 1941), 3–5.

119.   "The Value of Airborne Forces," Memorandum by CIGS, January 11, 1943, "Churchill at War. The Prime Minister's Office Papers, 1940–45." Unit 1, reel 12, University Publications of America, Bethesda, Maryland.

120.   Breuer, *Geronimo*, 9; and Ridgway, *Soldier*, 54.

121.   U.S. War Department Operations Division, General Staff, Strategy Book, November 1942, 212–213 & 219. National Archives, Washington D.C., RG 165, entry 422, box 2, item 10A, exec 1, file OPD Strategy Book, November 1942. Sourced from the Joint Military Intelligence College Washington, D.C.

122.   1 Cdn Para Bn War Diaries, January 15, 1943. NA, RG 24, Vol 15298, January 1943.

123.   Brian Nolan, *Airborne: The Heroic Story of the 1st Canadian Parachute Battalion in the Second World War* (Toronto: Lester Publishing Ltd., 1995), 34.

124.   "Assembling Paratroopers At Calgary," *Globe and Mail*, Vol XCIX, No. 28916, August 18, 1942, 13, NL, Microfilm N-20035.

125.   Robert Taylor, "Paratroop Van Eager to be Tip of Army 'Dagger,'" *Toronto Daily Star*, August 12, 1942. 1 Cdn Para Bn Assn Archives, Lockyer, Mark, file 10-3.

126.   The term elite is often misused. In its purest form it represents "the choice or most carefully selected part of a group." David Guralnik, ed., *Webster's New World Dictionary* (Nashville: The Southwestern Company, 1972), 244. Eliot Cohen, a former Harvard University scholar, developed specific criteria to define elite military units. He stated, "First, a unit becomes elite when it is perpetually assigned special or unusual missions: in particular, missions that are — or seem to be — extremely hazardous. For this reason airborne units have long been considered elite since parachuting is a particularly dangerous way of going into battle." Cohen's second criterion was based on the premise that elite units conduct missions that "require only a few men who must meet high standards of training and physical toughness, particularly the latter." Finally, he maintained that "an elite unit becomes elite only when it achieves a reputation-justified or not-for bravura and success." Eliot A.

Cohen, *Commandos and Politicians* (Cambridge: Center for International Affairs, Harvard University, 1978), 17. For strategist Colin Gray, the designation "elite" pertained directly to the standard of selection and not to the activity that soldiers were selected to perform. Colin S. Gray, *Explorations in Strategy* (London: Greenwood Press, 1996), 158. Conversely, military historian Douglas Porch utilized conventional measures of performance to determine elite status. As a result, he relied on such benchmarks as "battlefield achievement, military proficiency, or specialized military functions." Douglas Porch, "The French Foreign Legion: The Mystique of Elitism," in *Elite Formations in War and Peace,* eds. A. Hamish Ion , and Keith Neilson (Wesport: Praeger, 1996), 117. 1 Cdn Para Bn was clearly a military elite unit. Members underwent rigorous selection and were required to maintain high standards of physical fitness and toughness; the unit was assigned a unique mission and received specialized training and equipment. Finally, it earned a well-deserved reputation for battlefield accomplishments.

127. Lieutenant-Colonel E.M. Flanagan, "Give Airborne Spurs," *Infantry School Quarterly*, Vol 39, No. 2, October 1951, 33.

128. Flanagan, "Give Airborne Spurs," 33.

129. *Parachute Corps* (New York: British Information Services, 1942), 1 Cdn Para Bn Assn Archives, Storey, W.E., file 32–3.

130. Saunders, *The Red Beret*, 103; and William Cockerham, "Selective Socialization: Airborne Training as Status Passage," *Journal of Political and Military Sociology*, Vol 1, No. 2, Fall 1973, 216.

131. Taylor, "Paratroop Van Eager to be Tip of Army 'Dagger.'"

132. James C. Anderson, "Tough, Hard-As-Nails Paratroopers Arrive to Open Shilo School," September 22, 1942, 1. Cdn Para Bn Assn Archives, Firlotte, Robert, file 2-11; "Toughest in Canada's Army Back for Paratroop Course," *The Star*, September 21, 1942. 1 Cdn Para Bn Assn Archives, Firlotte, Robert, file 2-11; and Ronald K Keith, "Sky Troops," *Maclean's Magazine*, August 1, 1943, 18–20 & 28. This is simply a representative sample. Virtually every article in newspapers nation wide used similar adjectives to describe Canada's "newest corps elite."

133. "Assembling Paratroopers At Calgary," *Globe and Mail*, Vol XCIX, No. 28916, August 18, 1942, 13. NL, microfilm N-20035; and Taylor, "Paratroop Van Eager to be Tip of Army 'Dagger.'"

134. "Assembling Paratroopers At Calgary," *Globe and Mail*.

135. James C. Anderson, "Canada's Paratroopers Don't Have Stage Fright," *Saturday Night*, No. 11, December 12, 1942, 11. NL, microfilm 56A.

136. "Major Hilton D. Proctor," *Globe and Mail*, Vol XCIX, No. 28911, August 12, 1942, 1. NL, microfilm N-20035; and Memorandum, DMT to DCGS (B), October 30, 1942, "1 Cdn Parachute Battalion." NA, RG 24, series C-1, file HQS 8846-7, No. 1, 2, Reports on Parachute Troops, microfilm reel C-8379.

137. Taylor, "Paratroop Van Eager to be Tip of Army 'Dagger.'"

138. "Assembling Paratroopers At Calgary," *Globe and Mail*.

139. Memorandum, DND HQ MD No. 2, "Serial 1351 - 1st Parachute Battalion," November 27, 1942. NA, RG 24, series C-1, file HQS 8846-1, Vol 21, Parachute Troops. Organization, Training 1941–45, microfilm C-5278.

140. Letter, DCGS to District Officers Commanding, "Canadian Parachute Battalion," July 29, 1942. CAFM, AB 1, 1 Cdn Para Bn, Vol 2, File 19.

141. Letter, Major-General H.F.G. Letson (Adjutant-General), "1st Parachute Battalion - Serial 1351." NA, RG 24, series C-1, file HQS 8846-1, Vol 12. Microfilm C-5278, Vol 12.

142. Draft letter, Air Chief Marshal C.F.A. Portal, Air Ministry to GHQ Home Forces, January 1942. PRO, AIR 39/26. Air Ministry: Army Cooperation Command: Registered Files. Airborne Forces Organization, February 1941–43.

143. Major-General R.N. Gale, Pamphlet — "To All Officers in the 6th Airborne Division," June 1943. CAFM, AB 1, 1 Cdn Para Bn, Vol 6, file 21.

144. "Training Paratroops," *Canadian Army Training Memorandums*, No. 20, November 1942, 10.

145. Miksche, *Paratroops*, 133.

146. Letter, The Secretary DND (Army), "1st Canadian Parachute Battalion - Accounting of Personnel," 17 December 1942. NA, RG 24, series C-1, file HQS 8846-1. Microfilm C-5277, Vol 17; Memorandum, A.P. 3, "1st Canadian Parachute Bn - Documentation, Relinquishment of N.C.O. Appointment, February 11, 1943. Ibid, Vol 1; and Letter, Military Attache Canadian Legation to the Secretary, Department of National Defence (Army), "Organization - 1st Canadian Parachute Battalion," February 20, 1943. NA, RG 24, series C-1, file HQS 8846-8, Promotions 1 Cdn Para Bn, 1942–43, microfilm C-8379.

147. "Canada's Jumping Jacks!" *Khaki: The Army Bulletin*, Vol 1, No. 22, September 29, 1943, 1.

148. Letter, A.E. Moll, "Selection of Airborne Personnel," 52/Psychiatry/4/3 S.P.5. — November 24, 1943. 1 Cdn Para Bn Assn Archives.

149. Letter, November 15, 1985, from Dr. Bill McAndrews (DHH Historian) to Brigadier-General E. Beno. CAFM.

150. Letter, Adjutant-General to all District Officers Commanding, "Parachute Battalion, Serial No. 1351," July 10, 1942. DHH, file 171.009/ D223. The Army definition of "A.1." category was: "The man shall be able to see to shoot or drive, and can undergo severe strain without defects of locomotion and with only minor remediable disabilities. Age — between 22 and 32 years of age; Height — usual heights — minimum 5'2", max 6'; Weight — minimum 125lbs, maximum 196 lbs; Visual Standards — 20/40 both eyes without glasses. Colour vision should be 'defective safe'; Hearing W.V. — 10ft. both ears, i.e. a man standing with his back to the examiner and using both ears, must be able to hear a forced whisper 10 feet away. Must have patent Eustachian Tubes; Dental — Men must not drop with false teeth, consequently there must be eight sound or reparable teeth (including two molars) in the upper jaw in good functional opposition to corresponding teeth in lower jaw; Injuries of limbs — it was agreed that men with old fractures of the lower limbs or spine, however well recovered, were not suitable. Flat-feet not acceptable. Must have full movements in all joints of lower limbs; Mental and intelligence standard: It was agreed that men with alert minds are required for these duties and that men with doubtful intelligence should be eliminated by an intelligence test." Medical Standards for Paratroops. NA, RG 24, series C-1, file HQS 8846-1, Vol 15. Microfilm C-5277.

151. Letter, Adjutant-General to Commanders, "1st Parachute Battalion - Serial 1351," October 2, 1942. NA, RG 24, series C-1, file HQS 8846-1, Vol 12. Microfilm C-5277. There were those who were ineligible to volunteer for the paratroops. They were: tradesmen who have completed trade training; personnel under instruction in Army Trade Schools, Technical Schools, or Vocational Schools; and personnel earmarked for trades such as surveyors, instrument mechanics, wireless mechanics, radio mechanics, electricians, and fitters.

152. "Paratroops' Instructors are Selected," *Globe and Mail*, August 14, 1942, Vol XCIX, No. 28912 2. NL, microfilm N-20035.

153. Ibid. Rifleman H.G. Ives asserted, "They all thought it was a great chance to get action and quick." "Toughest in Canada's Army Back for Paratroop Course," *The Star*, September 21, 1942. 1 Cdn Para Bn Assn Archives, Firlotte, Robert, file 2-11. Another common sentiment was that the unit "was the best way of getting at the enemy." Dave Campbell, "Parachuters' Reunion Raises Old Memories," *The Brandon Sun*, June 7, 1971, 3. Hector Allan stated he joined to "get to where the action is" and Doug Morrison felt it was "a more exciting way to get into the war." Interviews with Bernd Horn, January 31, 2002.

154. Brigadier S.J.L. Hill, Presentation to U.K. War College, November 1993, 12. In an interview with journalist and writer Brian Nolan, on April 25, 1994, Brigadier Hill explained that his Canadian soldiers also joined the paratroopers because they "were fed up, with no conscription; they wanted something perhaps slightly spectacular, others felt the sense of duty." Letter, HQ Military District 3 to all officers commanding all units, "Parachute Battalion - Serial No. 1351," July 17, 1942, Annex B. CAFM, AB 1, 1 Cdn Para Bn, Vol 2, file 19.

155. T.E. Gavinski, interview with Bernd Horn, November 25, 1998.

156. Jan de Vries, interview with Bernd Horn, January 9, 2001.

157. Letter, Major A.E. Moll, "Selection of Airborne Personnel," 52/Psychiatry/4/S.P.5. November 24, 1943, 3. 1 Cdn Para Bn Assn Archives.

158. Memorandum, Colonel W. Line, "Selection of Personnel — 1st Parachute Battalion," December 23, 1942. DHH, file 163.009 (D16); and NA, RG 24, series C-1, file HQS 8846-1, Vol 16, microfilm C-5277.

159. Ibid. Many also volunteered to escape their current employment and not due to any real interest in parachute work.

160. Memorandum, Colonel W. Line, "1st Parachute Bn. (Serial 1351), December 26, 1942. NA, RG 24, series C-1, file HQS 8846-1, Vol 16, microfilm C-5277.

161. The personnel assessments consulted were found primarily in NA, RG 24, series C-1, file HQS 8846-1, Vol 19, microfilm C-5277. They spanned the period September 1942 to early 1943. It became evident that the cases in January to March 1943 were less rigidly assessed than those in 1942. This is a reflection of the difficulties that the Army experienced in filling the necessary quotas of aspiring paratroopers to undertake the necessary training in Fort Benning.

162. Ibid.

163. This detailed breakdown was done to provide greater visibility into the selection process. Many of these categories actually fall into the definition of "instability" as given in endnote 35. The remainder of the reasons with percentages were as follows: health reasons, 10 percent; voluntary withdrawal, 9 percent; mentally slow, 7 percent; non-swimmer, 1 percent; poor military record, 2 percent; and other, approximately 6 percent.

164. Examples are drawn from Personnel Assessments, NA, RG 24, series C-1, file HQS 8846-1, Vol 19. Microfilm C-5277.

165. Letter, Adjutant-General to GOCs, "Selection of Personnel — Canadian Parachute Troops," May 11, 1943. NA, RG 24, series C-1, file HQS 8846-1, Vol 24, microfilm C-5277.

166. Ibid. In the early months of 1943 there appears to have been numerous cases where medical examiners and psychiatrist recommended sending individuals as trial cases, yet they were overruled by the "OC of the Para Bn." It is unclear from the documents whether the OC is fact an improper acronym for the Commanding Officer (Lieutenant-Colonel) or whether if refers to an OC (Major - sub-unit commander) who was assigned as a liaison/standards officer to the selection process.

167. H.R. Holloway, interview with Bernd Horn, November 4, 1998.

168. Albert Kemshead, recollection in unpublished manuscript, "A Portrait of a Paratrooper," by David Owen, 18. 1 Cdn Para Bn Assn Archives, David Owen fond. Another veteran, John Feduck, is quoted in the same source as stating that a hidden fan was often used to create air currents that would make the paper shake. The candidate would then be told he was too nervous to be accepted in an attempt to discourage the volunteer and judge their reaction to an obstacle. John Feduck, interview with Michel Wyczynski, December 19, 2001.

169. John Simpson, interview with Michel Wyczynski, December 13, 2001.

170. Owen, "A Portrait of a Paratrooper," 15–20; Larose and Bill Talbot, interviews with Michel Wyczynski, January 10, 2002 and December 28, 2001, respectively; and Doug Morrison, interview with Bernd Horn, January 31, 2002.

171. Lieutenant-Colonel Fraser Eadie, interviews with Bernd Horn, June 23, 1998 and November 20, 2000.

172. Ibid.

173. Jan de Vries, interview with Bernd Horn, January 9, 2001.

174. "A.35 Canadian Parachute T.C.," November 19, 1943. DHH, file 112.21009 (D197) folder 6. Sergeant R.F. Anderson stated that, based on his discussions with others, a minimum of 60–70 percent of volunteers failed the selection/training process. Interview with Bernd Horn, June 11, 1998. This is consistent with the recollection of other veterans.

175. Letter, Adjutant-General, "1st Parachute Battalion - Serial 1351," August 10, 1942. DHH, file 171.009 (D223).

176. Telegram, Defensor to CanMilitry (Murchie to Stuart), October 1, 1942. 1 Cdn Para Bn Assn Archives.

177. Telegram, GS 3430, CanMilitry to Defensor, Ottawa, October 5, 1942. 1 Cdn Para Bn Assn Archives.

178. Report Flight Lieutenant Killick RCAF to M.T. 2, Major R.A. Keane, "Parachute Battalions," October 28, 1942. NA, RG 24, series C-1, file HQS 8846-7, No. 1, microfilm C-8379.

179. CMHQ Report 138, "Further Material Relating to the Organization and Training of the 1st Canadian Parachute Battalion," Appendix A, 56. DHH, file Hist 1B. By October 15, 1942, thirty Home Defence personnel had volunteered for parachute training.

180. Memorandum, DCGS to JAG, "1st Canadian Parachute Battalion," November 10, 1942. NA, RG 24, series C-1, file HQS 8846-1, Vol 11, microfilm C-5277.

181. Memorandum, JAG to DCGS, "First Canadian Parachute Battalion," November 10, 1942. NA, RG 24, series C-1, file HQS 8846-1, Vol 11, microfilm C-5277.

182. Letter, Military Attache Canadian Legation to DMT, "Parachute Troops, NRMA Personnel," December 18, 1942. NA, RG 24, series C-1, file HQS 8846-1, Vol 19, Microfilm C-5277; and CMHQ Report 138, Appendix A.

183. "Physical Standards and Instructions for the Medical Examination of Serving Soldiers and Recruits for the Canadian Army - 1943," 1 Cdn Para Bn Assn Archives; and "Medical Standards for Paratroops — All Ranks," January 18, 1943. NA, RG 24, series C-1, file HQS 8846-1, Vol 19, microfilm C-5277.

184. PULHEMS stood for: P – physique; U – upper limbs; L – lower limbs; H – hearing; E – eyes; M – mental; S – stability. Soldiers were graded from 1 to 5 for each of these factors, 1 being fit for any military employment, 5 being fit for none. Major-General F.M. Richardson, *Fighting Spirit. A Study of Psychological Factors in War* (London: Leo Cooper, 1978), 165.

185. Letter, Adjutant-General to GOCs, "Selection of Paratroops — Specifications General Instructions," May 17, 1944. 1 Cdn Para Bn Assn Archives; Letter, Director of Personnel Selection to All District Army Examiners, " Selection of Paratroops — Specifications General Instructions," May 22, 1944. 1 Cdn Para Bn Assn Archives; and Letter, Director of Personnel Selection to All District Army Examiners, " Selection of Paratroops," March 2, 1945. DHH, file 163.009 (D16).

186. Letter, Director of Personnel Selection to All District Army Examiners, "Selection of Paratroops — Specifications General Instructions," May 22, 1944. 1 Cdn Para Bn Assn Archives.

187. Ibid.

188. Memorandum, DMT to DCGS, "1st Canadian Parachute Battalion," October 22, 1942. DHH, file 112.3M300 (D99).

189. Ibid.

190. "Training Paratroops," *CATM*, November 1942, No. 20, 10.

191. *Canadian Parachute Training Centre — Standard Syllabus 1944.* DHH, file: 145.4036 (D2).

192. Taylor, "Paratroop Van Eager to be Tip of Army 'Dagger.'"

193. Otway, 29.

194. Ibid., 25. During that period the Air Ministry and the War Office focused all their energies, resources and manpower to counter the incessant Luftwaffe night and later day raids. With this ongoing battle to ensure Britain's survival, "many doubted whether there was yet time to spare for the creation of a force which could exert no major influence on the war for some time to come."

195. Ibid., 25, 29. The three main factors that hampered the maturation of the British airborne forces from the outset were the priority to manpower, priority to material, and the lack of policy. Britain was bracing for a possible invasion, and vast numbers of troops were required to guard its coasts and patrol vast areas to counter potential airborne and parachute insertions. In 1940, England was gearing its war industry, and the focus of its efforts was to supply planes and armaments to the RAF. Initially, the School had six obsolete Mark II Whitley bombers and one thousand RAF training type parachutes.

196. Introduction to The Central Landing Establishment's Operational Record Book, 1949-1945. PRO, AIR 39/58, Air Ministry: Army Co-operation Command: Registered Files, Airborne Forces Training, May-November 1942, 2.

197. Otway, 29-30. The Central Landing Establishment now comprised a Parachute Training School, a Technical Unit, and a Glider Training Squadron. The Establishment's mandate was to train aircrews, glider pilots, and parachute troops in the various technical and operational aspects of airborne warfare, conduct technical research, and develop operational requirements.

198. Air Ministry, *By Air To Battle: The Official Account of The British First and Sixth Airborne Divisions* (London: The Whitefriars Press Ltd., 1945), 7.

199. Maurice Newnham, *Prelude To Glory: The Story of the Creation of Britain's Parachute Army* (London: Sampson Low, Marston & Co., Ltd., 1948), 65.

200. Otway, 30.

201. Robin Hunter, *True Stories of The Paras: The Red Devils at War* (London: Virgin Publishing, 1999), 14–15.

202. Otway, 27-28.

203. Newnham, 55-56. Newnham recruited his future parachute instructors from the RAF Physical Fitness Branch.

204. Ibid.

205. Air Ministry, *By Air To Battle*, 16.
206. Otway, 31.
207. Ibid., 37.
208. Ibid., 38.
209. Ibid., 39.
210. Saunders, *The Red Beret*, 25-26.Even though all current efforts were geared towards the development of large airborne and air-landing units, smaller units were being trained and deployed on operations such as "Colossus" (Tragino Aqueduct, Italy) on February 10, 1941, and the later Bruneval Raid, on the coast of France, February 27–28, 1942. These two small-scale airborne operations provided valuable information used to re-assess and improve airborne training. Intelligence gathering and planning had to be improved. In Operation Colossus the soft-skinned containers were unsatisfactory. This led to the development of metal containers as well as a series of equipment changes on aircraft used for smaller parachute missions. Despite the limited tactical success achieved during these two raids, they nevertheless were great morale boosters for the British paratroopers and training staff alike. These incursions forced the Axis to deploy large numbers of troops to guard coastlines, industrial sites, and military installations and to monitor the skies for enemy aircraft. Furthermore, additional aircraft were required to patrol their vast air space. See also Otway, 5.
211. Otway, 52-53.
212. Ibid., 50.
213. Memoranda on the Organization and Employment of the Airborne Division by Major-General F.A.M. Browning, D.S.O., Commander — The Airborne Division, Headquarters, HOME FORCES, January 24, 1942. NA, RG 24, series C-1, file HQS 8846-7, No.1, Promotions, 1 Canadian Parachute Battalion, microfilm C-8379.
214. Otway, 53-54.
215. Ibid., 52.
216. Ibid., 52-53.
217. Norton, 208–210. By autumn 1942, the British Airborne Forces comprised the following units: 1st Parachute Brigade (formed September 1941), which contained the 1st Parachute Battalion (September 15, 1941), 2nd and 3rd Parachute Battalions (November 1941) — the 4th Battalion was formed later; 1st Air-Landing Brigade Group (October 10, 1941); the Army Air Corps, including the Glider Pilot Regiment (December 21, 1941); HQ 1st Airborne Division (Fall 1942), Airborne Forces Depot and Battle School – Hardwick Hall (unofficially established April 1942 and officially approved by the War Office December 1942); 2nd Parachute Brigade (July 17, 1942) — 4th Battalion was transferred to this Brigade in August 1942; 7th Battalion The Cameron Highlanders became the 5th (Scottish) Parachute Battalion, the 10th Battalion The Royal Welch Fusiliers became the 6th (Royal Welsh) Parachute Battalion; a second Glider Pilot Regiment (August 1942). All parachute battalions that had no parent corps or regiments were formed by the War Office into the Parachute Regiment as part of the Army Air Corps. On November 5, 1942, the formation of the 3rd Parachute Brigade was authorized and comprised the following units: 10th Battalion The Somerset Light Infantry, becoming the 7th (Light Infantry) Battalion The Parachute Regiment; 13th Battalion The Royal Warwickshire Regiment becoming 8th (Midland) Battalion The Parachute Regiment; 10th Battalion The Essex Regiment becoming 9th (Eastern and Home Counties) Battalion The Parachute

Regiment; 33rd Parachute Squadron RE; 224th Parachute Field Ambulance RAMC. In November 1942, the 4th Parachute Brigade was formed in the Middle East. It comprised the 151st Parachute Battalion (renumbered 156th) from India. The 10th and 11th Parachute Battalions were raised from the theatre.

218. Devlin, 40.

219. Devlin, 81; and Gordon Rottman, U.S. *Army Airborne, 1940–1990* (London: Osprey Publishing, 1990), 6.

220. Ibid., 42.

221. Ibid., 42, 44.

222. Breuer, *Geronimo*, 1–7; Rottman, 4–7; Carl Smith, *U.S. Paratrooper, 1941–1945* (London: Osprey Publishing, 2000), 4-5; and Devlin, 42, 44.

223. Devlin, 44–46.At that time the only parachute that was available in the U.S. Army was a free-fall type developed by Sky High Irvin. Safety regulations stipulated that all training jumps be carried out at 1,500 feet, thus this parachute could not be used. By May 1940, the Air Corps had designed the T-4 model and a parachute reserve. The T-4 was a backpack static-line activated parachute. The canopy measured 28 feet in diameter. Comparatively, the reserve parachute was 24 feet in diameter and was worn in front. To activate the reserve chute the paratrooper had to pull on a small ripcord handle located on the right side.

224. Rottman, 6. The Parachute Test Platoon was organized in four squads of 12 men each. Later, nine additional candidates were selected to cover off injuries. The first three weeks focused on the physical training and classes on the history and theory of parachutes. During the next three weeks the Platoon used the training facilities and the parachute High Towers of the Safe Parachute Company at Hightstown, New Jersey. By the end of their course each member had successfully trained on the various apparatus and were able to pack their own parachutes. The seventh and eight weeks (August 17–29) focused on single and mass parachute jumps from altitudes ranging between 1,500 and 750 feet. Following their last jump the Platoon was split up. Some members went to Chanute Field, Illinois for the Air Corps' rigger course while the remainder returned to Lawson Field, Fort Benning and became part of The Parachute School's instructional cadre. John C. Andrews, *Airborne Album, Volume One: Parachute Test Platoon to Normandy* (Williamstown, N.J.: Philips Publications, Inc., 1982), 3–6.

225. Rottman, 6.

226. Devlin, 114–115.

227. The American Parachute Infantry units activated between February and July 1942 were: 501 Parachute Infantry Regiment (PIR), activated February 15, 1942, Fort Benning; 502th PIR, 24 February 1942, Fort Benning; 503rd PIR, February 24, 1942, Fort Benning; 504th PIR, May 1, 1942, Fort Benning; 505th PIR, July 6, 1942, Fort Benning; 506th PIR, July 20, 1942, Camp Toombs, Georgia; 507th PIR, July 20, 1942, Fort Benning; 509th Parachute Infantry Battalion (PIB), February 24, 1942, Fort Benning. The American Glider Infantry units activated between February and July 1942 were: 88th Glider Infantry Regiment (GIR), activated October 14, 1941, Fort Benning; 325th GIR Redesignated August 15, 1942, formed in Camp Clairborne, Louisiana and moved to Fort Bragg; 327th GIR Redesignated August 15, 1942, formed Camp Clairborne, and moved to Fort Bragg; 401st GIR activated August 15, 1942, Fort Bragg; 550th Airborne Infantry Battalion, activated July 1, 1941, Howard Field, Panama Canal Zone. The American Airborne Divisions activated between February and August 1942 were: the 82nd Airborne Division and the 101st Airborne Division, August 15, 1942, which moved to Fort Bragg. Rottman, 11–16.

228. Report on Tour of Military Camps (U.S.A.) by Chief of Combined Operations, June 7–9, 1942. PRO, AIR 39/58 Air Ministry: Army Co-operation Command: Registered Files, Airborne Forces Training, May-November 1942.

229. The unit designation number for this new battalion was Serial No. 1351. Also indicated in this document were the criteria selections for the battalion's commanding officer, officer cadre, and NCO cadre. Two appendices were attached. Appendix A was titled Physical Requirements for Officers. Appendix B was titled Physical Requirements for Other Ranks. Memorandum from Major-General H.F.G. Letson, Adjutant-General to all District Officers Commanding, Commandant of Petawawa Military Camp, Commandant RMC, GOC Atlantic and Pacific Commands. NA, RG 24, seroes C-1, file HQS 8846-1, microfilm C-5278.

230. "Paratroops Will Be Picked From Canadian Army," *The Evening Citizen*, No. 44, August 10, 1942, 1, 10. NL, microfilm, N-17993.

231. Ibid., 1.

232. "Canadian Parachutists Thrill Colonel Ralston, Twenty-Seven Soldier Leave For Georgia to Learn 'Jumping' Tricks With the U.S. Army," *Globe and Mail*, Vol XCIX, No. 28913, 14 August 1942, 17. NL, microfilm N-20035.

233. The group sent to the Parachute School, Fort Benning, Georgia was composed of 7 officers and 20 Other Ranks. Letter from Lieutenant-Colonel (unidentified) to Adjutant-General, Commandant, Ottawa Area Command, and Officer Commanding No. 3 District Depot, Lansdowne Park, August 12, 1942. NA, RG 24, series C-1, file 8846-1, Vol 2DD, microfilm C-5277. The group that was sent to the Parachute Training School, Ringway, was raised from Canadian Army units in the UK. The initial group was composed of 90 candidates. However, when the course commenced, there were a total of 85 candidates, 25 officers, and 60 Other Ranks. Letter from Wing Commander Maurice A. Newnham, Commanding Parachute School, Royal Air Force, Ringway to G.S.O., E. M.T. Parachute Training — Canadian Personnel — August 17, 1942. NA, RG 24, CMHQ, Vol 9830, file 2/Para Tps/1. Report on Parachute Training - Canadian personnel from Wing Commander M.A. Newnham, Wing Commander, Commanding, Parachute Training School, RAF Ringway, to CMHQ, M.T. Branch, London, September 15, 1942. NA, RG 24, CMHQ, Vol 9830, file 2/Para Tps/1.

234. At the initial meeting of the Inter-Service Committee on Air Borne Troop, held at NDHQ on July 25, 1942, the RCAF representatives reported that the Brandon or Douglas aerodromes would be the best locations for aircraft that were to be used for parachute training. The Army representatives agreed and investigated the construction requirements to build accommodations at Camp Shilo for the 1st Canadian Parachute Battalion and the Parachute School. Minutes of a Meeting of The Inter-Service Committee on Air Borne Troops, Held At NDHQ, 1000 hours, July 25, 1942. DHH, file 112.3M2 (D232), Airborne Troops, November 14, 1941–October 1951. On July 29, 1942, Brigadier Weeks sent a letter to the Army Directorate informing them that Camp Shilo had been selected as the 1st Canadian Parachute Battalion's Camp, and the home of the Canadian Parachute Training Centre. When the Battalion completed its parachute training it would move to Wainwright to commence its collective training. RCAF aircraft used for parachute qualification would be stationed at the Brandon Aerodrome. Letter from Brigadier Weeks to Army Directorates, Ottawa, July 29, 1942. NA, RG 24, series C-1, file HQS 8846-1, Vol 2, microfilm C-5277.

235. Darrel L. (Bucky) Harris, "Close Up, and Stand in The Door," Unpublished manuscript. (River, Manitoba, 1996), 6.

236. George Wright, interviews with Michel Wyczynski, February 1, 15, 2001.

237. "Paratroopers' Course Divided Into 4 Phases. But Official Designations of Parachute Packing, Jump Training, Tower Training and Qualifications Don't Begin To Tell Story of Crowded Program," *The Evening Citizen*, No. 54, August 21, 1942, 3. NL, microfilm N -20035.

238. Report on Parachute Training — Canadian personnel from Wing Commander M.A. Newnham, Wing Commander, Commanding, Parachute Training School, RAF Ringway, to CMHQ, M.T. Branch, London, 15 September 1942. NA, RG 24, CMHQ, Vol 9830, file 2/Para Tps/1.

239. In Fort Benning, one officer and one NCO qualified one week after the course. One had been ill, and the other had been injured. Four officers and two ORs failed to qualify on the British parachute course. Two officers refused, one was injured, and one could not complete his course due to illness. Of the ORs, one refused and another could not obtain his qualification due to injury. Parachute Training — Canadian personnel, M.A. Newnham, Wing Commander, Commanding. Parachute Training School, Royal Air Force, Ringway to CMHQ, 13 September 1942. NA, RG 24, series C-1, file HQS 8846-1, Vol 11, microfilm C-5277.

240. "Canadian Paratroops' Commander Meets Death in His First Jump," *Globe and Mail*, September 16, 1942, Vol XCIX, No. 28935, 3. NL, microfilm N-20036. "Maj. Hilton D. Proctor Killed When Airplane Shears Into Parachute," *The Evening Citizen*, No. 70, September 9, 1942, 1, 2. NL, microfilm N-17994.

241. "Canadian Paratroopers Earn Praise of High U.S. Officer," NA, RG 24, series C-1, file HQS 8846-1, microfilm C-5277. Parachute Training — Canadian personnel, M.A. Newnham, Wing Commander, Commanding. Parachute Training School, Royal Air Force, Ringway to CMHQ, 13 September 1942. NA, RG 24, series C-1, file HQS 8846-1, Vol 11, Paratroops: Organization and Training, microfilm C-5277.

242. "Paratroops Fit, Ready For Duties in Manitoba," *Globe and Mail*, Vol XCIX, No. 28944, September 21, 1942 17. NL, microfilm N-20036.

243. During the summer and early fall of 1942, Army Directorates were studying the various training, construction, and accommodation requirements to set up the 1st Canadian Parachute Battalion and the Parachute Training Centre in Camp Shilo. It was a slow administrative process that required input from NDHQ, Military District 10, Winnipeg, the Canadian Military Attaché in Washington, the Safe Parachute Company (who built the High Towers in the United States), and the selected Canadian companies that were to supply the material and labour the erect the High Tower in Shilo Camp. Numerous delays hampered the initial target date of fall 1943. Some administrative and training buildings were partially ready. The work on the High Tower commenced during November, and the structure was completed on December 7, 1943. The Tower's working parts were installed and tested in April 1943. The tower was ready to be used in late May and early June 1943. Correspondence from various Directorates, the Safe Parachute Company, the Dominion Bridge Company in Montreal, Inspector M.W. Julian, Charles and Warnock and Co. Limited, Engineer and Major R.F. Routh (Acting Commanding Officer, 1 Cdn Para Bn, July 1942–August 1943). NA, RG 24, series C-1, file HQS 8846-5, No. 2 and No. 5, Accommodation and Construction, Canadian Parachute Battalion, Shilo. Microfilm C-8379.

244. Chief of the Air Staff Air Marshal C.S. Breadner informed the Chief of the General Staff that due to the shortage of transportation-type aircraft, the forecasted tactical training of paratroopers could commence on December 8, 1942. Memorandum from Air Marshal C.S. Breadner, Chief of the Air Staff, to the

Chief of the General Staff, Ottawa, September 18, 1942. NA, RG 24, series C-1, file HQS 8846-1, Vol 5, microfilm C-5277. As of this date no aircraft had yet been selected to conduct basic parachute training in Canada.

245. Letter from Brigadier Ernest Weeks, DCGS (B) to DQMG (E), Ottawa, September 23, 1942. NA, RG 24, series C-1, file HQS 8846-5, No. 5, microfilm C-8379.

246. The directors of various Army branches met weekly and discussed, during the directors' co-ordinating meetings, matters relating to the training and the organization of the 1st Canadian Parachute Battalion. Issues relating to pay, equipment, insignia, medical, training, selection, supplies, RCAF collaboration, and the construction of the parachute school were examined and addressed. The initial meeting was held during the first week of September, 1942, and the subsequent meetings went on well into 1943 until the battalion and the school were fully operational. Memorandum of the Directors' Co-ordinating Meeting 1st Canadian Parachute Battalion, September 17, 1942. DHH, file 112.2M2 (D232), Paratroops, Airborne Troops, Directorate of Military Operations and Planning, 1941–1951.

247. Memorandum from Colonel R.H. Keefler to the Deputy Chief of the General Staff (B), Ottawa, October 8, 1942. NA, RG 24, series C-1, file HQS 8846-1, Vol 11, microfilm C-5277.

248. Groups of trainees were to be sent until the week of December 12, 1942. It was anticipated that by January 1943, the Parachute School in Camp Shilo would be ready to commence training. NA, RG 24, Vol 13240, Directorate of Military Training, War Diary, September 28, 1942.

249. The proposed War Establishment (Cdn. III/1940/127/1) of the 1st Canadian Parachute Battalion was based on the British War Establishment (BWE X/127/2). The Battalion was to consist of a battalion hadquarters, a headquarters company, which included an intelligence section, a signal platoon, a mortar platoon of four detachments, a protective aection, and an administration platoon. Three rifle companies would consist of a Company Headquarters, two mortar detachments, an anti-tank section, three rifle platoons, each having a platoon headquarters, and three rifle sections. The Battalion's War Establishment was notified in General Order 452/42. NA, RG 24, CMHQ, Vol 12260, file 1/Policy/Parachute Troops/1. As the war progressed, the Battalion's War Establishment underwent several modifications.

250. Report of Visit to U.S.A. by Lieutenant-Colonel R.H. Keefler, (MT), (L), June 1–14, 1942. NA, RG 24, series C-1, file HQS 8846-1, Vol 21, microfilm C-5278.

251. Dan Hartigan, interview with Bernd Horn, October 30, 2000. There was no preferential treatment for the American parachute candidates. They underwent the same training regimen. Donald R. Bugett, *Currahee!* (Boston: Houghton Mifflen Company, 1967), 10–34.

252. Tom Gavinski, interview with Bernd Horn, November 1, 1998.

253. Letter from Albert Kemshead to David Owen, March 3, 1985. David Owen Fonds, 1 Cdn Para Bn Assn Archives. Kemshead described the run that concluded "A" stage. "The highlight was the 10 mile run on Saturday, the end of 'A' stage. It rained Friday night before our 10 mile run and believe me if you have ever run 10 miles in that red Georgia clay. It was something else to behold. We stumbled, bumbled and half carried each other along the way."

254. Ibid.

255. Ibid. See also letter from E.J. Scott to David Owen, February 3, 1985.

256. Interviews, letters, and recollections complied by Gary Boegal. 1 Cdn Para Bn Assn Archives.

257. Report of Visit — 25th to 28th November 1942 to 1st Canadian Parachute Battalion, Now Training at U.S. Army Parachute School, Fort Benning, GA. NA, RG 24, series C-1, file HQS 8846-7, No. 4, microfilm C-8379.

258. In his Weekly Parade State of December 5, 1942, Bradbrooke reported that 31 officers and 501 Other Ranks had been sent to Fort Benning. Of these, 1 officer and 45 Other Ranks had failed the course. NA, RG 24, series C-1, file HQS 8846-1, Vol 18, microfilm C-5277.

259. Bradbrooke recommended that such a tower be built in No. 4 District Depot, Montreal, where the candidates underwent their selection tests. Thus, those who were unable to jump could immediately be disqualified. This additional testing method ensured that only adept trainees were sent to Fort Benning, who could in fact undergo and successfully complete their course. By the time NDHQ approved this proposal the Battalion was preparing to return to Canada. Letter from Lieutenant-Colonel G.F.P. Bradbrooke to Directorate of Military Training, 30 November. NA, RG 24, series C-1, file HQS 8846-1, Vol 16, microfilm C-5277. Bradbrooke's observations were confirmed and supported by Lieutenant-Colonel W.B. Wedd, Military Attaché, Canadian Legation. Report of Visit — 25th to 28th November 1942 to 1st Canadian Parachute Battalion, Now Training at U.S. Army Parachute School, Fort Benning, GA. NA, RG 24, series C-1, file HQS 8846-7, microfilm C-8379. The building of the Mock Tower in D.D. No. 4 was approved and the file was forwarded to DWC, December 10, 1942. Summary of Action Form, Directorate of Military Training to DCGS (B) Brigadier Ernest Weeks, Ottawa, 11 December 1942; Letter of DMT to Department of Works, Canada, Ottawa, January 14, 1943. NA, RG 24, series C-1, file HQS 8846-1, Vol 17, Paratroops: Organization and Training, microfilm C-5277. As the last group of volunteers was preparing to leave for Fort Benning on February 4, 1943, there was no longer a requirement to build such a training structure to test potential candidates.

260. Letter from the Office of the Directorate of Military Training to D.C.G.S. (B), Ottawa, November 25, 1942. NA, RG 24, series C-1, file HQS 8846-1, Vol 15, microfilm C-5277.

261. Letter from Lieutenant-Colonel G.F.P. Bradbrooke to the Director of Military Training, Fort Benning, November 6, 1942. NA, RG 24, series C-1, file HQS 8846-1, Vol 17, microfilm C-5277.

262. Memorandum from Colonel R.H. Keefler to DCGS (B), Ottawa, October 22, 1942. DHH, file 112.3M3009 (D99), Training 1st Cdn Para Bn, October 1942-July 1943.

263. Ibid.

264. Letter from Colonel W. Line, Director of Personnel Selection to all District Army Examiners and All Army Examiners, Ottawa, 23 December 1942. NA, RG 24, series C-1, file HQS 8846, Vol 16, microfilm C-5277 and "Selection of Personnel - 1st Parachute Battalion," 23 December 1942. DHH, file 163.009 (D16).

265. Ibid. Colonel W. Line wrote that further information regarding the true nature of parachute training could be found in *Canadian Army Training Memorandum No. 20.*

266. Darrel Harris, who was one of the twenty-seven candidates of the Benning group, provides the best description of the shock harness training. "The student was obliged to lie face down on the mat with the parachute harness on. His legs were strapped together (to keep from tangling in the risers) and a small cable, which looked as small as a piece of sting, was attached to the trooper's parachute harness just behind the shoulders. By the right hand, there was a rip-cord simulating the rip-cord of the reserve chute. The student was hoisted upward in a hor-

izontal position with his head slightly below his heels. Up he went, up and up, until the whim of the instructor was satisfied. It could be, usually was, right to the top. He was left to hang there admiring the beauty of the countryside just long enough to get the wind up for sure. The rip-cord was dangling around on the right hand side of the chest. On a command, he was expected to grasp the rip-cord and give it a good firm yank. This action made the release, then he plummeted towards the earth while counting 'one thousand, two thousand, three thousand'. At the same time as he was counting and falling, he passed the rip-cord from his right hand to his left. This exercise was in place to keep one thinking while falling and counting .... The 'three thousand count' was to be used later when jumping from the aircraft. It one didn't feel the mighty tug of the main chute opening by the time one had counted three thousand, that meant there was likely some trouble brewing in the form of a malfunction in the main pack. So then the rip-cord was pulled and the reserve chute came into play." Harris, 7-8.

267.   Boyd M. Anderson, *Grass Roots* (Saskatchewan: Windspeak Press, Wood Mountain, 1996), 240–241. The *Canadian Army Training Memorandum* No. 20 issued in November 1942 provided the following additional information regarding the qualification jumps made during the "D" Stage. "The second jump is still not too difficult, as part of the emotional stimulation of the first carries over to the second. Another factor involved is that the man feels that, if he does not make the second jump, his comrades will think he was scared by the first. But, by the time the third, fourth, or fifth jump, the excitement is over, his curiosity is satisfied, and he has proved he has the nerve. Now he realizes clearly that jumping is a tough and sometimes a painful job."

268.   Of the 20 who failed the course, 7 were jump refusals, 3 refused to continue training, 2 were injured and hospitalized, 3 were sick in quarters, and 5 were held back for a later class. Letter from Lieutenant-Colonel G.F.P. Bradbrooke to Director of Military Training, Fort Benning, November 7, 1942. NA, RG 24, series C-1, file HQS 8846-1, microfilm C-5277.

269.   Since the graduation of the first Canadian paratroopers in Fort Benning, the issue of jump pay was a constant source of frustration. On numerous occasions Bradbrooke brought this subject to the attention of NDHQ. The response was always the same, stating that they were studying this file. Lieutenant-Colonel Wedd was in favour of granting parachute pay stating that such intense training and successful qualification "brings with it tangible benefits." Wedd recommended that the gap between jump pay for officers and ORs be narrowed. The officers received $2.00 while the OR.s received $0.75 per day. He proposed that the ORs' parachutist pay be increased to $1.00 per day so as to bring both "in the dollars range." Report by Lieutenant-Colonel W. B. Wedd, Military Attaché, Canadian Legation to the Adjutant-General, Washington, December 8, 1942. NA, RG 24, series C-1, file HQS 8846-7, microfilm C-8379. Wedd sent a follow-up letter, explaining the American jump pay. The U.S. parachute qualified enlisted men earned an extra $50.00 a month. Furthermore, the American Congress introduced a Bill amending the Pay and Readjustment Act so that the enlisted man's jump pay would be increased to $100.00 per month. Wedd speculated that the reason why the Canadian parachutist pay issue took so long to resolve was because the Adjutant-General was attempting to find a middle ground so as not to upset RCAF pilots and aircrews who earned flying pay. Wedd recommended "that it [jump pay] be divorced from flying pay, as parachute work is, in fact, infinitely more dangerous." Letter from Lieutenant-Colonel W.B. Wedd, Military

Attaché, Canadian Legation to the Adjutant-General, Washington, February 27, 1943. NA, RG 24, series C-1, file HQS 8846-1, Vol 20, microfilm C-5277.

270. 1 Cdn Para Bn War Diary, Daily entry of January 15, 1943. NA, RG 24, Vol 15,298.

271. Letter from Joe Nigh to his parents, February 1943. David Owen, "Joe Nigh — Portrait of a Parachutist, Part 5 of 13" *Fort Erie Weekend Edition*, December 19, 1987, 8. 1 Cdn Para Bn Assn Archives, David Owen Fonds, Series 2, Research Notes.

272. Ibid. See also letter from Lloyd Ford to David Owen, June 12, 1986.

273. Ibid. See also letter from Laurence V. Heal, June 14, 1986.

274. Bradbrooke was promoted to the rank of lieutenant-colonel on October 12, 1942. That same day he was appointed officer commanding of the 1st Canadian Parachute Battalion. He was posted on course to the Parachute School in Fort Benning, Georgia on October 28, 1942. NA, RG 24, Part II, Order, 1st Canadian Parachute Battalion, Order No. 26, October 29, 1942.

275. This was an important training initiative the qualified volunteers had come from a various Canadian Army non -infantry units. It was imperative for the commanding officer to confirm each soldier's military qualifications and aptitudes. Bradbrooke proposed to set up training wings staffed by officers and senior NCOs. Each wing would focus on a specific subject matter. Once all personnel had passed all prescribed subject matter, they would then proceed to the advanced training wings. Upon completion the candidates would be formed into platoons and companies. Officers and NCOs would also be rotated between wings to keep them up to date and proficient in all subject matters. Letter from Lieutenant-Colonel Bradbrooke to the Director of DMT, Fort Benning, November 9, 1942. NA, RG 24, series C-1, file HQS 8846-1, Vol 12, microfilm C-5277.

276. The Canadian Army Headquarters and the Directorate of Military Training were still familiarizing themselves with the weekly arrival of American and British airborne and parachute literature. As of this date they still had not devised a Canadian Airborne Training Syllabus. Bradbrooke submitted a series of recommendations to amend the Advanced Training Syllabus — Infantry to develop an Advanced Training Syllabus — Parachute Infantry. DMT studied these proposals but did not have enough time to draft such a training syllabus for the Battalion while it was at Fort Benning. DMT recommended that in the meantime the Battalion use the Advanced Training Syllabus — Infantry. Letter from Lieutenant-Colonel H.S.J. Paterson, DMT to Lieutenant-Colonel G.F.P. Bradbrooke, Ottawa, January 27, 1943; Progress Report, 1st Canadian Parachute Battalion, for the week ending February 6, 1943. NA, RG 24, series C-1, file HQS 8846-7, No. 8, microfilm C-8379.

277. As of November 28, 1942, twenty-nine officers had reported to the Battalion. Of these eighteen were still on course and would not be available for training or instruction for at least two weeks. It would possibly take even longer to incorporate these officers into various training wings because their personnel files had not yet been sent to Fort Benning. Bradbrooke was not familiar with these officers and their military qualifications. He chose to delay assigning them to specific unit posts and awaited their personnel files. Letter from Lieutenant-Colonel Bradbrooke to the Adjutant- General's Branch, Fort Benning, November 28, 1942. NA, RG 24, series C-1, file HQS 8846-8, No. 2, Promotions, 1st Canadian Parachute Battalion, microfilm C-8379.

278. This new unit designation was in fact an administrative cover for Canadian military personnel that were recruited and sent to train and later fight with the newly formed American unit, the First Special Service Force.

279. Herb Peppard, *The Light Hearted Soldier: A Canadian's Exploits with the Black Devils In WWII* (Halifax: Nimbus Publishing Ltd., 1994), 28.

280. Ibid., 27.

281. The newly trained Canadian paratroopers seemed confused as to the Battalion's operational mandate. Every day numerous questions were raised regarding the unit's future. Was the Battalion a Home Defence unit or would it be deployed to the UK? Was the Battalion a reinforcement unit for the 2nd Battalion? Would there be additional volunteer quotas to replace those who left? Would the Battalion's stay in Fort Benning be extended? Letter from Lieutenant-Colonel G.F.P. Bradbrooke to the Director of Military Training, Fort Benning, December 3, 1942. NA, RG 24, series C-1, file HQS 8846-1, Vol 17, microfilm C-5277. From the outset, in NDHQ, it was agreed that the 1st Canadian Parachute Battalion was slated for a Home Defence role. Brigadier-General Ernest Weeks, DCGS (B) stated that the policy regarding parachute troops "should be to organize a parachute force for employment in Canada only with operational role to recapture of aerodromes and reinforcing remote localities." Telegram from Weeks to GOC-in-Chief, Pacific Command, Victoria, Ottawa, June 20, 1942. NA, RG 24, series C-1, file HQS 8846-1, Vol 5, Paratroops: Organization and Training, microfilm C-5277. Major-General H.F.G. Letson, Adjutant-General, informed all District Commanders that the 1st Canadian Parachute Battalion "is being assigned for operational employment in Canada" Letter from Major-General H.F.G. Letson, Adjutant-General to All Districts Commanding, Commandant Petawawa Military Camp. GOG-C Atlantic and Pacific Command, Ottawa, August 6, 1942. NA, RG 24, series C-1, file HQS 8846-1, Vol 5, Paratroops: Organization and Troops, microfilm C-5277. By November 1942, the inclusion of Home Defence personnel had an adverse reaction on 1st Canadian Parachute Battalion. Weeks rectified this situation and emphasized that it was still not the "intention to announce that the 1st Canadian Parachute Bn. is for service anywhere." Memorandum from Brigadier Weeks, DCGS (B) to the Judge Advocate General, Ottawa, November 10, 1942. NA, RG 24, series C-1, file HQS 8846-1, Vol 9, Paratroops: Organization and Training, microfilm C-5277. By the beginning of December 1942, the threat of enemy raids on Canadian territory was perceived as minimal. The Directorate of Military Operations and Planning recommended, "Personnel volunteering for this service will represent the best type of highly trained Canadian soldier. It is considered that the permanent allotment of a whole battalion composed of this type of soldier for employment in Canada is not warranted under the present forms and scale of attack. In view of foregoing, it is recommended that the 1st Parachute Bn be not included in the operational troops required for the defence of Canada, but that this unit be considered as being available for use elsewhere overseas as the need arises." Letter from the office of the Directorate of Military Operations and Planning to the Chief of Defence Staff, Ottawa, December 2, 1942. NA, RG 24, series C-1, file HQS 8846-1, Vol 13, Paratroops: Organization and Training, microfilm C-5277. Another factor that came into play for the removal of the Battalion from Home Defence was that the RCAF at that time did not have enough planes to transport and drop large numbers of paratroopers. By the beginning of December 1942, the Battalion was directed to proceed with its collective training, provide reenforcements to the 2nd Canadian Parachute Battalion, and "be considered as available for operational employment in Canada when its training has progressed sufficiently and aircraft can be provided." Memorandum from the office of DCGS (A) to the Chief of The Defence Staff, Ottawa, December 6, 1942. NA, RG 24, series C-1, file HQS 8846-1, Vol 14, Paratroops: Organization and Planning,

microfilm C-5277. From December 1942 to February 1943 correspondence exchange between the various Directorates at NDHQ now reconfirmed, "The role of the battalion is at present 'operational duty in Canada.' This will be reviewed in April 1943." In March 1942, Chief of the General Staff Stuart informed General Officer Commanding-in-Chief General McNaughton that the 1st Canadian Parachute Battalion could be made available to the British. It was now just a matter of time before the Battalion sailed to the U.K. Message (CGS 142) from C.G.S. Stuart to GOC-in-Chief, First Canadian Army. Ottawa, March 6, 1943. NA, RG 24, CMHQ, Vol 12260, file 1/Policy Parachute Troops/1.

282. 1 Cdn Para Bn War Diary, December 3, 1942. NA, RG 24, Vol 15298, December 1942. The entry of December 4, 1942, added, "From all comments, a majority of these men decided to leave the 1st Battalion because they felt that the 2nd Battalion or Special Service group would be first to see overseas action. Furthermore, most of them being impatient, wanted to go to a fully organized and equipped unit, rather than submit to 'New Battalion Growth.' Of course, it must not be overlooked that every soldier has the ever present desire to see new lands and experience new training methods."

283. Letter from Lieutenant-Colonel W. B. Wedd, Military Attaché, Canadian Legation to Adjutant-General, Washington, December 8, 1942. NA, RG 24, series C-1, file HQS 8846-1, Vol 19, Paratroops: Organization and Training, microfilm C-5277.

284. 1 Cdn Para Bn War Diary, January 11, 1943. NA, RG 24, Vol 15298, January 1943.

285. Ibid.

286. The Parachute School in Fort Benning also provided the following courses: Parachute Communications (Signals) — 4 weeks; Rigger Course — 4 weeks; and Demolition Course — 2 weeks. Ten percent of the Canadian paratroopers were sent on the communications course. Ten men from every Canadian graduating parachute class were sent on the riggers course. Personnel were sent on the demolition course, but it was still being determined if in fact every jumper was required to attend this course. Ideally, it was argued that every man should be familiar with the manipulation of explosives and be taught sabotage tactics and operations. Report of Visit — 25th–28th November 1942, to the 1st Canadian Parachute Battalion, now training at U.S. Army Parachute School, Fort Benning, Georgia. Report was sent to the Directorate of Military Operations and Planning, Washington, December 5, 1942. NA, RG 24, series C-1, file HQS 8846-7, No. 4, microfilm C-8379. Candidates were also sent to train as instructors at the Parachute School. This training was carried out to enable Canadian personnel to set up their own parachute school in Fort Benning. Progress Reports for the weeks of January 11–16 and 18–23, 1943, 1st Canadian Parachute Battalion, Fort Benning. NA, RG 24, series C-1, file HQS 8846-7, No. 8, microfilm C-8379. Some 1st Cdn Para Bn personnel were posted to various operations and headquarters offices to observe the American methods of operations and management. 1 Cdn Para Bn War Diary, January 25, 1943. NA, RG 24, Vol 15298, January 1943.

287. Bradbrooke contacted General G.P. Howell, the commanding officer of the Parachute School, to work out arrangements to send selected Battalion Officers to be attached the American parachute regiments. Some would act as observers while others would take part in tactical training. Progress Report 1st Canadian Parachute Battalion for the week ending February 13, 1942. NA, RG 24, series C-1, file HQS 8846-7, No. 8, microfilm C-8379.

288. Report for the week ending January 9, 1943, 1st Canadian Parachute Battalion, Fort Benning, Georgia. NA, RG 24, series C-1, file HQS 8846-7, No. 8, microfilm C-8379.

289. Letter from Lieutenant-Colonel C.M. Drury, Military Attaché, Canadian Legation to Director of Military Training, November 24, 1942. NA, RG 24, series C-1, file HQS 8846-1, Vol 15, microfilm C-5277.
290. Company training schedules were now prepared. Training was given from Monday to Saturday noon. The day started with an early morning run, 6:15 to 6:45. The first class started at 8:30 and the last class finished at 17:00. Training Syllabus, January 11–16, 1943. NA, RG 24, series C-1, file HQS 8846-7, No. 6, Report on the Parachute Troops, microfilm C-8379. During the first few weeks the main focus was on weaponry. The average training week in January consisted of 30 hours of training: Rifle, 3 hours; Light Machine Gun (LMG) Bren, 4 hours; Anti-Tank, 2.5 hours; Grenade (36 type only), 3 hours; 2-inch mortar, 3 hours; Gas training, 3 hours; Route march, 4 hours; PT, Assault Course 4 hours; the balance was identified as miscellaneous time to be used by Company Commander "...where he sees most required." Training Syllabus (January 18–23, 1943) memorandum from Captain Nicklin to Company Commanders, Fort Benning. NA, RG 24, series C-1, file HQS 8846-7, No. 8, microfilm C-8379.
291. Training Syllabus, 1st Canadian Parachute Battalion, week of February 1–6, 1943, Fort Benning. NA, RG 24, series C-1, file HQS 8846-7, No. 8, microfilm C-8379.
292. Progress Report for the week of February 8–13, 1943, Fort Benning. NA, RG 24, series C-1, file HQS 8846-7, No.8, microfilm C-8379.
293. 1 Cdn Para Bn War Diary, daily entries of December 9, 10, 15, and 31 1942. NA, RG 24, Vol 15298, December 1942.
294. These were the numbers reported as of March 6, 1943. There were 40 officers and 705 other ranks at Fort Benning. Memorandum on the State of Training of 1st Canadian Parachute Battalion from the Lieutenant-Colonel E.C. Brown, DMT to DCGS (B), Ottawa, March 6, 1943. DHH, file 112.3M300 (D99), Training of 1st Canadian Parachute Battalion, October 42–July 43. The numbers submitted by Lieutenant-Colonel Bradbrooke as of March 20, 1943, prior to leaving for Canada, were 41 officers and 671 other ranks. NA, RG 24, series C-1, file HQS 8846-1, Vol 22, microfilm C-5278. By January 21, 1943, every paratrooper outfitted with a full pack could walk twelve miles in two hours. This was now considered the normal travel speed. 1 Cdn Para Bn War Diary, January 21, 1943. NA, RG 24, Vol 15298, January 1943.
295. By February 27, 1943, 199 ORs had qualified on the rifle on the 100-yard range, while 40 ORs had qualified on the Bren gun. Another 356 ORs had qualified on the rifle on the 30-yard range, and 202 ORs had qualified on the Bren gun. Progress Report for the week ending February 27, 1943, 1st Canadian Parachute Battalion. Fort Benning. NA, RG 24, series C-1, file HQS 8846-7, No. 9, Report on Parachute Troops, microfilm C-8379.
296. Memorandum on the State of Training of 1st Canadian Parachute Battalion from the Lieutenant-Colonel E.C. Brown, DMT to DCGS (B), Ottawa, March 6, 1943. DHH, file 112.3M300 (D99), Training of 1st Canadian Parachute Battalion, October 1942-July 1943.
297. Talks regarding this issue started between the Chief of the General Staff Stuart and McNaughton CMHQ during the first week of March. Since the operational role of a parachute battalion for Home Defence tasks had fallen through it seemed logical to offer this unit to the British. McNaughton spoke to General Sir Bernard Paget, Commander-in-Chief, Home Forces, GHQ, Home Forces, who was very receptive to this offer. Message from McNaughton to Stuart, CMHQ, (GS 583), March 18, 1943. A few days later, Stuart even considered the possibility of sending

the Battalion to North Africa to complete its training, however this idea was shelved. Message from Stuart to McNaughton , Ottawa, (CGS 170), March 22, 1943. Letter from Major-General P.J. Monatgue, Senior Officer CMHQ to Headquarters, First Canadian Army, London March 23, 1943. Message from CMHQ to NDHQ, (GS650), 27 March 1943. On 1 April, the War Office Director of Staff Duties sent a memorandum to CMHQ asking if the offer for the provision of a parachute battalion for the 2nd Airborne Division was still valid. On 5 April, CMHQ inquired if the Battalion was still available to be sent to the U.K. (GS 719), 5 April 1943. This was followed by yet another message (GS 728) from McNaughton to Stuart dated April 5, 1943 in which he stated that he had spoken with Sir Alan F. Brooke, Chief of the Imperial General Staff, who welcomed the idea of such an offer and even suggested that it could be deployed in North Africa at a later date. NA, RG 24, CMHQ, Vol 12260, file 1/Policy Parachute Troops/1.

298. Message from Stuart to McNaughton, (CGS 212), Ottawa, April 7, 1943. NA, RG 24, CMHQ, Vol 12260, file 1/Policy Parachute Troops/1; Letter from the Chief of the General Staff, Lieutenant-General Stuart to the Adjutant General, the Quarter Master General and the Mater General Ordnance, Ottawa, April 9, 1943. NA, RG 24, series C-1, file HQS 8846-1, Vol 24, microfilm C-5278. Originally this division was designated as the 2nd Airborne Division, however, the designation was quickly changed shortly to 6th Airborne Division to confuse German Intelligence.

299. The Battle Drill was introduced in the Canadian Army training program in June 1942. This new operational thinking was inculcated with the implementation of five elements. The first focused on developing team spirit. It was imperative that each man know his exact role and what was expected of him. The second featured battle discipline. The soldiers were taught how to act and react to battlefield surrounding noise and disturbances caused by enemy action and fire. The third made use of live fire to battle teach both commanders and soldiers to think and work while under fire. The fourth consisted of developing a series of drills that can be instinctively carried out in a series of different types of operations. The fifth and final element is the implementation of realism and enthusiasm during every step of the Battle Drill training. Individual initiative was now regarded as a very important 'in-theater' quality. Every man regardless his rank was encouraged to bring forward ideas and recommendations. A Canadian Training School Battle Drill manual further explained that "we have been so bound by old and well tried methods of training that we have hesitated to take what at first glance appeared to be fanatical ideas but which were, in many cases, the sound inventions of young enthusiasts. As a result the German, who has largely used our own Training Manuals, has been able to employ our ideas with a new technique and has been able to best us." In conclusion, the introduction of the Battle Drill was seen as a means "to enable us to overcome the staleness and boredom in training from which our men suffer at the present time." Memorandum explaining the Battle Drill from Colonel R.G. Whitelaw, Office of the Chief of the General Staff to the General Officers in Command of the Atlantic and Pacific Commands and the District Officers Commanding, Ottawa, May 18, 1942. DHH, file 171.009 (D187), Special War Course — Battle Drill Training, August 24, 1942–March 17, 1943.

300. NDHQ Parachute Training Instruction — No.1, prepared by Lieutenant-Colonel H.W.J. Paterson, GS for the Chief of the General Staff, Ottawa, March 26, 1943. DHH, file 168.009 (D42), Organization and Administration of 1st Cdn Para Bn.

301. All Company personnel attended: .303 Lee Enfield; Bren gun; .45 pistol; PIAT anti-tank weapon; grenade; and two-inch mortar courses. 1st Canadian

Parachute Battalion, Training Syllabuses for "A", "B", "C" Companies, week of April 19–24, 1943. 1 Cdn Para Bn War Diary. NA, RG 24, Vol 15298.

302. The new subject matter featured field craft, camouflage, movement with and without arms by day and by night, locating the enemy and control of fire and section attacks. "A", "B", and "C" training syllabus for the week of April 25 to May 1, 1943. 1 Cdn Para Bn War Diary, May 1943. NA, RG 24, Vol 15298, May 1943.

303. Ibid., Training Syllabus, Week ending May 8, 1943.

304. Staff writer, "Paratroopers Knuckling Down To Tough Training Schedule," *The Winnipeg Free Press*, Vol 49, No. 210, May 29, 1943, 6. NL, microfilm N-24550.

305. Training Syllabus, week of April 26–May 1, 1943. 1 Cdn Para Bn War Diary, June 1943. NA, RG 24, Vol 15298.

306. Training Syllabus, week of May 3–8, 1943. 1st Canadian Parachute Battalion. Ibid.

307. Training Syllabus, week of May 10–15, 1943. 1st Canadian Parachute Battalion. Ibid.

308. Training Syllabus, week of May 24–29, 1943. 1st Canadian Parachute Battalion. Ibid.

309. Ibid.

310. Ibid.

311. Training Syllabus, week of June 7–12, 1943. 1st Canadian Parachute Battalion. Ibid.

312. Training Syllabus, week of June 14–19, 1943. 1st Canadian Parachute Battalion. Ibid.

313. Ibid.

314. Ibid. The rifle range qualifications as of 19 June 1943 were: Rifle "A" Coy. 1st Class shot, 16; 2nd Class shot, 62; failed 27. "B" Coy. 1st Class shot, 17; 2nd Class shot, 51; failed 37. "C" Coy. 1st Class shot, 7; 2nd Class shot, 50; failed, 5. Bren "C" Coy. 1st Class shot, 2; 2nd Class shot, 25; failed 77.

315. Training Syllabus, week of June 21–26, 1943. 1st Canadian Parachute Battalion. Ibid.

316. Training Syllabus, week of 28 June–3 July, 1943. 1st Canadian Parachute Battalion. Ibid.

317. Ibid.

318. Report of Trip to Camp Shilo, Manitoba, (Canadian Parachute Training School, 1st Canadian Parachute Battalion) by Major R.A. Keane, May 17, 1943 to May 22, 1943. NA, RG 24, series C-1, file HQS 8846-1, Vol 23, microfilm C-5278. It must be noted that a great percentage of the men who were now part of this new unit came from numerous non-infantry units. Thus, their exposure to infantry training, weapons handing, and field craft was very limited. A great part of the training given during the Battalion's stay at Camp Shilo was in fact new training rather than refresher training. Furthermore few NCOs and officers possessed the required knowledge and experience to train their men. Everyone at every level was learning. This explains why the Battalion was falling behind in its projected training program.

319. Report on the 1st Canadian Paratroop Battalion, by Major-General J.P. Mackenzie, Inspector-General Western Canada, Brandon, Manitoba, July 4, 1943. DHH, file 169.009 (D212) Inspector-General's Reports of 1 Cdn Para Bn, July 1943.

320. The original 1st Canadian Parachute Battalion War Establishment called for 26 officers, 73 warrant officers, staff sergeants and sergeants, and 590 rank and file totaling 616 all ranks. 1st Canadian Parachute Battalion, War Establishment, effective July 1, 1942, Cdn. III/1940/127/1. NA, RG 24, CMHQ, Vol 12260, file 1/Policy Parachute Troops/1. NDHQ informed CMHQ of the Battalion's status as of July 3,

1943. The unit counted 512 members. All had completed their basic training, 502 were parachute qualified, and 411 had finished their Advanced Special and Arm Training. Only 30 underwent collective training and no company-level training had been initiated. Message from NDHQ to CMHQ, (Trg 4475), Ottawa, July 3, 1943. NA, RG 24, CMHQ, Vol 9830, file 2/ParaTps/1. On July 20, 1943, 30 officers and 574 other ranks of the 1st Canadian Parachute Battalion boarded the *Queen Elizabeth* in Halifax. 1st Canadian Parachute Battalion, embarked at Halifax, July 20, 1943, E-714. 1 Cdn Para Bn Assn Archives, De Vries, Jan, file 14-4. The under-strength Battalion and its projected casualty rate during future airborne opera-tional deployments had positive implications for the S-14 Canadian Parachute Training School. Not only were they to train volunteers using the American para-chute training program and equipment, but the School was now also responsible for developing and training a Parachute Troop Reinforcement Company and spe-cialists throughout the duration of the war. The S-14 Canadian Parachute Training School, (S-14 CPTS) was officially authorized on May 22, 1943. (HQS 20-1-18, F.D. 33; HQS 20-4-18, Vol 9, Mob. 9). 1 Cdn Para Bn War Diary, May 26, 1943. NA, RG 24, Vol 15298. The School's Home War Establishment was 30 officers and 218 Other Ranks. In the NDHQ Parachute Training Instruction No.1, dated 26 March 1943, it was stipulated that the parachute training phase now be the transferred to the S-14 Canadian Parachute Training School. After parachute qualification the successful candidates would proceed to undergo a further eight-week Advanced Infantry Training course. Upon completion qualified personnel were to be posted in the Trained Soldier Company. They would continued their training until rein-forcement requests were received by the 1st and 2nd Canadian Parachute Battalions. DHH, file 112.3M300 (D99), Training of 1st Canadian Parachute Battalion October 1942-July 1943. The School was re-designated as A-35 Canadian Parachute Training Centre on August 1, 1943. Part II Order, No. 87, September 17, 1943. NA, RG 24, Vol 17137, War Diary, S-14 /A-35 Canadian Parachute Training Centre. By mid-July 1943, the Centre's mandate was extended to include driver, demolition, and three-inch mortar training. Message from NDHQ to CMHQ (Trg 4590), July 12, 1943. NA, RG 24, CMHQ, Vol 9830, file 1/Para Tps/1. By the end of the war over 1,808 paratroopers had been qualified and had undergone advance training. 1st Canadian Parachute Battalion Class Numbers, Camp Shilo, Manitoba. 1 Cdn Para Bn Assn Assn Archives, Feduck, John, file 6-4. They were sent on a reg-ular basis to England and posted to the 1st Canadian Parachute Training Company (later redesignated as 1st Canadian Parachute Training Battalion). The reinforce-ment paratroopers were transferred to the 1st Canadian Parachute Battalion to replace injured personnel who could not resume their duties, and also during and following operations to replace casualties.

321. Lieutenant-General R.N. Gale, *With the 6th Airborne Division in Normandy* (London: Sampson, Low, Martson & Co., Ltd., 1948), 12.

322. The following issues were addressed: the Battalion's training and operational relationship with the 6th Airborne Division; hospitalization of injured para-troopers; maintaining the Battalion's documentation and records; role and responsibility of the Battalion's Paymaster; and the application of legal and administrative regulations. Brigadier E.G. Weeks, CMHQ, Memo to file, London, July 13, 1943. NA, RG 24, CMHQ, Vol 12260, file 1/Policy, Parachute Troops/1.

323. Letter from Lieutenant-Colonel D.C. Spry to Senior Officer, CMHQ, London, July 5, 1943. NA, RG 24, CMHQ, Vol 12260, file 1/Policy, Parachute Troops/1. Gale, *With the 6th Airborne*, 13.

324. CMHQ Administrative Instruction No. 10, Administrative Arrangements, 1 Cdn Para Bn, London, July 21, 1943. NA, RG 24, CMHQ, Vol 12517, file 6/1 Para Bn/1/2, Organization and Administration, 1 Cdn Para Bn. Directive by the Senior Officer CMHQ, in the U.K. to Lieutenant-Colonel G.F.P. Bradbrooke, Officer Commanding 1st Canadian Parachute Battalion, and to any officer who may succeed to the command of the said battalion while it is in the United Kingdom. Enclosed with this directive were copies of the following three documents: Privy Council Order 3464, April 29, 1943; Designation signed by the Minister of National Defence under Order In Council of April 29, 1943, PC 3464 as varied by order of the Minister of May 19, 1943; and the Order of Detail No. 13 by Major-General P.J. Montague, Senior Combatant Officer of CMHQ in Great Britain. Other issues that were explained to Bradbrooke were: attachments; general courts martial; field general court martial; instructions regarding administration; appointment, promotions and retirements; recommendation for honours and awards; selection of candidates and arrangement for OCTU; discipline – disposal of ORs for reasons connected with parachute jumping, reasons not connected with parachute jumping; reviews of sentence awarded by courts martial; absentees and deserters; detention; courts of inquiry; personal injuries; legal aid; British and civil and criminal law; instruction respecting civilian claims; regimental funds; auxiliary services; reinforcement system in the United Kingdom; transfer; trade testing; permission to marry; return and leave to Canada in compassionate grounds; pay and finance and reports.

325. Gale, *With the 6th Airborne*, 8–12. Orders to form the 6 AB Div were issued on May 2, 1943. Gale assumed command of this Division on May 7, 1943. The first unit to form the nucleus of this Division was the under strength 3rd Parachute Brigade commanded by Brigadier James Hill. The Brigade consisted of the 7th (Light Infantry), the 8th (Midland Countries), and the 9th (Eastern Counties) Parachute Battalion.

326. Ibid. 12. Previous to his airborne service, Brigadier Hill had served as a regular officer in the Royal Fusiliers before the war. During the Battle of France in 1940, he was on staff with Lord John Gort's command post. Hill was awarded the Military Cross (MC). After his return to England, he joined the Airborne Forces in late 1941 as a major. He was then appointed second in command of the 1st Parachute Battalion and fought in the North Africa. It was an arduous campaign in which the Battalion suffered heavy losses. Not being one to shy away from the action, Hill led his men on numerous missions and was ultimately wounded. His gallant service earned him the Distinguished Service Order (DSO) and the French Legion of Honour. Max Arthur, *Men Of The Red Beret: Airborne Forces, 1940–1990* (London: Century Hutchinson Ltd, 1990), 135.

327. Arthur, 135.

328. Dan Hartigan, *A Rising of Courage, Canada's Paratroops in the Liberation of Normandy* (Calgary: Drop Zone Publishers, 2000), 16. Every Battalion veteran interviewed had the highest admiration and respect for Brigadier Hill. All to a man stated that his standards were high and he was very demanding; however, he was encouraging, fair, and accessible to all troops. Brigadier Hill was a superior leader, but more importantly he was a great teacher. He made it a point to pass on his observations to all paratroopers regardless of their rank or position within the unit. Hill knew that in combat situations, and if a team sustained severe losses, the mission's success could depend on the initiative and stamina of a private or a corporal. Furthermore, during the initial contact Hill wanted to ensure

that the Canadians felt at home with the Brigade and the Division. He personally wrote a welcome note to each Battalion officer. "With my best wishes and a very warm welcome from all of us in the 3rd Parachute Brigade." Note from Brigadier James Hill to Lieutenant N. Toseland, Bulford, August 5, 1943. Lieutenant N. Toseland, 1st Canadian Parachute Battalion , Officer Training Folder. Canadian Airborne Forces Museum, CFB Petawawa, CAFM, AB 1, 1st Canadian Parachute Battalion, Vol 3, file 44.

329. Taped recollections of Captain John R. Madden. DHH, file: Biography, Major John R. Madden, 1st Canadian Parachute Battalion, non-dated. 42 pages.

330. Notes on The Training Of Parachute Troops, 3rd Parachute Brigade, Training Instruction No. 3, 7 June 1943. DHH, file: 145.4036 (D1), Training and Administration, 1942–1943.

331. Ibid.

332. Lieutenant-Colonel Fraser Eadie, interview with Bernd Horn, December 6, 2000.

333. The Battalion was ordered to send fifty paratroopers to undergo a special leg kit bag course. The staff of the No. 1 Parachute School and the British paratroopers who had previously been involved in airborne operations were not satisfied with the current equipment container delivery system. In past operations, the paratroopers had experienced difficulties locating and retrieving their containers. Quick access to these was vital because they contained heavy weaponry, extra ammunition, radios, and supplies. Thus, the leg kit bag delivery system was created. This enabled designated section or platoon personnel to jump into battle with the above-mentioned items. At the end of the course each candidate took part in one qualifying leg kit bag jump. The leg kit bag was attached to the paratrooper's right leg. It was designed to hold between 60 and 80 pounds of equipment. The paratrooper then jumped with the kit bag and executed the prescribed in flight release drill. Airborne Liaison Report No.11, Part II-Training 1Cdn Para Bn, Item 9, Programme, 5-7, October 5, 1943. NA, RG 24, CMHQ, Vol 9830, file 2/Para Troops/1.

334. After November 1, 1944, one brigade-level exercise was organized, per month, to observe the officers in their respective command settings. James Hill, 3rd Parachute Brigade, Training Instruction No.3, item 23, Training of Officers, July 23, 1943, 9. DHH, file 145.4036 (D1), 1 Cdn Para Bn, Training and Administration, 1942-1943.

335. Ibid.

336. Hill ordered that special attention be particularly paid to the development of the junior leader. Once every six weeks he proposed to hold a Subaltern Officers Day. During this day, he planned to test all Brigade subalterns on subjects relating to the various aspects of their profession. James Hill, 3rd Parachute Brigade, Training Instruction No.3, item 23, Training of Officers, Junior officers/leaders, July 23, 1943, 9. DHH, file 145.4036 (D1), 1 Cdn Para Bn, Training and Administration, 1942-1943.

337. Airborne Liaison Report No.11, Part II-Training 1 Cdn Para Bn, Item 12, Training in Explosives, October 5, 1943, 6. NA, RG 24, CMHQ, Vol 9830, file 2/Para Troops/1.

338. Ibid., Item 9, Programme, B, November–December 1943.

339. Ibid. By mid-October the Battalion pulled the mortar, the anti-tank, and the machine-gun platoons from the rifle companies and assigned then to the Headquarters Company. Major E.W. Cutbill, Airborne Liaison Report No.11, Part II, Training 1st Canadian Parachute Battalion, Item 13, Organization of a Parachute Battalion, 7. The Battalion's specialized platoons and sections were: Intelligence Section, Signal Platoon, Anti-Tank Platoon, No. 2 and 3 Mortar

Platoons, and the Machine-Gun platoon. The other sub-units were "HQ", "A", "B" and "C" Companies. The last three companies were rifle companies. Training was carried out throughout the day. If further instruction was required, additional classes were added in the evenings. Short night exercises organized to confirm certain aspects of the training were also added to the weekly schedules. Platoon, Section, and Company Weekly Training Syllabuses, September, October 1943. 1 Cdn Para Bn War Diary, daily entries, September 1–31, October 1–31, 1943. NA, RG 24, Vol 15298, September–October 1943.

340.   Lieutenant-Colonel Fraser Eadie, interview with Bernd Horn, November 20, 2000.

341.   Ibid. All members who had previously parachute qualified in Fort Benning or Ringway only had to undergo the conversion parachute training at the No. 1 Parachute Training School, RAF Station Ringway. Those who had joined the Battalion in Camp Shilo, and had not parachute qualified were first sent to Hardwick Hall for their physical hardening phase, and then proceeded to Ringway. 1 Cdn Para Bn War Diary, September 1–31, 1943. NA, RG 24, Vol 15298.

342.   Boyd M. Anderson, *Grass Roots* (Moose Jaw: Windspeak Press, Wood Mountain, 1996), 254.

343.   The School's motto was "Knowledge Dispels Fear." Newnham, v.

344.   See Chapter 4 for an in-depth comparative analysis of the American and British parachute training methodology.

345.   Due to other British airborne units currently undergoing parachute training, the 1st Canadian Parachute Battalion could not be sent to Ringway as an entire unit. The Battalion was asked to send its personnel by sub-units. Thus, each company and specialist platoon was ordered to devise their training syllabus for the month of September, taking into account the parachute conversion course. The first to undergo the parachute conversion training were two sections of the 3-inch Mortar Platoon and the Intelligence Section. Their training commenced on September 8. On September 20, 200 paratroopers were sent to Ringway and another 100 to Hardwick Hall for preparatory physical training. On September 28 part of "C" Company was sent to Ringway. As these groups underwent their parachute training, the remaining personnel commenced their courses, night training, 10-mile forced marches, and weapons training. 1 Cdn Para Bn War Diary, September 1–31, 1943. NA, RG 24, Vol 15298 — Daily entries listing the parachute conversion courses attended by the 1st Canadian Parachute Battalion and 1st Canadian Parachute Training Company/Battalion. Between September 18, 1943 and September 25, 1944, 1,160 Canadian paratroopers had successfully completed the British parachute conversion course. Daily course entires, September 18, 1943–September 25, 1944. PRO, AIR 29/512, Air Ministry and Minister of Defence, Record Books, Miscellaneous Units, Training Units.

346.   Letter from John Kemp to David Owen, May 3, 1985. 1 Cdn Para Bn Assn Archives, David Owen Fonds, Series 1: Correspondence. British parachute instructors were sent during the course of the war to coordinate the parachute training conducted at A-35 CPTC with that of the No. 1 Parachute School, Ringway. The first British reports revealed that they were concerned by the training techniques used by the instructors of the Canadian Parachute Training Centre. "It was found that the American methods of instruction were in vogue with the punitive elements almost more strongly developed than at Fort Benning. The wastage figures were very high. No less than forty per cent of the volunteers were turned down during pre-selection and approximately the same proportion was lost during training through 'washouts', injuries, men refusing to

continue and so on. With Canada's limited man-power situation and the volume of volunteers was relatively small so that the output of trained paratroopers was almost negligible." In Ringway the parachute instructors were monitored very closely. "The first duty of a British was to get to know his pupils as intimately as possible," explained Newnham, "so that he could apply his teaching craft in the most effective ways, by explanation, by example and by encouragement — never by threat of punishment. If a pupil showed inaptitude or lack of interest he was returned as unsuitable. As a volunteer for specially hazardous duties we felt he was entitled to every assistance and consideration. There were no men to spare and the best use had to be made of those available whether they had the physique of a Goliath or he ardour of a David." Newnham, 257–258. These observations were confirmed by Fernand A. Poupart, who graduated from A-35 CPTC on January 14, 1944. Poupart recalled that many of his classmates simply left the course because of exaggerated "gung-ho" attitude. "They were in great shape. They could have easily passed the course, but they were fed up with the childish nonsense." Conversation with Michel Wyczynski, August 15, 2002.

347. Training Syllabus —Week ending September 25, 1943, Item 2, Ranges. 1 Cdn Para Bn War Diary, September 1943. NA, RG 24, Vol 15298.

348. In Brigadier Hill's 3rd Parachute Brigade Training Instruction No. 3, he explained that successful training depended on firm decentralization to subordinates and that every man be briefed in minute detail as to the action expected of him. He underlined that passing adequate information down the line was extremely important. Every man on or near the battlefield had to be "in the picture" and "know the mind of his commanders."

349. Ibid., Item 3, Battle Drill. Hill had always maintained that effective training depended on two very important factors: forethought/careful planning and decentralization of authority to subordinates. Brigadier James Hill, 3rd Parachute Brigade, Training Instruction No.3, item 2, July 23, 1943, 1. DHH, file 145.4036 (D1), 1 Cdn Para Bn, Training and Administration, 1942–1943.

350. Training Syllabus — Week ending September 25, 1943, Item 7, General. 1 Cdn Para Bn War Diary, September 1943. NA, RG 24, Vol 15298. Bradbrooke also noted that uniformity of dress for training parades was poor. Troops wore a variety of items of dress and equipment.

351. Brigadier James Hill. Notes on The Training Of Parachute Troops, 3rd Parachute Brigade, Training Instruction No.3, June 7, 1943, 1-2. DHH, file 145.4036 (D1), Training and Administration, 1942–1943.

352. Upon the Battalion's arrival at Carter Barracks, Brigadier Hill gave each officer a training folder. Inside the folder's front cover was a small pocket on which was written in bold black letters, "Discipline the only road to victory." It contained the following items: a handwritten note from Brigadier Hill welcoming the officer to the Brigade, Bulford, August 5, 1943; a pamphlet titled *Airborne Forces*, by Major-General F.A.M. Browning, June 1943; and a pamphlet titled *Airborne Forces, Discipline The Only Road to Victory*, Major-General F.A.M. Browning, June 1943. In it, Browning enumerates the fundamental principles of discipline: drill; esprit de corps; cleanliness and smartness; physical fitness; confidence in his own and his comrades fighting efficiency; trust in his leaders; self-sacrifice; loyalty and faith in the cause. In the pamphlet titled *To All Officers in The 6th Airborne Division*, June 1943, Gale listed what he expected from each officer. "Resourcefulness, courage, endurance and discipline; these are the characteristics that must be developed by all in this division." These four documents explain in

detail the comportment that was expected of a professional, disciplined para-trooper. Battalion officers were instructed to bring the folder with them to each course and insert all provided literature and handouts. The folder also contained tests and results of Brigade Tactical Exercises Without Troops (TEWTs), as well as training session notes distributed during the Brigade Commander's Subalterns Days. Also included was an exhaustive list of Army Training Manuals and pamphlets required for the preparation of all airborne related courses and training. Lieutenant N. Toseland, 1st Canadian Parachute Battalion, Officer Training Folder. CAFM, AB 1, 1st Canadian Parachute Battalion, Vol 3, file 44, and unidentified Battalion officer's training folder, Vol 3, file 34.

353. Battalion Training Syllabus, September 5–11, 1 Cdn Para Bn War Diary, September 1943. NA, RG 24, Vol 15298.
354. Anderson, *Grass Roots*, 252.
355. Brigadier James Hill. 3rd Parachute Brigade, Training Instruction No.3, Item 13, Night Training. Bulford, July 23, 1943. Five copies of this document were sent for distribution to the 1st Canadian Parachute Battalion.
356. Brigadier James Hill, "By Night Every Time — Notes on ... in Active Operations." Bulford, June 7, 1943. This document was distributed as a training directive to all officers in the 3 Para Bde. DHH, file 145.4036 (D1), 1st Canadian Parachute Battalion. Training Instructions, 6AB Div, 3 Para Bde.
357. Battalion Training Syllabus, September 19–25, 1943. Item no. 6, Night Training. 1 Cdn Para Bn War Diary, September 1943. NA, RG 24, Vol 15298.
358. Brigadier James Hill, 3rd Parachute Brigade, Training Instructions No. 3, Item 17, Physical Training, (F) Physical standards. DHH, file 145.4036 (D1), 1st Canadian Parachute Battalion. The original physical training standards comprised two different sets of forced marched road tests. The first applied to young soldiers (all men under 19 1/2 years): 10 miles, on road and cross country, carrying full equipment, time 2 hours; 35 miles on road in 24 hours, carrying full equipment, less Anti-tank rifles, PIAT projectors and 3 inch mortars. The second test applied to the trained parachutists: 10 miles on road and across country, carrying full equipment, time 2 hours; 15 miles across country and on road in P.T. kit and boots, 3 hours; 50 miles on road in 24 hours carrying full equipment, less Anti-tank, rifles, PIAT projectors, 3inch mortars. Battalion Training Syllabus, September 19–25, 1943. Item 17, Physical Hardening.
359. Ibid.
360. Owen, 39. The march started at 1000 hours on October 19. The Battalion moved off in "Ack Ack" formation, with Major Nicklin, the 2 I/C, in command. At noon there was a one-hour rest and lunch. At 1500 hours rained started and continued for the next six hours. By 1815 hours they had reached the halfway mark and had supper. Due to the increasing cold and rain, the rest period was cut to 45 minutes. The march resumed at 1900 hours. "Spirits were low at this time though the rations and a hot drink made a remarkable difference in morale for an hour or two." The rain stopped around 2300 hours and due to the darkness the Battalion closed up in columns of route. At midnight the paratroopers were given a 35-minute rest period and hot cocoa. On October 20 at 0001 hours the weather cleared up and became windy. The troops were tired, cold, and wet but morale was improving. At 0200 hours, the troops were given a 30-minute rest and hot cacao. The march ended at the barracks at 0500 hours. The remainder of the day was spent resting. 1 Cdn Para Bn War Diary, October 19–20, 1943. NA, RG 24, Vol 15298.

361. Training Syllabus, 1st Canadian Parachute Battalion, Week of September 27 to October 2, 1943, Item 3, Weapons Training & Range Classification: Rifle, Bren Light Machine Gun & Sten. 1 Cdn Para Bn War Diary, October 1943. NA, RG 24, Vol 15298.

362. Brigadier James Hill, "Notes On The Training of Parachute Troops, Base On The Experience Gained By Many Commanders In Active Operations." Item 4, Fire Effect. Bulford, June 7, 1943, 3. DHH, file 145.4036 (D1), 1st Canadian Parachute Battalion, Training and Administration, 1942-1943.

363. Brigadier James Hill, " 3rd Parachute Brigade, Training Instruction No. 3." Item 16, Weapons Training, Bulford, June 23, 1943, 6-7. All paratroopers had to qualify on the .303 Lee Enfield. They would then proceed to pistol, Bren gun, and Sten gun qualifications. Once the paratrooper had qualified on all these weapons he took part in field and night firing range exercises. Field firing exercises consisted of handling and firing weapons over and around ground cover. The standards specified that "every shot must be fired to kill." All targets were inspected after each firing drill so as to immediately point out the candidates' weaknesses. Night firing drills were conducted at night as well as at first light, early in the mornings, and at last light in the evenings. DHH, file 145.4036 (D1), 1st Canadian Parachute Battalion. Training and Administration, 1942–1943.

364. Training Syllabus for Week Ending October 17 1943. 1st Canadian Parachute Battalion, Item 3, Weapons Training & Range Classification. Initially it was hoped that the rifles qualifications would be completed by October 17, 1943. Regrettably the qualifications were not completed and had to be extended into the month of November. Training Syllabus for Week Ending October 21, 1943. 1st Cdn Para Bn War Diary, October 1943. NA, RG 24, Vol 15298.

365. Training Syllabus For Week Ending November 6, 1943. 1st Canadian Parachute Battalion, Item 5, Training General. Ibid.

366. The daily figures for paratroopers who were hospitalized in November 1943 ranged from 1 to 2 officers and 23 to 44 ORs. Paratroopers admitted to the unit's medical inspection room varied from 1 to 5 ORs. Paratroopers relegated to light duties ranged between 3 to 28. Those excused from duty varied between 1 to 5 ORs. The daily figures for paratroopers who were hospitalized in December 1943 ranged between 1 to 2 officers and 21 to 36 ORs. Paratroopers admitted to the unit's medical inspection room numbered 1 officer and between 2 to 13 ORs. Paratroopers relegated to light duties ranged from 1 to 30 and those excused from duty ranged between 1 to 5 ORs. Weekly Parades States for November and December 1943. 1 Cdn Para Bn War Diary, November–December 1943. NA, RG 24, Vol 15298.

367. Airborne Liaison Report No.11, Part II-Training 1st Cdn Para Bn, Item 9, Program. B) November–December, 1943; C) Physical Standards. October 5, 1943, 5-6. NA, RG 24, CMHQ, Vol 9830, file 2/Para Troops/1.

368. Lieutenant-Colonel Bradbrooke, his HQ staff and company commanders had to constantly juggle their officer and NCO slates because of shortfalls due to personnel away on courses. Brigade directives required that Battalion officers and NCOs be sent on various courses to expand their combat and administrative knowledge, as well as improve their teaching and operational leadership skills. Bradbrooke agreed that it was imperative to send his personnel on these courses, regardless of the problems their absence would cause during the ongoing training. Their knowledge, he felt, would enhance the level of instruction. Thus, above and beyond sending personnel on the Parachute conversion course, para-

troopers were selected and sent to attend and qualify in the following courses during the September to mid-November period: Night Fighting Wing, School of Infantry, Middleton House, Middleton-in-Teesdale, Co. Durham, 1 major, 1 captain, and 1 private; Street Fighting Wing, London District of Tactics, 1 captain, 1 lieutenant, and 2 privates; 6 AB Div Battle School, Para Wing, Hardwick, 2 lieutenants, 1 sergeant, 4 corporals, and 3 privates; HQ, No.1 Cdn Rly, Op Groups, RCE, 1 sergeant and 1 private; 55 Field Hygiene Section, RAMC, Chitterne Lodge, Chitterne, Nr., Warminster, Wiltshire, 1 corporal, 1private; Airborne Forces Depot and School, 3 privates; attached to 9 Para Bn, 6 AB Div., 1 sergeant, 1 corporal, and 4 privates; War Intelligence Course Wing, Matlock, Derbyshire, 2 lieutenants; attached to Bde HQ, 3 Para Bde, 1 lieutenant; attached to Leuchars Airfield, 1 corporal, 3 privates; Night Firing Wing, School of Infantry, 1 captain, 1 private; Army School of Hygiene, Keogh Barracks, Mytchett; School of Signals, Catterick Camp, 1 lieutenant, 4 privates; School of Military Engineering, Daverell Barracks, Ripon, 1 lieutenant-colonel, 1 private; Night Firing Wing School of Infantry, 1 major; Hythe Wing, Small Arms School, Bisely Camp, Brookwood, 2 sergeants, 1 corporal, 1quartermaster sergeant; AB Depot and School, AB Forces, Hardwick Hall, Chesterfield, Derbyshire, 2 lieutenants; School of Military Engineering, Deverell Barracks, Ripon, York, 1 lieutenant, 2 privates; No. 22 (NW London) Tech Trg Gp, Henlep Ltd, 3 privates; 1CSRU, HQ Coy, 1 sergeant, 1 private; Rangefinder Course, 1 lieutenant; Infantry D&M School, Keswick, 1 sergeant; Night Fighting Wing , School of Infantry, 1 lieutenant; Battle Drill School (Para Wing), Depot and School AB Forces, 1 lieutenant; London District School of Tactics, Street Fighting Wing,, 1 sergeant; SM Command Weapons Training School, Plymouth, 2 privates; Battle Drill School (Para Wing), Depot and School, AB Forces, 1 company sergeant-major, 2 corporals, 3 privates; Divisional Battle School, Course No. 10, 2 lieutenants, 4 sergeants and 5 corporals; School of Military Intelligence, (Course on German Army), 1 captain; Army School of Physical Training (British Army), 2 company sergeant-majors; and Fieldcraft, 1 Lieutenant. NA, Part II Orders, September to November 1943, 1st Canadian Parachute Battalion.

369. Ibid.
370. Brigadier James Hill, "3rd Parachute Brigade, Training Instructions No. 3." Item 11, Ground Training, (G) Information. DHH, file 145.4036 (D1), 1st Canadian Parachute Battalion, Training.
371. 1 Cdn Para Bn War Diary, November 7, 1943. NA, RG 24, Vol 15298, November 1943.
372. John Simpson, interview with Michel Wyczynski, December 13, 2001.
373. Operational Orders No.1 and 2, Exercise Schemozzle, November 4–7, 1943. 1 Cdn Para Bn War Diary, NA, RG 24, Vol 15298, Appendix II.
374. Ibid., 1 Cdn Para Bn War Diary, November 15, 1943. A Battalion level debriefing was conducted by Lieutenant-Colonel Bradbrooke. "Many mistakes in procedure were brought out."
375. Ibid.
376. Brigadier James Hill, "3rd Parachute Brigade, Notes On The Training Of Parachute Troops, Based On the Experiences Gained By Many Commanders In Active Operations," Bulford, June 7, 1943. DHH, file 145.4036 (D1), 1st Canadian Parachute Battalion Training.
377. As of November 20, 1943, the average Battalion score was: Rifle 93, Bren 98, and Sten 48. The rest of 3 Para Bde was Rifle 111, Bren 120, and Sten 72. Battalion

Training Syllabus, Week Ending November 20, 1943. Appendix 4, Training Syllabus, 1 Cdn Para Bn War Diary. NA, RG 24, Vol. 15298, November 1943.

378. Ibid.

379. Ibid.

380. Brigadier James Hill, 3rd Parachute Brigade, Training Instructions, No. 3, Item 18, Signals Training, B, C, Bulford, July 23, 1943.

381. Ibid.

382. Item 1, (e) Fieldcraft. 1 Cdn Para Training Directive, for period November 27–December 31,1943, Bulford, November 24, 1943. NA, RG 24, Vol 15298, War Diary, 1st Canadian Parachute Battalion, November 1943. From November 23 to 26, Lieutenant-Colonel Bradbrooke was away on course. During his absence, Major J.A. Nicklin took over, as Acting Commanding Officer.

383. Anderson, *Grass Roots*, 256.

384. Ringway and Camp Bulford Training. Interview with Alcide H. (Sid) Carignan. Interviews, letters and recollections compiled by Gary Boegal, 1 Cdn Para Bn Assn Archives.

385. Nolan, *Airborne*, 49.

386. Brigadier James Hill. Report on Inspection of 1st Canadian Parachute Battalion, held at Carter Barracks, Bulford, on December 6, 1943. Item 24, Snap Exercise "C" Company, Bulford, December 9, 1943. NA, RG 24, CMHQ, Vol 9830, file 2/Para Tps/1.

387. Ibid. Brigadier Hill assessed the Battalion's ceremonial parade, dress and equipment, arms drill, and march past. He also carried out a detailed quarters and kit inspection of "B" Company. "A" Company was assessed on drill, TOETs, and guard mounting parade. Officers' and sergeants' messes were inspected, barracks and cookhouse were verified for cleanliness. Hill remarked that the feeding schedule had to be improved. The separate units were using this facility. The following administrative records were examined and numerous suggestions were made as how to improve the entering and control of information: weapons training results; TOETs records; library's control of distribution and signing out of pamphlets and training manuals; records of courses attended; ammunition records; jumping records; platoon commanders folders; store ledgers and records (QM); store ledgers (Coy); postage book; pay books; clothing deficiencies and 1954 charges (losses by neglect); duty rosters; bath books; inspection of transport; adjutant's records; and bill book and men's messing meetings ledger.

388. Operation Order No. 2, Exercise Procedure, 1Cdn Para Bn, December 4, 1943. The previous 3 Para Bde exercises were Schemozzle, Schemozzle Two, and Preparation for a Para Exercise. NA, RG 24, Vol 15298, War Diary, 1st Canadian Parachute Battalion, December, Appendix 2.

389. A total of twenty administrative phases were carried out before the paratroopers emplaned. Exercise Procedure, Appendix 1, Routine Time-Table, December 4, 1943. Ibid.

390. Gale, *With the 6th Airborne*, 13.

391. 1 Cdn Para Bn War Diary, December 19, 1943. NA, RG 24, Vol 15298, December 1943.

392. Ibid. Synopsis of Brigadier Hill's comments regarding Exercise Shilo, December 23, 1943. Appendix 1.

393. Ibid.

394. Nolan, *Airborne*, 49.

395. Urgent memorandum from War Office to various commands and 6 AB Div, London, January 5, 1944. DHH, file 145.4036, Reports on visits to Cdn Para School, Jan/March 1944.

396. Memorandum on 1 Cdn Para Bn serving outside Canada from Colonel W.A.I. Anglin, DJAG, CMHQ to ADAG (A), London, January 8, 1944. Memorandum on mobilization of 1Cdn Para Bn, Brigadier M.H.S. Penhale, General Staff, CMHQ to DAG (AG 1), London, 17 February 1944. NA, RG 24, CMHQ, Vol 12260, file 1/Policy Parachute Troops/1.

397. Mobilization Order No. 98, CMHQ issued by Major-General P.J. Montague, February 23, 1944. The 1Cdn Para Bn to mobilize on WE Cdn III/127/1 at present location on February 29, 1944, under the supervision of HQ Southern Command, in collaboration with HQ First Cdn Army. This order contained special instructions as to completing requests for stores and equipment deficiencies, the manning of the unit's rear party, preparation,and coding of records and the submissions of progress reports. See also Ibid.

398. Major J.A. Nicklin, 2 I/C, Training Forecast and Instructions for January 1944, December 29, 1943. Items 6 and 11, Radio Transmission, and Map Reading. 1 Cdn Para Bn War Diary, December 1943. NA, RG 24, Vol 15298.

399. Major J.A. Nicklin, Training Forecast and Instructions for January 1944, December 29, 1943. 1 Cdn Para Bn War Diary, NA, RG 24, Vol 15298. See endnote 358 to compare the old and new 3 Para Bde physical training standards.

400. Preventive Air Defence (P.A.D.) Exercise Boomer. 1 Cdn Para Bn War Diary, January 1944, Appendix F. NA, RG 24, Vol 15298.

401. Ibid. During this jump, the Battalion tested new equipment and practised the post-jump reporting drill. A selected number of paratroopers within each stick jumped with rifle valises and leg kit bags. Furthermore, upon reaching the rendezvous (RV) point each platoon commander was ordered to report the strength and condition of his men to company commanders who in turn reported the state of their companies to Battalion Headquarters. Exercise Manitoba, Operation Order No.1, January 17, 1944, Appendix G.

402. Report by Lieutenant G. C. Tinning, war artist, to Lieutenant-Colonel C. P. Stacey, Historical Officer, CHMQ, on Attachment to 1st Canadian Parachute Battalion., January 7–29, 1944, February 17, 1944. NA, RG 24, CMHQ, Vol 12758, file 24/Reports/2, Reports-War Artists. This was also the first time CMHQ officials visited the Battalion and witnessed a parachute jump. "They expressed a great deal of satisfaction at the way in which the Battalion cleared the aircraft and move off the DZ to the RV." 1 Cdn Para Bn War Diary, January 20, 1944. NA, RG 24, Vol 15298.

403. Ibid., Major J. Nicklin, Acting Commanding Officer to Brigadier S. J. L. Hill, Quarterly Morale Return for November 1943 to January 1944, Item 2, Confidence, January 25, 1944. Ibid.

404. Anderson, *Grass Roots*, 255.

405. "One fine spring day we lost our company commander," recalled Corporal Anderson. "Every soldier in the battalion had to make a fifty-mile march carrying his battle pack and weapon. There were no exceptions to this regulation." Anderson recounted one specific example: "[Major Taylor] had injured his knee on a parachute landing several months previously, but he was up front leading us all the way. After an early morning start we had marched about twenty-five miles or half way by noon. He never showed up after lunch. His knee had swollen and it was impossible for him to carry on. This was his second try and he was finished as far as going into

action with us. We all felt badly about losing him because he was looked upon as being one of our best officers." The march in which Major Taylor aggravated his knee injury took place on December 13, 1943. It was a 20-mile march that had to be completed in 4 hours. See Anderson, 257. Also War Diary, 1st Canadian Parachute Battalion, "B" Company Weekly Training Schedule, December 12–18, 1943, NA, RG 24, Vol 15298. On December 14, Taylor was struck off strength and posted to No. 1Canadian General Reinforcement Unit and ceased to draw parachutist pay. 1 Cdn Para Bn War Diary, October 1943, Part II Order, Order No. 65, December 23, 1943, Section A, Officers, Item 1 Strength and Decrease and Parachutist Pay. NA, RG 24, Vol 15298 He was then appointed commanding officer of the 1st Canadian Parachute Training Company on December 31,1943. Ibid., Part II Order No. 71, December 31, 1943. Item 2, Attachment and Parachutists Pay. During the first week of January 1944, both Bradbrooke and Hill recommended that Major D.H. Taylor be considered for posting to Canada to command the A-35 CPTC. Major-General R.N. Gale agreed with their recommendation. Memorandum from Major-General R.N. Gale to MGA and CMHQ, January 8, 1944. DHH, file 145.4036 (D2). Reports on visits to Cdn Para School, Ringway, January to March 1944. Major Taylor was promoted to the rank of lieutenant-colonel and replaced Lieutenant-Colonel R.F. Routh as commanding officer of A-35 CPTC. He commanded the CPTC from May 25, 1944 to August 11, 1945. DHH, file 367.039 (2), Unit History Questionnaire completed by Major G.A. Flint, Commanding Officer, A-35 Canadian Parachute Training Centre, Camp Shilo, July 24, 1946.

406. The jump took place during late afternoon. This was followed by DZ and RV drills. The paratroopers then set up and occupied defensive positions. Once their perimeter was secured, patrols were sent out. When enemy forces were located counterattacks were launched using various specialized platoons. Other training objectives that were tested involved dropping a parachute brigade. Each paratrooper jumped "with a maximum number of weapons on a man." In order to practise this, paratroopers were rigged with kit-bags and rifle valises. Once on the ground they practised the re-organization drills on the DZ. Other training objectives were to practise a parachute force of approximately one battalion (35 C-47s) in dropping en masse at night on one DZ in conjunction with the arrival of Air Landing troops by glider on two LZs; and to practise a Parachute Brigade Group in taking up anti-tank defensive positions during the hours of darkness. Warning Orders, Exercise Co-operation, January 9, 1944; Operation Order No.1, Exercise Co-operation, January 29, 1944, 1 Cdn Para Bn Assn Archives, Firlotte, Robert, file 1-2. Brigadier James Hill, Lesson Learned from Exercise Co-operation, Bulford, February 11, 1944. DHH, file 145.4036 (D2), Reports on visits to Cdn Para School Ringway.

407. Anderson, *Grass Roots*, 256.

408. Transcript of interview with Brian Nolan, April 25, 1994, 18. Brian Nolan Fonds, 1 Cdn Para Bn Assn Archives.

409. Richard Hilborn, interview with Bernd Horn, April 27, 2001.

410. Sergeant R.F. "Andy" Anderson, "From the Rhine to the Baltic," 1 Cdn Para Bn Assn Archives, Anderson, R.F. "Andy," file 11-2.

411. John Feduck, interview with Michel Wyczynski, December 19, 2001.

412. Otway, 153.

413. Brigadier James Hill, Lesson Learned from Exercise Co-operation, Bulford, February 11, 1944. DHH, file 145.4036 (D2), Reports on visits to Cdn Para School Ringway.

414. The Battalion also participated in Brigade Exercise Bizz II, March 24, 1944 and

in Corps Exercise Mush in which the 6 AB Div was pitted against the 1 AB Div. The war diary entry reported, "The Battalion performed very credibly on this exercise." 1 Cdn Para Bn War Diary, March–April 1944. NA, RG 24, Vol 15298.

415. Ibid., April 1944.
416. "Appreciation of Situation" by Brigadier Hill, Bulford, April 14, 1944. The 20-page appreciation covered the following 12 points: 1) Object, by priorities; 2) Factors, Ground, a) Relief, b) Anti-tank Obstacles, c) Roads; 3) Relative Strengths and Dispositions-Enemy, a) Costal Sector, b) Local Defence in Area; 4) Relative Strengths and Dispositions — Own Troops; 5) Air; 6) DZs; 7) Air Support and Diversions; 8) Time and Space — Own Troops; 9) Time and Space — Enemy; 10) Courses; 11) Own Troops; 12) Outline Plan. Nine copies of this document were made and distributed. Lieutenant-Colonel Bradbrooke received copy number 3. 1 Cdn Para Bn War Diary, June 1944. NA, RG 24, Vol 15298.
417. Ibid., Daily entries for April 1944.
418. "Appreciation of Situation" by Brigadier Hill, Bulford, April 14, 1944. Factors, Ground. 1 Cdn Para Bn War Diary, June 1944. NA, RG 24, Vol 15298.
419. Swimming tests had been devised for the 1st Canadian Parachute Battalion on October 13, 1943. The tests were to be conducted by January 1, 1944. Due to the busy training schedule and the emphasis on collective training, these courses were temporarily pulled from the training schedule. However, with the upcoming invasion of Normandy and the Battalion's operational tasks these were once again added to the schedule. The swimming standards to be attained were: for young soldiers, under 19 ? years old, swim 100 yards in swimming kit and 50 yards with clothes on. The same criterion applied for trained paratroopers. Airborne Liaison Report, No. 11, Part II — Training, 1st Canadian Parachute Battalion, (C) Physical standards, October 13, 1943. NA, RG 24, CMHQ, Vol 12260, file 1/Policy Parachute Troops/1.
420. Ibid. Each company was sent to the Yeovil Baths for a few days to undergo swim training. During this period, parachute water jumps conducted in the U.K. were at the experimental stage. They were organized by No.1 Parachute Training School staff at Ringway. Testing revealed that a paratrooper's chances of surviving a water jump were better when using the "X"-type parachute rather than the American T-type parachute. "The American parachute was a far less efficient arrangement than ours," explained Wing Commander Newnham, Commanding Officer of the No.1 Parachute Training School, "and it was in fact extremely difficult to extricate oneself from it when in the water." Newnham, 256.
421. John Baynes, Urquhart of Arnhem: The Life of Major General R.E. Urquhart, CB, DSO, (London: Brassey's, 1993), 70. The 1st British Airborne Corps consisted of the 1st and the 6th Airborne Divisions. With the creation of the 6th Airborne Division in April 1943, Browning was promoted to command this new corps. Later, in August 1944, the 1st British Airborne Corps was to become one of the two Corps that made up the 1st Allied Airborne Army. The other was the 18th United States Airborne Corps. The 1st Allied Army was commanded by Lieutenant-General Lewis H. Brereton, of the United States Army Air Force (USAAF). Browning was appointed the Army's deputy commander, while still commanding his own Corps.
422. Gale, With the Sixth Airborne, 65–66.
423. 1 Cdn Para Bn War Diary, non-dated daily entry, April 1944. NA, RG 24, Vol 15299.
424. In order not to expose the men to any unnecessary injuries, the Battalion did not jump during the King and Queen's Bulford visit on the May 19, 1944. The 1st Canadian Parachute Training Company participated in a demonstration jump.

After, the men of both the 1st Canadian Parachute Battalion and the 1st Canadian Parachute Training Company were inspected by the Royal Couple and took part in a series of weapon and exercise demonstrations. 1st Canadian Parachute Training Company War Diary, May 1944. NA, RG 24, Vol 15300.

425. The CMHQ Administrative Order Number 175, Paragraph 5, December 9, 1943 authorized the mobilization of "No.1 Canadian Parachute Training Company." On May 22, 1944, Captain D.W.W. Mascall relinquished command of the company to Major G.F. Eadie. The unit strength was 41 officers and 390 ORs. 1st Canadian Parachute Training Battalion War Diary, May 31, 1944. NA, RG 24, Vol 15300. The initial proposed establishment of the 1st Canadian Parachute Training Company was 19 Officers and 370 ORs. The establishment of this new unit was based on the organization of a British holding unit. Memorandum from Brigadier Hill to 6AB Div, Recruiting for 1Cdn Para Bn, Bulford, January 4, 1944. DHH, file 145.4036, Reports on visits to Cdn Para School, Jan/March 1944.

426. Brigadier Hill and Lieutenant-Colonel Bradbrooke agreed that all parachute reinforcements must have the following training completed prior to being accepted into the 1 Cdn Para Bn, 3 Para Brigade: have completed basic training; undertaken at least two months of advanced training; possess a good knowledge of their platoon weapons and firing range courses as laid out for these weapons. Letter from Brigadier James Hill to HQ 6AB Div pertaining to recruiting for 1 Cdn Para Bn, Bulford, February 17, 1944. DHH, file 145.4036 (D2), Reports on visits to Cdn Para School Ringway.

427. Owen, 41.

428. Ibid., 43.

429. Interview with Brian Nolan, April 25, 1994, 15–16. Brian Nolan Fonds. Brigadier James Hill File, 1 Cdn Para Bn Assn Archives.

430. Nolan, *Airborne*, 48–49. As the war progressed "A", "B", "C" and "HQ" Companies developed their own distinct characters. "'C' Company were real pirates," stated Lieutenant-Colonel Fraser Eadie "'B' Company were professional soldiers, no doubt about it. They were tremendous. 'A' Company was bloody good. 'HQ' Company comprised the specialist platoons. They were hellish good fighters as well." Interview with Brian Nolan, May 17, 1994. Brian Nolan Fonds, Fraser Eadie File, 1 Cdn Para Bn Assn Archives.

431. Gale, *With the Sixth Airborne*, 59–60.

432. Ibid., 61.

433. Major-General Gale was first informed of the 6th Airborne Division's Normandy invasion role by Major-General Browning on February 17, 1944. The initial plan called for the insertion of one brigade only. This limited drop was due to the lack of air transport. This part of the plan worried Gale. He had preferred a divisional size airborne operation. Having no voice in the matter, Gale selected Brigadier Hill's 3rd Para Brigade, the division's senior brigade. Later on February 23, Browning contacted Gale and reassured him that now the entire 38 and 46 Group RAF were available for transport duties. Thus, Gale upgraded his planning to include his entire Division. The next day, the 6th Airborne Division was officially placed under the command of the 1st British Corps for "Operation Overlord." Gale, *With The Sixth Airborne*, 32–33; and Gale, *Call To Arms*, 136.

434. 1 Cdn Para Bn War Diary, May 18, 1944. NA, RG 24, Vol 15298.

435. Hartigan, *A Rising of Courage*, 20–21; the transit camp's security directives were explained in detail in 3 Para Bde Op Instruction No. 2, Copy No. 5, 20 May 1944 titled Exercise Rampant. A copy of this instruction was issued to all units of the

3 Para Bde. Two copies were sent to 1 Cdn Para Bn. 1 Cdn Para Bn War Diary, June 1944. NA, RG 24, Vol 15298.

436. "Ad Unum Omnes," handout given to British and Canadian officers serving under Major-General Richard Gale during World War II. CAFM, AB 21, Vol 1, file 47, CAFM Staff Airborne Research Notes, file, mystique-airborne.

437. The Director of Military Training stated, "…due to the fact that this type of work requires unusual stamina and mental attitude by personnel, parachute battalions must be considered as elite units. Therefore, in the early formative period of such a corps, volunteers should be selected who by reason of physical and mental standards and previous Military training are most likely to be able to succeed in this unnatural and difficult work." Memorandum, DMT to DCGS (B), October 30, 1942, "1 Cdn Parachute Battalion," NA, RG 24, series C-1, file HQS 8846-7, No. 1, 2, microfilm C-8379.

438. CIGS, Airborne Operations, Pamphlet No. 1, General — 1943 (London: War Office, 1943), 1. Airborne troops include all those carried by air to battle, whether parachute troops or air landing troops. Parachute troops are trained and equipped to land by parachute, and air landing troops are those that land by either aircraft or glider.

439. CIGS, Airborne Troops — Military Training Pamphlet No. 50 - 1941 (London: War Office, 1941), 1.

440. "Notes on German Airborne Troops," CATM, No. 11, February 1942, 14.

441. CIGS, Airborne Operations, Pamphlet No. 1, General — 1943 (London: War Office, 1943), 6–9.

442. Ronald A. Keith, "Sky Troops," Maclean's, August 1, 1943, 19.

443. "Ad Unum Omnes" handout. CAFM, AB 21, Vol 1, file 47.

444. William B. Breuer, Drop Zone Sicily: Allied Airborne Strike, July 1943 (Novato, CA: Presidio, 1983), 71, 89.

445. Ibid., 57.

446. Clay Blair, Ridgway's Paratroopers: The American Airborne in World War II (New York: The Dial Press, 1985), 88.

447. Flanagan, The Angels, 47.

448. Breuer, Drop Zone Sicily, 45.

449. Napier Crookenden, Drop Zone Normandy (London: Ian Allan Ltd., 1976), 110.

450. Blair, 314.

451. David Owen, "A Portrait of a Parachutist," unpublished manuscript, 1 Cdn Para Bn Assn Archives, David Owen fonds.

452. Richard Armstrong, "The Bukrin Drop: Limits to Creativity," Military Affairs, July 1986, 130. See also David Glantz, The Soviet Airborne Experience (Fort Leavenworth: U.S Army Command and General Staff College, 1984), 124; The History of Soviet Airborne Forces (Portland: Frank Cas & Company, 1994); and, Steven Zaloga, Inside the Blue Berets (Novato: Presidio Press, 1995), 99–116.

453. Stephen E. Ambrose, Pegasus Bridge (London: Touchstone Books, 1985), 109.

454. John Feduck, interview with Michel Wyczynski, December 19, 2001.

455. Centre of Military History, Airborne Operations — A German Appraisal (Washington D.C.: U.S. Govt Printing Office, 1989), 21; John Toland, Battle — The Story of the Bulge (New York: Random House, 1959), 40–44; Michael Reynolds, The Devil's Adjutant (New York: Sarpedon, 1995), 67–68. Air Chief Marshal Sir John C. Slessor made reference to the drop in a most uncomplimentary manner describing it as "the fiasco of Heydt's single ill-fated battalion's [drop] during the Ardennes

offensive." Taken from an article "Some Reflection of Airborne Forces," *Army Quarterly 1948*. DHH files.

456. The paratroopers must quickly regroup prior to carrying on with their mission, but the defender must try and determine what has happened, how many have landed, where, what is their objective and who is available to counter the alleged attack. The problem of regrouping is actually offset by a phenomena that was noted by senior German commanders who defended against many successful airborne operations. "It is a unique characteristic of airborne operations," they insisted, "that the moment of greatest weakness of the attacker and of the defender occur simultaneously. The issue is decided by three factors, who has better nerves, who takes the initiative first, and who acts with the greatest determination." Centre of Military History, *Airborne Operations — A German Appraisal* (Washington D.C.: U.S. Govt Printing Office, 1989), 28.

457. Ralph Allen, "Canadian Paratroops Create Proud History," *Globe and Mail*, No. 29, 495, June 26, 1944, 1, 3. NL, microfilm N-20057.

458. "How to Deal with Parachute Troops," *CATM* No. 17, August 1942, para 96.

459. WD/HF/180/1/A Div Comd's Directive 26.1.42 contained in "The Airborne Forces 1940-1943," PRO, CAB 101 /220, 25.

460. Much of the blame has been levelled at Major-General Roy Urquhart, who was appointed division commander with no prior airborne experience. He made the fateful decision to go with DZ locations between 5 and 8 miles from the objective, distances contrary to airborne doctrine. He preferred good DZs at a distance compared to bad DZs close to the objective. He later admitted this was unnecessary and a fatal error. It cost the division the advantage of surprise and forced it to divide its forces to maintain DZ security for follow-on operations. John Warren, *Airborne Operations in WWII, European Theatre* (Kansas: USAF Historical Division, Air University, 1956), 149.

461. Flanagan, *The Angels*, 247.

462. DND Historical Section, *The 1st Can Para Bn In France, 6 June-6 September 1944, Report 26*, 23 August 1949, 7. DHH and CAFM files.

463. Cornelius Ryan, *A Bridge Too Far* (London: Touchstone Books, 1995), 244.

464. This time frame became the doctrinal framework that was used during the establishment of the British Airborne Division in 1941. Extracts from "Memorandum on the Organization and Employment of the Airborne Division. by Major-General F.A.M. Browning, D.S.O., Commander, The Airborne Division." DHH and CAFM files.

465. Brigadier Hill, battlefield tour, Canadian Land Forces Staff College, April 1991and 50th anniversary of D-Day, June 1994. See also Brian Nolan, *Airborne*, 73.

466. Lucas, *Storming Eagles*, 42–47; and Kuhn, 33–40.

467. James E. Mrazek, *The Fall of Eben Emael* (Novato, CA: Presidio, 1970), 138.

468. Lucas, *Storming Eagles*, 75 and Kuhn, 52–55.

469. Captain F.O. Miksche, *Paratroops* (London: Faber and Faber Ltd, 1942), 38-39.

470. Norton, 254; and Philip Warner, *The Special Forces of World War II* (London: Granada, 1985), 8.

471. Eric Morris, *Churchill's Private Armies* (London: Hutchinson, 1986), 163.

472. David Eshel, *Daring to Win* (London: Arms and Armour Press, 1992), 33-34.

473. Breuer, *Drop Zone Sicily*, 113.

474. F.H. Hinsley, *British Intelligence in the Second World War, Vol 3, Part II* (New York: Cambridge University Press, 1988), 797. The units which were brought in specially from Germany were: 101 Werfer Regt, 206 Panzer Bn, 70 Army Assault Bn,

17 MG Bn, 100 Panzer Training Bn.

475. Dwight D. Eisenhower, *Crusade in Europe: A Personal Account of World War II* (Garden City, NY: Doubleday & Company Inc., 1948), 358.

476. Ryan, 217.

477. Martin Wolfe, "This Is It," *Air Power History,* Vol 41, No. 2, Summer 1994, 32; and Heike Hasenauer, "Airborne's 50th Anniversary," *Soldiers,* Vol 45, No. 9, September 1990, 49.

478. Flanagan, *The Angels,* 256.

479. J.A. Easterbrook, *Fatigue in Mobile Striking Force Parachutists, JSORT Memorandum No. 55/8* (Ottawa: DND Joint Services Operational Research Team, 1955), 1-8.

480. Ryan, 423.

481. Ridgway, *Soldier,* 1.

482. John Talbot, "The Myth and Reality of the Paratrooper in the Algerian War," *Armed Forces and Society,* November 1976, 73.

483. MacDonald, *The Lost Battle,* 37.

484. Mrazek, 164.

485. Eric Morris, *Guerillas in Uniform* (London: Hutchinson, 1989), 45-46; Brigadier M.A.J. Tugwell, "Day of the Paratroops," *Military Review,* Vol 57, No.3, March 1977, 48; and Centre of Military History, *Airborne Operations - A German Appraisal,* 21-23. Another account reported German casualties at 44% and aircraft losses at 170 out of 530 operation (32%). Blair, 29.

486. Lucas, *Storming Eagles,* 94.

487. Hilary St. George Saunders, *The Green Beret: The Story of the Commandos 1940–1945* (London: Michael Joseph, 1949), 193; and Lieutenant-Colonel Robert D. Burhans, *The First Special Service Force. A History of The North Americans 1942–1944* (Toronto: Methuen, 1975), 162.

488. Kunzmann-Milius, *Fallschirmjäger der Waffen — SS im Bild* (Osnabrück: Munin Verlag GMBH, 1986), 7.

489. F.H. Hinsley, *British Intelligence in the Second World War, Vol 3, Part II* (New York: Cambridge University Press, 1988), 382-389.

490. Ridgway, *Soldier,* 102 & 295.

491. Personal letter Major-General M.B. Ridgway to General G.C. Marshall, 1 November 1944. *Marshall Papers,* 31:086, University Publications of America, Bethesda, Maryland.

492. Kurt Gabel, *The Making of a Paratrooper* (Lawrence: University Press of Kansas, 1990), 268.

493. Breuer, *Drop Zone Sicily,* 43.

494. Crookenden, 101.

495. Dan Hartigan, interview with Bernd Horn, October 30, 2000.

496. Ridgway, *Soldier,* 7.

497. Blair, 27. See also Saunders, *The Red Beret,* 317. "With the end of the German Campaign in sight, interest is widespread in airborne units as to the disposition and future use of American airborne troops. That there are no better fighting troops in the theater is evidenced by the wholesome respect accorded these unit by all other combat troops. With a high esprit de corps and morale second to none they firmly believe they are unbeatable. Headquarters Army Ground Forces, Army War College, "Report on Temporary Duty, Visit to European Theater of Operations," 5 May 1945, 11. CAFM, AB 21, Vol 2, file 37.

498. Larry Gough, "Parachutists Want it Tough," *Liberty,* December 4, 1943. 1 Cdn

Para Bn Assn Archives, Harris, Darryl, file 3-1.

499. "Assembling Paratroopers At Calgary," *Globe and Mail*, Vol XCIX, No. 28916, August 18, 1942, 13. NL, microfilm N-20035.

500. Flanagan, "Give Airborne Spurs," 33. General-Leutnant Bruno Brauer, who commanded a German parachute regiment during the invasion of the Low Countries in 1940, captured the essence of the "airborne" allure. Parachuting, he said, "compresses into the space of seconds feelings of concentrated energy, tenseness and abandon; it alone demands a continual and unconditional readiness to risk one's life. Therefore the parachutist experiences the most exalted feelings of which human beings are capable, namely that of victory over one's self." Brauer concluded, "For us parachutists, the words of the poet, who said that unless you stake your life you will never win it, is no empty phrase." Maurice Newnham, "Parachute Soldiers," *RUSI*, Vol 65, No. 580, November 1950, 592.

501. "3rd Parachute Brigade — Training Instruction No. 3," July 23, 1943, 2 & 6. DHH, file 145.4036 (D1). American Major-General A.S. Newman believed that parachuting proves the "will to dare." He further elaborated, "Parachute jumping tests and hardens a soldier under stress in a way nothing short of battle can do. You never know about others. But paratroopers will fight. You can bet on that. They repeatedly face danger while jumping and develop self-discipline that conquers fear. Subconsciously every trooper knows this. That's why he has that extra cocky confidence." Major-General A.S. Newman, *What Are Generals Made Of?* (Novato, CA: Presidio, 1987), 197. Similarly, another American, Major-General Willard Pearson, declared, "If you want to select a group of people who are willing to fight, well, one of the best criteria I know is whether or not they will jump out of an airplane. Now that is not to say that some of the others won't fight, but sure as hell the airborne will." Ward Just, *Military Men* (New York: Alfred A. Knopf, 1970), 130.

502. Breuer, *Drope Zone Sicily*, 35. Historian Clay Blair wrote that the 82nd Division emerged from Normandy with the reputation of being "a pack of jackals; the toughest, most resourceful and bloodthirsty infantry in the ETO." Blair, 295.

503. Letter, Marshall to Ridgway, December 18, 1944, *Marshall Papers*, 31:0876.

504. Ryan, 237.

505. Ibid., 415.

506. S.L.A. Marshall, *The Soldier's Load and the Mobility of a Nation* (Quantico: The Marine Corps Association, 1950), 16.

507. Brigadier Ridgley Gaither, Headquarters Army Ground Forces, Army War College, "Observer's Report, Airborne Operations, European Theater of Operations," April 19, 1945. CAFM, AB 1, 1 Cdn Para Bn, Vol 5, file 18.

508. Lieutenant-General Michael Gray, "The Birth of A Regiment," *Illustrated London News — Red Berets '44*, 19. Gale also wrote, "He [the paratrooper] is aware, too that once on the ground his future lies in his own skill. The gun which he carried down in his drop and the small supply of ammunition on his person are his only weapons for support in either attack or defence. His water and food are what he can carry when he jumps. His sense of direction, his field-craft and in map reading and his physical strength must all be of a high order. He may be alone for hours, he may be injured, he may be dazed from his fall. But it is his battle and he knows it." Gale, *With the 6th Airborne*, 2–3.

509. Saunders, *The Red Beret*, hand-written foreword by Field-Marshal Viscount Montgomery of Alamein.

510. Speech by Brigadier Hill to 1st Canadian Parachute Battalion personnel in the

transit camp, June 5, 1944. Brigadier S. James L. Hill's speaking notes, November 1993, Section V, Lead Up to D-Day and D-Day, 14. Brian Nolan, Brigadier Hill file, 1 Cdn Para Bn Assn Archives.

511. Major-General R.H. Barry, "Build -Up for D-Day, The Allied Armada," *History of The Second World War*, Part 63, June 1974, 1740. During the months of April and May 1944, the Allies co-ordinated their efforts to launch a series of very successful air operations against the Luftwaffe over France. A total of 1,858 German aircraft had been destroyed, thus explaining the absence of German counter air offensive during D-Day.

512. Ibid., 1739.

513. R.W. Thompson, *D-Day, Spearhead of Invasion* (New York: Ballantine Books Inc., 1969), 152–153. The U.S. 1st Army comprised two corps. The U.S. 7th Corps was commanded by Major-General J. Lawton Collins. His units landed on Utah Beach. The U.S. 5th Corps was commanded by Major-General L.T. Gerow. These units disembarked on Omaha Beach. The British 2nd Army was also composed of two corps. The British 1st Corps was commanded by Lieutenant-General John Crocker. His force landed on the Sword and Juno Beaches. The British 30th Corps was led by Lieutenant-General Gerard Bucknall. His units landed on Gold Beach.

514. *Report by Dwight D. Eisenhower to Combined Chiefs of Staff*, 1946, 11–16. A grand total of 10,000 aircraft took part in the various D-Day air phases. These included preparatory bombing runs, fighter escort duties, tank hunting activities, transporting paratroopers to their dropping zones, towing air-landing units and their support equipment and vehicles, reconnaissance flights and artillery observation missions.See also R.W. Thompson, "D-Day, The Great Gamble," *History Of The Second World War*, Part 63, July 1974, 1796.

515. Field Marshal the Viscount Montgomery of Alamein, *21 Army Group, Normandy To The Baltic By Field Marshal the Viscount Montgomery of Alamein* (Germany: British Army of The Rhine, 1946), 30. The initial American and British elements to land on the French beaches were: the First United States Army (three infantry divisions; five tank battalions; two ranger battalions; corps and army troops; and naval and air force detachments); the Second British Army (four infantry divisions, less two brigade groups; three assault tank brigades; one armoured brigade; two Special Service brigades (Commando), corps and army troops; and naval and air force detachments). Eisenhower anticipated landing and deploying 37divisions: 23 infantry, 10 armoured, and 4 airborne within the first 48 hours. The breakdown of the vehicles to be landed within this time period was: 1,500 tanks, 5,000 tracked vehicles, 3,000 guns, and 10,611 assorted vehicles. See also *Report by Dwight D. Eisenhower to Combined Chiefs of Staff*, 1946, 11–16.

516. Montgomery, *21 Army Group*, 29.

517. Carlo D'Este, *Decision In Normandy* (New York: Konecky & Konecky, 1994), 120–121.

518. 6th Airborne Division Operations Instruction No. 1, May 17,1944. Neptune-Bigot, Copy No. 36. Intention, Item 5. NA, RG 24, Vol 10955, file 252B6.016 (D1), Op Instructions, 6 AB Div.

519. Hartigan, *A Rising of Courage,* 21.

520. 3 Para Bde, Operational Orders, No.1, Method, 8 Para Bn, 5. 1 Cdn Para Bn War Diary, Appendix B. NA, RG 24, Vol 15299.

521. 3 Para Bde, Operational Orders, No.1, Method, 9 Para Bn, 5. Ibid. According to the larger Allied plan, upon completion of its initial tasks 3 Para Bde was to defend their areas until relieved by Brigadier Lord Lovat's 1 SS Bde. This

seaborne brigade was to fight its way from Sword Beach, cross over the previously captured Caen Canal and Orne River bridges, and link up with the paratroopers. Subsequently, Lovat's men were to relocate and occupy the area between Le Plein and Troarn. There, defensive positions were to be set up and manned. Elements of 1 SS Bde would then be sent to engage enemy forces in the costal area of Frenchville Plage. Meanwhile, all units of 3 Para Bde were to dispatch reconnaissance patrols on a regular basis to confirm the enemy's actions, intentions and positions. 6th Airborne Division Operation Instruction No.1, 17 May 1944. 1 SS Bde, 14; Appendix "F", Major-General Gale's Instructions to Commander 1 SS Bde, Brigadier The Lord Lovat. NA, RG 24, Vol 10955, file 252 B6.016 (D1). OP Instruction 6 AB Div; and ibid., Neptune-Bigot, Copy No. 36. Intention, Item 10, 3 Para Bde Group. NA, RG 24, Vol 10955, file 252B6.016 (D1), Op Instructions, 6th AB Div. Attached to 3rd Para Bde were the following units: Section 4, Anti-Tank Battery, Royal Artillery; 3 Parachute Squadron, Royal Engineers; One Troop, 591 Parachute Squadron, Royal Engineers; and 224 Parachute Field Ambulance.

522. 1 Cdn Para Bn, Operational Order No.1, 28 May 1944, Copy 23, Intention, Item 3, 1 Cdn Para Bn, 4–5. 1 Cdn Para Bn War Diary, May–June 1944, Appendix 6. NA, RG 24, Vol 15298.

523. Hartigan, *A Rising of Courage,* 197. The other elements that were flown in with "C" Company were a ten-man reconnaissance patrol from 9 Para Bn to go to the Merville Battery, and the 22nd Independent Parachute Pathfinder Company to set up the Eureka devices on Drop Zones "V," "K," and "N."

524. Method, Item 4, "C" Company, 5. 1 Cdn Para Bn War Diary, May–June, Appendix 6. NA, RG 24, Vol 15298. The defence of the Le Mesnil crossroads was important because it was a central point that linked up to many roads systems: Troarn and Sannerville; Troarn and Esconville; Robehomme and Le Mesnil; Varaville and Le Mesnil; Merille Franceville Plage and Bréville; and Franceville Plage and Sallentelles. If this crossroads was successfully defended, it would force the Germans to make long detours. This extra traveling would result in the expending precious fuel, disruption important timetables, and exposing armoured vehicles to the Allied air force tank-hunting aircraft.

525. Ibid., Method, Item 5, "A" Company, 5–6.

526. Ibid., Method, Item 6, "B" Company, 6.

527. Ibid., Method, Item 7, Mortar and MMG Platoons, 7.

528. Ibid., June 2, 1944.

529. Dan Hartigan, interview with Bernd Horn, October 30, 2000.

530. Allied intelligence reports confirmed that Rommel had been appointed commander of Army Group "B" in February 1944. Under his command were the Seventh Army, located in Normandy and Brittany; the Fifteenth Army deployed in the Pas de Calais and Flanders area; and the 88 Corps stationed in Holland. Montgomery, 21.

531. The 21st Panzer Division was formed August 1, 1941. The Division operated in North Africa with the German Afrika Korps against British Commonwealth Forces 1941–1942. Very heavy losses were sustained by this Panzer Division in Alam Halfa and El Alamein in May and October 1942. It provided rearguard forces for retreating Axis forces to Tripoli and Tunis. The Division was virtually annihilated in Tunis in May 1943, where surviving elements surrendered. The unit was reformed in Normandy in May 1943 and fought Allied invasion troops during the Normandy Campaign. Martin Windrow, *The Panzer Divisions,*

Revised Edition, (London: Osprey Publishing Ltd., 1982), 11; and David C. Isby, editor, *Fighting the Invasion, The German Army at D-Day* (London: Greenhill Books, 2000),114–121, 221–222. The 711th Infantry Division had initially been employed as an occupying force at the frontiers of occupied and unoccupied France. By April 1943, it had already been deployed as the left wing division of the Fifteenth Army, in the coastal sector between the Seine and the Orne. This was its operational location during D-Day and the Normandy campaign. Isby, 145. The 716th Infantry Division was raised in May 1941. It was part of the 15th Army until June 1942, when it was sent to the 7th Army in the Caen area, where it remained until the Allied invasion. The Division did not have combat experience. Http://home.swipnet.se/normandy/gerob/infdiv/716id.html. The 346th Infantry Division was organized in October 1942 as a fortress division intended only for duty in the fortifications on the Channel coast. During 1943, it was used as a fortress division in the St Malo area in the northern coast of Brittany. In December 1943, it was converted to a mobile reserve division. It was then transferred to the 15th Army as a army reserve unit. The Division was stationed in the Le Havre and the Seine River areas during the invasion. Isby, 151–152, 175. Elements of the above-mentioned Division fought against the 6th Airborne Division during the Normandy Campaign.

532. Since 1942, France had been used by the German High Command as a rest and refitting area for units who had been removed from the Russian front. Located throughout France there were anywhere from 50 to 60 divisions. Of these no more that 25 divisions were "of reasonable quality and seldom at full strength." R.W. Thompson, "Fortress Europe, Building Up-for D-Day," *History Of The Second World War*, Part 62, June 1974,1727.

533. The average age of the Divisions' officers, NCOs and privates were: 711th Infantry Division: Officers, 37; NCOs 31 and privates 29; 716th Infantry Division: not available; 346th Infantry Division: Officers, 37; NCOs, not available; and men 32–33; and 21st Panzer Division, not available. Bundesarchiv, Gen. Kdo, LXXXI, A.K. IIb Nr. 398/44 geh, T314, R1590, F000849.

534. In 1942, foreign battalions were drafted into German divisions. These foreign nationals made up between ten to 25 percent of a division's strength. These battalions were commanded by German officers and NCOs. R.W. Thompson, "Fortress Europe, Building Up-for D-Day," *History Of The Second World War*, Part 62, June 1974,1727.

535. Isby, 114. The Division had a formidable re-fitting task following its arrival in France. Personnel were ordered to select French and British tanks that had been captured two years earlier during the Battle of France. These were left in special guarded open compounds. During the following two years no maintenance had been carried out on these armoured vehicles. Time and the elements had caused considerable damage to these vehicles. On average it took parts from two or three vehicles to build one of good quality.

536. Chris Ellis, *21st Panzer Division, Rommel's Afrika Korps Spearhead,* Spearhead Series, No. 1, (Surrey: Ian Allan Publishing, 2001), 65. After the invasion scare of May 20, 1944, the 21st Panzer Division's 1st Battalion was ordered to upgrade its tanks and be re-equipped with seventeen Mark IV's per company. The 2nd Battalion was to receive fourteen Mark IV's per company so as to replace the old French tanks. The 21st Division had a total of 167 armoured vehicles. The Division comprised three panzer regiments, two panzer grenadier regiments and supporting units totaling 16,000 men. Of these, 4,500 were fighting troops.

Special Interrogation Report of Lieutenant-General Edgar Feuchtinger, Comd, 21 Pz Div, non-dated. The Papers of Sir Basil Liddell Hart. Liddell Hart Centre for Military Archives, King's College, London.

537.   The constant arguing between Rundstedt and Rommel inevitably weakened the 21st Panzer Division's operational effectiveness. Feuchtinger was forced to position his Panzer Grenadiers near the Orne River to support the 716th Infantry Division. His armour was to be held back further to the rear as a tactical reserve. "This dual role," complained Feuchtinger, "resulted in neither being effectively carried out." Special Interrogation Report of Lieutenant-General Edgar Feuchtinger, Comd, 21 Pz Div, non-dated. The Papers of Sir Basil Liddell Hart. Liddell Hart Centre for Military Archives, King's College, London.

538.   1 Cdn Para Bn, Summary of Information , Number 1, 26 May 1944, Miscellaneous, 1) Air landing Obstacles; 2) Anti-Airtroops, 11. 1 Cdn Para Bn War Diary, Appendix 29. NA, RG 24, Vol 15299. Allied intelligence reports confirmed that the Germans had increased the installation of trip wires with warning devices, barb wire and concertina wire, and booby traps, and had set up mine fields on slopes of hills that could be occupied by paratroopers after their landings. Furthermore, as of May 15, 1944, Rommel ordered that special anti-paratroops guards and patrols be trained and operate in areas that could be used by the allies to drop paratroopers. To further complicate anticipated glider landings, large poles were planted throughout open field to damage the incoming gliders and injure or kill their occupants. French civilians were paid by the Germans to install these. Otway, 182. Italian troops who had been captured by British paratroopers admitted that they also had been involved in installing these anti-glider poles. Carl Shilleto, *Pegasus Bridge & Merville Battery, British 6th Airborne Division Landing in Normandy D-Day, 6 June 1944* (South Yorkshire: Battlefield Series Club Pen & Sword Books Ltd, 2001), 68-69. German troops nicknamed these "Rommel's Asparagus." Initially these poles were to be rigged with explosive shells. Rommel ordered 13,000 shells for these poles but they never arrived. Despite the resources and manpower committed to the building of air-landing obstacles, the goal of completing this project by May 1944 did not materialize. Following a May 1944 inspection, a disappointed Rommel stated that this projects was only in its initial stages. Shilleto, 37; and Thompson, 1734. Due to a great labor shortage personnel of the 711th Infantry Division were forced to participate in these never ending construction taskings. "The general training was now almost completely neglected," complained Generalleutnant Joseph Richeter. The whole division, including the supply units and the rear services, became construction troops ... Moreover, all large free areas up to a depth of 1 kilometres which seemed to be suitable for an air landing were strengthened with piles," wrote a frustrated Reichert. Isby, 147. However, the poles' anticipated effect was disappointing. Major General Sir Nigel Tapp was ordered to assist with the landing of the 6th Airlanding Brigade in an area east of St-Aubin. Seeing these poles, Tapp wondered if he should send his engineers to cut them down. As the first gliders were preparing their final descent, "The thought [of using engineers] seemed to be logical," noted Tapp. "But as I watched the whole operation [glider landings]," observed Tapp, "the gliders either snapped off the poles or the poles sheared off a piece of the wing." Tapp added, "None of the occupants appeared to be any worse for this contretemps." D'Este, 136.

539.   Isby , 145, 179.

540.   Ken Ford, *D-Day 1944 (3), Sword Beach & the British Airborne Landings* (Oxford:

Ospery Publishing Ltd, 2002), 16; and Isby, 33.

541. Martin Windrow, *The Panzer Divisions (Revised Edition)* Men-At-Arms Series No. 24, (London: Ospery Publishing Ltd, 1982), 2, 12. These refitted and restructured German armoured divisions positioned in proximity of the coastline were: the 2nd, the 21st and the 116th Panzer Divisions. Isby, 33. The great majority of these Divisions' personnel had not seen action. The 2nd was refitted in Amiens in early 1944 after seeing heavy action on the Russian front. The 116th was formed in France on March 28, 1944, from elements of the 116th Panzer Grenadier Division. The Waffen SS Armoured formations and divisions attached to Army Group "B" and held in reserve were: 1st SS Panzer Division and 12th SS Panzer Division. Also held back in a reserve capacity was the Panzer Lehr Division. Eric Lefèvre, *Panzer In Normandy, Then And Now* (London: Battle of Britain Prints International Limited, 1996), 78–95, 126–129, 149–159.

542. Hartigan, *A Rising of Courage*, 30.

543. Nolan, *Airborne*, 74.

544. 1 Cdn Para Bn War Diary, June 4, 1944. NA, RG 24, Vol 15299.

545. Anderson, *Grass Roots,* 264. Gale was pleased to note that his paratroopers "were in great heart, cheerful, expectant and ready for anything." Gale, *With the 6th Airborne*, 70.

546. Anderson, *Grass Roots*, 263.

547. Doug Morrison, interview with Bernd Horn, February 2, 2002.

548. Hartigan, *A Rising of Courage*, 62. 1 Cdn Para Bn War Diary, June 3, 1944. NA, RG 24, Vol 15299.

549. "C" Company and elements of the 3 Para Bde Hq emplaned in fourteen Albemarles, aircraft No. B, T, Q, E, R, I, Z, of 295 Squadron, and aircraft B, I, K, D, X, L, and P from 570 Squadron. These aircraft took off from Harwell between 2308 hours and 2314 hours. The other Airborne units that were part of this Advance Group were: twenty paratroopers from the Independent Parachute Company emplaned in two aircraft; twenty paratroopers of the 22nd Independent Parachute Company emplaned in two aircraft; and twenty paratroopers from the 8th Parachute Battalion who emplaned in two other Albemarles. Harwell Station entry June 5, 1944. PRO, AIR 28/342 Air Ministry and Minister of Defence: Operations Record Book, Royal Air Force Station, Harwell. Notes taken from 3 Para Bde Operational Order 1, included as an appendix to W.D. 3 Para Bde, May 1944, Appendix E giving allocation of airfields aircraft, Drop Zones and Landing Zones for 3 Para Brigade. 1 Cdn Para Bn War Diary, June 1944. NA, RG 24, Vol 15298.

550. Captain J.R. Madden, "Ex Coelis," *The Canadian Army Journal*, January 1957, Vol XI, No. 1, 51.

551. Ibid. "A", "B" and "HQ" Companies emplaned in thirty-six C-47 Dakota aircraft, Nos. 263–265 and, 278–303. These aircraft were flown by crews of the RAF 46 Group. Personnel of 3 Para Bde HQ boarded seven C-47, Nos. 268–274. The Down Ampney Station records state that a total of thirty-nine C-47 Dakotas from 48 and 271 Squadrons transported the Battalion and the 3 Para Bde HQ personnel into France. This airlift operation was called Operation Tonga. The operation comprised two tasks. Task 1 consisted lifting off at 2248 hours. The assigned aircraft were to tow and release seven gliders on landing zone "V" by 0045 hours. Task 2 consisted of lifting off at 2320 hours and transporting and dropping paratroopers at 0056 hours on selected dropping zones. PRO, 28/211 Air Ministry and Minister of Defence: Royal Air Force Station, Down Ampney.

552. 1 Cdn Para Bn War Diary, June 4–5, 1944. NA, RG 24, Vol 15299, June 1944. The

liftoff timing given by RAF Station Harwell was between 2308 and 2314 hours. Harwell Station records show that 117 paratroopers of "C" Company emplaned and 46 containers were loaded onto the 14 Albemarles. PRO, AIR 28/342 Air Ministry and Minister of Defence: Operations Record Book, Royal Air Force Station, Harwell.

553. Embarkation and Disembarkation of 1st Cdn Para Bn Officers and Other Ranks into France, June 6–9, 1944. Another thirty-six 1st Cdn Para Bn paratroopers arrived in France by parachute, glider and sea vessels: two jumped on June 6; four landed via gliders on June 6; twenty-eight embarked on a ship on June 4 and landed on June 8; nine embarked on a ship on June 9 and landed the same day; four embarked on a ship on June 3 and landed on June 9; one embarked on a ship on June 1 and landed on June 8. The grand total of Canadian paratroopers in France by June 9, 1944, was 577. NA, Part II Orders, 1st Canadian Parachute Battalion, issued by Canadian Section GHQ, 2nd Echelon, 21st Army Group, Order No. 19, 19 July 1944.

554. D'Este, 112. Between 0300 and 0500 hours of June 6, more than one thousand British aircraft had dropped in excess of five thousand tons of bombs on the German costal defences and in the surrounding area where the 6th Airborne Division would land.

555. Hartigan, *A Rising of Courage*, 71.

556. Hartigan, *A Rising of Courage*, 108–109. Of the 117 members of "C" Company who flew into France, 99 had exited their aircraft safely. Two aircrafts returned to Harwell with a total of 18 paratroopers. In one aircraft, an exit door accidentally unfastened and jammed a paratrooper in the aperture. All attempts to extricate him proved useless and the remaining members of the stick could not exit. Another aircraft experienced a similar problem; however, the paratrooper was freed. This incident resulted in part of the stick being dropped off course. Furthermore, some technical difficulties were experienced during the equipment container -releasing phase. Of the 46 loaded containers, 6 could not be jettisoned. RAF Station, daily entry, June 5, 1944. PRO, AIR 28/343 Air Ministry and Minister of Defence: Operations Record Book, Royal Air Force Station, Harwell.

557. Peter Harclerode, *"Go To It!" The Illustrated History of The 6th Airborne Division* (London: Caxton Edition, 2000), 88. A total of three advance parties with pathfinders were dropped to protect and mark three Drop Zones between the Orne and Dives Rivers. The units of the main body that jumped onto them were: Drop Zone "N," 5th Para Bde Gp; Drop Zone "V," 3rd Para Bde Gp, and Drop Zone "K," 8th Para Bn. The Drop Zone "V" pathfinder group consisted of two sticks. Stick No. 1 dropped directly onto the DZ. Regrettably this stick's DZ marking equipment was either damaged or lost in the marshes. Stick No. 2 landed a thousand yards north of the DZ. They finally reached the DZ as the main body was jumping. The DZ markings that were set up for the main body consisted of two green lights set up prior to the main drop. An additional two lights were installed by the paratroopers of the second stick during the main body's jump. 6 Airborne Division, Report on Operations in Normandy, 6 June – 27 August 1944. Part III, Conclusions, Appendix "H", Details of Pathfinder Drop. NA, RG 24, Vol 10955, file 225.B6.013 (D1), 6 AB Div Report. Simultaneously, two small forces of "D" Company Group 2 Oxford and Buckinghamshire Light Infantry were glider inserted to carry out a *coup de main*, which resulted in the ca pture of the bridges over the Caen Canal and the River Orne. Harclerode, *"Go To It!"*, 88.

558. Otway, Appendix D, Radar Homing Devices, 405–406. The "Rebecca/Eureka" was a two-part homing device. The first part, the "Eureka," was a beacon housed in a small rectangular box with a collapsible aerial. The Eurekas were operated by pathfinder units to assist the pilots transporting the main bodies in locating their DZs. This beacon was designed to receive on one frequency and transmit on another. The second part, the "Rebecca," was installed in the aircraft. It was designed to transmit and receive on the Eureka's transmitter frequency. When receiving the Rebecca's impulse signal, the Eureka responded by sending a signal. This enabled the pilot to confirm his approach and distance to the DZ. See also *Circumstances attending dispersion of the 6th Airborne Division on D-Day* from "The Liberation of North West Europe. Volume III: The Landings in Normandy." The Varaville Dropping Zone 'V', 2-3. NA, RG 24, Vol 10955, file 2255B6.013(D3), Circumstances attending dispersion of the 6th AB Div on D-Day.

559. Hartigan, *A Rising of Courage*, 109.

560. *By Air To Battle, The Official Account of The British First and Sixth Airborne Divisions* (London: The Whitefriars Press Ltd., 1945), 87.

561. Hartigan, *A Rising of Courage*, 114–115. The other paratroopers who were killed were: Major H.M. McLeod, Lieutenant H.M. Walker, Corporal W.E. Oikle, and Privates P.I. Bismutka and L.A. Neufeld. Major McLeod and Private Bismutka had been mortally wounded and died within a few minutes.

562. Ibid., 132.

563. 1 Cdn Para Bn War Diary, June 6, 1944, Varaville, "C" Company. NA, RG 24, Vol 15299, June 1944. 1st Canadian Parachute Battalion, Operational Order No.1, Method, 4. "C" Company, Phases 1-5. Ibid., May 1944, Appendix 6.

564. 1 Cdn Para Bn War Diary, June 6, 1944, Varaville, "C" Company. Ibid.

565. Ken Ford, *D-Day 1944 (3), Sword Beach & the British Airborne Landings*, (Oxford: Osprey Publishing Ltd, 2002), 32-39. The two bridges that were captured were the Caen Canal lifting bridge and Orne River bridge. At 0020 hours, June 6, 1944, Major John Howard and "D" Company of the 2nd Ox and Bucks Light Infantry landed on Landing Zone "X" in three gliders near Caen Canal bridge. They quickly overpowered the Germans and defended the bridge until relieved. At 0025 hours, two other gliders landed on Landing Zone "Y" near the Orne River bridge located approximately four hundred yard from the Caen Canal bridge. Elements of "D" Company, 2nd Ox and Bucks under the command of Lieutenant Fox captured the bridge unopposed.

566. "Circumstances attending dispersion of the 6th Airborne Division on D-Day" from *The Liberation of North West Europe. Volume III: The Landings in Normandy.* Dropping Zone 'V' – Drop of the Main Body of the 3rd Parachute Brigade, 4-5. NA, RG 24, Vol 10955, file 2255B6.013(D3), Circumstances attending dispersion of the 6th AB Div on D-Day. The RAF airlift to DZ "V" in Normandy consisted of a total of thirty-nine Dakotas from 48 and 271 Squadrons. These aircraft transported the 1st Canadian Parachute Battalion, less "C" Company, and elements of the 3rd Para Bde Headquarters into France. Despite all the problems encountered during the final approach and drop RAF personnel from RAF Station Down Ampney considered this drop "a very successful operation". PRO, AIR 28/211, Air Ministry and Minister of Defence: Operations Records Book, Royal Air Force Station, Down Ampney. The No. 46 Group unofficial history provided additional insights into the circumstances that led to the dispersal drop. "It will be recollected that the plan to employ Pathfinder techniques was a partial failure on this Zone [DZ "V"], too, because while one stick either lost its equipment or recovered it in

unserviceable condition, the other stick of troops dropped over half a mile away. The Main Body had arrived and commenced dropping before the Beacons and Lights were in operation." It was reported that "only two green lights were exhibited on Dropping Zone 'V' when the Dakotas crossed the coast and in the prevailing conditions few crews saw them. It was at first thought that some of the navigators had mistaken the River Dives for the Orne River which was the pinpoint. As an explanation of the scattered drop this is by no means clear. No. 46 Group Historian says that the lack of the expected ground signals, the pall of dust and smoke blown across the run-in and the Dropping Zone, and some troublesome flak combined to produce the scattered landings. It seem, however, that uncertain navigation, the lack of prominent land-marks and the prevalence of veering winds were also important factors in the failure of the Dakota Squadrons." A post-war analysis revealed that of the total thirty-four sticks that made up the main body of 1 Cdn Para Bn, seven were dropped on the DZ, five were dropped within a mile of the centre of the DZ, six were dropped within one to two miles of the centre of the DZ, and sixen were over two miles from the centre of the DZ. Extract from, "Report On The British Airborne Effort In Operation 'Neptune' by 38 and 46 Groups, n.d. DHH, file 145.4013 (D), 1 Cdn Para Bn – Information reference dispersion on D-Day, 6 June 1944.

567.   Harold Johnstone, *Johnny Kemp, DCM, His Story With the 1st Canadian Parachute Battalion, 1942–1945* (Nanaimo: Private Printing, 2000), 9.

568.   D-Day and Normandy. Interviews, letters and recollections compiled by Gary Boegal, 1st Canadian Parachute Battalion Assn Archives, Boegal, Gary, file 45-1.

569.   Recollections of a Canadian Parachuting Medical Officer in World War II, 6. Brian Nolan Fonds, Colin Brebner file, 1 Cdn Para Bn Assn Archives. Captain Colin Brebner, the Battalion's medical officer, landed in a tree. As he attempted to extricate himself from his harness, Brebner fell to the ground and broke his left wrist and pelvis. Another casualty sustained during this night drop was the Battalion's Padre, Captain G.A. Harris. The Padre's parachute got tangled with another parachute. Harris was killed upon impact while the other paratrooper survived.

570.   Doug Morrison, interview with Bernd Horn, February 2, 2002.

571.   Letter from Ted Kalicki to Brian Nolan, Warsaw, New York, February 7, 1994. Brian Nolan Fonds, Ted Kalicki file, 1 Cdn Para Bn Assn Archives. Kalicki gave a detailed description of what he carried and jumped with. "I had sewn two bandoliers of .303 rifle ammo onto the bottom of my Denison Smock and I also criss-crossed two more on my shoulders. We had felt bags strapped to our legs which we could release with a rip cord. And then lower it away from us on a 20 foot nylon cords. The bag held our .303 Lee Enfield rifle, more .303 ammo and some phosphorous grenades, several sticks of plastic high explosives, a couple of 2 inch mortar shells and several hand grenades. In our back packs, we had a change of underwear, socks 3 days supply of field rations which consisted of tinned corned beef, hard candy, cigarettes, razor, a plastic tube in which we put the PHE and make a bangalore torpedo, 1 or 2 75 anti-tank mines, prima cord and whatever else we could stow and felt we could carry. We couldn't climb into the aircraft on our own. There were two men, one on each side of the door that literally lifted and threw us into the plane."

572.   Hartigan, *A Rising of Courage*, 113.

573.   Ross Munro, "Nicklin's Feat, Lands In Nazi-Held Town," *Winnipeg Free Press*, Monday, June 26, 1944, Vol 50, No. 232, 1, 8. NL, microfilm N-24564.

574. Gale, *With the 6th Airborne*, 80–81, 83. By early morning of June 6, 1944, General Gale still had no situation reports from the 3rd Parachute Brigade headquarters and its battalions. By 1000 hours Gale had gathered from second-hand information that the Canadian paratroopers were at the Le Mesnil crossroads but he did not know their exact numbers.

575. Letter from Lieutenant-Colonel G.F.P. Bradbrooke (ret'd) to David Owen, March 6, 1985. David Owen Fond, Series 1: Correspondence, G.F.P. Bradbrooke file, 1 Cdn Para Bn Assn Archives.

576. Letter from Lieutenant-Colonel G.F.P. Bradbrooke (ret'd) to Brian Nolan, Ramsey, Isle of Man, August 19, 1985. Brian Nolan Fond, Lieutenant-Colonel G.F.P. Bradbrooke file, 1 Cdn Para Bn Assn Archives.

577. Ibid.

578. Jean E. Portugal, *We Were There — The Army: A Record for Canada, Volume #2 of Seven*. Toronto: The Royal Canadian Institute, 1998, 943–944.

579. Jan de Vries, interview with Bernd Horn, January 18, 2001.

580. Anderson, *Grass Roots*, 269–270.

581. H.R. Holloway, interview with Bernd Horn, November 4, 1998.

582. Letter from John Feduck to Dan Hartigan, non-dated. 1 Cdn Para Bn Assn Archives, Dan Hartigan , file 23-7.

583. Denis Flynn, interview with Bernd Horn, April 18, 2001. He added, "I began to meet up with others and we made our way towards our objective. Everyone knew what was required and we did whatever could be done under the circumstances."

584. Brigadier James Hill, interview with Brian Nolan, April 25, 1944, 20–21. Brian Nolan Fonds, Brigadier Hill file, 1 Cdn Para Bn Assn Archives.

585. Isby, 179.

586. Colonel C.P. Stacey, Historical Officer, Canadian Military Headquarters, *Report No. 19, The 1st Canadian Parachute Battalion In France, 6 June - 6 September 1944*, 13.

587. Shilleto, 81, 93.

588. 1 Cdn Para Bn War Diary, June 6, 1944, Protection of left Flank of 9 Para Bn , "A" Company. NA, RG 24, Vol 15299, June 1944. 1st Canadian Parachute Battalion, Operational Order No.1, Method, 5, "A" Company, Phases 1-3. Ibid., May 1944, Appendix 6.

589. Shilleto, 104. Of the 150 British paratroopers who participated on the attack of the Merville Battery, only 80 combatants were able to move on and prepare for their next task. The German defenders had sustained heavy losses. Battery Commander Oberleutenant Raimund Steiner confirmed that by the end of the battle, only 8 of his 130 men were still able to fight.

590. Ibid. 87; Saunders, *The Red Beret*, 185; and "Silent Guns," *Red Berets' 44, The Illustrated London News* 1994, 38.

591. Shilleto, 77; and "Silent Guns," *Red Berets' 44*, 36–40.

592. Ibid., 81. The Battery's surrounding area was defended by five camouflaged machine gun emplacements, fifteen5 additional weapons pits, and three light anti-aircraft positions that could also double as anti-tanks weapons. The Gammon Bomb was a grenade type anti-tank weapon. It was invented by Captain Arthur Gammon of 1 Para Bn in 1941. It consisted of a stockinette bag filled with plastic explosives. To arm this device one simply had to remove the screw cap and throw it at the armour vehicle or bunker. Ferguson, 29.

593. 1 Cdn Para Bn War Diary, June 6, 1944, Protection of left Flank of 9 Para Bn , "A" Company. NA, RG 24, Vol 15299, June 1944.

594. Napier Crookenden, *Dropzone Normandy, The Story of the American and British Airborne Assault on D-Day 1944* (New York: Charles Scribner's Sons, 1976), 210. The British engineers of 2 Troop, 3rd Parachute Squadron had also experienced difficulties with their drop. They had landed into the water east of Varaville. Furthermore, they lost valuable time searching for the explosive containers.

595. There are conflicting accounts from both British and Canadian sources as to how this bridge was destroyed. Canadian sources: Lieutenant N. Toseland recalled, "We attempted to blow the bridge with the plastic explosives each man carried in his helmet. We did not succeed in destroying the bridge as our charges were insufficient. Finally, the British Para Engineers appointed to do the job arrived and expertly dropped the bridge into the river." Interview of Normand Toseland, "Out Of The Clouds: The Story Of The First Canadian Parachute Battalion" *The Legion Bugle*, Vol 2, Issue 11, July/August 1988, 1. The Battalion's War Diary entry reads, " Captain Griffin waited until 0630 hours for the R.E.'s who were to blow the bridge. As they failed to arrive explosives were collected from the men and the bridge successfully demolished. 1 Cdn Para Bn War Diary, June 6, 1944, "B" Company. NA, RG 24, Vol 15299, June 1944; Captain Peter Griffin writes, "In the first two days I had fun blowing up two bridges ... So finally we pooled all the explosives we normally carry and no one knowing anything about engineering, we slapped it up against the bridge hoping against hope. Sure enough when I touched it off the bridge split in the centre and fell in the river — big thrill!" Letter from Captain Peter Griffin to his sister Margeret, Normandy, June 20, 1944. NA, MG 30, E 538, William M.R. Griffin and Peter R. Griffin fonds. British sources: Lieutenant Inman states that he arrived at the bridge at 0900 hours where he met Sergeant William Poole. The Sergeant stated that he had dropped nearby and collected thirty pounds of explosives from the paratroopers and "destroyed the span with a clean cut." Appendix C, Report on Operations Re. 6th AB Div D-Day + 1, Part 1, D-Day, 3 Parachute Squadron, Royal Engineers. NA, RG 24 Vol 10956, file 2556.018 (D2+3), War Diary 6AB Div, June-July 1944. Crookenden concurred with Inman recollections, but added that Lieutenant Inman used his explosives "to create a worse obstacle by preparing two carters on the near side abutment." 210; and Peter Harclerode wrote, "However, Sergeant Bill Poole of No.3 Troop of 3rd Parachute Squadron RE, who was one of the sappers who had joined up withe Lieutenant Toseland, collected all the plastic explosives carried by infantrymen to make Gammon bombs. This amounted to some thirty pounds in all. Sergeant Poole attempted to blow the bridge but, with the limited amount of explosive available to him, only managed to weaken it. At about 0600 hours, however, Lieutenant Jack Inman and five sappers of No.3 Troop arrived with 200 pounds of explosive charges and the bridge was duly destroyed." 72. It is most likely that during the course of the night, two charges had been set off. The first charge prepared with the explosives collected from the paratroopers only weakened the structure. The second , larger charge rigged by the British engineers destroyed the bridge.

596. 1 Cdn Para Bn War Diary, June 6, 1944, Protection of left flank of 9 Para Bn , "A" Company. NA, RG 24, Vol 15299, June 1944. As the group made its way to Le Mesnil, they met up with Lieutenant I. Wilson, a Battalion Intelligence Officer. Wilson guided the paratroopers back to the Battalion's defensive positions.

597. 1 Cdn Para Bn War Diary, June 6, 1944. NA, RG 24, Vol 15299, June 1944. The members of the Vickers platoon had packed their machines guns, spare parts and ammunition in their leg kit bags. This was the first time that they had used these kit bags to jump with their weapons. This method of transporting weaponry into

combat proved totally unsatisfactory. When the paratroopers released the bags, the shock generated by the full extension of the twenty-foot rope was so severe that the bottoms ripped. Within seconds, the contents fell out, scattered and crashed to the ground. Mortar platoon personnel also experienced the similar problem with their leg kit bags. Since most of these platoons members were mostly dropped over marshy and flooded areas, the conditions were such that it was impossible for the paratroopers to locate their heavy weapons. The signalers faired no better. All the radios had been lost. John Simpson, interview with Michel Wyczynski, December 13, 2001.

598. Isby, 145, 179.

599. Letter from Lieutenant-Colonel G.F.P. Bradbrooke (Ret'd) to David Owen, Ramsey, Isle of Man, March 6, 1985. David Owen Fonds. Series 1, Correspondence, G.F.P. Bradbrooke, file. 1 Cdn Para Bn Assn Archives.

600. Brigadier James Hill's speaking notes on the training and briefing of the 6th Airborne Division for their role in Operation Overlord. Talk given to Staff College, Camberley, June 7, 1968. Brigadier James Hill's speaking notes, November 1993. Brian Nolan Fonds, File Brigadier Hill, 1st Canadian Parachute Battalion Assn Archives. There were only three reported cases of battle exhaustion during the entire campaign. Furthermore, some of the wounded , after receiving medical attention, opted to return as quickly as possible to the front lines to be with their comrades. In one case a wounded paratrooper who had been evacuated to a beach front medical facility left without permission and returned to Le Mesnil. Ross Munro, "Canadian 'Chutists Held Crossroads In 11 Days and Nights of Fighting" *The Evening Citizen*, No. 321, June 26, 1944, 8. NL, microfilm N-18015.

601. Colonel C.P. Stacey, Director, Historical Section (G.S.). The 1st Canadian Parachute Battalion in France, June 6 – September 6, 1944. DHH, Report No.26 Historical Section (G.S), Army Headquarters, 23 August 1949, 21. On June 6, 1944, the casualties sustained by the 1st Canadian Parachute Battalion were: three Officers and eighteen ORs killed or dead of wounds; oneofficer and eight ORs wounded; three officers and eighty-three ORs captured

602. John Feduck, interview with Michel Wyczynski, December 19, 2001.

603. Hartigan, Map D-Day Plus One, 157. The 6th Airborne Division's roughly semi-circular defensive front extended from the outskirts of Les Marmiers, a small coastal village located in the vicinity of the captured Merville Battery, to the small village of Longueval and the portion of Caen Canal next to this village. The units deployed on this front from the sea to the Longueval area were: 1st Special Service Bde Commandos; 9 Para Bn; 1Cdn Para Bn; 8 Para Bn; 52nd Light Infantry (Oxs &Bucks) Glider Troops; and Royal Ulsters Regiment, Glider Troops.

604. Montgomery, 68-69. By early morning, Lieutenant-General Edgar Feuchtinger, commander of the 21st Panzer Division, refused to wait any longer for orders from Army Group "B" Headquarters. By 0630 hours, acting on his own initiative he ordered elements of his armoured units to prepare to move out towards 6th Airborne Division Landing and Dropping Zones. However, by 1000 hours, he finally received an Operational Order from Army Group "B" Headquarters. Feuchtinger was ordered to move west and assist the German units in Caen. See also Isby, 221–222.

605. Gale, *With the 6th Airborne*, 96. General Gale provided an interesting assessment of the effectiveness of the German artillery bombardments on the positions occupied by his paratroopers and air-landed infantry. "I said I felt little doubt

that we would hold our bridgehead, but, and this was the important part, that was provided the Germans tactics did not alter. Up to that moment, though we had been continually mortared and shelled by self-propelled guns, we had never been seriously registered. Without registration, that is to say careful ranging by all guns of all calibre, artillery fires, thought harmful admittedly, can never be really devastating. They enemy had never registered the bridges or the approaches to them: he had never registered our gun positions: he had never registered our headquarters: he had never registered methodically our forward posts. All he had done was to mortar indiscriminately where he believed the troops were dug in. He had shelled us twice with his 5.9s, but these guns shot wildly and just indiscriminately browned off into the villages. I knew, therefore, that no sudden and devastating accurate mass of artillery fire was likely to precede a methodically mounted divisional attack. This failure of the German to group his artillery and exploit the great potential of his arm is astounding. That he had the means of controlling and co-ordinating this fire I later found to be only too true."

606. 6 Airborne Division, Report On Operations In Normandy, 6 June – 27 August 1944, III) Second Phase, 14 June – 16 August, Paragraph 14. To provide the troops with adequate training during their defence of Le Mesnil, a divisional rest camp was established in Ouistreham. There, a School for Sniping, Patrolling and Mine lifting were set up. Ibid., Paragraph 15. NA, RG 24, Vol 10955, file 255 B6.013, 6 Airborne Division Report.

607. Lieutenant-Colonel Fraser Eadie, interview with Bernd Horn, November 20, 2000.

608. Summary of information No. 1, 1 Cdn Para Bn, Part 1, Topography, B) Roads, May 26, 1944. NA, RG 24, Vol 15299, War Diary, 1st Canadian Parachute Battalion, June 1944.

609. Montgomery, 26–27. The Americans paratroopers, just like their British and Canadian counterparts, encountered numerous problems fighting in the bocage. "Progress into the hedgerow country was bound to be slow, for each hedgerow became a separate objective, each enclosed filed a battleground. Their observation limited to a few hundred yards at most, offensive weapons lacking files of fire, troop control difficult to maintain, manoeuver hard to coordinate, the Americans would suffer the additional penalty of almost constant rain in June and July. Tanks could move cross-country only if preceded by bulldozers punching holes in banks. Vehicles on the country roads would often be in a labyrinth of sunken trails perfect for ambush. Every American division committed in Normandy had to learn to fight in the hedgerows, and the process was accomplished at great cost in lives and pain. Success depended on the initiative of the individual soldier, on the aggressiveness of small unit leaders, and on the ingenuity and persistence of those who overcame a multitude of obstacles to give supporting fire." Martin Blumenson, "St Lô: Battle of the Hedgerows" *History Of The Second World War*, Part 66, 1840.

610. John Madden, 1st Canadian Parachute Battalion. Taped recollections. Non-dated, 33. DHH, Madden , John, biographical file.

611. Personal account of Private Bill Dunnett, "A" Company, 1st Canadian Parachute Battalion. Portugal, *We Were There*, chapter 20. Sky Commandos: 1st Canadian Parachute Battalion, Vol 2, 953.

612. 1 Cdn Para Bn War Diary, Daily entry for Battalion Headquarters — Initial Stages, 6 June 1944. NA, RG 24, Vol 15299, June 1944.

613. Letter From G.W. Embree to Brian Nolan, non-dated. Brian Nolan Fond, G.F.P. Bradbrooke, file. 1 Cdn Para Bn Assn Archives.

614. Johnstone, 16.
615. Private Harold Croft, "C" Company, 7 Platoon. Interviews, letters and recollections compiled by Gary Boegal. 1 Cdn Para Bn Assn Archives, Boegal, Gary, file 45-1.
616. Hartigan, *A Rising of Courage*, 174, 222. Hartigan recalled that while training in England he and other paratroopers had had long conversations with many wounded Canadian soldiers who had been evacuated from Italy. The wounded soldiers told many stories of their stressful encounters with German snipers. To the man they were impressed by their deadly efficiency. Conversations with numerous 1 Cdn Para Bn veterans confirmed that throughout the Normandy campaign there were daily firefights with enemy snipers. However, in the Battalion war diary's daily entries of the June, July, and August there are only five references to German sniper activity: June 7, 8, 9, and 27, 1944; none for July, and only one for August (August 25). One must keep in mind that most of the information had been re-transcribed a few weeks after the events took place from a series of rough notes forwarded by the Bn HQ. Only the most notable events were logged. 1 Cdn Para Bn War Diary, NA, RG 24, Vol 15299.
617. Private Harold Croft, "C" Company, 7 Platoon. Interviews, letters and recollections compiled by Gary Boegal. 1 Cdn Para Bn Assn Archives, Boegal, Gary, file 45-1.
618. Interview with Brigadier Hill, Monday, April 25, 1994. Brian Nolan Fonds, Brigadier James Hill file, 1 Cdn Para Bn Assn Archives.
619. George Green's commentaries for the video production, *Lest We Forget: Canadians In Normandy* produced by the Canadian Battle of Normandy Foundation, 1994.
620. "D-Day: Parachuting Behind Enemy Lines," *Maclean's Special Edition*, January 1, 2000, 164.
621. Portugal, "Personal account of Private Mervin F. Jones, Battalion HQ, 1st Canadian Parachute Battalion," 953. Major-General Richard Gale also noted that his paratroopers changed their trench construction when they occupied positions in wooded areas or near tree lines. "Whenever their trenches were near trees they had constructed overhead cover. They had seen many of their number become casualties as a result of air-burst mortar bombs detonated by the branches overhead, and they knew that the downward bursts from this type of detonation could have the most devastating effect." Gale, *With the 6th Airborne*, 94.
622. Hartigan, *A Rising of Courage*, 222.
623. Doug Morrison, interview with Bernd Horn, January 31, 2002.
624. 1 Cdn Para Bn War Diary, June 7–17, 1944. NA, RG 24, Vol 15299, June 1944. No patrol reports were filed in the June portion of the Battalion's war diary. Thus, it was difficult to confirm the patrols' missions and results. The preparation of patrol reports and post-patrol debriefings would, however, change. Due to the nature of the terrain and the constant movement of enemy troops, it became increasingly important that all information gathered during patrols be brought forward accurately and completely. The correct logging and subsequent interpretation of the enemy's actions, positions, and type of weaponry located in these positions could prove vital for the elaboration of future strategies and, more importantly, for limiting casualties. In the last week of July five reports were completed and turned over to the Battalion's Intelligence Platoon. In August, when the Battalion was on the offensive, a total of thirty patrol reports had been completed and filed.
625. Letter from Captain Peter R. Griffin to his sister Margaret Norman, Normandy, July 6, 1944. NA, MG 30, E538, William M. R. Griffin and Peter R. Griffin fonds.

626. Letter from Major John P. Hanson to Lieutenant-Colonel G.W.L. Nicholson, Montreal, November 12, 1949. DHH, file 145.4013 (D5) Operations, Correspondence from 1st Canadian Parachute Battalion officers, reference 1st Canadian Parachute Battalion Operations. The counterattack took place on June 8 rather than June 7 as indicated in the War Diary. 1 Cdn Para Bn War Diary, 7 & 8 June. NA, RG 24, Vol 15299, June 1944.

627. Ibid., June 8. The enemy losses in the counterattack totaled approximately fifty killed and an unknown number wounded.

628. Brigadier Hill, interview with Brian Nolan, 18. Brian Nolan Fonds, Brigadier James Hill file. 1 Cdn Para Bn Assn Archives.

629. John Madden, 1st Canadian Parachute Battalion. Taped Recollections, Non-dated, 22. DHH, Madden, John, biography file.

630. Max Arthur, *Men of The Red Beret, Airborne Forces, 1940–1990* (London: Century Hutchinson, 1990), 163; 1 Cdn Para Bn War Diary, June 9, 1944. NA, RG 24, Vol 15299, June 1944.

631. Hartigan, *A Rising of Courage*, 171.

632. 1 Cdn Para Bn War Diary, June 9, 1944. NA, RG 24, Vol 15299, June 1944.

633. Gale, *With the 6th Airborne*, 99. The situation had deteriorated to the point that Major-General Gale personally came down on June 12 and 13 to assess the situation first-hand. Even though the initial and subsequent attacks had been contained, this was definitely the weakest link in the 6 AB Div's defensive front. From the outset, Brigadier Hill was very concerned the defence of Bréville and its surrounding areas. In the first few days after the drop, Hill urged Gale to take whatever actions required to once and for all liquidate the Bréville sore.

634. Brigadier Hill, interview with Brian Nolan, April 25, 1994, 20-21. Brian Nolan Fonds, Brigadier James Hill file. 1 Cdn Para Bn Assn Archives.

635. Jan de Vries, interview with Bernd Horn, January 18, 2001.

636. Letter from Major John P. Hanson to Lieutenant-Colonel G.W.L. Nicholson, Montreal, November 12, 1949. DHH, file 145.4013 (D5) Operations, Correspondence from 1st Canadian Parachute Battalion officers, reference 1st Canadian Parachute Battalion Operations.

637. Hartigan, *A Rising of Courage*, 233.

638. Jan de Vries, interview with Bernd Horn, June 20, 2002.

639. Michael Ball, interview with Michel Wyczynski. June 12, 2002.

640. Ibid.

641. Ibid.

642. Crookenden, 273–279. On June 10, German prisoners captured on the outskirts of Bréville revealed that the II Bn, 857 Grenadier Regiment was to capture the glider Landing Zone located on the other side of Bréville. The III Bn, 857 Grenadier Regiment would then pass through their positions and consolidate. The plan nearly succeeded. However, a few hours after the Canadian paratroopers left this sector, the Independent Parachute Company arrived at 2315 hours to reinforce the 12th Parachute Battalion. Following an aerial bombardment of enemy concentrations east of Bréville, the final British ground attack was launched during the evening of June 13. 6 AB Div War Diary, daily entries, June 10, 11, and 13, 1944. NA, RG 24, Vol 10956, file 255B6.018 (D2+3), 6–30 June 1944.

643. Ross Munro, "Canadian Paratroopers 11 Day Siege Remains Epic Of Invasion Fighting," *The Gazette*, Vol CLXXIII, No. 152, 26 June 1944, 1. NL, microfilm N-32626.

644. Portugal, *We Were There*, 953.

645. Joseph King, interview with Bernd Horn, January 31, 2002.

646. Jan de Vries, letter to Bernd Horn, January 21, 2001.

647. Ross Munro, "Canadian 'Chutists Held Crossroads In 11 Days and Nights of Fighting," *The Evening Citizen*, No. 321, 26 June 1944, 8. NL, microfilm N-18015. Ross Munro, "Invasion's East Flank Canada 'Chutists' Job," *Toronto Daily Star*, 26 June 1944, 1. NL, microfilm N-28589.

648. Brigadier Hill, interview with Brian Nolan, 16. Brian Nolan Fonds, Brigadier Hill file. 1 Cdn Para Bn Assn Archives.

649. Colonel C.P. Stacey, Director, Historical Section (G.S.). The 1st Canadian Parachute Battalion in France, 6 June–6 September 1944. DHH, Report No.26 Historical Section (G.S), Army Headquarters, 23 August 1949, 20. Between June 7 and 17, 1944, the casualties sustained by the 1st Canadian Parachute Battalion were: 3 officers and 28 ORs killed or died of wounds; 7 officers and 81 ORs wounded. No Battalion members was taken prisoner. Total losses 10 killed and 109 injured.

650. J.A. Collins. Interviews, letters and recollections compiled by Gary Boegal. 1 Cdn Para Bn Assn Archives.

651. Jan de Vries, letter to Bernd Horn, January 21, 2001.

652. 1 Cdn Para Bn War Diary, June 17, 1944. NA, RG 24, Vol 15299, June 1944.

653. Hans Von Luck, *Panzer Commander: The Memoirs of Colonel Hans Von Luck* (New York: Dell, 1989), 164. 21st Division German tank commander Werner Kortenhaus wrote, "On the evening of the 9 June we realized that we could no longer drive the British back into the sea."

654. 6th Airborne Division, Intelligence Summary No. 22, June 1944. NA, RG 24, Vol 10956, file 255B6.018 (D2+3), 6 AB Div, War Diary.

655. 6th Airborne Division, Intelligence Summary No. 22, Paragraph 1, June 1944.

656. 1 Cdn Para Bn War Diary, June 26, 1944. NA, RG 24, Vol 15299, June 1944.

657. Ibid., June 28, 1944.

658. Ibid., June 27, 1944.

659. Ibid.

660. Ibid., July 5–11, 1944.

661. Gale, *With the 6th Airborne*, 102–103. Even General Gale noted the ill effects of the mosquito bites on his paratroopers. "Pearson all this time was suffering from a wound; but he would not give in: he was too, I knew, a sick man; but held on. He became covered in small boils and sores, and his blood was so out of order that he looked ill and colourless. The mosquitoes were a plague and his men were bitten; they scratched their bites and got sore skin sores; they were blotchy with dolly blue which their medical officer had treated their poor skins with: but they never complained." Hilary Saunders writes, "They [mosquitoes] were so enormous in numbers, so many in fact that it was impossible to eat or talk without swallowing several of them." 209. Napier Crookenden added, "For most men the main enemies were boredom and the mosquitoes, which swarmed out of the flooded valley of the Dives and caused many swollen faces before face veils and cream began to come up with the rations." 283. The Germans troops faired no better. Colonel Hans Von Luck, Commander of the 125th Regiment of the 21st Panzer Division reported, "We all suffered from the mosquitoes; some had to receive medical treatment for their swollen eyes." Hartigan, *A Rising of Courage*, 244.

662. Recollections of Harold Croft. Interviews, letters, and recollections compiled by Gary Boegal. 1st Canadian Parachute Battalion Assn Archives. The paratroopers also set their fair share of booby traps. Tragically, many combatants detonated their own devices. On July 23, "Major Nicklin was wounded by one of our own

booby traps," revealed Company Sergeant-Major John Kemp. "One of our forward patrols," he explained, "had set up the trap against enemy patrols."
Although the device was "just a mess tin stuffed with high explosives and a trip
wire," its effect was deadly. Luckily Nicklin was only wounded, but he did require
evacuation to England. Johnstone, 15. Nicklin's medical reports state that he had
suffered multiple pen size wounds to his back arms, buttocks, and legs resulting
from metal mine fragments. The largest wound was the size of a quarter. It would
require a minor surgical intervention to clean and suture it. By the time Nicklin
resumed duty, August 30, 1944, it had still not healed properly. NA, Lieutenant-
Colonel Jeff Albert Nicklin's personnel file.

663. Gale, *With the 6th Airborne Division in Normandy*, 126. Gale readily took on the
challenge; however, he requested vehicles as well as additional artillery support
to supplement his meager resources. The Belgian Brigade and the Princess Irene
of The Netherlands Brigade were attached to Gale's Division for this pursuit.
Harclerode, *"Go To It!"*, 98.

664. Harclerode, *"Go To It!"*, 98.

665. Johnstone, 16.

666. Letter from Captain Peter R. Griffin to his sister Margaret Norman, Normandy,
August 23, 1944. NA, MG 30, E538, William M. R. Griffin and Peter R. Griffin
fonds.

667. Ibid., August 28, 1944.

668. Ibid.

669. Ibid.

670. 1 Cdn Para Bn War Diary, August 18, 1944. NA, RG 24, Vol 15299, August 1944.

671. Colonel C.P. Stacey, Director, Historical Section (G.S.). The 1st Canadian
Parachute Battalion in France, 6 June-6 September 1944. DHH, Report No.26
Historical Section (G.S), Army Headquarters, August 23, 1949, 20.

672. 6 Airborne Division, Report On Operations In Normandy, 6 June–27 August
1944, Paragraph 26. NA, RG 24, Vol 10955, file 255B6.013 (D1).

673. Stacey, *Six Years of War*, 20. 1 Cdn Para Bn personnel who required medical treatment during the push to the Seine totaled one officer and fifty Other Ranks.
Casualties Treated By Divisional Medical Units, Appendix 'R'. 6 Airborne
Division, Report On Operations In Normandy, 6 June-27 August 1944. NA, RG
24 Vol 10955, file 255B6.013 (D1).

674. Major-General Richard Gale's Special Order Of The Day, in the field, August 26,
1944. PRO, WO/171/426, War Office: Allied Expeditionary Forces, North West
Europe (British Element): War Diaries, Second World War, G, Divisions, 6th
Airborne Division.

675. Letter from Captain Peter R. Griffin to his sister Margaret Norman,
Normandy, August 28, 1944. NA, MG 30, E538, William M.R. Griffin and Peter
R. Griffin fonds.

676. *Pegasus, Goes To It!*, No. 86, Tuesday, 29 August 1944. Message from Lieutenant-
General H.D.G. Crerar, commander 1st Canadian Army, through Lieutenant-
General J.T. Crocker, commander 1st British Corps. CAFM, AB 1, 1 Cdn Para Bn,
Vol 4, file 35. Major-General Gale made it a point to publish in this daily news
sheet all letters congratulating the actions and accomplishments of his paratroopers. "I always put letters in it that would be of interest to the Division as a
whole. And sometimes, if I wanted to get something over to the troops, I would
publish it in the paper. I knew they'd all read it there and take if for what it was
meant to be." Gale, *With the 6th Airborne Division In Normandy*, 119.

677. Ibid.
678. Portugal, *We Were There*, 951.
679. Captains J. P. Hanson and P. R. Griffin were awarded the Military Cross. Sergents G. H. Morgan and J. A. Lacasse, W. P. Minard, Corporal William Noval, Lance Corporal R. A. Geddes, and Private W. S. Ducker were awarded the Military Medal. Casualties and Decorations, Colonel C.P. Stacey, Historical Officer, CMHQ, Report No. 139, The 1st Canadian Parachute Battalion In France, 6 June-6 September 1944, 13.
680. Letter from Captain Peter R. Griffin to his sister Margaret Norman, Normandy, July 6, 1944. NA, MG 30, E538, William M. R. Griffin and Peter R. Griffin fonds.
681. Letter from Lieutenant-Colonel G.F.P. Bradbrooke (Ret'd) to David Owen, Ramsey, Isle of Man, March 6, 1985. David Owen Fonds. Series 1, Correspondence, G.F.P. Bradbrooke file. 1 Cdn Para Bn Assn Archives.
682. 1 Cdn Para Bn War Diary, September 1-2, 1944. A small reinforcement group of 5 officers and 85 paratroopers from the 1st Canadian Parachute Training Battalion finally had arrived on September 2. They had experienced a series of difficulties to link up with the Battalion during the pursuit phase. 1 Cdn Para Bn War Diary, September 1944. NA, RG 24, Vol 15299.
683. NA, 1st Canadian Parachute Battalion Part II Orders. No. 19, 19 July 1944. Embarkation and disembarkation list of Battalion Officers and Other Ranks who parachuted into France, 6 June 1944. No. 42, 3 December 1944. Embarkation and Disembarkation of Battalion Officers and Other Ranks who embarked in France on 6 September 1944 and landed in U.K. 7 September 1944. A total of 334 paratroopers embarked on September 6 to return to England. There were 29 officers and 305 ORs. Of the officers only four remained of the original officer slate who had jumped into Normandy. Of the ORs who returned, 112 were reinforcements and the remaining 193 were part of the original group who had jumped into Normandy. The Battalion's losses including subsequent reinforcements provided by the 1st Canadian Parachute Training Battalion for the Normandy Campaign were: officers, 6 killed, 16 wounded, and 3 captured; Other Ranks, 77 killed, 171 wounded, and 84 captured. Total losses were 25 officers and 332 Other Ranks. Ibid. The total casualties suffered by the 6th Airborne Division for the Normandy Campaign were: 76 officers and 745 Other Ranks killed; 199 officers and 2510 Other Ranks wounded; and 41officers and 886 Other Ranks missing. 6 Airborne Division, Report on Operations in Normandy, 6 June–27 August 1944. Part III, Conclusions, Appendix "T", Casualties Suffered By 6th Airborne Division. NA, RG 24, Vol 10955, file 225.B6.013 (D1), 6 AB Div Report.
684. Richard (Dick) Hilborn, interview with Bernd Horn, April 27, 2001.
685. D'Este, 517–518. An equivalent of five panzer divisions were destroyed, and another six were severely mauled. A total of twenty infantry divisions were eliminated and twelve more (including three parachute divisions) were severely weakened. By late August 1944, one infantry division was trapped in Brittany and one infantry division was isolated in the Channel Islands.
686. Ibid., 517. The losses sustained by the 21st Army Group (British/Canadian/Polish troops) were: 15,995 killed, 57,996 wounded, and 9,054 missing. American losses totaled: 20,838 killed, 94,881wounded, and 10,128 missing. Royal Air Force reported 8,178 killed and missing, while the U.S. Army Air Force numbered 8,536.
687. The Official Services of the United Kingdom Government, *Despatches submitted by Field Marshal The Viscount Montgomery of Alamein to the Secretary for War describing the part played by 21st Army Group, and the Armies under his*

Command, from D-Day to VE Day (Ottawa: The United Kingdom Information Office, 1946), 74–75.
688. 1 Cdn Para Bn War Diary, September 7, 1944. NA, RG 24, Vol 15299, September 1944.
689. R.F. "Andy" Anderson, interview with Michel Wyczynski, February 7, 2002.
690. Johnstone, 17.
691. 1 Cdn Para Bn War Diary, September 11–24, 1944. Battalion personnel boarded three trains on September 11 for Scotland, London, and the Midlands. All personnel were ordered to return by September 24, 1944. NA, RG 24, Vol 15299, September 1944.
692. Major Jeff Nicklin was promoted to the rank of Acting Lieutenant-Colonel on September 8, 1944. NA, RG 24, Part II Orders, No. 37, 8 November 1944, 2) Appointments - Promotions. The promotion was posted in the Overseas Routine Orders 5103 dated October 16, 1944.
693. Ibid., September 26, 1944.
694. Brigadier James Hill, interview with Brian Nolan, 33–34. Brian Nolan Fonds, Brigadier James Hill file. 1 Cdn Para Bn Assn Archives.
695. Ibid., 41.
696. Brigadier James Hill's speaking notes, November 1993, 22. See also Ibid.
697. Interview of Brigadier Hill by Brian Nolan, 37. Brian Nolan Fonds, Brigadier James Hill file. 1 Cdn Para Bn Assn Archives.
698. Report On Operations, 6 Airborne Division, 5 June–3 September 1944. CMHQ, 18 July 1945. NA, RG 24, CMHQ, file HQS 9008-5-9, Airborne Forces — General. Microfilm C-5321.
699. Notes by Brigadier James Hill, CO, 3 Para Bde, 16 October 1944. Airborne Training Liaison Letter, May to October 1944. DHH, file 145.4036 (D2). Reports on Units to Cdn Para Schools, Ringway, January/March 1944.
700. 3 Para Bde War Diary, September 26, 1944. NA, RG 24, Vol 10993, September 1944.
701. Minutes of Brigadier Hill's Conference, September 26, 1944. DHH, file 145.4036 (D2). Reports on visits to Cdn Para School, Ringway, January–March 1944. Upon hearing this news, Brigadier W.H.S. Macklin DCGS, CMHQ, met with Lieutenant-Colonel Bird, GSO, I, SD, War Office. Macklin reminded Bird that the current "in combination" of 1 Cdn Para Bn with 6 AB Div was only for deployment in the European theatre. If the Battalion was to be deployed to Burma, then NDHQ and CMHQ would have to examine the legal and administrative implications of such a proposed deployment. W.H.S. Macklin memorandum to file, DCGS, CMHQ, London, 13 September 1944. NA, RG 24, CMHQ, Vol 12260, file 1/Policy Para Tp/1.
702. Minutes of Brigadier Hill's Conference, September 26, 1944. Part 1-General Staff, 2) Training, b) i. DHH, file 145.4036 (D2). Reports on visits to Cdn Para School, Ringway, January–March 1944.
703. The range allotments for 1 Cdn Para Bn for the month of October were: October 11, Beaches Barn; October 12, 14, Southampton Street Fighting; October 15, 20, 22, Larkhill OP 13; October 16–17, 23, Cranbounre Chase; October 18, Bulford 'B' range; October 19–21, 24, 27, 30, Bulford 'C' (MMG) range; and October 20, Bulford (Grenade). 1st Canadian Parachute Battalion Training Syllabus, October 1944. NA, RG 24, 1st Canadian Parachute Battalion War Diary, Vol 15299, October 1944.
704. Having confirmed that the heavy machine gun skills and marksmanship were weak, Hill made arrangements to send the Battalion's Vickers machine gunners

to the 5 Battalion Northumberland Fusiliers for additional instruction. Many lessons had been learned in Normandy with regards to weapons handling. These would prove useful in enhancing the Battalion's overall firepower during the fall 1944 training. This campaign had proven an excellent testing and training ground on how to efficiently use personal and support weapons under difficult combat conditions. "I didn't feel confident in the PIAT," confided Del Parlee. "But there wasn't anything else. It was a dangerous weapon," explained the anti-tank gunner, "the round was temperamental if it was banged around." The paratroopers also carried out experiments to find ways to improve their weapons' reliability and firepower. These positive results were quickly shared with the new paratroopers back in Bulford. Initially, the Sten Gun Mark V proved unreliable. Stoppages were frequent. To correct this problem, another spring was inserted into the magazine, and 28 instead of 30 rounds were now loaded into the magazine. The new pressure exerted by the double spring system significantly reduced the number of stoppages. Richard Hilborn also noted that some of the Mark V Sten guns were very temperamental when firing long bursts. Shell casings sometimes jammed the weapon's ejection slot. "However, when you used, German nine millimetre ammunition, it would resolve this frustrating problem," revealed Hilborn. "Lucky for us," he added, "enemy ammunition was lying about in great quantities." The manner of firing was also altered. Long bursts were ineffective and a waste of valuable ammunition. Even though this was an automatic weapon, "We taught our men to fire in twos, one-two, one-two," explained Roland Larose. Additional practice was also required to increase the level of marksmanship when firing the U.S. Thompson .45 Submachine Gun. "When you'd fire this weapon," stated Larose, "it had a tendency to pull to the left and go up." In order to hit the target accurately, " you had to lean into it and force it down so as to keep it from rising," recalled the paratrooper. Bren gunners also learned a valuable lesson. After a few days in the "bocage" country, the gunners noted that they were always subjected to intense enemy fire. The Bren guns' tracer bullets revealed their concealed firing positions. The experienced German snipers had picked up on this fact quickly. Waiting patiently they pinpointed the tracers' point of origin and fired into that exact area. It did not take long for the Bren gunners to abandon this type of ordnance. Another improvement made by the paratroopers involved the splaying of the safety pin on the No.36 Grenade. In Normandy, they hooked these grenades to various parts of their webbing. This manner of carrying grenades resulted in a few safety pins slipping out, causing the grenade to fall off. Greater attention was now given to splaying the cotter pin. However, this was a tricky procedure. If the ends of the pin were folded too far back it took additional time and strength to extract the pin and throw the grenade. Interviews with Bernd Horn and Michel Wyczynski, 2001 and 2002.

705. Furthermore, the Battalion also organized NCO courses that were given at the company level. However, only one NCO training syllabus had been located. This syllabus was prepared by "HQ" Company and listed five one-hour courses that were given on November 23, 1944. The courses were: 1330–1420 hours, Orders (Operation), Major E.C. Hilborn; 1430–1520 hours, Signal Procedure, Lieutenant Tucker; 1530–1630 hours, Lecturettes by NCOs (15 minutes duration) 36, 75 Grenades, Organization of Para Bn, and First Aid; 1630–1730 hours, Demolition and charges, Captain Madden, and 1830–1930 hours, Signal Procedures, Lieutenant Tucker. NCO Syllabus - Thursday, 23 November 1944, "HQ" Company, 1 Cdn Para Bn War Diary, November 1944. NA, RG 24, Vol 15299, November 1944.

706. The quality of the leg-kit bags used by the paratroopers of all three battalions of 3 Para Bde during the D-Day jump proved unsatisfactory. When the leg kit bags were released a 20-foot cord secured to the paratrooper unraveled. The ensuing shock generated by the rope's full extension coupled with the weight of the weapons or heavy equipment caused the bottom of the bag to rip. This resulted in the loss of a very high percentage of the Battalion's mortars, heavy machine guns, radios, and heavy equipment. To correct this problem, the Ringway Parachute School staff developed a new trial reinforced kit-bag to be used for carrying 3-inch mortars and machine-guns. 3 Para Bde Conference, October 12, 1944, Airborne Training Liaison Letter, May-October 1944. NA, RG 24, CMHQ, Vol 9830, file 2/Para Tps/1/2. Samples of these new leg kit bags were available for viewing at the Bde HQ on October 20, 1944. Notes of the Bde Commander's Conference — 12 October 1944, Part II-Administrative Staff, Equipment General. PRO, WO 171/593, War Office, Allied Expeditionary Force, North West Europe, (British Element): War Diaries, Second World War, Brigades, 3 Para Brigade. Furthermore, paratroopers were ordered to pack their Bren Guns in rifle valises. Ibid., Part I-General Staff , 3) Parachute Training Notes. B) and C).

707. Notes of the Bde Commander's Conference — 12 October 1944, Part II — Administrative Staff, Equipment General. PRO, WO 171/593, War Office, Allied Expeditionary Force, North West Europe, (British Element): War Diaries, Second World War, Brigades, 3 Para Brigade.

708. Airborne Training Liaison Letter, May–October 1944, 3 Parachute Brigade — Training during October 1944. Reports on visits to Cdn Para School, Ringway, January/March 1944. DHH, file 145.4036 (D2).

709. Ibid. Other issues address by Brigadier Hill dealt with stores, leave, Regimental Accounts, escaped prisoners of war and their service status, medical inspections, units returns, Security Fund, positing of Officers and NCOs.

710. John Feduck, interview with Michel Wyczynski, August 2002.

711. Harry Reid, interview with Michel Wyczynski, January 24, 2002.

712. R.F. Anderson, interview with Michel Wyczynski, February 7, 2002.

713. Roland Larose, interview with Michel Wyczynski, January 10, 2002.

714. Each company and specialized platoon (mortar, signal, machine gun, and anti-tank) and the Intelligence Section devised their own training schedule in line with the Battalion and 3 Para Bde training directives. 1 Cdn Para Bn Weekly Training Schedules for Specialist Platoons, Section and the three rifle Companies, October 1944. NA, RG 24, 1 Cdn Para Bn War Dairy, Vol 15299, October 1944.

715. Ibid., 1 Cdn Para Bn Weekly Training Schedules for Specialist Platoons, Section and the three rifle Companies, October 1944. NA, RG 24, 1 Cdn Para Bn War Dairy, Vol 15299, October 1944. The manner in which the Battalion command-ing officer forwarded weekly observations and comments regarding the unit's strengths and weaknesses along with recommendations and training notes to his company commanders and officers had changed. Gone were the written weekly training directives. To avoid unnecessary administrative duplication, Nicklin now posted the minutes of the Brigade commander's weekly CO Conferences. These contained the CO's and Brigadier's concerns regarding training issues and recommendations that were raised and discussed at theses conferences. Now that all the battalions had combat experience, Hill notified his Battalion COs that it was quicker to deal with and correct training concerns immediately, as they arose, rather than wait a week to draft and circulate a directive.

716. Notes on Brigade Commander's lecture, October 16, 1944. Reports on visits to Cdn Para School, Ringway, January-March 1944. DHH, file 145.4036 (D2).

717. Exercise Fog, Bde Orders Group, October 2, 1944. NA, RG 24, 1st Canadian Parachute Battalion , War Diary, October 1944, Appendix 6.

718. Ibid.

719. Ibid., October 9–10, 1944.

720. Conference 3 Para Bde, October 12, 1944. Reports on visits to Cdn Para School, Ringway, January–March 1944. DHH, file 145.4036 (D2). The other lessons learned included: reevaluating the role and the operational requirements of pathfinder groups; studying the possibility of combining the LZs and DZs so that all troops landed in one location; developing a delivery method to drop the paratroopers' six-pounder artillery pieces; evaluating the use of the American. 60-mm mortar to possibly replace the British three-inch mortar during the initial DZ combat phase; defining the role and dropping of the Royal Engineers and their equipment to be used during the initial deployment and the consolidation phases; testing various types of personal and unit containers to drop into battle weapons and heavy equipment; and testing the use of trolleys to transport this equipment after the DZ deployment and subsequent pursuit phases.

721. Richard Hilborn, interview with Michel Wyczynski, December 14, 2002.

722. Alf Tucker, interview with Michel Wyczynski, December 12, 2001.

723. Richard Hilborn, interview with Bernd Horn, April 27, 2001.

724. Alcide "Sid" Carignan, interview with Michel Wyczynski, February 13, 2002. Carignan was a member of 1 Cdn Para Bn, but he did not jump into Normandy. Each stick had two designated spare parachutists who were on the airfield, on stand-by, by each aircraft. They were to replace members of the stick who became ill or may have sustained a last minute injury. Luckily for Carignan and his colleague Stu Richardson, they were not called upon to replace anyone. The aircraft that they were attached to eventually dropped Lieutenant Marcel Côté's stick at the furthest point from the drop zone. The entire stick was captured within minutes of landing on French soil. Alcide Carignan, E-mail to Michel Wyczynski, December 8, 2002.

725. Richard Creelman, interview with Michel Wyczynski, December 27, 2001.

726. Roland Larose, interview with Michel Wyczynski, January 10, 2002.

727. 1 Cdn Para Bn War Dairy, October 26–31, 1944. NA, RG 24, Vol 15299, October 1944. This course was given at the platoon level. A total of five periods consisting of lectures, demonstrations, and hands-on practices were given each day. The subject matter featured: observation of fire and street craft; individual movement; house clearing drills; and defence in built-up areas. Moreover, the officers had to attend a pistol course. This was a dangerous course because live ammunition and explosives were used during the hands-on practice phase. Each man was given five rounds, and two Sten gun magazines. Each platoon was also given fifteen No. 69 grenades and fifty thunder flashes. Royal Engineers rigged booby traps in houses that were to be cleared or prepared for defence. Ibid, Appendix 1, November 1944. The street fighting courses were one-week courses. They were given by instructors of The Cold Stream Guards at the London District School of Tactics-Street Fighting Wing. Roland Larose, interview with David Owen, 1985. David Owen Fonds. Interviews, Roland Larose, 1 Cdn Para Bn Assn Archives.

728. R.F. Anderson, interview with Michel Wyczynski, February 7, 2002.

729. Interview with David Owen, 1985. David Owen Fonds. Interview with Roland Larose, 1 Cdn Para Bn Assn Archives.

730. Ibid.

731. Roland Larose, interview with Michel Wyczynski, January 10, 2002.

732. Ernie Jeans, interview with Michel Wyczynski, January 22, 2002.

733. 1 Cdn Para Bn War Diary, October 20, 1944. NA, RG 24, Vol 15299, October. Another version of this story that has been circulating throughout the years inferred that the men were protesting the quality of the food. Most paratroopers agreed that the food wasn't the best; however, it was not the cause of this hunger strike.

734. Telephone interview with Jan de Vries, December 8, 2002. John Madden, 1st Canadian Parachute Battalion. Taped recollections, non-dated, 21. DHH, Madden, John, biography file, 21.

735. Ibid., John Madden.

736. Jan de Vries, telephone interview with Michel Wyczynski, December 8, 2002.

737. DHH, Madden, John, biography file, 21.

738. Ibid.

739. William E. Jenkins, interview with Michel Wyczynski, December 19, 2001.

740. Many of the veterans that were interviewed confirmed that they did not go hungry during this period. They were provided with rations from other units, or had built up their own personal food stashes or had light lunches or snacks at the NAFFI's.

741. Brigadier James Hill, interview with Brian Nolan, April 25, 1994, 40. Brian Nolan Fonds, Brigadier James Hill file, 1 Cdn Para Bn Assn Archives.

742. Ibid.

743. Ibid.

744. R.F. "Andy" Anderson, interview with Michel Wyczynski, February 7, 2001.

745. The demolition training was conducted at the Ink Pen Range. There, staff of the Royal Engineers gave a series of lectures and supervised live demolition practices. The paratroopers practised breaching wire obstacles using the Bangalore torpedo; handling different types of explosives, booby traps, pole charges, and mines. Courses were also given on how to lay and clear mines. "A", "B" and "C" Companies Weekly Training Syllabus, 5–11 November 1944. NA, RG 24, Vol 15299, War Diary, 1st Canadian Parachute Battalion , November 1944.

746. Interviews with mortar platoon veterans confirmed that training on the U.S. mortar did take place. However, Canadian paratroopers did not jump with these at Operation Varsity. No reason was given why. It is possible that these mortars may have not been available to the British Airborne Division via the supply system in time for this operation. Notes on Brigade Commander's Conference, 12 October 1944. Part 1— General Staff; 1)Points for consideration; d) 60mm U.S. Mortar. Reports on visits to Cdn Para School, Ringway, January –March 1944. DHH, file 145.4036 (D2). Airborne Training Liaison Letter, 3 Para Bde Conference, 12 October 1944. Item 6) 60mm U.S. Mortar. The training plan outlined that each battalion would be issued with eight of these mortars for testing purposes. If the testing was positive the Brigade would used these during upcoming operations until their own three inch mortars could be transported to their positions. NA, RG 24, CMHQ, File 2/Para Tps/1/2. The Battalion's mortar platoon trained extensively on the U.S. 60mm mortar during the first three weeks of November 1944. Mortar Platoon's training syllabus, November 1944. NA, RG 24, War Diary, 1st Canadian Parachute Battalion, Vol 15300. The weight of the British 3-inch mortar was 125 pounds. It was carried by a three-man crew. Spare parts were also transported and brought the total weigh to 147.5 pounds. Comparatively, the U.S. 60-mm mortar weighed 42 pounds in total. A 60mm anti-personnel high explosive round weighed 3.7 pounds while a three inch mor-

tar bomb weighed 10 pounds. Ferguson, 48; Reader's Digest, *The Tools Of War 1939/45* (Canada: The Reader's Digest Association Ltd., 1969), 38; War Office, *Small Arms Training, Mortar (3-inch)* (Canada: December 1944), 1,7.

747. DHH file 145.4036 (D2). Item 2) Battalion level exercise prepared by the Brigade, October 12, 1944.

748. 3 Para Bde November 1944, Training, October 25, 1944. Reports on visits to Cdn Para School, Ringway, January-March 1944. DHH, file 145.4036 (D2).

749. Howard P. Davies, *British Parachute Forces, 1940–1945* (New York: Arco Publishing Company, Inc, 1974), 30. 6 AB Div was still experimenting and testing various types of leg kit bags, and containers to enable paratroopers to jump with heavy weaponry and equipment. During this jump selected 1 Cdn Para Bn paratroopers jumped with airborne folding bicycles and the Mark I trolley. NA, RG 24, War Diary, 1st Canadian Parachute Battalion, November, Appendix 15. Form AA, Exercise Eve. The folding bicycles were provided to messengers and members of reconnaissance teams. The trolley was a lightweight collapsible device designed to carry heavy equipment, ammunition, etc. that could be hauled by a three- or five-man team.

750. Roland Larose, interview with David Owen, 1985. David Owen Fonds. Interviews, Roland Larose, 1985. 1 Cdn Para Bn Assn Archives.

751. 1 Cdn Para Bn War Diary, November 21, 1944. NA, RG 24, Vol 15299, November 1944.

752. Ibid., November 22–30, 1944.

753. R. F. "Andy" Anderson, "The 1st Canadian Parachute Battalion in the Ardennes, 23 December 1944–26 February 1945." 1 Cdn Para Bn Assn Archives, Anderson, R. F., 'Andy,' file 11-1.

754. Montgomery, Map 38, The Battle of the Ardennes, 218. Peter Elstob, "Battle Of The Bulge: The Onslaught," *History Of The Second World War*, Part 80, October 1974, 2224. The German forces that took part in this winter offensive were: the 6th *SS* Panzer Army commanded by *SS-Obergruppenfuhrer* Josef "Sepp" Dietrich; the 5th Panzer Army commanded by Field Marshal Hasso-Eccard von Manteuffel; and the Seventh Army commanded by General Erich Brandenberger. Each of the two Panzer Armies fielded four Panzer Divisions. Also taking part in this operation were various elements of the German Parachute Corps under the command of Colonel von der Heydte. A total of seventeen infantry, parachute, and Panzer Grenadier divisions would assist the Panzer Divisions in this offensive.

755. Harclerode, "*Go To It!*", 110. The objectives of the three German armies were: Sixth *SS* Panzer Army located in the northern part of the front was tasked to capture Monschau and Butgenbach. Then they were to secure the road leading northwest to Eupen and Verviers. The Fifth Panzer Army positioning in the centre of the front was tasked to capture the cities of St Vith and Bastogne. Once these two cities captured they were to move out towards the River Meuse and Namur. The Seventh Army located on the southern portion of the front was to travel through the Ardennes between Vianden and Echtenach and protect the flank north of Luxembourg and Arlon.

756. Peter Elstob, *Bastogne: The Roadblock Battle Book, No. 4* (New York: Ballantine Books Inc, 1968), 13.

757. *SS-Oberstgruppenfuhrer* Josep 'Sepp' Dietrich, First Canadian Army Interrogation Report. PRO, WO 205/1021. 21 Army Group: Military Headquarters Papers, Second World War. Interrogation Reports, German Generals, Vol II, August 1945. Interrogation was carried out by Milton Shuman.

758. Elstob, "Battle of the Bulge," 2224–2225.
759. Harclerode, *"Go To It!"*, 219.
760. Harclerode, *"Go To It!"*, 109. Bols took over command of the 6th Airborne Division on December 19, 1944.
761. Del Parlee, interview with Bernd Horn, May 8, 2001.
762. Notes on Brigade Commander's Conference, 12 October 1944, Part II-Administrative Staff. 6) Clothing. Reports on visits to Cdn Para School, Ringway, January–March 1944. DHH, file 145.4036 (D2). The commander of 6 AB Div was informed in September 1944 that his division would possibly be deployed on the continent during the winter months. Thus, it was recommended that the following items be issued to every paratrooper: one heavy wool jersey; one pair of woolen gloves, three compartment; one pair of long woolen mittens; and one pair of heavy woolen socks. This clothing proved insufficient during the Battalion's deployment to the Ardennes.
763. Minutes of Brigade Commander's Conference, 1400 hours, 21 December 1944. NA, RG 24, Vol 10993, War Diary, 3 Parachute Brigade, December 1944.
764. Ibid., 2) Patrolling. Hill also made it very clear that the reconnaissance patrols were not to become involved in the fighting. No further details were given regarding this task at the Brigade Commander's Conference.
765. Notes on Brigade Commander's Conference, 12 October 1944, Part 1-General Staff. 1) Points for consideration, C) Clothing and equipmentLater, during the December 21, 1944 Brigade Commander's Conference, Hill advised that the paratroopers bring only the clothing that they could carry. The clothing was to be placed in their large backpacks. Other articles were to be stored in their small packs. Personnel who had greatcoats were to roll these up in their blankets and tie onto their large packs. A second blanket was to be packed in a kitbag. See also Minutes of Brigade Commander's Conference, 1400 hours, 21 December 1944. NA, RG 24, Vol 10993, War Diary, 3 Parachute Brigade, December 1944.
766. Lieutenant-Colonel Fraser Eadie, interview with Bernd Horn, November 20, 2000.
767. Harry Reid, interview with Michel Wyczynski, January 24, 2002.
768. Ernie Jeans, interview with Michel Wyczynski, January 22, 2002.
769. Richard Hilborn, interview with Bernd Horn, May 5, 2001.
770. Lieutenant-Colonel Fraser Eadie, interview with Bernd Horn, November 20, 2000.
771. 3 Para Bde Group, Instruction No.1, 29 December 1944. War Diary, 3 Para Bde, December 1944. NA, RG 24, Vol 10993, December 1944. The elements of 3 Para Bde that were deployed in the Ardennes were the following: HQ 3 Para Bde; Defence platoon; "J" Section Divisional Signals; Detachment Field Section Police; Sub-Section Provost; 8 LAD; 8 Para Bn; 9 Para Bn; 1 Cdn Para Bn; 224 Para Field Ambulance; 3 Para Squadron, Royal Engineer; 3 Airlanding Anti-tank Battery, Royal Artillery.
772. 1 Cdn Para Bn War Diary, December 26, 1944. NA, RG 24, Vol 15300, December 1944. 3 Para Brigade advance party went to he town of Antoine and set up Brigade Headquarters. 3 Para Bde HQ War Diary, December 26, 1944. NA, RG 24, Vol 10993, December 1944.
773. Art Stammers, interview with Michel Wyczynski, January 16, 2002.
774. 3 Para Bde HQ War Diary, January 2, 1944. NA, RG 24, Vol 10993, December 1944.
775. 3 Para Bde Operational Order No.1, 1 January 1945. Information; Intention; Occupation of Defensive Position; Artillery. Artillery personnel allotted to 1 Cdn Para Bn was: Battery Commander 53rd Light Regiment; Two Forward Observer Officers; and 1 Forward Observer Officer, Medium Regiment. See also ibid.

776. R.F. Anderson, interview with Michel Wyczynski, February 7, 2002.
777. Alf Tucker, interview with Bernd Horn, June 23, 2001.
778. Denis Flynn, interview with Bernd Horn, April 18, 2001.
779. Minutes of Brigade Commander's Conference, 1400 hours, 21 December 1944. Other issues of concern for winter deployments were: the issuing of maps and escape kits; type of transport available; drivers' coats; signal equipment; items that were currently in short supply; and appointing a rear party to prepare the transport of additional supplies for each Battalion. NA, RG 24, Vol 10993, War Diary, 3 Parachute Brigade, December 1944.
780. Ernie Jeans, interview with Michel Wyczynski, January 22, 2002.
781. Harry Reid, interview with Michel Wyczynski, January 24, 2002.
782. John Ross, interview with Michel Wyczynski, February 14, 2002.
783. Joe King, interview with Bernd Horn, January 31, 2002.
784. R.F. "Andy" Anderson, interview with Michel Wyczynski, February 7, 2002.
785. Richard Hilborn, interview with Michel Wyczynski, December 14, 2002.
786. Roland Larose, interview with Michel Wyczynski, January 10, 2002.
787. R.F. "Andy" Anderson, interview with Michel Wyczynski, February 7, 2002.
788. Richard Creelman, interview with Michel Wyczynski, December 27, 2002. Some paratroopers from "B" Company had also borrowed white sheets from 9 Para Bn, "to blend with the snow." War Diary, "B" Company, 1 Cdn Para Bn, 21 December 1944–22 January 1945. Daily entry of January 7, 1945. 1 Cdn Para Bn Assn Archives. Kemp, John, file 22-2.
789. Joseph King, interview with Bernd Horn, January 31, 2002.
790. R.F. "Andy" Anderson, interview with Michel Wyczynski, February 7, 2002.
791. William E. Jenkins, interview with Michel Wyczynski, December 19, 2001.
792. Confirmatory Notes Bde Commander's Conference, 09:00H, January 4, 1945. Intention; Method. NA, RG 24, 3 Para Bde War Diary, Vol 10993, January 1945,
793. Art Stammers, interview with Michel Wyczynski, January 16, 2002.
794. Jan de Vries, written submission to Bernd Horn, January 9, 2001.
795. Denis Flynn, interview with Bernd Horn, April 18, 2001.
796. Del Parlee, interview with Bernd Horn, May 8, 2001.
797. Lieutenant Jack Scott, "Canadian Parachutists Came to Battlefield By Boat. Hun's Don't Want To Play With Canuck Airtroops." Unidentified newspaper clipping, Tom Jackson scrapbook. CAFM, AB 1, 1st Canadian Parachute Battalion.
798. Harry Wright, interview with Michel Wyczynski, November 6, 2002.
799. Charles Whiting, Skorzeny (New York: Ballantine Books Inc., 1972), 98.
800. Throughout the war Skorzeny had planned and participated in a series of special operations. Amongst his most notable accomplishments was the daring rescue of Italian dictator Benito Mussolini on September 13, 1943. During the fall of 1944, Skorzeny recruited and trained eighty candidates who spoke English ranging from excellent to just a few words. These volunteers were mostly sailors who had previously served on American ships. The men were placed under the command of Captain Stielau and began their training session. This small unit was now referred to as Panzerbrigade 150. They were outfitted with captured American uniforms, vehicles, and weapons. The men were divided into two groups: a sabotage group consisting of eight jeeps, and a reconnaissance group equipped with six jeeps. The reconnaissance group was organized into four long-range and two short-range reconnaissance teams. Each vehicle transported three to four men. They included a driver, a radio operator, an interpreter, and a saboteur. All were issued with a phial of prussic acid or cyanide to be used in case they were cap-

tured. During the first few days the teams enjoyed remarkable success. The leader of one team had succeeded in directing an entire three-thousand-man American regiment down the wrong road, while his men were destroying signposts and cutting telephone wire. Another team, feigning terror, succeeded in stopping an armoured column and making them turn back. Another group cut the main cable linking General Bradley's headquarters in Luxembourg with that of Lieutenant-General Hick Hodges, commander of the U.S. 1st Army in Spa. While the tactical accomplishments were limited, the state of paranoia and confusion caused in the Allied camp was beyond the Germans' wildest expectations. A total of five teams returned safely to the German lines. The others were killed. Those who were captured in American uniforms were tried as spies and executed by firing squad. Ibid., 92–111.

801. Alcide Carignan, interview with Michel Wyczynski, February 13, 2002. Hitler's original directives to Skorzeny stated that he was to carry out his attacks with teams dressed in British and American uniforms. Whiting, 82. Having captured German soldiers wearing U.S. Amy uniforms, the Allies suspected that it was very likely that other teams could be disguised as British Army personnel. However, Skorzeny never deployed such teams.

802. Alf Tucker, interview with Bernd Horn, June 23, 2001.

803. Whiting, *Skorzeny*, 101. R.F. "Andy" Anderson, interview with Michel Wyczynski, February 7, 2002.

804. Lieutenant-Colonel Fraser Eadie, interview with Bernd Horn, November 20, 2002.

805. Charles B. MacDonald, "Battle Of The Bulge: The Allied Counterblow," *History Of The Second World War,* Part 81, October 1974, 2243. On January 8, 1945, Hitler authorized the withdrawal of troops from the village of Houffalize about ten miles from Bastogne. This signal the beginning of the German retreat from the Ardennes.

806. M.H. Halton, "Dare-devil airborne fighters are known as 'hell-damners'. Tough Canadian Parachutists Do 18-Hour Patrols In Ardennes," Unidentified newspaper clipping, Appendix No. 13, War Diary 1st Canadian Parachute Battalion, January 1945. NA, RG 24, Vol 15299.

807. Ibid.

808. Recollections of R.F. "Andy" Anderson. Interviews, letters, and recollections compiled by Gary Boegal. 1 Cdn Para Bn Assn Archives.

809. Lieutenant Jack Scott, "Canadian Parachutists Came to Battlefield By Boat. Hun's Don't Want To Play With Canuck Airtroops," Unidentified newspaper clipping, Tom Jackson scrapbook. AB 1, 1st Canadian Parachute Battalion, CAFM.

810. 3 Para Bde War Diary, January 9, 1945. NA, RG 24, Vol 10993, January 1945.

811. Confirmatory Notes, Bde Commander's Conference 2300 hours, 8 January 1945. Part 1), Move New Area, 1 Cdn Para Bn. NA, RG 24, Vol 10993, 3 Para Bde War Diary, January 1945.

812. Jan de Vries, interview with Bernd Horn, January 18, 2001.

813. Ernie Jeans, interview with Michel Wyczynski, January 22, 2002.

814. Johnstone, 20. On December 17, 1945, German troops under the command of SS *Obersturmbannführer* Joachim Peiper captured a convoy of American troops belonging to Battery "B" of the 285th Field Artillery Observation Battalion. More than one hundred prisoners were led into an adjacent field and machine-gunned. Approximately thirty soldiers survived. After the war Peiper and seventy-three of his men were tried by a U.S. Army court in 1946 for the Malmédy murders. Peiper and forty-three others were found guilty. All were sentenced to

death; however, none of these sentences were carried out. James J. Weingartner, "Unconventional Allies: Colonel Willis Everett and *SS-Obersturmbannführer* Joachim Peiper," *The Historian*, Fall 1999, 1.

815. 1 Cdn Para Bn War Diary, January 12, 1945. NA, RG 24, Vol 15299, January 1945.
816. "War Diary, 'B' Company, 1 Cdn Para Bn, 21 December 1944–22 January 1945." 1 Cdn Para Bn Assn Archives. Kemp, John, file 22-2.
817. Roland Larose, interview with Michel Wyczynski, January 10, 2002.
818. MacDonald, "Battle of the Bulge," 2243.
819. Richard Hilborn, interview with Michel Wyczynski, December 12, 2002.
820. 1 Cdn Para Bn War Diary, January 14, 1945. NA, RG 24, Vol 15299, January.
821. Richard Hilborn interview with Michel Wyczynski, December 14, 2002.
822. Michael Ball, interview with Michel Wyczynski, June 12, 2002. Some of the Panther's characteristics: crew 5; total weight 44.8 tons; overall measurements, 8.86m x 3.43m x 3.0m; armour, front 80-mm; sides and rear 40mm; armament 1gun 7.5cm 42L/70 and 3 machine guns (7.92mm) including an anti-aircraft machine gun; ammunition 82 rounds 7.5cm and 4,200 machine gun rounds; maximum speed 46km/h and range on road 177km. Will Fey, *Armor Battles of the Waffen-SS, 1943–1945* (Winnipeg: J.J. Fedorowicz Publishing, 1990), 355.
823. 1 Cdn Para Bn War Diary, January 15–16, 1945. NA, RG 24, Vol 15299, January 1945.
824. Bruce Quarrie, *The Ardennes Offensive, V Panzer Armee, Central Sector*, Order of Battle 8 (Oxford: Osprey Publishing Ltd, 2000), 14. The 47th Panzer Corps comprised the following units: 2nd Panzer Division; (130) Panzer Lehr Divisions; 26th *Volksgrenadier* Division; 9th Panzer Division; 15th *Panzergrenadier* Division; 182nd Flak-Strum Regiment; and the 10th SS Panzer Artilleries Regiment (attached).
825. John Feduck, interview with Michel Wyczynski, December 19, 2001.
826. Alf Tucker, interview with Michel Wyczynski, December 12, 2001.
827. William E. Jenkins, interview with Michel Wyczynski, December 19, 2001.
828. 1 Cdn Para Bn War Diary, January 19–20, 1945. NA, RG 24, Vol 15300, January 1945.
829. HQ, No.1 Forestry Group, December 1944, and Appendix 12. NA, RG 24, Vol 16413. There were several companies of the No.1 Canadian Forestry Group working in the Ardennes when the Germans launched their initial attack. However, this unit was not considered as combat unit. No.1 ,9, 14, 25 and 27 Companies were operation sawmills south-east of Namur, in the St-Hubert area. Another company, No.16 had been working in Spa, southeast of Liège.
830. Quarrie, 13.
831. MacDonald, "Battle of the Bulge," 2248. Montgomery estimated the enemy's losses to be 120,000 men, and 600 tanks and assault vehicles.
832. Letter from E. L. Burdon to Hugo Levels, Demorestville, August 19, 1992. 1 Cdn Para Bn Assn Archives. Burdon, E.L., 19-1.
833. "War Diary, B Company, 1 Cdn Para Bn", 21 December 1944–22 January 1945. Daily entry of January 9, 1945. 1 Cdn Para Bn Assn Archives. Kemp, John, file 22-2.
834. Montgomery, *Normandy to the Baltic*, 231–233.
835. 3 Para Bde Operational Order No. 10, 24 January 1945. Intention; Method. NA, RG 24, Vol 10993, 3 Para Bde War Diary, January 1945. 1 Cdn Para Bn War Diary, January 22–23, 1945. NA, RG 24, Vol 15299, January 1945.
836. Ibid., Patrols, Standing, Reconnaissance and Fighting. Ibid.
837. Ibid., 27. January 1945.

838. Johnstone, 20.
839. R. F. "Andy" Anderson, "The 1st Canadian Parachute Battalion In The Ardennes, 23 December 1944–26 February 1945." 1 Cdn Para Bn Assn Archives. Anderson, R. F. 'Andy', file 11-1, 8.
840. Lieutenant J. L. Davies, patrol report, January 30, 1945. NA, RG 24, War Diary, Vol 15299, Appendix No 8, Patrol Reports, January 1945. The construction of the Siegfried Line started in August 1934 on the Western German border. This fortification system was divided into two main parts: the Sharnhorst Line and the Schill Line. This first was built along the Hurtgen forest. It consisted of numerous anti-tank obstacles and the famous dragons' teeth. These were three staggered rows of concrete pyramids about three feet high. The Schill Line was located five miles behind the Sharnhorst Line. It also had a complex defensive system containing hundreds of pillboxes, log bunkers, trenches, minefields and wire obstacles. www.63rd infdiv.com/siegfriedline. Views of Germany's West Wall (The Siegfried Line).
841. Roland Larose, interview with David Owen, 1985. David Owen Fonds. Interviews, Roland Larose, 1 Cdn Para Bn Assn Archives.
842. Letter from E.L. Burdon to Hugo Levels, Demorestville, August 19, 1992. 1 Cdn Para Bn Assn Archives. Burdon, E.L., file 19-1.
843. William E. Jenkins, interview with Michel Wyczynski, December 19, 2001.
844. "Be Alert," pamphlet, February 4. NA, RG 24, Vol 15300, 4 February 1945. Appendix 5.
845. Instructions reference Forward Patrol Areas, 1, 2, 3 and 4. Lieutenant-Colonel J. A. Nicklin. 2 February 1945. Appendix 10, Ibid.
846. Incident With Enemy Recce Patrol on Night of 11–12 February 1945. Captain S.W. McGowan, "B" Company, 12 February 1945. NA, RG 24, Vol, 15300, War Diary, 1 Cdn Para Bn, Appendix 8, Patrol Reports, February 1945.
847. For security reasons, while in Holland, all 1 Cdn Para Bn observation posts and patrols were given code names.
848. 1 Cdn Para Bn War Diary, February 13, 1945. NA, RG 24, Vol 15300, February 1945.
849. Ibid. Other 1 Cdn Para Bn reconnaissance patrols conducted during this deployment were: Lieutenant E. J. Esling, February 7; Lieutenant D. J. Proulx, February 10; and Lieutenant C. B. Browne, February 14, 1945.
850. 3 Para Bde War Diary, February 16, 1945. NA, RG 24, Vol 10993, February 1945.
851. Joseph King, interview with Bernd Horn, January 31, 2002.
852. Doug Morrison, interview with Bernd Horn, February 2, 2002.
853. 1 Cdn Para Bn War Diary, February 20–22, 1945. NA, RG 24, Vol 15300, February 1945.
854. R. F. "Andy" Anderson, "The 1st Canadian Parachute Battalion in the Ardennes, 23 December 1944–26 February 1945." 1 Cdn Para Bn Assn Archives. Anderson, R. F. 'Andy', file 11-1.
855. Denis Flynn, interview with Bernd Horn, April 18, 2001.
856. 1 Cdn Para Bn, War Diary, January –February 1945. NA, RG 24, Vol 15300, January–February 1945. In the Ardennes, two paratroopers were killed and six were injured. In Holland, one paratrooper was killed and three were injured. During the research phase, it was noted that casualty figures for the battalions varied slightly depending on the source consulted. The figures of "B" Company for the Ardennes and the Holland campaigns were the following: two Other Ranks killed; one died of wounds; and ten wounded. Furthermore, a total of twelve paratroopers from "B" Company were evacuated due to: bad colds, throat

infections, influenza, flue, a poisoned knee, and an infected hand. All returned to duty following an absence ranging between eight and ten days. "War Diary, 'B' Company, 1 Cdn Para Bn, 21 December 1944 - 22 January 1945." Daily entry of January 7, 1945. 1 Cdn Para Bn Assn Archives. Kemp, John, file 22-2. No comparable information was uncovered regarding the health status of the paratroopers of the other three companies.

857. 1 Cdn Para Bn War Diary, March 17, 1945, Appx F, "Operation Varsity - Plunder, 1 Cdn Para Bn Operations Order No. 1." NA, RG 24, Vol 15299, March 1945.

858. Brigadier-General Denis Whitaker and Shelagh Whitaker, *Rhineland* (New York: Stoddart, 2000), 278–282. The Americans, on March 7, 1945, had by bold action and good fortune already secured a foothold on the west bank of the Rhine River by capturing the Ludendorff Bridge at Remagen. Within twenty-four hours a complete infantry division and a pontoon bridge had been established in the pocket Unfortunately, Remagen was in near impossible terrain to facilitate the massive armoured breakout that was required for the Allied assault into the industrial heartland of the Ruhr.

859. Headquarters First Allied Air Army (FAAA), "Narrative of Operation Varsity," 31 March 1945, 1. CAFM, AB 1, 1 Cdn Para Bn, Vol 5, file 12; 6th Airborne Division, "Report on Operation Varsity and the Advance from the Rhine to the Baltic, March 24 to May 2, 1945, 1. CAFM, 1 Cdn Para Bn, Vol 5, file 9; and Canadian Army Headquarters, Historical Section (G.S.), Report No. 17, "The First Canadian Parachute Battalion in the Low Countries and in Germany. Final Operations (2 January –18 February and 24 March –5 May 1945)," 12, DHH.

860. HQ British Army of the Rhine, "Operation Varsity. XVIII United States Corps (Airborne) in the Crossing of the River Rhine, 24 and 25 March 1945," November 1947, 7. CAFM; and Historical Section (G.S.), Report No. 17, 12.

861. Field Marshal the Viscount Montgomery of Alamein, *Despatch Submitted to the Secretary of State for War Describing the Part Played by the 21st Army Group, and the Armies Under Command, From D Day to VE Day* (London: U.K. Information Services, 1946), 62; and Montgomery, *21 Army Group*, 247–248.

862. Gavin, *Airborne Warfare*, 132; HQ British Army of the Rhine, "Operation Varsity. XVIII United States Corps (Airborne) in the Crossing of the River Rhine, 24 and 25 March 1945," November 1947, 23, CAFM; Historical Section (G.S.), Report No. 17, 13; Lieutenant-General Lewis H. Brereton, *The Brereton Diaries. The War in the Air in the Pacific, Middle East and Europe, 3 October 1941- 8 May 1945* (New York: William Morrow and Company, 1946), 405.

863. "HQ First Allied Airborne Army Outline Plan for Operation Varsity (Revised)," February 10, 1945. PRO, WO 205/204, War Office: 21 Army Group: Military HQ Papers, Second World War, 1942-47. Operation Varsity: Revised outline, plan and appreciation - March 1945; 1 Cdn Para Bn War Diary, 17 March 1945, Appx F, "Operation Varsity – Plunder, 1 Cdn Para Bn Operations Order No. 1." NA, RG 24, Vol 15299, March 1945; HQ British Army of the Rhine, "Operation Varsity. XVIII United States Corps (Airborne) in the Crossing of the River Rhine, 24 and 25 March 1945," November 1947, 23. CAFM; and Gale, *Call to Arms*, 152. 12th British Corps was tasked with assaulting across the Rhine on a two brigade front. 15th Scottish Division was responsible for capturing the bridges over the Issel River west of Dingden and relieving the 6th Airborne Division in the area of Hamminkeln. 1st Commando Brigade was tasked with the capture of Wesel.

864. "Operation Varsity – Plunder, 1 Cdn Para Bn Operations Order No. 1, 2-4; "Operation Varsity – Plunder, 3 Para Bde Operations Order, No. 20," 15 March

1945, 5. PRO, WO 171/4306, War Office: Allied Expeditionary Force, North West Europe (British elements): War Diaries, Second World War, 1943-46. HQ, January–August 1945; Whitaker, 320; and Willes, 125.

865. "Agenda for Airborne Conference on 9 February 1945 – Role of Airborne Troops," February 8, 1945, and "Minutes of Conference Held at Main HQ 21 Army Group, on 9 February 1945 to Consider Operation Varsity," February 10, 1945. PRO, WO 205/200, Operation Varsity — Part I. The staff also concluded, "The German Air Force will have a better opportunity to interfere with 'Varsity' if the operation is mounted at night." "Operation Varsity Revised Appendix 'C' — Appreciation of GAF, Part 1 — German Air Defences," HQ First Allied Airborne Army, 2 March 1945. PRO, WO 205/204. This is significant as it was estimated that the Luftwaffe could muster up to 570 fighters to oppose the airborne force. "Op Order No. 531 For Operation Varsity," HQ No. 38 Group RAF, March 16, 1945. PRO, WO 205/200.

866. Montgomery, *Normandy to the Baltic*, 254. In Normandy, for instance, approximately 75 percent of the paratroopers were missing for a considerable period of time. See Chapter 7 for a detailed account of 1 Cdn Para Bn (3 Para Bde) and their experience, where in most cases objectives were taken with a mere one third of the originally planned strength. In addition, during Operation Market Garden in September 1944, part of the failure to quickly capture the bridge at Arnhem was the fact that drops were made too far from the actual objective. This criticism was substantiated by the German defenders who were given time to mobilize their defence and respond to the threat. Much of the blame has been levelled at Major-General Roy Urquhart who was appointed Division Commander with no prior airborne experience. He made the fateful decision to go with DZ locations between five to eight miles from the objective, distances contrary to airborne doctrine. He preferred good DZs at a distance compared to bad DZs close to the objective. He later admitted this was an unnecessary and fatal error. It cost the division the advantage of surprise and forced it to divide its forces to maintain DZ security for follow on operations. Dr. John Warren, *Airborne Operations in WWII, European Theatre* (Kansas: USAF Historical Division, Air University, 1956), 149.

867. Stanley Maxted, "I Crossed the Rhine with the Glider Troops," *MacLean's Magazine*, May 15, 1945, 54.

868. "6th Airborne Division Report on Operation Varsity — The Advance from the Rhine to the Baltic, 24 March to 2 May 1945," 1. PRO, WO 205/947, War Office: 21 Army Group: Military HQ Papers, Second World War, 1942-47. Operation Varsity: 6th Airborne Division, March–May 1945.

869. FAAA, "Narrative of Operation Varsity," 1.

870. "Bomber Command Intelligence Digest, No. 30 — Operation Varsity," April 4, 1945. DHH, file 181.003 (D721); and Montgomery, *Normandy to the Baltic*, 255.

871. "Bomber Command Intelligence Digest, No. 30 — Operation Varsity," April 4, 1945. DHH, file 181.003 (D721). The numbers (loads) given for the initial drop are: troops — 14, 865; ammunition and explosives — 109 tons; vehicles - 695; artillery pieces — 113; and equipment and supplies — 765 pieces. During the three days prior to the landings 2090 effective sorties dropped over 5375 tons of bombs.

872. Ibid.

873. Sergeant R.F. "Andy" Anderson — Interviews, letters, and recollections compiled by Gary Boegal for the 1 Cdn Para Bn Assn, Boegal, Gary, file 44-1.

874. R.F. "Andy" Anderson, "From the Rhine to the Baltic," 1 Cdn Para Bn Assn Archives, Anderson, R.F., file 11-2.

875. FAAA HQ, "Narrative of Operation Varsity," 4–5.

876. Charles B. MacDonald, *The United States Army in World War II. The European Theater of Operations. The Last Offensive* (Washington, D.C.: Center of Military History United States Army, 1990), 309. Numbers on aircraft vary slightly. Whitaker, gives the numbers as 1,795 troop transports, 1,050 tug aircraft, and 1,305 gliders. See *Rhineland*, 325. General Gale gives the numbers at over 1500 troop carrying aircraft and 1100 gliders. See Gale, *Call to Arms*, 153. "Bomber Command Intelligence Digest, No. 30 — Operation Varsity," April 4, 1945. DHH, file 181.003 (D721) gives the numbers as 1589 aircraft and 1337 gliders with initial loads dropped as: troops — 14,865; ammunition and explosives — 109 tons; vehicles — 695; artillery pieces — 113; and equipment and supplies — 765 pieces. A resupply drop by 240 Liberator bombers after the troops had landed inserted an additional 582 tons of supplies and equipment into the battle zone.

877. MacDonald, *The Last Offensive*, 309.

878. Whitaker, *Rhineland*, 316.

879. 224 Parachute Field Ambulance, *Over the Rhine. A Parachute Field Ambulance in Germany* (London: Canopy Press, 1946), 8. 1 Cdn Para Bn Assn Archives, David Owen Fond, Series 2, Memoirs, Diaries and Scrapbooks.

880. Portugal, *We Were There*, 966.

881. Dan Hartigan, interview with Bernd Horn, October 30, 2000.

882. Joseph King, interview with Bernd Horn, January 31, 2002.

883. Douglas Amaron, "Paratroops Tell Story," *The Canadian Press News, London, England*, March 31, 1945.

884. "Mightiest Airborne Army Safely Landed By 6,000 Aircraft," March 26, 1945, newspaper clipping, CAFM.

885. Sergeant R.F. "Andy" Anderson — Interviews, letters, and recollections compiled by Gary Boegal for the 1 Cdn Para Bn Assn Archives, Boegal, Gary, file 44-1.

886. Jan de Vries, interview with Bernd Horn, January 18, 2001. Dan Hartigan wrote, "The pilots of U.S. 9th Troop Carrier Command fly straight and level. Probably, one of the clearest examples of mass, self-sacrificing airmanship in World War II." Dan Hartigan, "1st Canadian Parachute Battalion Assault on the Rhine. The Ride, The Drop, and the Objectives," 1 Cdn Para Bn Assn Pamphlet, 1988, 10. 1 Cdn Para Bn Assn Archives, Toseland, N., file 7-7.

887. Private M. Zakaluk's "Recollections of Rhine Drop — March 1945," 1 Cdn Para Bn Assn Archives, Gavinski, T.E., file 8-7.

888. William E. Jenkins, interview with Michel Wyczynski, December 19, 2001.

889. Lieutenant-Colonel Fraser Eadie, interview with Bernd Horn, November 20, 2000. The Carrier Command policy was that "<u>NO</u> evasive action will be taken between the IP and DZ - LZ area" and "<u>NO</u> paratrooper or gliders will be returned to friendly territory." Direction was given that "In the event that aircrews fail to locate designated DZ or LZ on first pass, paratroops and gliders will be released as near to the assault area as possible." Field Order No. 5, IX Troop Carrier Command, 16 March 1945, PRO, WO 205/203, War Office: 21st Army Group: Military HQ Papers, Second World War, Operation Varsity: Field Order No. 5, Briefing map information.

890. Lieutenant-Colonel Fraser Eadie, interview with Bernd Horn, November 20, 2000. The issue of drop altitude is an interesting one. Interviews and written accounts by veterans range from a low of 200 to 300 feet to a high of 1,000-plus feet. However, the most consistent and reliable accounts place the drop, for 3 Para Bde at any rate, at around 600 feet. There is also some disagreement on speed.

The 1 Cdn Para Bn War Diary states that the aircraft failed to slow down and lift their tails, resulting in wide dispersion. Yet most other accounts, including most veterans, state otherwise. The fact that the Brigade assembled so quickly and achieved their objectives so early would support a concentrated drop.

891. Dick Hilborn, interview with Bernd Horn, May 5, 2001. "You have so much to think about," noted Hilborn, " that I wasn't airsick." He also said, "I had faith in the pilot — you had to have faith in someone." Dick Hilborn, interview with Bernd Horn, April 27, 2001.

892. Private M. Zakaluk — Interviews, letters, and recollections compiled by Gary Boegal for the 1 Cdn Para Bn Assn, Boegal, Gary, file 44-1.

893. Jan de Vries, interview with Bernd Horn, January 18, 2001.

894. Max Arthur, *Men of the Red Beret* (London: Century Hutchinson Ltd., 1990), 291.

895. Lieutenant-Colonel Fraser Eadie, interview with Bernd Horn, November 20, 2000.

896. Sergeant R.F. "Andy" Anderson — Interviews, letters, and recollections compiled by Gary Boegal for the 1 Cdn Para Bn Assn, Boegal, Gary, file 44-1.

897. Douglas Amaron, "Paratroops Tell Story," *The Canadian Press News, London, England*, March 31, 1945.

898. Nolan, *Airborne*, 141.

899. Johnstone, 24.

900. "2 AB Div Intelligence Summary, No. 35, Estimate of the Enemy Situation on 17 March 1945," 1 Cdn Para Bn War Diary, 17 March 1945, Appx F, "Operation Varsity — Plunder, 1 Cdn Para Bn Operations Order No. 1." NA, RG 24, Vol 15299, March 1945.

901. Whitaker, *Rhineland*, 310. Hoehne conceded that material losses and lack of equipment hampered his Army Group. "At one time," he stated, "Army Group H had 50,000 men for whom there were no weapons." See also ibid.

902. R.D. Creelman, interview with Michel Wyczynski, December 27, 2001.

903. Lieutenant-Colonel Fraser Eadie, interview with Bernd Horn, November 20, 2000. Also quoted (but not attributed) in Whitaker, *Rhineland*, 333.

904. Johnstone, 24.

905. 1 Cdn Para Bn War Diary, March 24, 1945. NA, RG 24, Vol 15298.

906. Whitaker, *Rhineland*, 332.

907. Dan Hartigan, "1st Canadian Parachute Battalion Assault on the Rhine. The Ride, The Drop, and the Objectives," 1 Cdn Para Bn Assn Pamphlet, 1988, 1 Cdn Para Bn Assn Archives, Toseland, N., file 7-7.

908. Military Medal Commendation, G7194 Pte James Oliver QUIGLEY, Canadian Parachute Bn. 1 Cdn Para Bn Assn Archives, Green, Dwight, file 15-1.

909. Douglas Amaron, "Paratroops Tell Story," *The Canadian Press News, London, England*, March 31, 1945.

910. Distinguished Conduct Medal Commendation, B62282 Sergeant (Acting Warrant Officer Class II, Company Sergeant-Major) George William Green, Canadian Infantry Corps. 1 Cdn Para Bn Assn Archives, Green, Dwight, file 15-1.

911. 1 Cdn Para Bn War Diary, March 24, 1945, Appendix J. NA, RG 24, Vol 15298.

912. Portugal, *We Were There*, 968.

913. Johnstone, 25.

914. R.F. "Andy" Anderson, "From the Rhine to the Baltic: The Final Operation of The 1st Canadian Parachute Battalion, March 24th to May 8th, 1945, 2. Unpublished Diary. 1 Cdn Para Bn Assn Archives, Anderson, R.F., file 11-2.

915. Whitaker, *Rhineland*, 328.

916. Battle accounts, "Vickers Platoon D and D Plus One," "PIAT Platoon," and "Mortar Platoon," 1 Cdn Para Bn War Diary, 24 March 1945. NA, RG 24, file 15300, March 1945. Both the Vickers Platoon Commander and the Mortar Platoon Commander attribute the SP gun kill to mortars while the PIAT Platoon Commander claims the kill was done by his platoon.

917. MacDonald, *The Last Offensive,* 313.

918. "Operation Varsity — Losses in Vehicles and Guns," 6th Airborne Division, "Report on Operation Varsity and the Advance from the Rhine to the Baltic, March 24 to May 2 1945, Appendix F. CAFM, AB 1, 1 Cdn Para Bn Assn Archives, Vol 5, file 9.

919. HQ British Army of the Rhine, "Operation Varsity. XVIII United States Corps (Airborne) in the Crossing of the River Rhine, 24 and 25 March 1945," November 1947, 101. Total casualties for the airborne component of Operation Varsity was approximately 2,500 personnel. 1 Cdn Para Bn Assn Archives, Jenkins, William, file 38-1. Nolan, *Airborne,* 167.

920. Report No. 17, Historical Section (G.S.) Army Headquarters, October 27, 1947. DHH.

921. Letter, Jan de Vries to Bernd Horn, January 6, 2003.

922. Anderson, "From the Rhine to the Baltic," 3.

923. Alf Tucker, interview with Bernd Horn, June 23, 2001. Tucker, the Signals Officer, was normally the number one jumper.

924. Jack Karr, "I'll Go Into Hiding Until this Blows Over — New V.C." Newspaper Clipping, August 3, 1945, unknown publication, 1 Cdn Para Bn Assn Archives, Firlotte, Robert, file 11-2.

925. Ibid.

926. Canadian Army Headquarters, Historical Section (G.S.), Report No. 17, "The First Canadian Parachute Battalion in the Low Countries and in Germany. Final Operations (2 January –18 February and 24 March –5 May 1945)," 35, DHH; "Corporal Wins V.C." *The Maple Leaf,* August 3, 1945, Vol 1 No. 62; and Harclerode, *"Go To It!",* 125.

927. Hartigan, "1st Canadian Parachute Battalion Assault on the Rhine," 13.

928. 224 Parachute Field Ambulance, 20.

929. Captain J.E. Thomas, "Crossing the Rhine — March 1945," *The Army Quarterly,* Vol 1, No. 2, July 1945, 226.

930. "Interrogation Report on Maj Gen Fiebig, Commanding 84 Infantry Division captured near WISMAR 2 May 1945," 6th Airborne Division, "Report on Operation Varsity and the Advance from the Rhine to the Baltic, March 24 to May 2 1945, Appendix D. CAFM, AB 1, 1 Cdn Para Bn Assn Archives, Vol 5, file 9.

931. Otway, 154. "D" day often used in populist literature to describe the Normandy invasion in a definitive manner, is actually the military designation for the day a specific operation is to commence. For example, June 6 is D-Day for Operation Jubilee, and March 24 is D-Day for Operation Varsity.

932. Norton, 124.

933. Private E.H. Jackson — Interviews, letters, and recollections compiled by Gary Boegal for the 1 Cdn Para Bn Assn Archives, Boegal, Gary, file 45-1.

934. Chester Wilmot, *The Struggle for Europe* (London: Fontana Books, 1974), 783–789.

935. Ibid., 788–789. See also Omar Bradley, *A Soldier's Story* (New York: Eagle Books, 1951), 523; and Leo Kessler, *Kommando* (London: Leo Cooper, 1995), 151–161.

936. Address given by Brigadier S.J.L. Hill, June 1, 1997, at Bulford Garrison Church, on occasion of the unveiling of a plaque to the memory of the 1st Canadian Parachute Battalion. *Maroon Beret,* Vol 2, No. 2, August 1997, 56–57.

937. Alf Tucker, interview with Bernd Horn, June 23, 2001. He also recalled commenting to the Brigade signalers, "I hope that those pantywaists in London know what they're talking about" in regard to his concern with stopping the Russian armies.

938. Jan de Vries, interview with Bernd Horn, January 18, 2001.

939. Ibid.

940. William Jenkins, interview with Michel Wyczynski, December 19, 2001.

941. Jan de Vries, interview with Bernd Horn, January 18, 2001.

942. Private E.H. Jackson — Interviews, letters, and recollections compiled by Gary Boegal for the 1 Cdn Para Bn Assn, Boegal, Gary, file 45-1.

943. "6th Airborne Division Report on Operation Varsity — The Advance from the Rhine to the Baltic, 24 March to 2 May 1945," 23. PRO, WO 205/947, War Office: 21 Army Group: Military HQ Papers, Second World War, 1942–45. Operation Varsity: 6th Airborne Division, March–May 1945.

944. 3rd Parachute Brigade War Diary, March 28, 1945. NA, RG 24, Vol 10993, file 24 Mar to 30 Mar 45.

945. "6th Airborne Division Report on Operation Varsity — The Advance from the Rhine to the Baltic, 24 March to 2 May 1945," 24. PRO, WO 205/947.

946. Ibid. See also 3rd Parachute Brigade War Diary, March 29, 1945. NA, RG 24, Vol 10993, file 24 Mar to 30 Mar 45.

947. Dick Hilborn, interview with Bernd Horn, May 5, 2001.

948. Patrick Forbes, *6th Guards Tank Brigade* (Sampson Low, Marston & Co., Ltd), 144–146. See also "Extracts," DHH, file 145.404011 (D2).

949. Ibid.

950. 1 Cdn Para Bn War Diary, March 30, 1945. NA, RG 24, Vol 15300. March 1945.

951. Trent Frayne, "Monty Lauded 'Chutists,' Lt.-Col Eadie Reveals," June 20, 1945. Newspaper clipping, unknown publication, 1 Cdn Para Bn Assn Archives.

952. 3rd Parachute Brigade War Diary, 1 April 1945. NA, RG 24, Vol 10993, file 1 April 45 to 1 May 45; and 1 Cdn Para Bn War Diary, 1 April 1945. NA, RG 24, Vol 15300. April 1945.

953. "Canadian Paratroopers Go 145 Miles in 10 Days," April 12, 1945, newspaper clipping, unknown publication, 1 Cdn Para Bn Assn Archives, Firlotte, Robert, file 2-11.

954. Report No. 17, Historical Section (G.S.) Army Headquarters, 27 October 1947, 27. DHH.

955. Lieutenant-Colonel Fraser Eadie, interview with Bernd Horn, November 20, 2000.

956. 1 Cdn Para Bn War Diary, April 1, 1945. NA, RG 24, Vol 15300, April 1945.

957. Lieutenant-Colonel Fraser Eadie, interview with Bernd Horn, November 20, 2000.

958. Del Parlee, interview with Bernd Horn, May 8, 2001.

959. Alf Tucker, interview with Bernd Horn, June 23, 2001.

960. Lieutenant-Colonel Fraser Eadie, interview with Bernd Horn, November 20, 2000.

961. "Military Government — Relations with Civilians," Appendix C to March 1945, War Diary. 1 Cdn Para Bn War Diary. NA, RG 24, Vol 15300. March 1945.

962. Ibid.

963. Alf Tucker, interview with Bernd Horn, June 23, 2001.

964. R.F. "Andy" Anderson, "From the Rhine to the Baltic. The Final Operation of The 1st Canadian Parachute Battalion, March 24th to May 8th, 1945, 2. Unpublished Diary. 1 Cdn Para Bn Assn Archives, Anderson, R.F., file 11-2.

965. Nolan, *Airborne*, 161.

966. Ibid., 174.

967. 3rd Parachute Brigade War Diary, April 3, 1945. NA, RG 24, Vol 10993, file 1 April 45 to 1 May 45.

968. "Canadian Paratroopers Go 145 Miles in 10 Days," April 12, 1945, newspaper clipping, unknown publication, 1 Cdn Para Bn Assn Archives, Firlotte, Robert, file 2-11.

969. "Service of 1 Cdn Parachute Battalion in United Kingdom and North West Europe," 2. DHH, file 112.3HI.009 D4.

970. 3rd Parachute Brigade War Diary, April 4, 1945. NA, RG 24, Vol 10993, file 1 April to 1 May 1945; and Report No. 17, Historical Section (G.S.) Army Headquarters.

971. Lieutenant-Colonel Fraser Eadie, interview with Bernd Horn, November 20 and December 6, 2000.

972. Personal Diary, Fraser Eadie, April 4–5, 1945.

973. Ibid.

974. Ibid.

975. Ibid.

976. The "battle" for the city of Minden is somewhat of a conundrum. The 1 Cdn Para Bn official history, *Out of the Clouds* by Professor John A. Willes (Private Printing, 1981), and Harcelrode's *"Go to It!"* describe heavy street to street fighting. However, Harcelrode seems to rely heavily on Willes' account, who in turn seems to base his version on Sergeant "Andy" Anderson's "Rhine Diary," which is not always accurate, as Anderson himself admits as much of it was filled in after the war. The 3rd Brigade HQ War Diary mentions only "Enemy opposition in town"; this is reported at 1755 hours on April 4, a mere two hours after the initial contact, but nothing later on at the time of the actual night attack. The 1 Cdn Para Bn War Diary for 4/5 April and the Army HQ Historical Section report both state, "It [Minden] was found by a scouting party to be empty."

977. Report No. 17, Historical Section (G.S.) Army Headquarters; and 1 Cdn Para Bn War Diary, April 5, 1945. NA, RG 24, Vol 15300. April 1945.

978. Personal Diary, Fraser Eadie, April 4–5, 1945.

979. Lieutenant-Colonel Fraser Eadie, interview with Bernd Horn, November 20, 2000.

980. Letter, Jan de Vries to Bernd Horn, January 21, 2001.

981. Del Parlee, interview with Bernd Horn, May 8, 2001.

982. 6th Airborne Division, Intelligence Summary, No. 40, 6 April 1945. PRO, WO 171/4157, Part 2. War Office: Allied Expeditionary Force, North West Europe (British Element): War Diaries, Second World War, 1943-46. G. January–April 1945.

983. 1 Cdn Para Bn War Diary, April 6, 1945. NA, RG 24, Vol 15300, April 1945.

984. 3rd Parachute Brigade War Diary, April 8, 1945. NA, RG 24, Vol 10993, file 1 April to 1 May 1945.

985. Ibid.

986. Ibid.

987. Ibid.

988. Letter Brigadier James Hill to the Honourable P.J. Montague, Cdn Military HQ., April 9, 1945. DHH, file 145.4011 (D2) 1 Cdn Para Bn.

989. Report No. 17, Historical Section (G.S.) Army Headquarters. "Werewolves" was the title given to those who were members of the Nazi underground guerilla movement that would carry on the struggle to liberate Germany from occupation after the end of hostilities. See endnote 935.

990. 6th Airborne Division, Intelligence Summary, No. 41, 12 April 1945. PRO, WO 171 / 4157, Part 2.

991. 3rd Parachute Brigade War Diary, April 16, 1945. NA, RG 24, Vol 10993, file 1 April to 1 May 1945.

992. 1 Cdn Para Bn War Diary, April 17, 1945. NA, RG 24, Vol 15300, April 1945; and Report No. 17, Historical Section (G.S.) Army Headquarters, 29.

993. "Experiences of Capt (now Major) J.A. Clancy, POW from 24 March 45 until he escaped 15 Apr 45, and reached Allied lines 18 Apr 45," appendix to 1 Cdn Para Bn War Diary, March 1–31, 1945. NA, RG 24, Vol 15300. March 1945.

994. Memorandum, "Trg and Inspections," 3 Para Bde HQ to all its units, April 22, 1945. DHH, file 145.4009 (D4). The Brigade Commander inspected one company from each of the three battalions, all machine guns and all German vehicles in use by the units. "B" Company under Major Stan Waters was the subunit inspected. It received the highest marks in the Brigade for the standard of maintenance of the Company's weapons. However, Hill did direct that twenty-two Bren magazines per gun be carried instead of the fifteen that was used within the unit. He also found fault with the administrative discipline. "Where adm discipline is weak," he cautioned, "you will always find men deficient of small items of kit together with many of the larger ones, such as small packs, entrenching tools, toggle ropes, etc." He also noted that inspection of the administrative group indicated that its standard was "a long way below that achieved in other bns." Memorandum, "Inspection," April 26, 1945. DHH, file 145.4009 (D4).

995. 1 Cdn Para Bn War Diary, May 1, 1945. NA, RG 24, Vol 15300. May 1945; and Report No. 17, Historical Section (G.S.) Army Headquarters, 31.

996. Alcide Carignan, interview with Michel Wyczynski, February 13, 2002.

997. Johnstone, 26.

998. Alf Tucker, interview with Bernd Horn, June 23, 2001.

999. R.D. Creelman, interview with Michel Wyczynski, December 27, 2002.

1000. 1 Cdn Para Bn War Diary, May 2, 1945. NA, RG 24, Vol 15299, May 1945.

1001. Ibid.

1002. Ibid.

1003. Ibid.

1004. Ibid.

1005. Ibid.

1006. Jerry McFadden, OC Headquarters Company, letter to spouse, May 3, 1945, reprinted in 1 Canadian Parachute Battalion Newsletter, Vol 6, No. 14, April 1995, 48.

1007. 3rd Parachute Brigade War Diary, May 2, 1945. NA, RG 24, Vol 10993, May 1945.

1008. 1 Cdn Para Bn War Diary, May 2, 1945. The Battalion's official history (Willes) describes (page 149) an afternoon meeting with a Russian patrol and Major Simpson. The War Diary, however, explains this as the evening encounter and this explanation is in sync with the 3 Para Bde HQ War Diary.

1009. 1 Cdn Para Bn War Diary, May 3, 1945. NA, RG 24, Vol 15300, May 1945.

1010. Ibid.

1011. Transcript of interview, A. Anderson and Blake Heathcote, Testaments of Honour.

1012. Jan de Vries, interview (and written submission) with Bernd Horn, January 9, 2001.

1013. Alcide Carignan, interview with Michel Wyczynski, February 13, 2002.

1014. Roland Larose, interview with Michel Wyczynski, January 10, 2002.

1015. Jan de Vries, interview with Bernd Horn, January 18, 2001.

1016. Anderson, "From the Rhine to the Baltic."

1017. Doug Morrison, interview with Bernd Horn, January 31, 2001; and Joseph King, interview with Bernd Horn, January 31, 2002.

1018. Jim Peerless, interview with Bernd Horn, May 7, 2001; and William Jenkins, interview with Michel Wyczynski, December 19, 2001.
1019. Dick Hilborn, interview with Bernd Horn, May 5, 2001.
1020. Memorandum, "Relationship with Russian Troops," 6 AB Div, 2 May 45. DHH, file 145.4009 (D4), Instructions and Reports.
1021. Transcript of interview, A. Anderson and Blake Heathcote, Testaments of Honour.
1022. John Simpson, interview with Michel Wyczynski, December 13, 2001.
1023. John Feduck, interview with Michel Wyczynski, December 19, 2001.
1024. 1 Cdn Para Bn War Diary, 6-8 May 1945. NA, RG 24, Vol 15300, May 1945.
1025. Anderson, "From the Rhine to the Baltic."
1026. 1 Cdn Para Bn War Diary, May 11, 1945. NA, RG 24, Vol 15300, May 1945.
1027. Address given by Brigadier S.J.L. Hill, June 1, 1997, at Bulford Garrison Church, on occasion of the unveiling of a plaque to the memory of the 1st Canadian Parachute Battalion. *Maroon Beret,* Vol 2, No. 2, August 1997, 56-57.
1028. *Pegasus* (6 AB Div newsletter), No. 158, 8 May 1945. CAFM, AB 19, Robinson Hamilton fonds, Vol 1, file 2.
1029. Letter, Brigadier Hill to Lieutenant-Colonel Eadie, June 7, 1945. 1 Cdn Para Bn War Diary, June 1945, Appendix 3. NA, RG 24, Vol 15300, June 1945. See also Report No. 17, Historical Section (G.S.) Army Headquarters, 33.
1030. "Messages Of Welcome Given Paratroopers, On Garrison Grounds," *The Halifax Herald,* Vol 70, No. 145, 21 June 1945. NL, microfilm N-23620.
1031. Stacey, *Six Years of War,* 433. There were two reasons that led to the Battalion's early return to Canada. First, the entire Battalion was in England. CMHQ had a rule that only complete units would be repatriated to Canada. This greatly facilitated and accelerated the repatriation administrative procedures. Numerous Canadian units had been stationed in England since 1940, but they were passed over because many of their sub-units were still in Europe. The second reason had important financial implications. Each Battalion member received jump pay. 1 Cdn Para Bn and the 1 Cdn Para Trg Bn officers received an extra $2.00 per day. The Other Ranks earned $0.75 per day. Since there were no longer any operational requirements for the unit, a rapid disbandment represented for NDHQ a daily savings of $881.44. The repatriation process of Canadian Service personnel stationed in the U.K. was also further accelerated in June 1945 due to the sudden availability of a large quantity of ships
1032. 1 Cdn Para Bn War Diary, May 27, 1945. NA, RG 24, Vol 15300, May 1945.
1033. Alcide Carignan, interview with Michel Wyczynski, February 13, 2002.
1034. Alf Tucker, interview with Michel Wyczynski, December 12, 2001.
1035. Peter Harclerode, *Para! Fifty Years of The Parachute Regiment* (London: Brockhampton Press, 1999),193. With the end of the war in sight, it was no longer necessary for the War Office to maintain two airborne divisions. Thus, the 1st Airborne Division was disbanded and the 6th Airborne Division became part of the Army's strategic reserve. On September 15, 1945, 6 AB Div commenced its deployment to Palestine. The Division had also undergone many changes. 3 Para Bde was now commanded by Brigadier Gerald Lathbury. Furthermore, with the removal of 1 Cdn Para Bn from the Division's Order of Battle, 3 Para Bn was selected to replace the Canadian unit.
1036. Letter from Brigadier W. H. S. Macklin, Deputy Chief of the General Staff to Lieutenant-General P. J. Montague, London, 11 May 1945. NA, RG 24, CMHQ, Vol 12260, file 1/Policy Para Tp/1. The Deputy Chief of the General Staff CMHQ "intimated that such a proposal would be contrary to current Canadian policy

that Canadian contributions to operations in the Far East is to be restricted to the provision of a Canadian element within a U.S. force, (estimated at approximately one division)."

1037. Ibid. In a "Top Secret" letter, dated May 3, 1945, sent by the CMHQ's Chief of Staff, Lieutenant-General P.J. Montague to the War Office's Under Secretary of State, Montague explained the Canadian Army's plan to proceed with the "orderly reallocation and demobilization of the First Canadian Army," as well as the "withdrawal of the 1 Cdn Para Bn and the Cdn Para Trg Bn" from the 6 AB Div. NA, RG 24, Vol 12260, CMHQ, file 1/Policy Para Tp/1. This letter would be followed by numerous others providing additional information on 1 Cdn Para Bn's rapid repatriation to Canada. In the event that the services of 1 Cdn Para Bn were still requested, this unit would now have to get its reinforcements from Infantry reinforcement depots.

1038. See Bernd Horn, *Bastard Sons* (St Catharines: Vanwell Publishing, 2001), 34–35.

1039. Ibid., 34–35.

1040. On VE Day, May 8, 1945, the strength of the Canadian Army in the U.K. and in Europe totaled, 281,757 all ranks. By December 31, 1945 184,054 had returned to Canada. By March 31, 1946, only 17,745 remained in the UK. In Europe there were fewer than 800 personnel as well as the 17,000 men of the Canadian Army Occupation Force. Stacey, *Six Years of War*,434.

1041. Richard Hilborn, interview with Bernd Horn, May 5, 2001.

1042. Letter from Major-General A.E. Walford, Adjutant-General to General Officer Commander-in-Chief, Pacific Command, all districts Officers Commanding and Commander, Camp Borden, Ottawa, June 15, 1945. DHH, file 168.009 (D42) Organization and Administration, 1 Cdn Para Bn. The idea of a Canadian Amy Pacific Force was discussed by Allied leaders during the course of the "Octagon" Conference in Quebec City, September 12–16, 1944. On November 20, the War Committee agreed on a Canadian military participation in the Pacific theatre. The Pacific Force would comprise one division totaling 30,000 men. The division was to be raised from returning battle experienced troops. By the end of August 1945, 1,963 officers and 22,058 Other Ranks had been posted to the CAPF. However, with the dropping of the two atomic bombs on August 6 and 9 on Hiroshima and Nagasaki respectively, Japan had no other recourse but to surrender. On August 14, the Japanese ceased all hostilities. On September 1, 1945, a directive was issued by NDHQ calling for the disbandment of the Canadian Army Pacific Force. Stacey, *Six Years of War*, 512–519.

1043. Michael Ball, interview with Michel Wyczynski, June 12, 2002.

1044. R.F. "Andy" Anderson, interview with Michel Wyczynski, February 7, 2002.

1045. R.F. "Andy" Anderson, letter to Bernd Horn, December 19, 2000.

1046. Richard D. Creelman, interview with Michel Wyczynski, December 27, 2001. Later, Brigadier Hill wrote a letter to Lieutenant-Colonel Eadie expressing the sadness he felt seeing the Battalion leave. "It was very sad to return to Bulford last night, after the two very happy years we have all spent together in the 3rd Brigade, to find that the last member of the 1st Canadian Parachute Battalion had left ... Thanks to the wonderful spirit of co-operation and friendliness shown by every member of the 1st Canadian Parachute Battalion and Training Battalion, there has never been any friction at any level between any units within the Brigade..." Letter from Brigadier James Hill to Lieutenant-Colonel Fraser Eadie, Bulford, June 7, 1945. NA, RG 24, Vol 15300, 1 Cdn Para Bn War Diary, June 1945. After the Battalion's return to Canada, Brigadier Hill commanded and oversaw the demobilization of the 1st Parachute Brigade. In July 1945, Hill retired from the British Army and returned to civilian life. Curriculum Vitae, Brigadier Stanley James Ledger Hill, DSO, MC. Brian Nolan Fonds, 1 Cdn Para Bn Assn Archives, Brigadier Hill file.

1047. Letter from Brigadier James Hill to Major-General E.G. Weeks, CMHQ, 3 Para Bde HQ, May 24, 1945. NA, RG 24, CMHQ, Vol 12517, file 6/1Para Bn/1/2, Organization and Administration.

1048. Ibid. The 1 Cdn Para Bn totaled 31 officers and 566 Other Ranks. The 1 Cdn Para Trg Bn totaled 19 officers and 463 Other Ranks. The five-day trip was marred by a tragic accident. During the early evening of June 17, while lying in his bunk, a young paratrooper was examining a German side arm. Suddenly, a shot echoed through the cabin. The bullet went through the upper bunk killing, its occupant. "I was appointed to defend this poor guy," recalled Alf Tucker. "The ship's Captain said if we arrive back to port," explained Tucker, "with a death on board it would tie the ship up. We tried the poor guy and he was convicted." The regrettable incident cast a momentary shadow over the Battalion's homecoming. The rest of the voyage proceeded without an incident. The victim was Private Guy Payette. Corporal W. Krutow was the paratrooper responsible for the accidental discharge. 1 Cdn Para Bn War Diary, June 17–19, 1945. NA, RG 24, Vol 15300, June 1945. Corporal Payette was buried at sea.

1049. Ibid. The men of the 1 Cdn Para Bn and the 1 Cdn Para Trg Bn had been recruited from thirteen Military Districts located throughout out Canada.

1050. Tumultuous Welcome As 8,920 Heroes Arrive on Ile de France," *Daily Halifax Star*, Wednesday, June 20, 1945, 1. 1 Cdn Para Bn Assn Archives, Firlotte, Robert, file 2-11. The other troops on board the vessel were: 4,939 Army veterans; 3,200 Air Force personnel; and 460 Navy men. Also among these troops were the ground crews of the Pathfinders, Alouette, and Ghost Squadrons of No. 6 Bomber Command. A total of 8,920 veterans were on board. "

1051. Harry Wright, interview with Michel Wyczynski, January 24, 2002.

1052. R.F. "Andy" Anderson, interview with Michel Wyczynski, February 7, 2002.

1053. "Parade, Ceremony to Mark Welcome. Huge Reception Planned For Paratroopers Today," Unidentified Canadian newspaper clipping. 1 Cdn Para Bn Assn Archives, Firlotte, Robert, file 2-11.

1054. Richard D. Creelman, interview with Michel Wyczynski, December 27, 2001.

1055. "Battalion Fights Out of Job In Conflict." Unidentified Canadian newspaper clipping. 1 Cdn Para Bn Assn Archives, Feduck, John, file 6-8. Parade of 1 Cdn Para Bn, Order by District Officer Commanding, 2/1945, Halifax, 18 June 1945. 1 Cdn Para Bn War Diary, June 1945. NA, RG 24, Vol 15300.

1056. "Messages Of Welcome Given Paratroopers, On Garrison Grounds," *The Halifax Herald*, Vol 70, No. 145, 21 June 1945. NL, microfilm N-23620.

1057. Ibid.

1058. Ibid.

1059. "'Chutists Toast Of City As Ile De France Docks," June 21, 1945. Unidentified Canadian Newspaper Clipping. 1 Cdn Para Bn Assn Archives, Firlotte, Robert, file 2-11.

1060. T.A. Gavinski, interview with Bernd Horn, November 25, 1998.

1061. A great number of paratroopers remained in their Military Districts and awaited their demobilization. The discharge priority was as follows: those wounded, those who had signed up for university studies, and personnel who had a long service record.

1062. Stacey, *Six Years of War*, 432–433. The release of individuals from the Canadian

Army was devised on "a point score system". Each month of service in Canada counted for two points. Each month of service overseas counted for three points. The score of married personnel, widowers, or divorces with dependant children were increased by 20 percent. The order of repatriation to Canada was the following: personnel who volunteered to serve in the Canadian Army Pacific Force were given repatriation priority; the next groups to be repatriated were the men who had accumulated the most points. They returned to Canada in drafts. Finally, major (complete) units were repatriated in the same general order in which they came overseas: "First in, first out."

1063. Return from Overseas, 1 Cdn Para Bn. Instructions forwarded by Major S.H. Muton, M.D.10 to Officer Commanding No.10 District Depot, and Officer Commanding 1 Cdn Para Bn. District Headquarters, Fort Osborne Barracks, Winnipeg, Manitoba, 25 July 1945. DHH, file 168.009 (D42), Organization and Administration of 1 Cdn Para Bn.

1064. 1 Cdn Para Bn War Diary, July, August–September 1945. NA, RG 24, Vol 15300.

1065. "Toronto Paratrooper Wins Victoria Cross," Globe and Mail, No. 29839, 3 August 1945, 1, 2. NL, microfilm N-20071. "Toronto's Newest VC Prefers Rigors of War To Adulation of Public," Ibid., 4. "'Wasn't Much To It!' Says Toronto VC." Ibid., 5

1066. Directive issued by Major-General A.E. Walford, Adjutant-General to Deputies Officers Commanding M.D. 2, 10, Ottawa, September 4, 1945. DHH, file 168.009 (D24). Organization and Administration, 1 Cdn Para Bn.

1067. Ibid. The 1st Canadian Parachute Training Battalion was disbanded on 10 June 1945. General Orders (G.O.), Disbandment — Active Units, G.O. 321 September 1945. As for the parachute training activities at the A-35 Canadian Parachute Training Centre these had ceased on June 30, 1945. "Today saw the winding up of the jump training," wrote the war diary chronicler, "in the Parachute Training Wing ... 108 men and Lieutenant Stewart qualified. These men are probably the last men who will become Parachutists in Canada, at least during this war or unless the picture changes." A-35 Canadian Parachute Training Centre War Diary, 30 June 1945. NA, RG 24, Vol 17138, June 1945.

1068. 1 Cdn Para Bn War Diary, September 16, 1945. NA, RG 24, Vol 15300, September 1945.

1069. Hector Allan, interview with Bernd Horn, January 31, 2002.

1070. Art Stammers, interview with Michel Wyczynski, January 16, 2002.

1071. Ernie Jeans, interview with Michel Wyczynski, January 22, 2002.

1072. Lieutenant-Colonel Fraser Eadie, interview with Bernd Horn, June 23, 1998.

1073. Ernie Jeans, interview with Michel Wyczynski, January 22, 2002.

INDEX

INDEX